The Slave Girl

and Other Stories about Women

OTHER TITLES IN THE SERIES

On the cover: "The First Love" by Dušica Benghiat

The Slave Girl

and Other Stories about Women

Ivo Andrić

Edited by Radmila Gorup
Introduction by Zoran Milutinović

CEU PRESS

Central European University Press

Budapest • New York

Published in 2009 by

Central European University Press
An imprint of the
Central European University Share Company
Nádor utca 11, H-1051 Budapest, Hungary
Tel: +36-1-327-3138 or 327-3000
Fax: +36-1-327-3183
E-mail: ceupress@ceu.hu
Website: www.ceupress.com

400 West 59th Street, New York NY 10019, USA
Tel: +1-212-547-6932
Fax: +1-646-557-2416
E-mail: mgreenwald@sorosny.org

First edition, printed in 1000 copies

ISBN 978-963-7326-42-5
ISSN 1418-0162

Library of Congress Cataloging-in-Publication Data

Andric, Ivo, 1892-1975.
  [Short stories. English. Selections]
  The slave girl : and other stories about women / Ivo Andric ; edited by
Radmila J. Gorup.
       p. cm. -- (Central European Press classics)
  ISBN 978-9639776425 (pbk. : alk. paper)
  1. Short stories, Serbian--Translations into English. I. Gorup, Radmila
Jovanovic. II. Title. III. Series.

  PG1418.A6A6 2009
  891.8'235--dc22

                                              2009002729

Printed in Hungary by Akadémiai Nyomda, Martonvásár

For Wylie, Piper and Sophie

Contents

Acknowledgments

I owe my gratitude to the many who assisted in the preparation of this volume. This book would not have been possible without the help of my colleagues, students and friends who translated these wonderful stories: Marijeta Božović, Henry R. Cooper, Jr., John K. Cox, Ellen Elias-Bursać, Natalia Ermolaev, Savka Gajić, Kosara Gavrilović, Daniel Gerstle, John Gery, Celia Hawkesworth, Biljana Obradović, Bogdan Rakić and Milo Yelesiyevich. I am particularly indebted to Žaneta Perišić of the Ivo Andrić Foundation in Belgrade for her support and advice. The Harcourt Publishing very generously gave us permission to reprint "Anika's Times" while *Serbian Studies* allowed us to reprint "Ćorkan and the German Tightrope Walker," and "Olujaci". Special thanks are due to Dušica Benghiat for letting us use her illustration for the cover. I would like to thank the Harriman Institute of Columbia University for their generous financial support. My deep gratitude to Celia Hawkesworth who helped with editing this volume. Last but not least, I thank Linda Kunos, the editor of CEU Press, who was tremendously supportive throughout this process.

Acknowledgments

Several of the stories in this volume have been translated into English earlier. The majority, however, appear here in English for the first time.

I would like to dedicate this volume to my three granddaughters and all the female readers of these stories: be always the wondrous beings Andrić saw in you.

Radmila Gorup

Preface

As he breathes his last, the wise dervish monk Alidede in the story "Death in Sinan's Tekke" offers an unspoken prayer to his God, saying among other things: "I had forgotten that at the exit from this world, as at the entry, stands a woman like a gate." He had endeavored to live his life "purely," his eyes directed always heavenwards. But at the last he had "to pay his debt" to the laws of nature by acknowledging that his two last memories from his long life were of occasions when he was shaken to the core by encounters with women. Many of Andrić's male characters experience women in this way: as a profoundly disturbing phenomenon. There are two main aspects of this experience: social and personal. On the one hand the potential power of women over men must be socially controlled if the structure of the patriarchal hierarchy is to be maintained. On the other an individual's personal life may be disrupted, even destroyed, through his association with a woman or enriched to the point of rapture merely by his catching a passing glimpse of "beauty."

Many of the essential categories developed in Andrić's later works were first hinted at in his youthful prose poems *Ex Ponto* (1918):

> Women, your shadow lies on the slumbering desire of the ascetic and the dreamless craving of the libertine.[1]

> Women, I do not know for whom you have been soft morning rain, but you enter our lives like downpours borne on gales. Our lives foam loudly over your white bodies, are caught in whirlpools and fall headlong.
>   [...]
> Woman, why can we not see you clearly as the original man saw the female in the sun, but rather you have become a terrible vision and the poison of our blood, so that we run from you and when we think that you are far away, you keep watch over our thoughts, and when we wish to forget you in work—fine lines coil over all our deeds, the traces of your invisible fingers.[2]

In his introduction to this volume, Zoran Milutinović quotes the critic Zdenko Škreb: "If Andrić's main character from Turkish Bosnia should be named, then it is the *kasaba*." The Bosnian provincial town, small enough to be encompassed as a whole, may, like the prison setting in *The Damned Yard*, be seen as representing a system of social relations in miniature. The prison in particular emphasizes constraint as a fundamental law of social existence. In a less drastic way, the *kasaba* also establishes a firm structure of power relations and strict

---

[1] Ivo Andrić, *Ex Ponto, Nemiri, Lirika*, Prosveta, Belgrade, 1977, p. 26. Author's translation.
[2] *Ibid.*, p. 27.

rules of behavior. Power over subordinate members of this structure is essential to its survival. And in the patriarchal system of power relations, it is of course women who are most obviously subordinate and subject to sanctioned violence. This volume includes numerous examples of the oppression of women and the disaster that ensues if any should defy the established rules, as is vividly illustrated in "Anika's Times." Most submit to their fate as Mara does in "The Pasha's Concubine."[3] The most extreme illustrations of their fate are the stories in which individual women are forced into an impasse where their only choice is to take their own lives, like Rifka in "Love in the *Kasaba*" or the exceptionally stark image of constraint in "The Slave Girl."

In addition to evoking this society, Andrić has woven into it a more personal experience of the categories which society assigns to women. In this volume an extreme evocation of fear of women would be the terror provoked by the all-encompassing presence of the little figure in "An Ivory Woman." By contrast with such images of chaos and destruction, a woman may appear in a man's life as a vision of perfect beauty or the embodiment of pure joy. This vision enriches the man's life, transporting him into a different order of experience, as when the old roué Byron comes upon the innocent child in Sintra or when the despised Gypsy Ćorkan catches sight of the tightrope walker floating in space. Even the

---

[3] The contrast between these two characters is explored in detail by Jasmina Lukić in an unpublished article, "Two Stories by Ivo Andrić."

old tyrant Jevrem in "An Uneasy Year" is momentarily transformed by the presence of the beautiful young Gaga. Such an experience is in its nature fleeting.

This reflection of the European cultural tradition of personifying beauty, innocence and joy in a female form was again first expressed by Andrić in *Ex Ponto*. From the outset the female presence was given the name "Jelena." She represents an ideal of beauty and joy which is essentially elusive: the narrator is aware of her stepping silently through a snowy wood and walking past his door along a dark corridor, holding a flickering candle.

> That woman was called the Unadulterated Joy of Life, but in the language spoken with her by my soul that phrase was one resonant word. I arranged a meeting with that woman, in the center of town, in the middle of the day.
> I came. She did not come. [...]⁴

In the story "Jelena, the Woman Who is Not," she is associated with light and freedom, standing for a glimpse of another order of being engendered by the constraints of daily living in a structured, hierarchical, crowded, noisy society. In this story, and in many others, the experience of such transient rapture, while seeming more real than the mere daily routine, is expressed in the image of a swing. Like the tightrope, a swing transports one out of the world of daily life: "So I am borne on this cosmic swing, in breathtaking sweeps, from one perfect

⁴ Ivo Andrić, *Ex Ponto, Nemiri, Lirika,* Prosveta, Belgrade, 1977, p. 41.

bliss to another, from Jelena's and my presence to our disappearance along with everything around us into the joy of general existence."

These two basic types of women in Andrić's work could be roughly categorized as the traditional poles of 'Madonna' and 'whore.' Such an association emphasizes the fact that these categories are social constructs, imposed on women from outside. In all his work, Andrić is always more interested in the conditions which give rise to the 'main legends of humanity', the 'kernels of truth' around which they grow, than in the individual psyche. His characters are products of their times and the way they are seen, talked about and remembered is a function of the human impulse to shape experience and give it enduring form in stories. Anika tried to act autonomously, outside the constraints of society, with fatal consequences. Most of Andrić's other women characters are obliged to accept these constraints. But they are all portrayed, not so much as individuals with specific psychological traits, but as they are experienced by others: the individual men whose lives they enhance or disturb, and the society, the *kasaba* whose rules determine their fate.

Celia Hawkesworth

Introduction

The Wisdom Effect: Ivo Andrić
the Storyteller

Although readers who read English translations of Andrić's works would be more familiar with his novels *The Bridge on the Drina*, *Bosnian Chronicle* and *The Damned Yard*, than with his stories, such as "Anika's Times" or "An Uneasy Year," Andrić was a storyteller rather than a novelist. Even these three important novels are composed of what can be read as more or less autonomous stories. What connects the stories about various characters is a place: in *The Bridge on the Drina* they are diachronically threaded around the town of Višegrad, in *Bosnian Chronicle* they are synchronically connected around the town of Travnik, and in *The Damned Yard* they are linked in a spiral manner around the Istanbul prison described as "a whole small town of prisoners and guards." [1] Only his fourth novel, *The Woman from Sarajevo*, has a recognizable novelistic structure, centered on one main character and narrated in a linear manner—but it has never been read much, and today seems to be all but forgotten. The difference be-

---

[1] Ivo Andrić: *The Damned Yard and Other Stories*, ed. by Celia Hawkesworth, London/Belgrade: Forest Books/Dereta, 1992, p. 149.

tween Andrić's three celebrated novels, and the one which is less so, is indicative of the nature of the author's imagination and narrative interest. The unity of the former three novels is guaranteed by the places in which different and numerous characters enter the stage, but the places are always the same. Only in the fourth novel does the place of action change, when Rajka, its main character, moves from Sarajevo to Belgrade. *The Woman from Sarajevo* is a study of a single character and it focuses on her psychology: this is what gives it its unity even after the place changes. That which is of the greatest importance is preserved even after Rajka's move to another place. A similar device was used only in a small number of stories, and is entirely absent from the remaining novels; it was used in his earliest stories "The Journey of Alija Djerzelez" and "Mustafa the Hungarian," and in one of the later stories, "The Woman on the Rock," which are also studies of one character or one psychological trait. The majority of Andrić's stories however, and all three great novels, are not focused on a single dominant character, even if a proper name forms part of a title, as in "Mara the Concubine."[2] What matters most is not individual psychology.[3] Andrić tried to repress the interest in psychology as much as is possible when one writes about people. It means that he was never led by the question of what made somebody do

[2] The title of the story "Mara milosnica" has been translated as "The Pasha's Concubine." Milutinović refers to it as "Mara the Concubine."

[3] On Andrić's reduction of psychological dimension of his characters see Jovan Hristić: "Andrićeva pripovetka," in *Izabrani eseji*, Belgrade: Srpski PEN centar, 2005, p. 114.

this or that, but by the fact that something had been done, and that it had effects on the lives of others. This takes his stories out of the individualistic vision of the novel genre, and leads them into the vision characteristic of traditional storytelling: people living with one another.

Nevertheless, places such as Višegrad, Travnik or the Istanbul prison are much more than just formal compositional devices which link different stories together. "If Andrić's main character from Turkish Bosnia should be named, then it is the *kasaba*," wrote Zdenko Škreb.[4] The *kasaba* is the world of merchants and craftsmen, somewhere halfway between the world of the village—and its loyalty to the epic—and the world of the metropolis with its individualism and the novel as its appropriate literary expression. Not tied to the land and freed from the chains of the collective, and the mythical, which expresses itself in epic stories about heroes, but still not in the modern metropolis, in which a mobile individual's psychology is the beginning and the end of everything, these merchants and craftsmen are for the most part, directed to one another. They are what Aristotle called *politēs*, people living in towns, the inhabitants of a *polis*— the Greek version of the *kasaba*—with all the liberties and limitations that go with it. Although there is always a tyrant whose absolute power must be obeyed, a pasha in Travnik or the sultan in Istanbul, the townspeople regulate their day-to-day life themselves. They no longer

---

[4] Zdenko Škreb: "Što je Andrić unio novo u svjetsku književnost," *Sveske Zadužbine Ive Andrića*, 3/1985, p. 224. The Turkish word *kasaba* comes from Arabic *kasbah*—small town.

believe in the myth about Djerzelez Alija, but have not yet created their own myths about victors who can live independently of others, or even against them. In the master narrative of the nineteenth-century European novel, Balzac's *Le père Goriot*, self-confident Rastignac surveys the metropolis from the heights of Père Lachaise ready to come down and to challenge it. In a similar setting, Mihailo in "Anika's Times" surveys Višegrad from a hill equally determined to do what he must, but instead of challenging the town he runs away. For denizens of the *kasaba,* a tiny fissure of freedom opened up between, on the one hand, the monolith-mythical rural life in which they listened with awe and terror to a poem about an epic hero who alone had the right to act freely and to make his own decisions, and on the other hand, the freedom and indifference the inhabitants of a modern metropolis enjoy and suffer. Within that fissure anything they do has immediate consequences for the lives of others. They might not be shackled by the monolithic tradition which defines every one of them in a similar manner, but it does not mean that they are free to define themselves. It is as if they can step outside of the monolith and commit a sin or an offence, but cannot ultimately live with it. Since they are no longer controlled by myth, they control one another. This *directedness* to the other, surveilling and being surveilled in return, expresses itself in the stories which they tell one another, and about one another. The best stories are always about those who step outside the order which the *kasaba* tries to establish. In *Bosnian Chronicle* a young French diplomat Des Fossés explains it in the following manner:

The existence of such outcast and isolated people, abandoned to their passions, their disgrace and rapid ruin, just showed how firm the links were and how remorselessly strict were the laws of society, religion and family in patriarchal life. And this applied to the Turks as well as to the *rayah* of all faiths. In these societies everything was connected, one thing locked firmly into another, one thing supporting another, and watched over by everyone. Each individual took care of the whole, and the whole of each individual. Each house observed the next house, each street oversaw the next, for everyone was responsible for everyone else, and all were responsible for everything. Each person was closely linked with the fate not only of his relations and those in his household, but also of his neighbours, fellow-believers and fellow-citizens. This was both the strength and the enslavement of these people. The life of each individual was possible only within that pattern and the life of the whole only in accordance with those conditions. If anyone stepped outside that pattern, following his own instincts and will, it was as though he had committed suicide and, sooner or later, he would inevitably be destroyed. Such was the law of these communities, mentioned even in the Old Testament. It was the law of the classical world as well. Marcus Aurelius wrote somewhere: "Whoever avoids the obligations of the social order is an outcast."[5]

Andrić's Bosnian stories are set in a time before merchants and craftsmen had succeeded in creating the myth about the invincible and self-sufficient individual, and the sentence formulated by Aristotle in *Politics* still applies to them: "We thus see that the polis exists by nature and that it is prior to the individual. Not being self-sufficient when they are isolated, all individuals are

[5] Ivo Andrić: *Bosnian Chronicle*, translated by C. Hawkesworth and B. Rakić, London: The Harvill Press, 1992, p. 118.

so many parts all equally depending on the whole. The man who is isolated—who is unable to share in the benefits of political association, or has no need to share because he is already self-sufficient—is no part of the polis, and must therefore be "either a beast or a god."[6]

One of those who stepped outside the order and followed their own instincts is the main character of "Anika's Times." The narrator, however, never explicitly says which instincts Anika followed in particular, and what made her "*reveal* herself to the *kasaba*." All the reader is told is that she made her decision after waiting endlessly for Mihailo to make up his mind about taking her as his wife. Mihailo's hesitation is justified to a certain extent by what he had gone through before coming to Višegrad, but how Anika's disappointment turns into the drive to destroy the *kasaba* and herself, is left open to the reader's interpretation. The narrator's interest does not lie in the sphere of psychology, or at least not primarily. He is more interested in the consequences Anika's decision has for other people's lives. However, before beginning the story about the girl who came to believe that she could live against the others, and be "either a beast or a god," the narrator determines the story's true place and its real dimensions. The learned Mullah Muhamed recorded in his notebook all important events in the *kasaba* and the wider world. In the year of Anika's decision to step outside the order, he noted three more significant things: that somewhere in Germany a devil

---

[6] *The Politics of Aristotle*, translated by Ernest Barker, Oxford: The Clarendon Press, 1952, p. 6.

was born, (luckily it was such a small one that it could be captured in a bottle); that some Bonaparte challenged the Sultan's rule over Egypt; and that the *rayah* in Serbia rebelled. And then, closer to home:

> That same year a young woman, a Christian (God confound all the infidels!), was overtaken by evil, and created such commotion and gained such strength that her evil reputation spread far and wide. Numerous men, both young and old, had gone to her, and many a youth had gone afoul there. And she placed both authority and law under her feet. But someone was found to deal with her, too, and she was crushed according to that which she deserved. And people were again put straight and were mindful of God's commands.[7]

Of all that happened in that year the town chronicler Mullah Muhamed recorded four threats to the order: one clearly metaphysical, two political and one ethical—which all, due to Mullah Muhamed's interpretation, turn out to be metaphysical rebellions against the order God implanted on the earth—with the reassuring remark that all of them had been overcome, that the world was still in its proper place, and that the order was still as God wanted it to be. This is one of the stories, contracted into a formula of several sentences, which townspeople tell one another, or about one another, in order to pass on the experience of human life. "Anika's Times" represents a development of the formula into a story about Anika, but as it is told by someone who is not a merchant or craftsman, it becomes a story about the *kasaba* as well. Contrary to its original teller Mullah Muhamed,

[7] See p. 374 of present volume.

the narrator of "Anika's Times" is never tempted to convert evil into transcendence: for him, evil is always entirely human. Much as beauty is human as well, laying down one's arms and surrendering to it is also human. As Petar says: "We can resist any trouble, save *that*." *That* is Anika, whose beauty owes nothing to the place that had given her life, but which "happened" to the place much in the same way as miracles or disasters happen. However, if the merchants and craftsmen cannot resist this beauty, and thus do harm to themselves and others, the *kasaba* can:

> In the *kasaba*, where man and women resemble one another like sheep, it happens sometimes that chance will bring a child, as the wind brings seeds, who is deprived and stands out from the usual order of things, causing ill-luck and confusion, until it is cut down itself and the old order re-established.[8]

And after Anika's death,

> the *kasaba*, which had been momentarily deranged, could again sleep peacefully, walk freely, and breathe regularly. If a similar blight should occur—and it will at some point—the kasaba will again resist it, succumb to it, struggle against it, break it, bury it, and forget it.[9]

Until then the *kasaba* shall retell the story about Anika's beauty, evil and misery. Why? In order for other girls who eagerly await a proposal, or boys who come of age when they behave like the fish in the Rzav, to hear the story about Anika and learn something from it?

---

[8] Ibid., p. 375.
[9] Ibid., p. 440.

Hardly. The *kasaba* knows that something similar will happen again despite all the warnings, and that others' mistakes and misfortunes rarely help one not to be led astray. The telling of the story has a different purpose.

This purpose is represented in "Anika's Times" in the image we already touched upon. After he had decided to kill Anika, Mihailo climbed the hill above Višegrad, sat there and surveyed both rivers, the houses, the roofs, the sunset behind the pine trees, and the mountain tops disappearing as dusk fell. He saw even what could not be seen from such a distance: the doors of the shops, the people, and their smiles and greetings. Despite being detached from the hustle and bustle of the town, the people's greetings and the children's voices, Mihailo was still close enough to encompass everything in his gaze: this gaze, which encompasses everything, but which is not part of that everything itself, brought him peace of mind. "All this is life," repeats Mihailo three times. All this: the shops, people greeting one another, Anika's beauty, her evil and misery, children's laughter, Mihailo's own misfortune which first brought him to Višegrad, and the seven years of happiness which he lived through in the town. Mihailo's all-encompassing gaze and the sentence which accompanies it are the image of Andrić's poetics: they do not contain any attempt at totalizing, such as Mullah Muhamed's intention in his chronicle to find the hidden law behind world events. They do not even attempt to explain everything, because not everything in the world lends itself to explanations; but they do recognize that, although inexplicable, beauty and evil, seven good years and misfortune, co-exist side by side in the world. And that all that is contained in what we call the experience of human life. The peace of mind brought about by this all-encompassing gaze resembles wisdom.

Wisdom—this word disappeared from the discourse of literary criticism a long time ago. Philosophy abandoned it as well, keeping the second part of its Greek name as one would keep one's surname inherited from a long forgotten ancestor, in whom one is not all that interested. Thus wisdom began to resemble a drought-ridden territory claimed by no one, a realm which nobody is greatly interested in. We do not consider as wisdom any specialized or applicable knowledge, such as healing or building bridges, but only deep insights into the ultimate, most important questions of human existence. Here, language already betrays us, because it does not seem possible to explain what wisdom might be without resorting to foggy metaphors of 'depth' and 'end.' The simplest way of putting it might be to say that a wise person is someone who knows true answers to the questions of the meaning of existence and of the nature of relationships between people, who has succeeded in seeing past the rough waves at life's surface and has clearly seen the calm bottom of the ocean. It seems that the idea of wisdom cannot do without the parallel image of depth. This kind of knowledge never achieves anything practicable, it does not heal the sick nor does it build bridges, but it is a precondition of all other knowledge, because it teaches us which knowledge is worthwhile and what can be achieved with it. And, most of all, wisdom is believed to bring peace of mind, and take away the uncertainty and the tearing apart which accompany every misled quest for truth, and the disappointment arising from it. "Wisdom is the virtue of old age," says Hannah Arendt, it smells of oldness and experience, and not only of the individual but of the experience accumulated by generations.[10] That is why it is never to be found anywhere in the vicinity of innovation, revolution and experiment, and never at beginnings, but always at ends. Consequently, the title of sage tends to be reserved for those whose long lives are rooted in long-standing, most often religious traditions.

How can we be sure that something is endowed with wisdom, or that someone is a sage? Beauty can be recognized by those who are not beautiful themselves, but in order to recognize wisdom one has to be wise oneself. Only if we are in possession of true answers to the questions about the meaning of existence and the nature of human relationships can we declare someone else's knowledge and experience as wise. It means that the claim about someone's wisdom is always above all the demand that our wisdom be recognized and respected. This might be a reason why literary criticism shies away on the rare occasions when talking about wisdom seems to be possible.

Walter Benjamin was among the last critics to write about the wisdom of the storyteller: "Counsel woven into the fabric of real life is wisdom. The art of storytelling is nearing its end because the epic side of truth—

---

[10] Hannah Arendt: *Man in Dark Times*, London: Jonathan Cape, 1970, p. 109.

wisdom—is dying."[11] Benjamin is enigmatic here as usual. He uses the word wisdom in relation to the art of storytelling, but only after he has changed its meaning. "Counsel woven into the fabric of real life" cannot help one overcome a specific difficulty—for instance, how to save oneself from the dangers brought about by beautiful girls who have decided to "*reveal* themselves." Counsel is "less an answer to a question than a proposal concerning the continuation of a story"[12] and rests on one's ability to tell the story in the first place. Wisdom, then, has nothing to do with "depths," "meaning" or "old age"; it is the ability to tell a story which communicates human experience, whatever it might be. Wisdom has as its content no true answers to ultimate questions, but only "the fabric of real life." It is, following Benjamin, the ability to transform life into the experience laid out in the form of a story, and it belongs to a storyteller as much as to every reader or listener who accepts the storyteller's proposal and continues the storytelling—who takes over the storyteller's ability to see real life, his own and that of others, as experience communicable by means of a plot and characters.

Nevertheless, there are many storytellers whom no one would consider wise, although their ability to tell a story is never questioned. It is said that Goethe and Tolstoi are wise, but never Gogol' or Proust. Again, Thomas Mann is considered wise, but not Joyce or Beckett, although no one questions their abilities to rebottle life

[11] Walter Benjamin: "The Storyteller," in *Selected Writings*, Vol. 3, ed. by H. Eiland and M.W. Jennings, the Belknap Press of Harvard University Press, 2002, p. 146.

[12] Ibid., pp. 145–46.

into experiences exposed in the form of a story. In order to deserve this honourable title, a storyteller has to offer something more than this ability. That something can be called, similar to the reality effect described by Barthes, the *wisdom effect*.[13]

As for Andrić, the wisdom effect is produced by characteristics of his narration which largely correspond to the characteristics commonly found in the popular idea of wisdom. In his novel and stories one hardly ever finds traces of the great literary experiments and artistic revolutions which unfolded during his lifetime. Although classifying Andrić as a realist writer would raise eyebrows, no one would protest against the claim that his work belongs to that broadest narrative tradition in European literatures in which Flaubert and Chekhov, but also Gide and Thomas Mann feel comfortable. As in the novels and stories of Thomas Mann—a writer whom Andrić admired more than all his other contemporaries—in Andrić's works that which is specifically modern is achieved by a means which cannot be detected at the language level.[14] Both of them drew upon the accumulated experience of that long tradition, which in their works leaves an impression of living its last splendid days—the impression of old age and sunset. They leave such an impression even in their earliest published works: in "Death in Venice," and in "The Journey of Alija Djerzelez," Andrić's first published

---

[13] Roland Barthes: "The Reality Effect," in *The Rustle of Language*, translated by Richard Howard, Berkeley and Los Angeles: University of California Press, 1986, pp. 141–148.

[14] On Andrić's appreciation of Thomas Mann see Ivo Tartalja: *Put pored znakova*, Novi Sad: Matica srpska, 1991, pp. 74–90.

story. What is felt as old and experienced in these stories, written by relatively young people, is the old age and experience of the tradition, not of the authors.

What is more, more than any other writers of the same tradition, Mann and Andrić seem to be authors whose stories come from the depths of memory (these depths again!), from legend and history. Mann's medieval and oriental stories, the Biblical paratext of *Joseph and His Brothers*, the modern version of the legend of Faust, Andrić's story about the Muslim epic hero Djerzelez Alija, his transformations of the legend of two brothers in *The Damned Yard*, historical wefts in *The Bridge on the Drina* and *Bosnian Chronicle*—are all the result of reliance on what has already been told in the past. In the case of Andrić, this distancing of the subject in the past is accompanied by a cultural distancing, as in the oriental exoticism of "Torso" and "The Story of the Vizier's Elephant," or in all other stories from Ottoman Bosnia, which was already a distant past in his time. In "A conversation with Goya," in which the foundations of Andrić's poetics are formulated, "the old gentleman" Goya says that "it is useless and mistaken to look for sense in the seemingly important but meaningless events taking place around us, but that we should look for it in those layers which the centuries have built up around the few main legends of humanity. These layers constantly, if ever less faithfully, reproduce the form of that grain of truth around which they gather, and so carry it through the centuries."[15] So not contemporary life,

---

[15] Ivo Andrić: *Conversation with Goya. Bridges, Signs*, translated by Celia Hawkesworth and Andrew Harvey, The Menard Press, 1992, p. 16.

but what is distant in time, or made to look distant because it is felt as culturally different, offers a basis for a story which can achieve the wisdom effect.

A legend is something that comes to the storyteller as already transformed by previous storytelling. *Mythos*, a story, is what someone has already told to someone. Andrić does not narrate from the tradition of folklore storytelling, which was very rich among the South Slavs, but he fully embraces the tradition of oral narration. The story about Anika is a story about what the old people of the *kasaba* have remembered from the tales of even older witnesses. In "Torso," the narrator retells what he heard from Fra Petar, who in turn had heard the story from Hafiz Čelebi's servant, who could not have witnessed the events in Syria himself, but must have learnt about them from someone else's story. Fra Petar is Andrić's archetypal storyteller; old and ill, lying on his deathbed:

> (…) Fra Petar was still able to tell long and beautiful stories, but only if he could find listeners whom he liked. No one could say what the beauty of his stories consisted of exactly. In everything he said there was something 'smiling and wise' at the same time. But, in addition to that, around every word he said there hovered a special overtone, as a sound nimbus, which, missing from other people's speech, remained in the air and flickered even after the words he uttered died away. This is why every word that Fra Petar said, meant more than it did in everyday speech. This is now lost forever.[16]

Through traveling the world, and living a long life, wise Fra Petar had seen "good and evil," but the narra-

---

[16] Ivo Andrić: "Trup," *Žedj*, Belgrade: Prosveta, 1967, p. 135.

tor of "Torso" does not say what his wisdom consisted of exactly, save his ability to transform Benjamin's "fabric of real life" into experience exposed in the form of a story. In doing this, Fra Petar would draw upon what he had experienced himself, as well as what he had heard in stories told to him by others. In *The Damned Yard* every character has a story to tell: at times a simple one, such as the athlete's, at other times a false one, such as Zaim's, and also profound and wise ones, such as Kamil's. Fra Petar listens to them all, and says:

> For, what would we know about other people's souls and thoughts, about other people and consequently about ourselves, about other places and regions we have never seen nor will have the opportunity of seeing, if there were not people like this who have the need to describe in speech or writing what they have seen or heard, and what they have experienced or thought in that connection? Little, very little. And if their accounts are imperfect, coloured with personal passions and needs, or even inaccurate, we have reason and experience and can judge them and compare them one with another, accept or reject them, partially or completely. In this way, something of human truth is always left for those who listen or read patiently.[17]

Fra Petar is a listener and a storyteller at the same time: in the Istanbul prison he listens to stories, and upon his return to his monastery in Bosnia he retells a story composed of Zaim's, Haim's, Kamil's and his own stories. Since *The Damned Yard* is narrated as a recreation of Fra Petar's story by a young monk Rastislav, the "counsel" of which Benjamin wrote seems to have been taken. A chain

[17] Ivo Andrić: *The Damned Yard*, p. 174.

of storytellers was created, a chain in which the next listener accepts the storyteller's proposal and continues the
storytelling by taking over the previous storyteller's ability
to see real life, his own and that of others, as an experience communicable by means of stories. It would be possible to say that what they pass on further is the tradition
of storytelling, which in any event is already implicit in
the other: a tradition, that which is given over or handed
down, is possible only thanks to the act of continued storytelling, and the other way around—storytelling is the
effect of inserting oneself into tradition, into the chain of
storytellers and listeners who, when their time comes,
become storytellers themselves.

It is thus fully comprehensible why the central narrative consciousness in Andrić's stories is always repressed
into the background.[18] The voice which tells the story—
if it is not individualized as one of the characters—
remains concealed in the background, for the story is
not about him, but about us, and it is not his, but ours,
everybody's and no one's. If we are to continue with
spatial metaphors, it would be better to say that the narrator is high above the level of events: like Mihailo in
"Anika's Times," the narrator also seems to be up on
the hill above a town, from where he can see everything,
but remain detached from it, calm and tranquil—in a
word, epic. He can also say, as Mihailo does, "All this is
life": passion and ecstasy, but also the downfall which

---

[18] On the narrative voice in Andrić's novels and stories see Zdenko
Lešić: "Ivo Andrić—pripovjedač. Izmedju naratologije i hermeneutike,"
Novi izraz, Vol. 7, No. 30, 2005, pp. 25–39.

follows afterwards. This calm of the narrating voice contributes to the wisdom effect as well. From his elevated position, the voice is able to tell of things that surpass the individual position of those included in the events. Since he narrates from the tradition in which the memory of other events is preserved, he knows about similar or even identical occurrences, which happened before the one which is narrated. This is how the story about Pop-Vujadin in "Anika's Times," "before it had completely disappeared into oblivion, provoked memories of other disasters and other times which have been long forgotten," and the story goes back to Anika, and in conjunction with her even deeper in the past to "Tijana's riot." The storyteller knows about them all, and he also knows that Anika's story is far from being unique: sooner or later, it will all happen again with some other girl in the *kasaba*. However, the storyteller also knows that both Anika's and Tijana's times are in the past and forgotten. At the end of the story we see how the veil of oblivion falls on all events. Mara in "Mara the Concubine" begins to be eclipsed while those who attended her funeral are still returning home from the cemetery. Rifka in "Love in the *Kasaba*" was remembered only until the following spring, when a new beauty appeared in the *kasaba*. Only a few months after her marriage, no one mentions the beautiful Gypsy girl Gaga ("An Uneasy Year"). The memory of a story resists the oblivion of humans: a story can recognize a pattern and a rule in the constant cropping up and disappearing of everyday life, the calm bottom of the ocean under the turbulence above. Marta L., the opera singer in "The Woman on the Rock," resurfaces from the sea "powerful as the world, which constantly changes but remains the same."[19] Those who insert themselves into chains of storytellers and hand down what they receive, who shun individual perspective in order to carry through what has endured for centuries, are entitled to such claims. Who else, apart from them, could pretend to have grasped what was and what will be, and to have understood the dynamics of change and sameness in it? When they write such a sentence, it does not sound gnomic in the way that a formula which sums up individual experience does, but as a universal truth. By sounding as a universal truth, it achieves the wisdom effect.

But what exactly have we determined about the world by establishing that it constantly changes but nevertheless remains the same? What the storytellers hand down to one another, and what reaches us as if from the depths of the past, lacks any specific content. It is not the shaping of individual experience in a novel, which no matter how polyphonic it might be nevertheless tends to follow a handful of lives, consciousnesses and worldviews, and thanks to that does achieve a specific meaning. And, contrary to religious traditions, which also come from afar and for the most part remain oral, the storytelling tradition claims neither this nor that about the nature of the world and human relationships. Instead of advocating any specific content, the tradition of storytelling merely validates itself as an ability of

---

[19] Ivo Andrić: *"Žena na kamenu," Jelena, žena koje nema*, Belgrade: Prosveta, 1981, p. 225.

shaping human experience in stories. If the "story of the human condition [...] that men never weary of telling one another"[20] has any content, message or counsel, then it can be expressed only by the sentence which Mihailo silently tells himself while surveying houses, people, smiles, hills, children's laughter, pine trees, Anika, beauty and evil: "All this is life." All: the paradox of the character in "A Letter from 1920," who escapes Bosnia, "the land of hate," only to find death in the Spanish civil war (which is one more version of the old oriental folk story "Death in Samara"). It is also the madness of Mustafa the Hungarian, who disgusted by people and by himself begins to kill everyone who happens to come his way, until he is killed himself; the suppressed erotic desire of Alidede in "Death in Sinan's Tekke," which still surfaces as a bitter regret in his final hour; the comedy of a struggle with an elephant which accompanies servitude to the elephant's master in "The Story of the Vizier's Elephant"; the decision of Vizier Jusuf to leave the bridge bereft of any inscription in "The Bridge on the Žepa." And most of all, it is the destiny of beauty, which harbors the seed of destruction and tragedy in "Mara the Concubine," "Anika's Times" and "An Uneasy Year": beauty and evil stay side by side, as extremes which touch one another.[21]

---

[20] Ivo Andrić: "O priči i pričanju," the Nobel Prize acceptance speech, in *Istorija i legenda*, Belgrade: Prosveta, 1981, p. 68.

[21] On female beauty in Andrić's stories see Radmila Gorup: "Women in Andrić's writing," in *Ivo Andrić Revisited. The Bridge Still Stands*, ed. by Wayne S. Vucinich, Berkeley: University of California Press, especially p. 165, and Dragan Stojanović: *Lepa bića Ive Andrića*, Podgorica/Novi Sad: CID/Platoneum, 2003.

This simultaneous and contiguous existence of beauty and evil prevents the storyteller from passing final, unambiguous judgment on the world. Instead of giving the world closure, as religion does, the wisdom of the storytelling tradition opens it up to the multitude of its phenomena, and to the irreducibility to a closed and final meaning. "Truly wise," wrote Andrić in his notebook, "would be a man who would on every occasion and in every moment keep before his eyes the infinite and immeasurable multiplicity and diversity of phenomena in human life and social relations, and who would be constantly and consistently guided by this knowledge in his thinking and acting."[22] It is almost as if someone whom you approach for advice, counsel, guidance, and an answer to the question of why we are here and where we are heading replies: open your eyes wide and you will see wonders, as I saw them.

The ability to see humans simultaneously as innocent, beautiful beings, such as Mara the Concubine, and as embodiments of monstrous bestiality, such as Mustafa the Hungarian, was crucial in Andrić's choice of Goya for a figure of an artist with whom to identify. What was it that Andrić could see at Goya's centennial exhibition when he visited the Prado in 1928? An artist of unrivalled success, who rose up from a modest background to the position of King's Painter saw the misery of the hovels of the poor, and the splendour of the Spanish court, the sensuous joys of life in Madrid, and the horrors of famine in the war from 1808 to 1812. Two of

---

[22] Ivo Andrić: *Znakovi pored puta*, Belgrade: Prosveta, 1977, pp. 167–168.

Goya's paintings, both still in the Prado, illustrate the breadth of vision which both Goya and Andrić shared. Both paintings share the same subject: the 15th of May, the day of St. Isidro, the patron saint of Madrid. On that day the Madridians crossed the Mazanares and went to the spring of healing water. However, the two paintings represent two very different visions. On the one hand, *La pradera de San Isidro* (St. Isidro's Meadow, 1788) portrays a splendid spring day, with white Madrid houses across the Mazanares, and under the blue sky a bridge over the river, resembling the one in Višegrad. Closer to us we can see houses, roofs, people going about their business, and Andrić's Mihailo might add "and people's greetings and smiles." In the foreground a group of young men and women sit on the grass, in elegant, graceful positions. A girl pours wine into a young man's glass; the others exchange a kind word, or a smile—and this binds them together. This is a world without suffering, fear or evil. On another wall hangs *Peregrinación a la fuente de San Isidro* (The Pilgrimage to the spring of St. Isidro, 1821–1823) which portrays the same landscape, but plunged into a darkness which conceals the sky, Madrid and the river. Out of the darkness crawls a long column of weary and tormented people. They are crowded together, one on top of another, as if shackled together. And in the foreground, we see human faces disfigured from suffering and evil, their own and that of others. Both visions belong to the same painter.

In that exhibition Andrić could also see Goya's beautiful *Majas*, nobly relaxing in the anticipation of sensual pleasures; the smile of the beauty in *El quitasol*; the demure beauty of his *La aguadora* (The water seller), who might easily have been a woman from the bazaar in Sarajevo; the Duchess of Alba, a self-conscious beauty who seems to be wondering why her orders have yet to be obeyed. And at the same time and on the same walls he could see the spectacles of madness in *Corral de locos* (Yard with Lunatics) or *Manicomio o Casa de locos* (The Madhouse); a man just about to stab a helpless woman lying on the ground; humor emanating from the grotesque scenes of *Los caprichos*; and most importantly, *Los desastres de la guerra*, the scenes of violence, suffering and death with title-commentaries such as *Yo lo ví* (I saw it), *Y son fieras* (And they are like wild animals), and *Porque?* (Why?). On one of them, *Popolacho* (Mob), one sees a man lying on the ground being beaten to death by a man and woman, while the mob cheers them on; on another, parts of a dismembered body hang on a tree; on yet another, a group of men and women being shot by an invisible firing squad. And finally *Saturno devorando a su hijo* (Saturn devouring his son): *mythos*—a story which people have been telling one another different versions of— comes in at the end to give the final comment on the meaninglessness of horror, violence and death. Those beautiful girls, and these horrors, all this is life.

Zoran Milutinović

Love in the Kasaba

The town lies in the hollow of a basin. It is enclosed by the Rzav hills, the rocks at Olujaci, and the Lijestanski slopes of Lijeska. The high and almost perfectly round ring they form is no more than half an hour across on foot. On a sandy and flood-prone peninsula, two fickle and threatening mountain rivers come together; they deliver devastation twice a year in the form of floods. There the town—so squeezed by the ring of heights that the last of its small houses lean against the first inclines—is battered by droughts in summer, avalanches in winter, and unexpected frosts in spring.

If the great stone bridge, a vital point on the route to the east, had not existed, no town would have ever originated at this spot, or elsewhere, in circumstances like these. Thus life was not easy for anyone in this town; it had been created by necessity and acquisitiveness, not by natural development in favorable conditions. For as long as it had existed, the town had never known uncontested property, a secure room, or a placid year. Indeed fortunes had been made here, but one could neither show off one's wealth nor enjoy it quietly. Instead it was necessary, once wealth was acquired, to conceal it,

1

and every day to capture more; it was all actually nothing more than security for the turbulent and lean years that could always hit.

The restricted horizon, the barren soil, the raw climate, and the frequent raids and wars left even the children the pugnacious, manic appearance of provincial Bosnian townspeople. When a young man had grown up, married, had children, and completed his twenty-fifth year, he was outfitted for life in the *kasaba*. And his character was set: sullen, stooped, wiry, matter-of-fact, squinting sharply—and above all taciturn and careworn. Having grown old so early, he then lived another fifty years or more and proved almost impervious to change. He simply became grayer and more stooped.

The people knew no mirth. Their pent-up vitality and joy came out as violent passions and provocations, individual and collective. Whatever humanity they retained in the face of this difficult life soothed in its pitiless struggles, they tranquilized with religious ceremonies, or established, simple modes of familial devotion, and shopkeepers' notions of honor. But in exceptional cases, they did demonstrate unexpected solidarity, daring, gratitude, and greatness.

Thus they were born, took husbands and wives, earned their livelihood, and went on and on with their hard, numbed existence.

But, once, love did make an appearance: when Rifka fell in love with Ledenik.

Ledenik was from an aristocratic Croatian family. He had grown up in Vienna and had been a lieutenant in the dragoons, but owing to his many amatory adventures and some financial troubles, he had been obliged to leave the service. By making use of his good connections and his knowledge of languages, he took refuge in Bosnia, where he was appointed forestry superintendent in the *kasaba*.

Rifka was the daughter of old Papo, a Jew who had arrived from Sarajevo fifty years earlier. He was a poor glazier then, but now he was the town's foremost merchant. Rifka was not even sixteen, but for quite a while now she had not been able to pass through the center of town in peace. No matter how she altered her gait, everything about her was forever quivering, bouncing, or swaying—her dress, her breasts, her hair. The young shopkeepers, who were always on the lookout for a hot beauty like her (whenever one of them got married, another was just about grown up), raised their heads from their work, whistled, cleared their throats, and called out to each other. Danilo, the butcher, bellowed and bit off a chip of the pinewood doorframe in his shop. Meanwhile his customers, munching on their grilled liver, laughed and clapped their hands. And paralyzed Murat Bektaš, who was all skin and bones, sat motionless by the charcoal stove and simply followed her with his eyes.

Someone said: "Ah, she shines like glass, all right. You can see she belongs to the glazier."

They sent her to school in Sarajevo. When had she and Ledenik first caught sight of one another? What words had they first exchanged? The lovers themselves forgot that.

In letters he called her his "star of the heavens"; he asked her to arrange a nocturnal meeting "when the world and its insane curiosity are asleep." She responded: "Why do you call me 'star of your heavens,' when you are my sun?" She informed him that her love did not know the difference between night and day. He sent her colorful candies and she sent him a pressed flower. He strolled up and down in front of her house, and she did not draw back from the window. The townspeople noticed all this and started to talk.

Papo, a quiet man of small stature who had an enormous beard, deliberated with his wife about what they should do to prevent this disgrace. They wanted to marry Rifka to the rabbi of Bijeljina. Through a relative they were negotiating about the dowry. Nonetheless the scandal grew; the Jewish community was abuzz and Rifka's brothers made threats. Rumors were spreading through the town. They locked the girl in the house. No one noticed the two of them together any more, but they exchanged letters and saw each other every day, even if only from a distance.

This was in the spring. After a day of rain, there was a great deal of haze hanging in the air. It was hard to breathe. The town turned gray and hunkered down even further between the mountains and the plum orchards. Only the trunks of the trees turned green, came to life, and branched out, and every leaf sparkled in the sun, which appeared briefly just before evening.

Ledenik took his binoculars and scrambled up the hillside next to the bridge. Rifka climbed up onto the foundation of the wall in her courtyard. They were separated by the river. His side already lay in the shadows, but, for a few moments, the sunlight glistened on hers.

Her red hair was fluttering in the wind and gleamed from time to time, and her white apron shone in the sun.

It was only darkness that broke the two of them apart. That is when Rifka went into her dark room, where, chewing on her fingernails, she sat on the divan and watched the shadows lengthen outside. She found it unbearable to have such a long night ahead of her and to know he was so close, but that nothing would happen. She wanted to write to him, but she choked at the very first "My dearest." Her chest swelled, her breath disappeared, and she was trembling. Her mother looked in and reprimanded her for letting a candle burn needlessly. Then she chased Rifka into bed.

At the same time, Ledenik, not knowing what to do with the long evening hours awaiting him as well, wrote to a friend from his old military unit, Baron Geza Durnajes:

Dear Geza,

I have already written you about my new posting, as well as the new officials I am compelled to work with and the forests I am condemned to roam. And so I repeat once more: I have been too severely punished. But have no fear—I have not yet lost hope, although that day might not be far off.

All the things I told you about the people here, the natives, were not just first impressions; they are confirmed day after day. I live among savages, filthy and unlettered. These people are not only uncivilized, but—I am firmly convinced—can never be civilized, because they use what little spirit and intellect they possess to confound every such attempt. And those who seem to me to possess a little understanding are so introverted that you'd have to strike them with a steel bar to see a spark of intelligence. Naturally, they don't open up to us.

I've already written you enough about the dirt, the lack of the most basic comforts, the tedium, and the brutality that surrounds me here. Nothing has changed in this regard, except that maybe it's gotten worse.

But, that said, extraordinary things are happening to me here. And that's what I want to write to you about now. In this wild and desolate setting, there are two things that console and delight me.

The first is the great Roman bridge with its eleven massive, splendidly vaulted arches. In this barbaric corner of the world, among the emaciated livestock and dull-witted people, it stands there, isolated, like a stray messenger from some distant and radiant world. Many evenings, when one cannot walk on the street for the dust and the animal droppings—when it becomes clear to me what I have lost and what I am up against now—I feast my eyes on these enormous arches and on the marvelously hewn materials.

The second unusual thing—you will have guessed it already—is a woman, or rather, a girl. She seems just as out of place here as the bridge. One of the petty local merchants, a Spanish Jew, has a daughter who is not yet seventeen. Her hair is dark red, and luxurious, in that Semitic way; her skin is amazingly pure and soft. And her eyes are dark brown, almost black. Do you recall the wife of Captain von Greising? This one reminds me a bit of her, but just twenty years younger. And a hundred times more beautiful. And a thousand times more innocent. In short: ambrosia for the gods. Among all the women here, who are impossible and anyway almost invisible, this young Spanish girl is my sole hope and my only solace. She is educated, too. And it would appear that she is in love with me, but out here that is not sufficient justification for a woman to be accessible. They never leave her unattended. We see each other on the street, and even if we exchange a few words (she can hardly speak due for embarrassment), they look at us like we are freaks of nature. When I walk past her house, I hear her mother furiously slamming the shutters. We write to each other, and for the time being that is all.

If you could only read these letters! The very essence of innocence! But my clerk—a local, who carries our letters back and forth—says that in the *kasaba* there is already far too much talk about us and that the Jews, who are quite fanatical, are furious with me. He told me that the family is trying to get the girl married as quickly as possible. To hell with them! Let them marry her off! That will be the end of those letters that so move me and make me laugh. And there will be no more little redhead, no more touching of fingers and coy glances. Then all I'll have is this bridge with its harmonious lines. That much is certain.

And now you see what a sentimental ass I've become in this wasteland. What's next?

Ach, Geza, you old dodger! Write me often, and at length, so that at least a little of the magnificence of life there reaches me.

As summer began, the messages to and from Bijeljina crossed more frequently. Preparations were under way in Papo's house. Rifka decided to yield to Ledenik and come to a night-time rendezvous in the garden.

At first they spoke through the fence, with their fingers convulsively intertwined. They kissed for a long time through the enclosure, and the crimson impression of the slats remained on their faces. Finally, on the third night, Ledenik leapt over the high fence. As he was climbing up, she was still protesting and calling out fearfully, but ever more feebly: "No, no, no…"

When he landed in the soft flower bed next to her, from on high like that, she swooned and lost herself in his embrace.

And again the next night: Ledenik dropped from the fence, and wide-open arms interlocked. But on the third night, the brother broke in on them. A frowning, rather short young man, he showed up in his underwear and nightshirt, looking totally bedraggled. Ledenik fled, Rifka collapsed into the flowers, and the brother shot twice into the night.

The next day Hajmo Romano appeared, leading a group of prominent Jewish men. They requested of the district superintendent that Ledenik be punished and removed from his post. The superintendent promised them he would do so. And then he had a talk with Ledenik, clapping a hand on his shoulder as he spoke:

"My dear Herr von Ledenik! I am quite sorry to have to spoil your little adventure with the Jewess. But her father is a respected citizen, and the Jews are threatening to lodge an official complaint. The girl, it seems, is love-crazed. You rascal! In a nutshell: it would be advisable for you to get away for a while. I shall send you on an assignment."

Ledenik assured him that the whole affair was meaningless, a minor flirtation. But if things were really as the superintendent said, then he was willing to leave. There was no end to their mutual amazement at these people who could fabricate some big romantic tragedy from absolutely nothing. Their resounding laughter lasted a long time, and then they concluded that the matter was worth neither the bother nor the scandal. With that, they said a fond good-bye to each other and parted.

Ledenik went off to the woods on Mount Setihovo. From his log cabin there, he wrote to his friend in Vienna:

My dearest Geza,

I've been in the forest for eight days. If I were to tell you how things are going, it would only mean repeating and doubling my personal misery. I don't want to do that. It's better if I just come out with it right away: I've lost both the Jewish girl and that beautiful bridge!

A scandal has erupted. To hell with all the Jews of this world! And this insane country too! First the slander, and then complaints to the district superintendent, conversations and love through the fence (can you imagine me in that pose?) and then, one night, her brother with the revolver. The superintendent requested that I break off this flirtation for the sake of the prestige of the authorities and for my own safety. He asked me to take this assignment here in the forest until things calm down in that stinking provincial town. Oh, please, what kind of people are these!

Here I have no choice but to wash down the peasant girls... but even then the whole thing smacks of bestiality. But they'll marry off the little Jewess, and she'll get fat and have six kids. God help her!

I am obliged to remain here until autumn. Maybe by then I will have arranged a transfer to Sarajevo. I am supervising the surveying of these accursed forests, and I'll be damned if I understand anything at all about this work. Write me, so that I don't go completely feral.

9

Rifka, however, lay sick in bed.

Through the shuttered windows and the thick drapes, one could still sense the blazing heat outside. Inside her room, a dense coolness prevailed, the kind one finds in ground-floor rooms with thick walls and iron shutters. There was also the deep silence of spaces crammed with rugs and clothes that are forever being fumigated and having the dust knocked out of them; the room seemed more like an altar than living quarters. In here the sound of steps was lost, and in the presence of so much fabric, voices did not carry: everything suffocated and was silenced.

The semidarkness was only penetrated when Rifka jerked on her mattress at the end of the room; her skin and hips and shoulders would flash as she tried with feverish motions to throw off her blanket. Then the gypsy woman, Hata, emerged above her from out of the shadows, quickly covered her up, and disappeared back into the darkness. In fact, Rifka had not regained consciousness since that night. She saw what was going on around her. She heard the doctor, her teacher, and her mother; she could make out what they were saying to her, and she herself would even utter an occasional word. But everything was like a dream.

She was no longer intent upon sneaking a letter out to Ledenik or justifying herself to her relatives. That all lay in the past. Now her only reality was the jerking, which came along every ten minutes. It began with an unbearable tickling in her calves and then made her knees bend and stiffen; her chest shook and she gagged. And when the spasm passed, she lay there trembling in anticipation of the next one; it was so inevitable that she started twitching and writing as soon as she thought of it.

She had no memory whatsoever of the love affair. There was only Ledenik, in his white trousers, fleeing again and again over the fence. And beyond that, there was nothing except the convulsions and the darkness, where an unfathomable shame rained down on her. If only it would stop pouring down through this dark, narrow space! If only it would cease! She tried to get up, but Hata, who was keeping watch over her, kept putting her back in bed. And once again came the fall into the bottomless depths, and then the spasms.

One night just before dawn, she heard one of her brothers leaving the house; he did not lock the door behind him. She waited a bit and then got up. Hata had been overcome by sleep. Rifka crept across the room; twice she tumbled to the floor as she made her way out of the house. She left the door wide open behind her, clung to the wall of the courtyard, and then pushed away and ran off down the steep street.

In the market-place she fell down again. As day emerged from night, a sharp wind was blowing from the east; it carried the dust and garbage to one side of the street.

She stood up again, her arms and palms bloody. She walked past the Great Han and went down the steps leading to the Drina River. She fell to her knees, remained there bent over for a moment, and then staggered on. From the bottom step she hurled herself into the water. Her nightshirt spread out around her, and she

11

remained there, motionless, for some time. Then the current caught her and carried her away.

Although day was just breaking, the street-sweeper Liskić and the dim-witted porter Hubo saw her from the edge of the market-place. As the stores opened up, they went into one after another, saying that they had seen the half-naked Rifka rushing past.

"The Captain probably had his way with her last night."

"For sure! And how!" cried Hubo, smacking his palms together and hopping on one leg. The shopkeepers clicked their tongues and laughed.

But it soon came to light that the girl had vanished. The next day the body was found among the logs in a cove. Fish had already bitten into the corpse.

The Jews scurried about busily. A team of officials quickly appeared and made an investigation. Then Rifka was buried towards evening that very day, right next to the street at the far end of the Jewish cemetery. All of this was carried out in silence and in haste.

Summer had barely reached its midpoint, and already the drought had begun.

One could see processions of Turks moving along the Drina; they went with their *hodjas* to pray for rain. The Orthodox priest clambered up the hill with the old women and peasants behind him, all of them drenched in sweat; they proceeded up to the cemetery and held special services there. Their candles drooped and melted before they were used up. There was no breeze and it was not cool even in the shade. The forests were begin-

ning to catch fire up on the mountains; on the horizon
one could see the smoke. Down below it was black, and
up high, where it merged with the sky, it was whitish.
And above everything hung the bleached-out heavens,
which were as hot as the lid of a baking dish.

The flies and gnats were biting. The butcher shops,
ditches, and gutters reeked. The cattle bellowed in their
stalls, but they couldn't be let out, because the gadflies
would not leave them in peace. In addition, there was
nothing on the burnt slopes for them to graze on. The
people were gasping as they stood at the double-doors to
their homes and shops. They did no business, but the flies
wouldn't let them sleep. Sluggish, disheveled, and half-
naked, they trembled with irritation. With curses and slaps
they vented their spleen on their wives and apprentices.

Both rivers were drying up. They grew narrower and
greener, and their murmur was audible all across the
somnolent city.

The gardeners on Mount Okolište stopped watering
their orchards and melon patches. The stems on the
melons curled up from the drought, and the fruit fell to
the ground and rotted.

Then, one evening, Milan Glasinčanin called together
his neighbors and confided in them that a man named
Petar, who had moved there from Hungary, had said
that no rain would fall until the drowned girl was
thrown back into the Drina, or at least until they emptied seven buckets of water into her grave.

They conferred for a long while. On the steep slope
underneath them the tombstones of the Jewish cemetery
shone white. The men smoked and talked and waited

until it grew completely dark. When the lights of the *ka-saba* went out below them, they drew together; each of them brought a helper. Carrying their tubs on poles, they departed for the Bektaš fountain. The fine stream of babbling water only gradually filled the buckets. The men sat nearby, fighting drowsiness, and the tips of their cigarettes ignited in the darkness.

They filled all their containers and hoisted the poles to their shoulders. The tubs swayed and water sloshed onto their bare feet.

When they reached the graveyard, one of them used a pick to dig up the dirt alongside the large gravestone, and they began pouring in the water. The parched, loose earth at first soaked it up, but by the time they had emptied the fifth bucket, the water began to flow back out of the grave. A puddle formed all around. At this point, a feeling of horror started to overcome them. In great haste they dumped out the last two buckets and scurried away. They all knocked the mud from their feet. No one said anything.

The next day, early in the morning, the gravedigger appeared and saw that the earth around the tombstone had been displaced and was still wet. He cursed and summoned Staniša, the road guard, who happened to be walking past with a pick and shovel. They threw the dirt back and stamped it down with their feet. Then they sat down and leaned against Rifka's gravestone, which was still cold from the night. They took out their tobacco pouches, slowly rolled themselves cigarettes, and lit up.

"Pouring water into graves—that's utter nonsense! It doesn't depend on the dead but on the will of God. It's a drought, that's what."

"Of course it's stupid, but the people think it's necessary. If I knew it would help, I'd dig up every grave in the *kasaba* and water each one of them. Take my corn, for instance: it had barely come up before it got burnt, and that was the seed that I had bought from Pavle on credit…"

They kept smoking, spitting, and looking up at the sky, and in that way they chatted for another hour or two about the drought.

But no rain came. People slept out on the grass in front of their houses, but the earth no longer cooled off even at night. Women fainted walking across the meadow, and children were constantly getting sudden nosebleeds. The *kasaba* shimmered, reddish and overheated, in everyone's eyes.

Milan Glasinčanin, who had led the men to water Rifka's grave, was unable to sleep. He had locked his doors and did not dare open his windows. He was sweating in the stuffy room but would suddenly get cold each time he thought back to the way the saturated grave had gurgled and spat out the water. He jumped up and laid one of the poles across the door. The lamp flickered on the wall. A yellowish moth was fluttering around the sooty glass. 'Now how did that get in here? The witch! Isn't that the barefooted, wet Jewish girl?' He chased the moth, but he was shaking and his fingers were so swollen and hardened from labor that it was able to evade him. He kept on waving his arms and lunging at the moth, and he knocked over the lamp, shattering the globe so that the wick went out. He panicked when he found himself in the dark. He retreated into a corner and groped about for his ax. There he squatted and stared around the room, straining his ears for any sound in the darkness. He was trembling as he pressed his face against the cold iron blade.

Papo's house was sealed up and quiet. Inside, everyone was bathed in sweat, choking on tears, and feigning sleep in front of each other.

On Mount Setihovo, Ledenik wrote to his friend:

> I'm going to kill myself, Geza. I am definitely going to kill myself. If I could just endure this red-hot, filthy Siberia till autumn, then everything would be all right. But I fear that I won't make it that long...

He lay all day long in the shade, fending off the gnats with little walnut boughs. He was surrounded by tall fir trees, straight as icicles; large amounts of resin were leaking out of all of them in big, heavy beads. The crickets—which didn't quiet down the entire day—irritated him, as did the peasants' drawling songs which rang out every now and then from their shady resting places:

> "Thirsty for water,
> thirsty for water,
> I yearn for girls."

Towards evening an animal call could be heard from the dried-up marsh: hoo-hoo, hoo-hoo, hoo-hoo. It seemed to be calling down the darkness. Foxes yelped in the night, and the dogs grew alarmed. It was never peaceful. There was only sweat and sap and an unrelenting pressure in his benumbed brain.

Nobody could remember a drought like this one. Many people fell ill. In addition to Milan Glasinčanin, two Turks went mad, and were sent away to Sarajevo. There was no hay or other fodder, and the wheat failed completely. The cows and goats stopped giving milk; people were already worrying about food for the winter.

It was not till right at the end of the summer that the heat broke. An icy wind came up and rain storms blew in; then the heavens cleared, and large, bright stars were visible in the night sky. One day after another passed this way in the tranquil autumn light. The people in the town put on their clothes and shoes. The merchants resumed their travels and profiteers moved through the villages. Everyone was on the lookout for wheat and hay; sellers rejoiced, while buyers scowled.

Papo, the glass merchant, held weddings for two of his sons simultaneously. One of his daughters-in-law was from Sarajevo, the other from Rogatica; both of them were wealthy. The tambourines shook in his courtyard, and his house resounded with wedding guests.

Ledenik had finally succeeded in getting himself transferred to Sarajevo. He came down from Mount Setihovo, all gaunt and sunburnt, and he did not hear about Rifka's death till he spoke with the district superintendent.

"That poor creature!"

They each smoked a cigarette. The superintendent congratulated him again on the promotion that would take him to Sarajevo, bringing him access to good society and a state-owned apartment with a bath. Ledenik left town early the next morning, still a bit saddened by the memory of the young Jewish girl.

That fall, the daughter of Perko the cobbler reached maturity. In summer she had still been swarthy and disheveled, with traces of early apples around her mouth. Now all of a sudden her skin became fair and she grew so thin that she nearly broke in two at the waist; when she walked through the market-place, the shopkeepers got agitated and called out to each other.

At one end of the rows of shops, Faisal the Albanian, who was making pastries for Ramadan, got the ball rolling; he banged his hand against the hot copper baking sheet and yelled out:

"Here's a hot one! Hot, hot, hot!"

And from store to store the responses rang out: "Oh, yes! Oh, yes!"

Danilo the butcher bellowed and bit off a sliver of wood from his toothmarked doorframe. His customers laughed so hard that they choked on their liver. The girl pressed her hand to her breasts to keep them from jiggling. Then she quickly adjusted her gait and blushed, as her steps resounded on the cobblestones.

Translated by John K. Cox

An Uneasy Year

The first half of March marks the beginning of a special season in Bosnian towns, which has no name in either the calendar or popular speech. These are days when the sun begins to strengthen; when the snow melts, there is no rain, but a south-westerly wind dries out the soil in the gardens and the mud on the roads and streets; when there is no sign yet of leaves or visible buds, blades of grass or flowers, only the wheat just sprouting on the winter ploughed land looks like a diluted, thin, greenish light; and in the clear morning a coral-green, ruffled halo plays round the occasional rare tree, a peach, or early plum, hinting at future buds and distant, uncertain fruit. All the rest, fields, copses, meadows, gardens, the façades and roofs of houses, everything has the same austere grey-brown tone. The sky and the surfaces of the river and ponds are grey, and even the wind—which carries with it rotted matter and dust, and a person feels it in his throat, his lungs, on his skin, and with all his senses—appears to be the same color.

Caked, dry, barren, grey. The eye roams in vain seeking for some other color. In the pupils a painful unease and in the mouth a dryness that fits in with the general dry deprivation and monotony. In an effort to overcome the dryness, a person swallows his saliva, and finds in its taste that same dry dreariness that he sees and feels everywhere around him.

This is the time of the greatest shortages and deepest gloom in the town. Even the best winter stores have passed their prime, loans have dried up, people's reserves of energy, joy and patience are exhausted. The animals' coats are dull and their eyes gummed up. The housewives cannot think what to prepare for lunch. The children have nothing to play with. Peasants come down from the mountains, looking in the town for a little food, whatever the conditions, until "the new comes through."

Perhaps the only creature in town whom this season suits is the money-lender, the usurer. Only, his joy is invisible and lost in the general gloom.

Neither shortages nor the grey gloom of the pre-spring season penetrate into the room where Master Jevrem sits. This year less than ever. This year too the need for money or wheat is great and conditions very hard for the one who wants them, but very favorable for the one making the loan. Master Jevrem's affairs are going well. His men go round the town and villages, making down-payments on wheat that is just beginning to sprout and plums that have not yet begun to bud. Master Jevrem can be satisfied, as he is, more or less, every year at this time. But the joy that now fills his room is not of just one kind. In this room there is a strange, new and joyful change, so strange and so new that it both is and is not joyful, not the whole time and not for everyone.

It has been fifteen years now that this grey-haired, burly man has been unable to use his legs. He was not much more than forty when the lower part of his body became paralyzed. Since then he sits at home, virtually entirely immobile, cared for by his wife and his widowed daughter with her little girl, and all his close and distant relatives, and all those who work in the house and shop. And not only them. It could be said that he is served by this entire town, all the villages around it, and even by many people from other more distant towns and communities. For, Master Jevrem may be sitting motionless, but, as everyone says, "he is sitting on money." And money either attracts or repulses people and makes Master Jevrem a living, immovable center, around whom a whole little world revolves.

And so the town has grown accustomed to seeing Master Jevrem as a real master on whom everything and everyone invisibly and indirectly depends, and this goes not only for those who have been baptized but also for many of the Muslims, and even the Turkish authorities themselves. And everything he possesses, he himself has earned and made. Jevrem's father, Master Marinko, was a small-scale merchant, a timid man, without enterprise, respected in the town more because of his goodness and honesty than because of his property and trading skills. Towards the end of his life he had completely lost heart.

It so happened that Master Marinko sent the youngest of his four sons, Jevrem, to be an apprentice in the famous house of the Ćuković merchants in Sarajevo.

The boy spent four years in Sarajevo and proved himself exceptionally gifted and quick in business affairs.

Old Ćuković used to say of him:

"This child is brighter than all the other apprentices, and it is a pity for him to go back to the wilderness and sink there without trace like old Marinko. He is made for Sarajevo and the wide world."

But Jevrem's father would not hear of it, saying that he knew that his son was bright and able, and that was precisely why he wanted him at his side, for he had not sent him away to be Ćuković's lad, but a merchant and a man in his own town.

And Jevrem really did become all that it was possible to be in a small town in those days. And that was more and different from what the quiet, conscientious Marinko had in mind. Jevrem succeeded his father in the shop, surpassed all his brothers, borrowed, married into a rich household, achieved status, what is called "status" in the commercial world, which is the right to be just as he wished in his business dealings, and meant that no one could do anything to him and other people needed him and not he them, that he did not depend on their opinion or their goodwill. And Master Jevrem protected and nurtured that "status" of his, which was both a secure defense and a powerful weapon; he cared about it as much as money itself.

From the very beginning, he worked most with money, and for a long time now it has been his only real work. His money circulates round the whole of eastern Bosnia. In the villages around the town every fourth household is in debt to him, and in the town itself there is hardly a merchant who does not depend on Master Jevrem or did not do so at one time, at least in the first years of his business.

He is now a strong, heavy man with a large head of grey hair. He has large brown eyes, eyes which know everything and have only one kind of look, their expression varying simply with the lowering or raising of his slanting lids, which are folded and heavy, like old, formal curtains. His thin, white moustache falls over his youthfully full, pink lips, which are always motionless because a spoken word does not move them, and they are never known to smile. He is wrapped in a blanket up to his waist, but the upper part of his body is always dressed in clean, neat clothes. There is always a fez on his head. And so he sits, on a raised place and on a specially made cushion. Around him lie cashboxes, registers, keys and all kinds of small objects, all within reach, should he need them when he is alone. But Master Jevrem is rarely alone.

First, there is his family. His wife Staka, his daughter Draginja and granddaughter Jevra. At least one of them is always in the room or nearby, so that he can call. And he calls them by banging a stick on a small, copper dish which hangs beside him like a gong. Several times a day, all three women stand in front of him, afraid and submissive in the face of his heavy, stern gaze, before which, everyone believes, nothing can be hidden and which confuses and disturbs even those who have nothing to hide. And he looks at his house slaves: three women so similar and yet so different in shape, clothing and age. Before his penetrating gaze, those three women are like some kind of inter-connected vessels. He can see the way the life force is being poured from one to the other with every passing day. Everything that the grandmother has lost with the years she has passed on to her daughter, a sturdy widow, and she is already passing part of that on to her little girl, who is twelve, and just beginning to fill out and come into her own.——A limited amount of life's juice that is not lost, but simply changes the vessel in which it is contained.

There are the lads from Master Jevrem's warehouse, who come several times a day to stand in front of him, their eyes lowered, trembling with fear in case they become confused and get something wrong. For then Master Jevrem lowers his heavy eyelids and just says, through his teeth:

"Come here!"

And no one can remember that there was ever anyone—old or young, man or woman, relative or servant—to whom those words have not been spoken. They each come forward, although they know all too well what awaits them. And Master Jevrem takes them by the ear, draws them towards him and shakes and knocks their head against the wall, more or less forcefully, for a longer or shorter time, depending on the mistake and the degree of his cold anger. And that man with the paralyzed legs has extraordinary strength in his arms.

Then are his relatives, close or distant, and friends from the town, or business associates. It is well known that to do business with Master Jevrem means to suffer both loss and shame. (For he first reduces a person and weakens him by his scorn, and then takes from him as much as he needs and believes he can take.) But still they all come seeking him and his help, for at this time it is impossible to undertake any business in the town without meeting Master Jevrem or his money on one's path.

And, finally, there are numerous strangers who drop in on all kinds of business, because everything is connected with money; people who needed a loan, or the extension of a deadline, or an introduction, or advice. Others come to visit: the bishop and the mufti, the rabbi and the Turkish administrator and other leading figures in the town and prominent travelers and passers-by, for a chat—or for information. Because this immobile man knows people and circumstances, changes and events better than all those who spend the whole day walking around on their own two feet. And he wants and likes people to come, although he never shows it in any way. Whenever one of his visitors opens the door of his room, no matter who it is, he is greeted with one single word, always the same:

"Well?"

And there is not a soul who can resist the commanding tone of that word. As though hypnotized, the visitor spills out all he knows. And Master Jevrem looks at him with that heavy gaze of his, thoughtful, as though he could at once, even as the words are being spoken, distinguish deceit and fallacy from truth and reality. Like this, confined to his room, he knows everything better than any individual who comes to give him information, and more than all of them put together. And in the same way, he has accumulated wealth more quickly, has more and keeps it more securely than any healthy, mobile person in this town and the whole region.

Such is Master Jevrem's power, which everyone acknowledges and respects, both the state authorities and the church, and not only people who depend directly or indirectly on him. No one can see the limits of that power, because he has succeeded in making it into a monster, and all the people around him, who are in any case quick to be reconciled, have reconciled themselves to the thought that, as long as he sits on his cushion and merely moves a finger, no one can resist him and that his power must be older than everyone else's.

"Who can do anything to him!" say people from the town, who both know Master Jevrem well and hate and despise him deeply.

"God doesn't wish to, and people can't!" they shrug their shoulders to one another.

And that is how all discussion of Master Jevrem in the town ends.

But nevertheless, life does not stand still, as it seems to the powerless, and no one's strength and power is so great and enduring as it appears to those who want or have to endure it.

A few years ago Master Jevrem's wife Staka took in an orphan girl who had literally been "left in the street." That year there was hunger throughout the country. The roads were full of Gypsies whom the lean year had driven to change their location more rapidly than usual. There were all kinds, coming from all over the place, those who considered themselves Muslim and those other Gypsies, tinkers, who rarely appeared and whom the people called "Karavlah", and who thought of themselves as Christian. They were all fleeing from the same misery. Their tents kept springing up around the town and disappearing again. That year one of them was ill with typhoid fever, and they brought him into the town as well. The townspeople fell on them, to kill them. As they fled, they died beside the roads and hamlets which would not let them in. It happened that in the wake of these various groups of Gypsies, sick, driven on by hunger and the embittered people, parentless children would be left, abandoned. So one little girl, of perhaps seven or eight, was found. It was thought that she was one of the baptized tinker Gypsies, although it was hard to tell by the rags and filthy state of the abandoned, sickly and hungry child, and she herself, weak and frightened as she was, could not say much about herself or her people. Master Jevrem's wife took the little girl in as a good deed and also a way of coming by a cheap servant. It should be said in passing that these contradictory impulses satisfied this woman's basic moods, and that they colored not only this, but almost all her actions.

In the first year of their marriage, she had borne Master Jevrem a daughter. The birth had been difficult; she had been ill for a long time afterwards and barely survived. She had never been either beautiful or cheerful; now she aged prematurely and excessively. Wizened and bony before her time, she ran the household zealously, immersing herself completely in her chores. After a few years, Master Jevrem said, as though incidentally: "She has dried up!" Just that, but it was a definitive judgment

27

on her and her life. And the more she worried and toiled, the more superfluous and small she felt in the face of that husband who grew increasingly in her eyes until he had finally become a malicious and fantastic deity whom she served with all her strength, but with no hope of ever being able to satisfy him. Seeing that she was unable any longer to serve him with her body and fertility, she served him all the more zealously in whatever way she could. She kept the house, acquired things, saved and protected what she had acquired, until her saving turned into a cruel, pointless miserliness through which the mistress of the house avenged herself for her ill fortune, unwittingly, on the whole world and herself. But still she was never able to attain not merely kindness and recognition, but even the smallest sign of gratitude from her terrible master.

Women like this, cold by nature and unhappy in marriage, such as Jevrem's wife, are blinded by their misfortune to everything else in life, and that blindness brings them new unhappiness. Mired in the dark and for her the only world of eternal household concerns and insensitive to all other human needs and instincts, she could not have imagined that this little girl would bring neither benefit nor the rewards of charity.

The foundling, on whom, as the mistress put it, there was neither cross nor name, was known in the house as Gaga. To start with, the child was wild and unyielding. She did not remember her earlier life or any of her family, but she bent and adapted slowly and with difficulty. A year passed in scolding, smacking, tears, and going to bed with no supper, but the child remained as stubborn and underhand as on the first day. However, the mistress so ground and wore her down that the child had to either give in or climb down, as did everything else that Staka grasped with her dark, powerful will and her bloodless, gnarled hands which, like the claws of a bird of prey, were incapable of letting go of what they had caught. It was not until the third year that the little girl began to "change her nature" and bend to the demands of the house into which she had fallen, to accept their lessons and their family language, and to serve without answering back. And by the time the mistress's "success" was complete, the child had already entered her fifteenth year and barely resembled the little Gypsy who had come into Master Jevrem's household like a small, bristling wild creature a few years earlier.

Gaga "obeyed" her mistress, she worked from dawn to dusk, humming something barely audible and incomprehensible all the while, carrying out all her chores ably and competently. But Gaga was also growing, and strangely, suddenly and before her time. The mistress's tight fist did not feed anyone she did not need to palatably or plentifully, and that included Gaga, but with her everything she ate struck root and was transformed at once into blood and strength. Her waist grew slender and her face longer, and she began to swell luxuriantly in the hips and breasts. Her clothes became shorter and tighter on her so that the mistress had to get her new ones or, more often, alter something old of her own or her daughter's. It was not, of course, either expensive or lavish, because it was measured with the mistress's eye, but whatever Gaga wore glowed on her in new colors, and swirled in unexpected folds. Everything on her blossomed, as though she herself were in flower. Her face grew narrower and thinner, and her eyes larger, her hair acquired a new sheen and fell in waves of its own accord. She hid her eyes and tied up her hair, but she could not conceal her walk, and her walk changed from one day to the next, as did her movements as she worked, becoming ever stronger and more graceful, without her knowledge or her will. So her whole bearing and appearance began to contrast increasingly with the other women in Master Jevrem's household.

It goes without saying that this was all a slow and gradual process, the way things in nature come to fruition: each individual stage of maturing passes immediately into the next, higher one, and it is hard to see them separately, for as we study them ("yes—no," "yes—no") and as we hesitate on that inconstant line that separates "yes" from "no," it has not only become what it appeared to be but it is already more than that. That is how everything in the world matures, and womenfolk particularly.

By nature cold-blooded, and entirely submerged in her molehill, the mistress observed nothing of all this; all the beauty in the world might bloom beside her, without her noticing any of it. But her daughter, gifted with somewhat more femininity, which widowhood had suppressed and strengthened, had a better eye and more understanding. But the first to notice and immediately judge the change in Gaga was Master Jevrem, silent and immobile on his cushion. During the first years she appeared before him only rarely and exceptionally, with great wariness, fearful and fluttering, like a bird which flies in at one window and out at another. But since last autumn it began to happen more frequently and to last longer.

That autumn day, Gaga had taken something in and turned immediately towards the door, her new wide trousers billowing as though they were wafting her along.

"Stop!" called Master Jevrem unexpectedly and hoarsely.

She stopped, turned and looked him straight in the eye. Her gaze was uncertain, cloudy and moist, with a hint of a smile somewhere in its depths. He looked at her for a few moments. Nothing could be observed on his face, but—something unheard of—Master Jevrem was surprised, frightened, one might say, if it were at all possible that anything could make him afraid.

"Leave!" he said then, in a quieter, softer voice.

And then, from day to day—"stop!," "leave!"— Master Jevrem summoned Gaga more and more frequently, finding something to ask of her or chide her with. Between the old master and his servant, whom he had not even been aware of until recently, there began a secret game without pause or end.

Gaga was still fearful and submissive, and paid in her words and movements the usual tribute of fear, which every living human being had to pay to Master Jevrem.

"Come near!" said the master, after he had forced himself to find some cause for anger.

The girl approached.

When his uncertain hand had found her ear in her thick, unruly hair, he took lengthy revenge on it, squeezing it cruelly, convulsively.

31

This happened once, twice, until one day, on precisely one of those dry, grey pre-spring days, the following took place:

"Come near!"

The words were spoken sharply, perhaps too sharply, but with too much breath, so that they were followed by something like the hint of a sigh, like a muffled sob.

At this the girl, as she walked, turned, twisting unexpectedly and strangely, with just the top part of her body, like a young poplar in the wind, and from that incredible position, which confused all the old man's thoughts, she replied briefly and gruffly:

"No!"

Only the moisture in her eyes was smiling.

And the master, in his immobility, became still more immobile, quite forgetting that there was anything healthy and moveable about him. Everything in him and on him suddenly seized up: his thoughts, his tongue, his hand. Only his eyes watched the twisted, turning girl, but they too were fixed in astonishment. For, it seemed to Master Jevrem that he was suddenly seeing a being from a different world, which did not resemble in any way the people who had moved around him up to now, and was not subject to any of the laws that reigned in this town or in his house.

And then something miraculous happened. For the first time since this little, closed world of Master Jevrem's had been going the way it went and Master Jevrem had been directing it from his cushion, for the first time ever he had to repeat what he had just said,

32

because he had not been instantly obeyed. But his words now had an altered sound, as though fractured.

After that everything was once again as it ought to be and apparently the same as before.

"Come near!"

And she would approach, but with a kind of smile and easily, without a shadow of fear and as though of her own accord. It even happened that she approached without his having called or asked her. Then he could not conceal the fact that his hand trembled. With that she had completely disarmed him. But often the reverse would occur, the very next day. She did not want to approach him at all, deaf to all his threats and pleas and hoarse summons. She would simply slip like a weasel through the barely open door and close it soundlessly behind her.

This strange and apparently innocent game drew the unapproachable and immobile Master Jevrem into its vortex as well. What neither events nor people nor the years had been able to achieve, was achieved, without her having any inkling of it, by this Gypsy lass of not quite fifteen; she insinuated herself into him, piercing him and beginning to gnaw away at him as a worm eats at wood, invisibly, from inside. In the eyes of strangers he was still just as he had always been, no milder or more human in his speech or bearing, there was no sign of change or weakness anywhere in him. But the people in the household, who were around him all the time, particularly his daughter Draginja, could from time to time observe on his face an unusual expression, both carefree and thoughtful. This was brief and transient. A second of forgetfulness. But still, that expression confused them more than any of his fits of anger, it alarmed them, as though they had caught sight of the mark of some terrible, unacknowledged illness, the beginning of decay.

Draginja was the first to give any sign of alarm. Jevrem's wife, insensitive to these things, as always, was mistaken again, not seeing or understanding that she was least well qualified in matters of this kind or that her will or her hand did not help here, nor could they achieve anything. Horrified, as though she had discovered a serpent in the house, she ordered Gaga to collect her rags and go back to the Gypsies she had come from. The girl just shrugged her shoulders. But then Master Jevrem blocked her way with an energy that the mistress could never have guessed he had, let alone understand or resist. Powerful, as he had always been, but even stronger and more terrible, he fell from his cushion onto his knees, crushing both his wife and daughter, threatening to force them to roam the highways and byways should "anything happen to the child."

After that, everything, apparently, returned to normal. The master continued to ask, increasingly often, that Gaga should serve him in his small needs.

Ever since he had heard her soft singing outside his door, from time to time he would stop her in the room:

"Sing!"

She would look at him, hesitate for a time, then lean against the wall, let her arms fall in front of her, one wrist over the other, so that they appeared tied, and, tilting her head slightly to one side, begin to sing softly. She sang mechanically and a little resentfully, like children whom their parents drive to sing in front of guests, but she sang each song she started conscientiously from beginning to end. As she sang, he watched rather than listened. And sometimes he would stop her in the middle:

"Enough!"

She would look at him in surprise, as though awoken, her mouth still open.

"Enough. There's no need for more!" he said dryly, just the way he spoke when she poured water over his hands or into his glass, and the girl would withdraw, a little uncertainly.

But it also happened that she did not feel like singing, and instead of the song he had requested all he would hear was the rustling and flashing of her wide trousers through the room, the click of her small slippers and the muffled bang of the door closing behind her.

But the next day she would sing again, at length and with dedication, if he asked her to. She would not start either a song or a conversation without his request, nor would she stay in the room longer than essential. And it would happen that he did not say anything or ask anything of her for days at a time. Never again did he grab her by the ear as he did others. There was no physical contact between them, barely even a word. Just her presence and his glances. He became still more silent and motionless, and she came in and out at times according to his wish, at others at her own whim, because for her, if she did not want to, there was no such thing as "Come here" or "Stop!." She fluttered around him, and for the most part he just watched her movements in

35

silence, as though reading them and as though in his old age he was learning from them what one really needed to know about life, but that he had never guessed, even in his youth.

And that realization without name or limit seemed to bring everything to life, give it wings and lift it up, and enable it to move and rise to unimagined heights, carrying him with it, immobile as he was. In the face of this girl, the world had a thousand faces. And it was all new and unknown. Sweet and seemingly dangerous, although you did not know exactly what kind of sweetness it was and could not see where any danger might lie; you could not make out anything at all. Because none of that had ever before had any meaning in his life, or influence on his thoughts, moods or actions. And his response to it all was a kind of cheerful energy, ready for anything, that Master Jevrem felt within himself, his response was the bitterness he felt towards his wife and daughter because of their malice and hatred of the little Gypsy. He would defend her, not from those loud-mouthed, brainless women, but, it seemed to him, from different, far greater forces. And not because of the little Gypsy herself, but because of that cheerful resolve within him. But of course all this was unknown and invisible, just for him and just in him, while he himself remained, with each and every person, just as he had always been, scowling, rigid and relentlessly calm.

And the women in the house appeared calm too, as though there were no breath in their bodies. But it was an illusion. With barely concealed hatred, they followed with watchful eyes every step and every movement of this new and dangerous creature, which had suddenly broken out of the cocoon of Gypsy Gaga and begun in her own way to rule in their house. And at the same time they discussed it all with the aunts and uncles and all the other older and more experienced members of their very widespread family both close and more distant. As though by chance and under the guise of commercial dealings, the mistress's brothers and cousins came from as far afield as Foča. The vast but powerful family mechanism had been silently set in motion and was now functioning, slowly, but resolutely.

That spring there was waged one of those family battles in which no one truly acknowledges their intentions and no one calls things by their proper name, but everyone does what he can to thwart his opponent's aims and achieve his own, not choosing the means and sparing no one.

In this battle, the women were restless and talkative (at least in whispers), while the men were silent and sullen.

"He's under a spell!" said Jevrem's wife tearfully, under her breath, "she's a tinker, she's cast a spell on the man. And what a man!"

"A spell, a spell!" sighed the women with her.

And together they all sought ways of using different, stronger sorcery to drive out the sorcery with which Gaga had enchanted Master Jevrem. Meanwhile the men looked on askance and contemptuously, although they were themselves worried, for although they knew better than the women what Master Jevrem's "sickness" consisted of and what kind of sorcery it was, it still made them anxious. It was a question of their standing and

37

interests. Master Jevrem's wealth and position made him the founder of their clan, the shared pride of the whole extended family, and now, if word got round that a little Gypsy girl was capable of casting a spell over *that* Master Jevrem, he would lose much of his standing in the world, and so would they along with him. For such weakness is not forgiven in the town or the commercial world and indicates the first sign of loss of power and the beginning of decline. Jevrem's strength had always lain in the fact that he had never taken anyone else into account, he had never focused on any individual person, whoever he was, for he needed no one. But now: it was a woman and a Gypsy, and in his own house. And then, it was well known that an old man is always open-handed towards a young woman, and once he starts making gifts, you never know where it will end, for when such a man gives he has the illusion that he is receiving. And they knew how bloody and furious Jevrem had always been in receiving and taking.

So the family tormented and contorted itself like an organism trying to reject a foreign body that has entered it and is torturing and threatening it. Many lengthy conversations took place, but nothing emerged into the outside world, because such families, otherwise so easily excited and loud-mouthed, also know how to pretend and to stay firmly silent when their reputation, or their interests, which was the same thing, were at stake. Only Master Jevrem saw through them and behaved even more sternly and inflexibly towards them. He did not so much as notice his wife, he only said to his daughter on one occasion:

"Listen you, viper! You and that mother of yours, and all the rest of you, you are to hold your tongues and stop thinking what you're thinking, because you'll all go to the devil."

Draginja pretended not to understand and asked him what he was talking about, but he knew how to silence her with just one glance. And, holding her by the ear, added through his teeth, speaking right into her lowered eyes:

"I created you, I can destroy you as though God had never given you!"

And he spoke briefly, tautly, and as though incidentally. But nevertheless, his threat remained hanging between them like a real force, confusing their thoughts and putting a brake on every decision.

In family conversations and discussions, which were endless, the words "we" and "she" were constantly repeated.—When someone in these large family communities says "we" he is always in fact, above all and first of all, thinking of himself and his wife and children; but nevertheless, they can in exceptional circumstances, such as these, pull together temporarily into a strong community to unseat and eliminate even a stronger opponent than Gaga, a Gypsy girl and a servant. But Gaga had Master Jevrem's backing. Days and weeks passed in whispering and forging plans, but things in Master Jevrem's household were not improving. On the contrary. Prayers and sorcery achieved absolutely nothing. Then the men of the family began to think up more drastic measures. Master Jevrem's nephew, a tall, dark youth, with large eyes and a fixed stare, one of the closest future inheritors, had already begun to mention, through clenched teeth, a certain Kajtaz, a murderer and brigand, who, for good money, could remove without trace or sound even someone quite different from a penniless foundling without family or roots. But initially the other men and particularly Jevrem's wife Staka shrank from such a step. There was no torment that she did not wish on Gaga, but to take her blood on her soul so openly, that she could not do. "It's not in our nature," she said. And her daughter Draginja, dumb with horror, affirmed with a nod that this was true. In fact, they were not so much afraid of the sin and crime as the thought of what they would do after that and how they would remain alive in the house with Master Jevrem.

It seemed that the affair had no end, that it could not after all pass without great evil and someone's destruction. The town had got through that grey, lean pre-spring period and real spring had arrived. The world burst into leaf and flower, and the fruit was already beginning to form. Everything looked nicer and people were more cheerful, but the secret battle in Master Jevrem's household had not let up. Master Jevrem, hard and unyielding, as only he could be. Gaga full of life. She blossomed before Master Jevrem's eyes, up there, on the first floor, while down on the ground she felt at every step that the women were tormenting her as much as they dared and were able, and that their hostility was driving her from the house; but still she worked and sang, carefree in her innocent beauty, which was changing from day to day, and as it changed—increasing. In the family the conspiracy was progressing; even the most measured of them were giving in and all beginning more and more to lend their support to the most terrible solution.

But it was precisely then that life, of its own accord, decided matters that those involved were unable to decide. Life, which never stands still, and least of all in times such as these, suddenly altered the course of things in the town, and therefore also in Master Jevrem's household, turning them in an unexpected direction.

The army arrived.

Since the spring word had been spreading through Bosnia about the imperial army that was to come, led by General Omer-Pasha to carry out *reforms* and subdue the insubordinate local lords and leaders, to introduce the order and justice that had been talked about for so long but which no one had yet seen or experienced for himself. They had seen and experienced only the other armies that had come before, under other generals, trying to achieve the same things, and those armies had brought with them all the burdens and troubles that they always bring.

For the ordinary people of these parts, peasants and townspeople, "the imperial army" denoted only partly and vaguely what the same term denoted everywhere else in the world, that is an organized force with a certain number of soldiers and officers from a state, with living and moveable assets, with a certain tradition, flag, uniform, rules of service, etc. For them this word had a far wider meaning, or, rather, a whole series of meanings. On the basis of their experience, the word "army" meant the same here as "war," violence and plunder, forced labor and hunger, flood and drought, and all of that together; in short: every evil and misfortune, the reverse of life and everything that a person could find pleasant, precious and sacred in life.

And when these people heard that an army had been assembled and was approaching, they did not ask what army, marching on whom, and why, but followed their inherited habits, saving their lives and their families and as many of their possessions as could be saved. Above all, they endeavored to keep as far as possible away from the highway and all traffic. But, if a peasant was able to conceal himself in woods and the urban poor to clamber uphill to a thicket which the approaching army had no time to search, the established townspeople rarely, hardly ever did the same. Their position and understanding of things were such that they were connected to their houses and property like snails and would not part from them as long as they lived. So they tried to get by with as little damage as possible.

At one time, armies used to pass through this little town in both directions, from Bosnia further on to the east and from the east into Bosnia. Not a single army could pass Bosnia by. But, over the last twenty or so years, armies had rarely come this way. Only the old people remembered the damage and trouble that large armies had caused to this area as they passed through the town and stopped there for a while. That is why it was the old people who showed the most alarm and anxiety now, and why their precautionary measures seemed exaggerated and their elderly fears a little comic to the younger people, who remembered little. But when one day the army really did appear, it was clear that all those measures had been inadequate and that not even the worst fears were entirely unjustified, for even if everything that people had feared did not come about, many things did happen that were worse and harder to bear, things that no one had anticipated.

The army that came was just the advance guard of Omer-Pasha's main force. A battalion of regular soldiers in new regulation uniforms and contemporary European equipment. In addition, a cavalry unit and two cannon, new and shiny, of the latest type.

They came in good order, as had never before been the case with Turkish troops, accompanied by the blaring of trumpets and the commanders' snapped instructions. The troops were settled on the slopes above the town, and the officers billeted in houses. Some shops were emptied for the medical corps, the like of which had never been seen before. It all looked stern and deadly, but orderly and disciplined.

That is how it was when they first arrived. But by the very next day even the last, uneducated townsperson had realized that what the better informed people had been whispering was true: that this was not an army "passing through," but that Bosnia was its target and that this was to be its base for future operations. It became clear that all its orderliness and modern equipment was only for its own benefit, while its relationship with the land and its behavior towards the people did not greatly differ from earlier imperial armies. In the space of twenty-four hours these five or six hundred men had swollen, as though with yeast, and spread through all the roads and hamlets. They requisitioned stock and food, just like the earlier imperial army with no uniforms or western training, and the only difference was the fact that now they gave out receipts which those who had lost possessions usually could not read, and which no one believed, and which made no distinction among the population by faith or reputation or status.

During the first two days there were still uninformed peasants who would come along with horses, unaware of the danger, and suddenly find themselves confronted by a dozen soldiers in black uniforms, as though by a terrible court from which they could not escape. The same scenes kept being repeated, both on the main highway and on the minor roads.

The soldiers waved their arms and guns and shouted, while the peasant, transfixed, did not know what to do, he shot glances all around, pretending that he did not understand. And when, instead of explaining in words, they began tearing the halter from his hands, he planted his feet wide apart in the ground and resisted with all his strength, stretching his arms, straining, doing whatever he could to keep hold of the little horse they were taking from him with their incomprehensible cries. To start with he held it by the halter right by its head, but then he had to give way in the face of their greater strength, but only bit by bit. Centimeter by centimeter, the taught lead-rope slid from his desperately clenched fist, but he still felt that the horse was his, although less and less so. Finally, the rope slipped from him and he was left for another moment or two, standing like that, his feet apart, his arms outstretched; the image of powerlessness, a bit of human dust, whipped up in an unequal struggle with the whirlwind known as "the imperial army." Then he looked around him to see how he could turn off the road, which he had stepped onto so unfortunately, and lose himself in the bushes, but the soldiers made him stay to take the receipt which the sergeant was writing on his knee, sitting by the side of the road. The peasant waited patiently, feeling this was another part of the great ill that had befallen him, he took the piece of paper as though blind, and thrust it mechanically into his belt, while his eyes were still fixed on the little horse they were leading away from him.

After two days of this, the roads emptied; word had reached even the remotest villages. Then the army had to go to the houses and shops in the town and the neighboring hamlets in search of what it needed.

But the land through which an army passes does not suffer only from official requisitions. An imperial army needs a great deal; with thousands of eyes and thousands of hands, it seeks, snatches and uses what it needs, or destroys things pointlessly. An army does not need only bread and dripping, meat and salt, packhorses and harness beasts and animal feed, but also drink and entertainment and women. For an army consists for the most part of young men, with little to do, with hungry senses; and the exceptional exertion, the constraints of army life and the constant proximity of sickness, wounds and death, simply sharpen that hunger of the senses. In a foreign land and far from his own home, a soldier loses control and, feeling that no one spares him, he in return spares no one and nothing; poorly supplied, irregularly paid and fed, he helps himself as best he can, requisitioning mercilessly, often stealing, sometimes snatching things by force.

Such an army brings into the land it passes through a whole series of temptations of all kinds. Wherever its flood waters reach, everything, living and dead, is exposed to danger, but not all in the same way or to the same degree. Those flood waters break off and sweep away first and most easily what is within reach, exposed and poorly secured: fruit trees hanging over a fence, stock in grazing pasture, goods that cannot be hidden or locked away, people with no one to protect and defend them, who do not know how to get away or have nothing to offer as ransom. While everything that has stronger roots, that is connected by social and family ties, is less vulnerable and defends itself more easily when it encounters danger.

The older and wealthier people knew that and acted accordingly. Master Jevrem knew it all very well. At the time of the great uprising in Serbia, he had already been a grown lad and then a young man. Then for years armies would pass through the town, often setting up camp, and he well remembered helping his father to conceal property and people. He learned from him that there was no joking with an army, that it had to be given what was essential immediately in order to preserve whatever could be preserved. And now, from his cushion, remembering that experience, Master Jevrem gave orders to the lads and instructions and advice to his associates and relatives, which were brief and sharp, but usually accurate and useful. He arranged everything so that he and his were damaged as little as possible by this advance guard and prepared in the same way to receive and wave off the main army of that terrible general about whom such evil reports abounded.

In his head, Master Jevrem added up all the losses he had suffered in connection with this army's passage, and so far everything corresponded exactly to his expectations. He had always been proud of this ability of his to anticipate and calculate everything in advance; and the older he became, the truer this was. His sense of pride at this capacity went some way to mitigating the unpleasantness of the losses.

And what was asked of Master Jevrem, as the leading man in the town, was not little; sometimes even quite unexpected things. On the very first day he had to make a gift in person to the commander, Ali-Bey. The commander had asked him to find somewhere in town a barrel of good wine. There was general consternation. No one here had ever sinned so openly against the rules and good customs of the Muslims. From time to time one would hear of some Turkish civil servants or officers who secretly drank wine, people knew that Christians kept it in their houses, but no one in the town had ever obtained it or poured it for them. The authorities became agitated. Wine had to be found, and it was found where it was to be expected, in the wealthiest Christian house, that of Master Jevrem.

In connection with this request there was quite a lot of talk about the commander, and Jevrem was able to learn what kind of man this Ali-Bey was. He belonged to the unit known as the "renegade troop," which Omer-

Pasha, himself a convert, had put together. It consisted of various foreigners, genuinely or ostensibly converted refugees of various kinds, from various parts of the world. Most of them were Poles and Hungarians, who had fled to Turkey after the failed uprisings of 1836 and 1848. Ali-Bey himself was a member of the Polish gentry, an able officer and courageous man. He had been in the Turkish army for some ten years now; he had already been promoted to colonel and, with his abilities, he would have risen still higher had he not been a heavy drinker, a despondent man and an eccentric.

People in the town talked a lot about the fact that a Turkish commander asked for and drank wine. Among the Muslims, the affair provoked unspoken, profound consternation and increased the weight of the impression made on them by this strange army, composed of converts from all over the world, but sent not against the enemies of the Empire and Islam, but against the Bosnian beys. Some, the more prominent people, spoke about this openly and even complained to Master Jevrem. As he listened to them, he began to smile, an inner smile, of course, that did not alter a single line of his face. He sent a barrel of wine, with relish and no regret, rubbing his hands and thinking all the time about the possibilities there could be for the *rayah* in such times as these, when a Turkish commander drank wine openly and without a qualm.

The greatest unpleasantness for Master Jevrem did not lie in the fact that this army had taken goods and stock from him, as from all merchants, but that the army doctor had been billeted in their "small house."

That "small house" was on the other side of the large courtyard, quite separate, but sharing the entrance to the yard, and in the middle of the yard there was a well which was used equally by the doctor's staff and Master Jevrem's household. Master Jevrem resisted these guests as far as he could, but then the local prominent men begged him to make this sacrifice, for it was after all less awkward for the strange officers of different faith to move into his house, than into one of the Muslim families, where the women had to conceal themselves. Master Jevrem weighed up his chances of resistance and all the possible consequences of such resistance and—took in the unwanted guests.

The doctor, a Polish Jew, now Junuz-Effendi, was a quiet, decent, already elderly man, but his two assistants and the soldiers in his service took wood from the pile in the yard, washed themselves and their clothes at the well, and their general behavior irritated the household. As a result, the womenfolk hardly emerged from the house. In so far as the women had to pass from one of the house doors to another, they would run across the space, covering their heads with a scarf. And one of the young men of the house was sent to fetch water from the well.

One day, when there were no soldiers in the yard, the mistress sent Gaga as well as the lad Jevto to bring water for the whole day. (Afterwards she always said that God Himself had "given her the wit" to do so.) As they stood beside the vessels that were filling with water, the main courtyard gate was flung open and into the yard came the Commander Ali-Bey, with his entourage. They

49

swept brilliance and movement in with them. The men in their shining uniforms were cheerful: laughing and talking loudly among themselves. Their long sabers clinked on the white cobblestones. The whole yard was filled with unusual noise. They made their way to the house where the doctor lived, banged on the door and windows, but there was no one at home. The commander, a tall, fair-haired, middle-aged man, red in the face, of lordly bearing and abrupt movements, stood with his legs apart, gazing at the well. Then one of the men in his entourage went over to it and asked in a few broken words whose the girl was. Jevto, alarmed, was able only to wave his hand towards the main house, while Gaga, leaning against the well, bowed her head and pulled her scarf down around her face, but it merely framed her face, which was more confused than afraid, and all the lovelier for that confusion.

Just by the gate, the commander turned once more and glanced at the girl at the well. They left more quietly than they had come.

That was all. But on the same day, towards evening, strange negotiations began that disturbed the whole town, but Master Jevrem's household most of all. The commander had sent word that he wished to marry the girl from the well, immediately. At first, the idea appeared senseless and incredible. Master Jevrem resolutely refused the strange demand. The girl had no family, she served in his house, and he was responsible for her as for his own child. The commander was persistent. He sent word that he was asking for the girl's hand as order and custom decreed, that he was no worse than any other suitor, that he would not use force or abduction, but wanted everything to be done nicely, according to the law. But he would not give up his demand and he would not leave town without marrying the girl in the presence of the kadi or until she declared that she refused him. But the girl would have to be asked before witnesses, it was not enough for the master to speak for her.

Master Jevrem received this message with apparent calm, although he felt his blood pulsing under the skin in his temples and the cushion beneath him rising and falling, rising and falling, and so rapidly that it took his breath away and made his head swim. And when he was left alone, he raised both his hands with difficulty, lifted the fez from his head and placed it in front of him, as carefully as though it were made of glass. (This happened only in moments of great excitement, when there seemed to be no way out, and those were very rare in Master Jevrem's life.) Then he passed his fingers several times through the thin grey hair on his reddened temples.

That night he did not sleep, but he felt as though he were dreaming. As he passed through the town, through his, Master Jevrem's town, a drunken officer from who knows where entered his house, pushed him out of the way, and sat down on Master Jevrem's cushion, with his saber and boots on. And everyone knew all about it. And people said to one another that Master Jevrem had been outwitted and outflanked.

Dawn came, but the dream was still there. That rosy summer dawn resembled the distant and long-since for-

51

gotten cold dawns from his difficult days in Sarajevo, it took him back to the years when he was a young man and an apprentice, lean, thankless years in which life was full of desires and fears, but without power or prospects. It was only when the sun came up that he pulled himself together and prepared himself so as to be able to continue to negotiate with the commander about his crazy desire and unexpected demand, in a way that was worthy of Master Jevrem.

In the space of twenty-four hours the commander's demand created a whirlpool, which spread ever further, drawing into it an ever greater number of people.

All kinds of intermediaries came to Master Jevrem. There were the liars and blackmailers and pimps that sprang up on such occasions. But there were also reputable townsmen of both faiths, who wanted to find a solution and so rid themselves of the army that was oppressing the town and would apparently not leave until the commander's will was done.

Master Jevrem's good, old acquaintances, such as Sulejman-Bey Osmanagić and Daut-Hodja, came to him, sat silently, lowering their eyes in their perplexity, then they spoke about recent times and altered natures, but in the end their whole bearing showed that they thought Master Jevrem ought to give in, although their cheeks burned with shame.

The zealous local authorities became involved as well; not on Master Jevrem's side, of course. The commander's representatives and various friends of Master Jevrem's spread news that uninformed and anxious people received without verification and passed on. First they said that the girl had not even been a Christian, but had been snatched from some Muslim Gypsies, given to Master Jevrem's household and there baptized. Master Jevrem therefore ought to be glad that no one was looking into it more closely and that the most favorable outcome to the whole affair would be her satisfactory marriage. Then they changed tactics and said (in confidence) that the commander was a Christian and only ostensibly a Turk, and that the girl, whom unexpected good fortune had befallen, would be able to keep her faith. In short, people said whatever came into their heads, and they would do whatever they dreamed up, just to satisfy the whim and fancy of a crazy, wild man, who was never entirely sober, but who now held the fate of this town and everyone in it in his hand.

As a result, the impression was rapidly created among the people that this army, that lay like a burden on the town, would leave the moment Master Jevrem relented and handed over the girl. Their embittered impatience grew. The men, many of whom remembered Master Jevrem for some evil deed, and all of whom, secretly, envied him his wealth, power and unwavering rise, could barely conceal their malice. ("What is this Master Jevrem thinking? That the army can burn the whole town, but he won't go back on his word!") While the women added their own note, which the man dismissed angrily with a contemptuous wave of the hand: "What does this Gypsy of Master Jevrem's want? She's probably waiting for the Vizier to come and ask for her hand!"

It was only now that Master Jevrem was able to see that not even his experience included everything, that

53

not even his power of anticipating and his shrewdness were always valid and did not reach everywhere, that what was called by one name, "the imperial army," had a hundred faces and a thousand demands, and concealed in itself so many dangers that no one could foresee or avoid them. It was not only that it plundered and beat and killed, but it lied and deceived and penetrated into a person's life, touching him in his most hidden and tender place. And its rough soldier's hand did not simply take animals or goods, on the road or in warehouses, but dragged what was most secret and most precious out of one's house, before one's very eyes, out of one's heart. And it did so through the unseen and irresistible power of imperial authority, with the help of the fear it spread around itself, which you could not see or weigh up, and which no one could escape. And even what remained was no longer what it had been: unreliable, it no longer pleased you, as though it were not yours.

Those days of strange negotiations were hard and uneasy. The negotiators were, of course, unequal in power and position. On the one hand, an unpredictable man who at this moment could do anything, and who in any case had nothing to lose and for whom law and consideration did not exist, of whom his own people said that on his campaigns he had already married several times in this same way, and on the other Master Jevrem's laborious but determined resistance.

The commander kept sending new messages, through new intermediaries. Master Jevrem looked at them and listened, and was simply amazed. He had never had a high opinion of people, but he had never guessed that there were so many good-for-nothings, capable of anything, in the world. And as though there weren't enough of them here, new, unfamiliar ones had arrived with the army.

Towards evening on the third day an unknown man came to Master Jevrem, a kind of secretary to the commander for affairs of this kind. You could not tell where he came from by his speech, nor what he was by his dress. He was tall, thin, red-haired, with a small head and a face as speckled as a bird's egg, with a cold, shameless expression and a quiet, icy voice. He announced his message without drawing breath and without shifting his gaze from his victim. The message contained the following: Master Jevrem appeared to be of the opinion that bad people had come with the imperial army who wanted to bring harm and shame to the town. But Master Jevrem was a merchant who knew the world and must be aware that there were bad people always and everywhere, including certainly also in this town or around it. Such people could always do great and irreparable harm to prosperous and prominent citizens, and there was no need to bring them in from outside. But if Master Jevrem nevertheless thought that the imperial army had brought such people with it in its ranks, let him say so openly. Let him complain and the matter would be investigated. The path of every complaint was known. None was left unanswered, and nor would his be either. And Master Jevrem could be certain that he would *receive a reply*.

That was all. And Master Jevrem, who, himself silent, knew how to drive everyone to speak, was unable to drag a single word more out of this sinister visitor. The man left as though that message were the only thing in the world that he had to say. Besides, Master Jevrem did not himself know what he could still have asked him. The message was conveyed in a mysterious manner, but the threat that was contained in it was perfectly clear, clearer than Master Jevrem found agreeable.

That evening, when the commander's man left his room like a shadow, Master Jevrem did not call for light to be brought, and none of the household dared to go upstairs and appear before him without being summoned. He sat in the half-dark, with the commander's threat beside him, as alive as though the one who had sent it was here as well. Master Jevrem spent the whole of that night with it in silent conversation, and when day dawned, he made an abrupt decision and gave in. Firmly, briefly and without many words, he cut the matter short, as he always did in his life. And then everything went simply and as though of its own accord, like a stone when it breaks off a hill and rolls down a steep slope. It was still going on, but it was already over. And everything finished, as in a dream, quickly and easily, as though even for this exceptional affair there had long since existed an established order and pattern.

The town, which had wished for such a decision and tried to hurry it, condemning Master Jevrem's hesitation and reveling in the fact that there was a master above Master Jevrem, was suddenly surprised. People seemed all at once to see and be ashamed of the violence they had favored and the many lies they had themselves spread. There was no more conversation or gossiping, and suddenly that unusual silence set in that always accompanies exceptional events. And everything was done in silence. It was impossible to know what anyone was thinking or feeling; all that was known was what the commander wanted, and that this had been carried out.

The army left and with it its commander Ali-Bey and the little Gypsy Gaga, and, so people said, as his lawful wife at that.

In the town there was a lull and sense of relief, and the desire for rest and forgetfulness, which always follows great excitement. Everyone tried not to think of the main army that was on its way, and particularly not of the one that had left and everything that had happened in connection with it. For everyone wanted to live, making up for what he had lost or acquiring replacements, to live his own life, in his own way and in the space in which he found himself, even if that space was no wider than the palm of a hand, between two armies passing through.

That second, main, army came sooner than the town had hoped. But, surprisingly, it came and went more easily and with less upset and damage than anyone could have imagined. No one actually saw the famous, terrible Omer-Pasha, the general, as though that interesting and dangerous sight was intended only for larger towns. The people who said "The little officers are worse than the big ones!" were proved right.

Everything was calm in the town. Master Jevrem's household was settling down as well. The women worked. Relatives dropped in. Conversations were once again loud and ordinary, as they had previously always been. Those conversations buried the little Gypsy who had so disturbed and concerned them all. Only the mistress Staka could not stop herself from mentioning the affair with Gaga in front of her daughter. She did not pronounce her name. She just let out a long sigh, in some way a victorious one, and said:

"The plague brought her, war took her away; she was theirs in any case."

When some time had passed since Gaga's departure, the mistress asked the priest, Pop Jevrem to read a prayer and fumigate the house. This was all carried out on the lower floor, without Master Jevrem's knowledge. They even closed the door onto the staircase so that the smell of the incense did not reach him. The priest did not wish, in any case, to climb the stairs up to his namesake without great need. There was a reason for this.

During those few difficult days, when Ali-Bey and his army were sitting in the town and when Master Jevrem, without saying a word to anyone, was trying to resist and not give Gaga up, he thought at one moment of summoning the priest and talking over the whole thing with him, as a man of God. It was not Master Jevrem's custom to seek help and advice from his townspeople, and least of all from his namesake the priest, whom he did not particularly respect, but the times were really hard, the matter exceptional and, after all, it was a matter of a baptized soul, and that was, after all, the priest's business. He sent for him, but the priest was nowhere to be found. He had wisely disappeared, finding that it was precisely during those days that he had to bless the water in the high villages around the town. ("The good-for-nothing!" said Jevrem to himself.) As soon as the army had left the town, the priest appeared the very next day. He went straight to Master Jevrem.

"I heard that you wanted me for something."

"Not me!" said Master Jevrem coldly, but naturally.

"But they told me at home."

"No!"

"Ah well," said the priest, wanting to initiate some kind of conversation, and in his awkwardness he kept undoing and doing up a button on his waistcoat.

And so he left, muttering something all the while, but thrust from behind by Master Jevrem's contemptuous silence, as though by a real and tangible force.

That was why the priest was in no hurry to appear so soon again in front of his namesake.

And, up in his room, Master Jevrem was already calmer and more self-possessed on these summer days. He had not come to terms with his loss, because he could not yet do so, nor did he try to weigh it and determine its extent, and nor did he gauge exactly what it was he had had and what he had now lost. His thoughts stopped at that point, it was still a darkened space, to be passed over. He had not come to terms with it, but he was calmer. He was no longer tormented by that oppressive sense of having been set back, returned to his starting point, to the immature, hateful years of his youth and apprenticeship. Similarly, now he was certain that he had given in at the right time, that no one in the town had guessed the true reason for his resistance, but that, on the contrary, this resistance had done him credit

59

in the eyes of the people. His reputation was saved. And that was the main thing.

What loss and misfortune he had sustained lay in himself. No one could see or know that, and it was therefore as though they did not exist, and that made things easier, or if not easier then brighter. As a summer's night passes by open windows and a steady candle flame, which only the pre-midnight breeze begins to bend, so Master Jevrem was beginning to see that everything that flutters (how it fluttered!) had one day to fly away. He had expected nothing from that late, great joy; nothing, least of all that it should endure. But still, it had never occurred to him that it would end so quickly and abruptly and in such an unusual way. He felt that he ought to regret it more. He felt, but he did not regret. Beauty departs and is easily lost. Nothing in life is constant, and that—least of all. Beauty fortifies. And that cannot last. Beauty had gone. Gone with the army. A new army had come and gone. A third might perhaps come, bringing new losses; he was prepared in advance for them; he would endeavor, of course, to ensure they were as slight as possible, but they would be as they would be. One of those losses was this lost beauty, and what it had appeared to promise so capriciously and uncertainly.

As he thought about that lost beauty, he saw the Gypsy girl once more, but not as she had been as she came in and out over the last year, always different and increasingly lovely, he saw her now transformed, prepared to leave, standing before him and declaring for a second time that she agreed to marry Ali-Bey. "Yes," the changed girl had said, as though she had learned from him that every question and everybody should be answered with one single word. There was a cold decisiveness and something like defiance and a threat in her voice, and a new, firm expression on her face, while her eyes looked somewhere over his head into some world that only she could see. That world was full of unknown masters and potentates, who all outshone one another. But she was not afraid of that and was prepared to go, and she wanted to prove her readiness to everyone through her bearing.

That was how she came up to his hand and kissed it, the way one kisses a deceased person to whom one is indifferent. And that was how she left, without a backward glance.

Master Jevrem thought about Ali-Bey as well, sometimes, on these still warm late summer nights, but he thought about him more calmly now too, and without that dark, impotent rage of the first days. On the contrary, the more often and the more he thought, the more he became accustomed to him. And strangely, but truly, that unknown, distant man without a country, without a house or home, even without a true faith or true name, that drunkard, unpredictable sick man and saber-rattler of bloody occupation, began to seem somehow close, sometimes like the closest of men, like a kind of kinsman, like a double.

He sat here, in his own place and among his own people, welded to his cushion, imprisoned in his room out of which through two quite small windows he knew and followed the course of the seasons. He lived for his

61

shop and his house, for his reputation in the town and among people involved in commerce, for what his name and his money meant to people. While that other man flew, with his soldiers, over the length and breadth of the Empire; one moment he was in Arabia, the next in Albania, the next in Bosnia, he attacked whoever he was ordered to and struck down whoever stood in his way, snatching from life and its beauty whatever could be snatched in flight like that, getting drunk so as to forget who he was and in order to be what he was. Whatever he possessed he carried in two saddle-bags, and everything he needed, from food and drink to a woman and a bed, he found wherever he happened to be, constantly changing place and circumstances. This changing of everything around him clouded his awareness of himself, and what change could not achieve, wine and brandy certainly could. He did not remember himself or who he was or how he had once been, he did not see blood, he was not afraid of wounds or death, he did not pity himself or anyone else. And, in moments of rest—Gaga poured water over his hands.

(Here Master Jevrem's thoughts passed over that forever darkened place and continued their course.)

That was what his double's life was like, or something like that. Well, that was life too. But the closeness and kinship that he sometimes felt in the hours of night for that double of his were so great that it seemed to him that he was not sitting on his cushion, but on a small, hot, Circassian saddle, that what was coming in through the open window, through the vine leaves and over the flowers in their pots, was not a nocturnal breeze, but a powerful current of air drumming in the face of a galloping horseman, and that what was pulsing and beating inside him was not his own excited blood, but the knocking of his broad saber against his thigh.

Here Master Jevrem came to, waved his hand, surprised himself by his boyish fantasies and dreams. And he blew out the candle, wishing to seek in the darkness a dreamless sleep.

The summer passed, and with it a kind of summer sickness and all these memories of Master Jevrem's. The autumn was well advanced. Winter was already in the air.

The year had not been particularly fruitful, although it was not one of the worst either. And the army had done considerable damage. But there was no hunger either in the villages or in the town, and there would not be—until the first days of spring. (Then, of course, those who had nothing would seek, and those who had and were able to would give, and set conditions.) Everyone was engaged in all kinds of important autumn tasks. At such times everything changes and one thinks ever more calmly of what once was.

By now Master Jevrem was completely calm. He sat thoughtfully, smoking and watching the smoke as it dispersed, but this was not a man thinking of beauty and loss, of Gaga and Ali-Bey. His thoughts were quite different and they moved in a quite different direction— news came that Omer-Pasha was breaking the resistance of the beys and local leaders, he was beginning to lock them up and execute them, or send them into exile and confiscate their lands. And he was preparing for worse and blacker things. It was becoming increasingly clear that he would not leave Bosnia without finishing the job and that many a bey's household would be left without a head and many properties without owners and for sale. Many men had bowed them, but this one, it seemed, would break them. And where some lost, always the strongest and wealthiest, there was work for others and money to be made.

Master Jevrem followed all of this from his room. People came to him for news and to hear his opinion. He told them as much as he wished, little or nothing, while they, unwittingly, gave him the information he needed, or filled out what he already knew.

When the arrogant Šemsi-Bey Alagić from Okolište tried to get to him, Master Jevrem knew quite well what it meant, but learned still more from their conversation. The Bey was elderly, but slender, with regular features, an aquiline nose and large blue eyes. He asked nothing, said little himself, but what he wanted was clear. He had two houses, one in the town itself and the other in the village of Okolište. He would like to sell the one in town. It no longer suited him, he said, and he was spending more on it than it was worth. But who, nowadays, had so much ready cash that he could buy such a house? And he would not ask much.

Master Jevrem looked at him and everything was clear. People who had never been fearful before, including this Šemsi-Bey, had now become so. There was no escape from the rank of people to which he belonged, and, besides, that would not be what he wanted, but the times were such that it was not good to be among the leading people or to have a house in too prominent a place. And what use was a house in which he did not live? Even this skin of his was beginning to feel increasingly tight and heavy. A man had to insure himself. Who would not understand him and who would hold it against him.

And when the bey left, Master Jevrem looked at the door which had just closed behind him.

"They're starting to sell up. They're starting!"

Then he lowered his gaze and stared at the brightly colored carpet spread over the floor; he looked at its pattern, and, the more he looked, the more that pattern seemed to be transformed into the map and disposition of the town and all the houses, properties and land in and around it. That map was becoming ever more accessible and Master Jevrem was able to read it easily, and at the same time he ran through in his mind what belonged to whom, what it had once sold for, what it was worth now, whose it had been before and whose it might still be. He heard the clink of the money with which it was paid for and the rustling of the documents passing from the previous owner to the new one. He heard and saw it all and thought about everything clearly and energetically, and, however he looked at it, in the end it turned out that times were coming of great and sudden losses for some and of course of careful and steady acquisition for others. And among those others was he.—And Master Jevrem looked, and looked, and calculated, and shifted and rearranged the properties, and changed their owners, bought and resold them, went ever further and deeper, losing himself in calculations and all sorts of ruses until his eyes were blurred and the pattern began to dance in front of his gaze, and everything began to merge and mingle, so that he no longer knew who was who or what was whose.

This filled both the winter days and evenings for Master Jevrem, and it made the season easier and more agreeable. For Master Jevrem did not like the winter, an evil season, with short days and long nights that sleep could not fill. In winter, in his opinion, a person withered like an apple on a shelf, and it was only summer that restored his lost strength.

This winter too, as every winter, when you open the door of Master Jevrem's room, the scene is always the same. Bright and warm. The air smells of burning apple peel. Master Jevrem will be sitting on his cushion, wrapped up to his waist, wearing a fur-lined cloak and a dark red fez. He will greet you with a sharp look and one word or none, but always hard and commanding. But if you sit for a while and look more closely, you might see that there is some change in him and that this year has not passed without trace. At least that is what people say who go to visit him. For the townspeople, merchants who have borne Master Jevrem for years as a nightmare oppressing them, and his relatives who in their plans often take into account the possibility of his death, keep a constant eye on him. They observe every smallest change in him with that dry, merciless shrewdness with which people in the town watch one another. And often, two of them, when they meet, after their initial greetings and, in the silence that regularly follows them, say a few words to one another about Master

Jevrem's health, without mentioning him by name or drawing any conclusions.

"His complexion is ruddy, but I'd say he was losing weight, melting away somehow."

"That's how it seems to me too, but you never know with him. Have you noticed the way his mouth twists when he speaks?"

"No."

"Well, take a closer look."

And they part, wishing one another good health.

Heavy snow and sharp frosts marked the end of the year in which Omer-Pasha's army passed through the town. And the town began to forget that army, remembering it only occasionally, for the damage it had done. No one had mentioned Gaga for a long time now, nor did anyone remember her, for she did not appear in anyone's calculations as a loss. Not even in Master Jevrem's. It happened that winter, only once, that he dreamed that he was healthy, on his feet and that he walked like Gaga, but he did not see her herself in that strange dream. In a thick, ceremonial cloak, reaching to the ground, he was walking across soft, green grass, easily and briskly. But he suddenly stopped, as though transfixed, because something held him, dragging him back. Although he could not see, he knew, in his dream he knew, that Gaga had come up to him from behind, stepped with both feet on his cloak, and now he could not move forward.

The sense of surprise and unease of this dream did not last long; Master Jevrem forgot it as soon as he woke and disentangled himself from the sheets in which he had wound himself. For, dreams have no power over a man who, when he wished, would easily and quickly forget real events, and did not remember dreams at all.

Translated by Celia Hawkesworth

Ćorkan and the German Tightrope Walker

T he circus' arrival was quiet and innocent. While
the stakes were being hammered in and the
ropes stretched and tightened, no one but children gathered around the site. It was not until the next
day, after they had erected the big-top for the performances, and a smaller tent with the rifle targets, that the
circus people paraded through the center of town: a
clown with white face-paint and a drum, a tightrope
walker whose short skirt was made of yellow silk, and
the manager wearing a threadbare tailcoat and shabby
boots. They had hired Sumbo the Gypsy to walk in
front of them playing his *zurna*. Following behind came
scores of children and Boško, the policeman. Even the
shopkeepers paid attention, and the women were peering through the windows of their houses.

The first few evenings passed quietly, but then the
boys began gathering in the shooting-gallery. They took
aim at the targets and, when they hit them, little tin figures would appear: a blacksmith striking a ringing blow

against an anvil, or a girl waving her handkerchief. Gradually this target practice developed into public passion.

Avdaga Sarač—once a well-known drunkard and rowdy, but now a sedate married man—was constantly closing the door of his shop and rushing off to the rifle range. The wife of the manager, stout and wrinkled beneath her blonde wig, loaded the rifles and handed them out. Avdaga would lean over the counter and slowly drew a bead on the target. There was only one target he ever aimed at: the one in the middle. When he hit it, up came Leda and, pressed up against her, a swan; after the bird flapped its wings two or three times, everything dropped back out of view. When he missed, he cursed under his breath and reached impatiently for another loaded rifle. But whenever he hit it, he took a step back in order to get a good look at the naked woman made of white sheet-metal and the swan on top of her. He muttered under his breath:

"Look how white she is, the bitch!"

And his eyes glistened like those of a man who is a connoisseur of both good rifles and beautiful women.

The passion spread and rose to a new pitch. Schoolchildren joined in, as did young bachelors and shopkeepers. Apprentices often showed up and called out to their masters, who in turn just swore absent-mindedly and chased them away. Avdaga's apprentice got such a thrashing that he dared not enter the shooting-gallery any more; instead, he yelled from a distance:

"Master, Mullah Mujo from Okrugla is here to see you. He's waiting at the shop."

But his master did not even turn around; he just set his sights on Leda and the swan. And if he missed them, he would drive the apprentice away and try to hit him with whatever was at hand.

"May the devil take you! And tell the man to get lost, too. What do I need with some old Mullah Mujo?"

And he picked up another loaded rifle.

But in the evenings, it was the tightrope walker that made the small town delirious and held all the menfolk spellbound.

In her short skirt and black stockings that stretched up to her hips, and swinging a little green umbrella, she walked across the entire circus tent on a wire up in the air, gliding forward sometimes on one foot and sometimes on both. Everyone gaped at her, slack-jawed and amazed. The lights of the tent flickered in their staring eyes. And, at the end, when she leapt into the director's arms and disappeared behind the canvas screen, everyone was worn out and enthralled, as though they had been stargazing. But afterwards they went out on terrifying binges, marked by all sorts of singing and brawling.

This second-rate tightrope walker in a little circus took on an ominous and mysterious grandeur in the *kasaba*. She filled it with turmoil, provoking whispers and tears in the homes and stirring huge, delirious desires in men's hearts. In the minds (and even the dreams) of the wives and the older daughters, she figured constantly as a faceless, slimy, mysterious monster.

The little children were the only ones who were taken by the acrobat and the clown in this same way. They

71

talked about them constantly and practiced their tricks on the town square: balancing sticks on their noses and giving each other resounding slaps that didn't really hurt.

But people had been seized by a collective madness and frenzy of the sort that sometimes crops up in sleepy, isolated communities.

This had happened from time to time in the past: the whole town, for some trivial reason or another, would suddenly lose its head. Those sagging little houses, which usually looked as serene as a worker at the end of the day, became a kind of hell. But this time even the quietest people, and folks who had long ago sworn off carousing, began to drink and brawl. Some of them did not come home for whole days and nights; others were brought home bloody or unconscious.

That fall the plum trees bore more fruit than they ever had before. People sold vast quantities of them and still all the wooden tubs were chock-full; plums overflowed onto the ground and spread far and wide the alcoholic aroma of fermentation. That fall a song came into vogue, too: "Oh, my necklace, my necklace, oh pure gold of mine." At the Nativity of the Virgin, more women walked up to Čajniče, to the Mother of God, than ever before. And even the Turkish women slipped them a few coins for oil or candles, thinking it might help ward off evil spells and other troubles from the town.

The first man to see the tightrope walker and start talking about her was Ćorkan, the one-eyed; he was also the one who was to be involved in the most foolishness and scandal on her account.

He was the son of a Gypsy woman and an Anatolian soldier. A miserable, fatherless half-caste, Ćorkan worked as a porter and a servant and more or less functioned as the village idiot. For all the weddings and celebrations, he would get decked out in a ragged red and green outfit and a big hat with a fox-tail hanging down the back. He was a kind of master of ceremonies and would dance and drink until he passed out.

He worked for everybody, at every type of job, and it almost seemed as though he never aged; this is how people remembered him, and this is how one generation passed him along to the next.

He also worked at odd jobs in the circus. He swept up and brought sawdust and water by day, and as soon as it grew dark he was the first to get drunk. With tears in his eyes he watched the dancer up on the wire, and he kept time with the music with his trembling hand. And after the performance, he kept on drinking and waiting on the prominent shopkeepers, because as long as anyone could remember he had been a constant presence whenever the village got down to serious drinking. When he was in his cups he babbled on about the dancer and boasted that he was the only one who spoke with her "in German, like some military officer." The shopkeepers put a paper hat on his head and set it on fire; they mixed gunpowder into his cigarettes; they doused him with plum brandy and beat him until it all ended in a horrible and vulgar scene.

Ćorkan was the first to burst into flames, and then the whole town caught fire. Everybody talked only about the tightrope walker. She was in every song and in every whisper.

73

The mayor closed the cafés and threatened to kick both the circus and the dancer out of town, but nothing seemed to work. The carousing was repeated daily, and it grew more and more rabid.

But Ćorkan's personality completely changed, as if he had been hit by some kind of calamity. He could barely bring himself to do the most basic tasks, and he moved like a sleepwalker. He forgot things easily. His songs no longer rang out in the marketplace, and neither did he dance around at the crossroads any more, as he used to do almost every day. He had spells of dizziness and he trembled in his sleep; he was dangerously elated and dwelt on the edge of a widening abyss. And from aloft he looked down on his life and the town. Love was growing inside him, and it felt as though this love was making him stronger.

The dawns were accompanied by heavy dew. The shopkeepers slept, but Ćorkan would get up from his bed in the hay and go to work, sweeping out the shops, carrying water for the circus. One day he woke furious and resentful at himself.

The night before he had only eaten sauerkraut, out of a barrel of brine, and he hadn't drunk much at all. And yet—how heavy and slow he felt this morning! He was barely able to put one foot in front of the other, and the ground before him seemed to be rising. His legs carried a load meant for three men. Or for ten—but even for them it would've been too much. How leaden he felt!

"And she dances on the tightrope!" And she's light as a feather and she swings her leg around up there, and she's practically flying around like one of those golden beetles that buzz through the shimmering, overheated air above pine-wood shingles. There is indeed so much to behold in this world. One cannot even imagine everything that's in it. So many things! All sorts of things! Ćorkan felt thoughts like these fill his heart and expand it, as if it were inflating.

The evenings preserved for a long while the rosy glow of the autumn sun above the town. As soon as night fell and the lights came on, the drunkards revived. That was when the circus began. And then later, when the lanterns in front of the circus were put out and the dancer, worn out by poverty, the passing years, and traveling, fell asleep in the green circus van, everybody thronged to the tavern.

There Ćorkan poured drinks for the shopkeepers. He himself drank excessively and explained to them the meaning of love, which none of them had apparently ever known.

"This is nothing for you to laugh at! I can't read and I don't have much money, but I know it all, and I see everything. I've only been so messed up since she got here. With her in town, I'm done for. Finished. Know what I mean?"

The old Ćorkan was nowhere to be found. Now he sat in the half-light. His head sank down onto his chest in the posture of a military commander or a man lost in contemplation. Once in a while, he would emit a quick sigh and let loose a torrent of words.

"Oh well, what can you do? I've slaved away here harder than anybody. If I piled up all the sacks of salt, bags of grain, and pails of water that I've toted around on my back, it would be enough to bury two towns like this one, without a trace. But nobody knows what old Ćorkan is made of! Hey, listen, for sixteen years I toiled like a slave for Suljaga. You know, he had four sons and I raised all four of them myself. Those kids were spoiled, like all rich kids, so they would climb on my back and ride around on me, kicking me in the chest. And then their father provided them with spurs and a whip so they could really go at me. So I ran around, neighing like a stallion. It was all I could do to shield my eyes with my hand so they wouldn't blind me. Oh Lord, I don't have a single friend anywhere. If somebody's cow dies—call Ćorkan, to skin it and bury it! If a puppy comes down with rabies—come on, Ćorkan, kill it and toss it in the stream! And for years and years nobody has cleaned out as many cesspools as me."

With that, he held his head up high and spoke with bitterness and pride, like a man who had worked hard and he knew it.

"Hey, all of you guys lock up your houses at night and go to bed, but that's just when I'm heading out. I pull on those trousers, the ones I got from Sumbul when he passed away, and I take my helper with me, and all night long we carry away the gunk, barrel by barrel. The next morning, when folks come by, they still have to pinch their noses. My eyes stay red and I shake all over until I down a shot of something."

The shopkeepers laughed and slapped their sides. Ćorkan groaned. He was ever more afflicted by that painful and peevish sincerity that so often causes drunks to cry. This is because part of paradise is revealed to a drunk. But it's a part he will never enter.

That is how Ćorkan had felt ever since he was smitten by the German tightrope walker. White and airy, new vistas opened up before his eyes, and he was plagued by the need to pour out his soul to someone. He was in love, and the moment he got drunk he "looked into his heart" and saw himself "as he really was." He also saw the other Ćorkan, the one who dug ditches and graves and pits for dead animals, the one who did his daily dance in the middle of the marketplace and played the fool for the amusement of the shopkeepers. And the tremendous contrast between the two Ćorkans caused him great pain; it was due to this gulf between them that he now sat with his head in his hands, lost in thought. He was trying in vain to give voice to his pain. But it was bigger than anything a person can imagine, let alone express. He went on:

"But what courage I have!"

He smacked his chest loudly and his one eye grew round and roamed across all their faces.

"Your whole marketplace doesn't have as much courage as I do. You see, the mayor issues a warning and you're all ready to abandon her. And for a hundred *forints* you'd pillory her in public. But Ćorkan says 'Hell no! Over my dead body!' I will not give her up. Not even the Emperor himself could lay a hand on her."

He was panting with asthmatic excitement. The shopkeepers laughed a little, but they listened a bit, too.

On other evenings he lost his head completely and spoke about nothing except the tightrope walker, or else he brought up people who had died, weeping wildly as if they had passed away just yesterday.

And so the days passed as copies of one another: circus performances, shooting, the shouting of children, hidden tears inside the houses, and drinking bouts. These were wild binges that started by themselves the moment night fell and pulled everyone into their midst. The whole town drank. Some shops did not open at all. This went on until, early one evening, someone spread a rumor that the mayor had finally ordered the circus to get out of town within twenty-four hours.

At noon that day, Ćorkan went out into the countryside while everybody else was still asleep. Right beside the river he made a little hut out of willow branches. In the afternoon he slaughtered a lamb and placed watermelons and bottles of brandy in the water. Then he waited for the guests. The first to arrive was Avdaga Sarač.

Green plants cloaked the banks. Under the men's feet the water gurgled. Over the course of the day the leaves on the hut had dried out, and now they rustled continuously in the wind that always picks up towards evening.

They pulled off some meat for a snack before the others arrived. Ćorkan ate, while Avdaga just nibbled; he dipped his moistened index finger into the salt and barely touched the cheese. They drank in moderation. They lit up, and then smoke streamed out of Avdaga's moustache.

"Hey, Ćorkan! What would you do if they just gave her to you? If they said, simple as you please, 'Here you

go! She's yours. Now do whatever you want with her!'
Huh?"

"Maybe I wouldn't do anything."

"What?"

"Well, I don't think I would touch her. That's just the
way it is."

"You're lying, you sonofabitch. You'd grind the life
out of her."

A faint grin rested on Avdaga's lips as he reproached
Ćorkan with a slight nod of his head.

"No, I wouldn't do that. I swear it on my life. Good
grief, man ... I go to sleep every evening in Ragibey's
hayloft and dream about her: standing up on that wire,
on one leg, spreading her arms in the air while she does
like this with her other leg..." And, with this, he
stopped eating and used the palm of one hand and the
fingers of the other to show how the tightrope walker
balanced on one leg during her performance.

"Lord have mercy! And then I wake up and feel all
over the hay and knotted planks with my hands. Then
sadness takes hold of me and my heart just seems to
swell and swell until I fall back to sleep."

At that point Master Stanoje and Kosta Mutapčija arrived with a few others. Sumbo had just wiped his
moustache and started warming up on his *zurna* when
Pašo the Butcher got there. It was he who brought the
news that the circus, and the tightrope walker, had to
leave town by noon the next day.

An embarrassed silence followed. Ćorkan turned
white and merely shifted his gaze from one man to the
next. The shopkeepers began a new conversation, but he

still couldn't pull himself together. Something in him was quivering so fast that it deprived him of his ability to speak. It also paralyzed his memory. He felt such a sharp, visceral pain deep inside him that he neither dared to move nor was capable of doing so. And his immobilized face took on a look of mad fright. The others had to nudge him to get him to cut the meat and pour the brandy for them.

Mist formed over the stubble in the fields, and the fire burned keenly now, without smoke. Sumbo set about playing and all at once everybody started shouting in unison. Avdaga was drinking brandy out of a small Turkish coffee cup, clinking it with the others and emptying It again and again.

"To your health! To your health!"

Night fell all around. No one spoke about either the tightrope walker or the mayor. Instead they struck up one new song after another. They drank rapidly and the time slipped by.

Ćorkan sat there, unresponsive. It was as though he was paralyzed, and his drinking and singing were in vain. He continued to shake incessantly, and his ears were filled with the painful screeching of his own voice.

At some point the fire went out. The stars glittered up above, and the men headed back to town. They stumbled frequently and grabbed hold of the fences, which in turn wobbled and sagged and cracked. And so they made it to town. Sumbo went in front, incessantly playing his reedy, high-pitched tunes, and behind him came the rest of them, making a great uproar. They slapped Ćorkan repeatedly on his skull-cap.

Nights like this made the town feel cramped to the heavy drinkers. The stars hung big and bright in the low autumn sky, and every few minutes one of them would split off from the others and fall. The drinkers felt both distant places and great heights roaring towards them. Feeling the rush in the air and in their heads, each of them merged his own voice with the wind and the roar. Their voices were now deep, altered, vigorous, and alien. With this sense of force and grandeur in mind, the town was like a lifeless plaything before their ambling stride and wide-open eyes.

The troop came to a halt and then somehow managed to file across a small wooden bridge. Their steps rang out loudly beneath them.

Then they burst like a torrent into Zarija's tavern. The windows fogged up immediately. Nothing could be heard over the *zurna*, yelling, and muffled stomping. Master Stanoje, whom the whole town called Zalumac, was leading the ring dance. He was bent and gray-haired, but he danced well, placing one foot precisely in front of the other. Next to him danced cross-eyed Šaha, a tomboyish Gypsy, and then came Manguraš, Avdaga, and Hadji Šeta. Further on was Santo the hardware dealer. The last dancer was Dimšo from Sarajevo, a fop with a Hungarian hairstyle.

Vapors and dust swirled above them.

The ring dance ended and Master Stanoje directed the musicians to play to the tune of Ćorkan's broken heart. There was more howling and laughter. They downed their drinks and spilled quite a few, too.

"Aiiieee!"

"Die, Ćorkan!"

"Your German girl is leaving!"

All this grieved Ćorkan even more.

"Well, now, I thank you, Master Stanoje, for your insults this evening. After all the bread and salt we've eaten together, you have to go and offend me? So I'm thanking you. By all means!"

Tears welled up in his single eye. Everything grew bigger and more significant. It was past midnight.

Stanoje calmed Ćorkan down by talking to him soberly and condescendingly.

"Be quiet, man! We'll get her up on that wire again this very night. She'll dance, all right, even if—"

Stanoje was interrupted by a wave of shouts.

"She'll have to dance!"

"A belly-dance!"

Everything plunged into confusion. Some new men joined up with them. The whole group then came flying out of the inn as if someone had tossed them. Master Stanoje was at the head of the pack. Ćorkan staggered along next to him, saying:

"You've insulted me, my friend. And that hurts me right here!"

But nothing could be heard over the song, the music, and the loud calls back and forth.

In front of the town hall, little pine trees and oak branches had been driven into the ground, and lanterns hung on them. The officers had held some celebration there earlier that evening. Without a moment's hesitation, the men ripped up the trees and branches. Master

Stanoje lined the group up in rows and issued commands. They moved along like a religious procession, with each man holding a little pine tree or paper lantern in front of him. He even stuck an oak branch into Ćorkan's hands, who tramped along oblivious to it, muttering constantly:

"So much love and friendship, and you stand there and tell me that…"

They arrived at the circus. Ćorkan discarded his branch and, with his hand, numb with cold, reached out to feel the canvas. It was still there, all of it. Some of the men were beating on the windows of the circus wagon. Others were looking for the entrance to the tent. They were all jostling each other and calling back and forth. The walls of the tent, shimmering in the gloom, swung gently back and forth.

The manager showed up with a candle. He had hastily thrown a cloak over his shoulders and now was trembling with cold and fright. The men surrounded him, waving their branches and lanterns.

"Open up!"

"Make her dance!"

"Hold on—I want to tell him!"

They were all yelling at once. Someone went off and banged with great force on the yellow sheet-metal of Mušan's barbershop, which stood right next to the circus.

By now, Ćorkan had also forgotten his misery. He regained his courage—and his strength—and, as he climbed up onto a stack of barrels, he screamed at the manager:

"Who gives a damn about the mayor? You and he can both go to hell! She's going to dance, and you and that chief are going to hold some candles for light. Make some light! Hold the candles for us!"

They all cursed the mayor. Ćorkan was the most enraged one of them all. Master Stanoje was standing closest to the manager. He grabbed hold of the man's coat and fixed his cold green eyes on him. Master Stanoje said to him, in a restrained, sober voice:

"Where is the girl that we want to dance? We have money."

Dimšo joined the conversation to translate. He spoke with a bit of a foreign accent, like soldiers do, and he told the manager:

"Your girl is going to dance for us."

"Please, please—all right! She'll dance!"

But others pushed forward, waving their arms.

"Where is she? Bring her here!"

"The rope! The rope!"

"Put up the tightrope!"

Finally the two men agreed that the crowd would go on in and sit down while the manager went to wake up the girl. She had to get dressed.

Some of the men stumbled over the ropes and boards; they lost their balance and fell down, or caught themselves on the canvas walls of the tent. The group made it inside with difficulty, where Ćorkan, after considerable effort, lit two lamps. They all blinked and looked around at each other.

"Sit down!" shouted Stanoje.

Some of them took a seat on the benches, others on the ground. Some weren't interested in sitting at all; they stood there waving their arms and singing. Ćorkan played the host. He was scraping the sawdust around with his foot and then trying to stamp it flat again, but he kept tripping and staggering. His shadow was inconstant, foreshortened, absurd. The others, confused by the light, blinked drunkenly.

Sumbo started up a song, but in vain, because he was constantly interrupted. Everybody demanded he sing something different. Pašo the Butcher fell asleep on a thin bench made of unplaned wood. It bent under his weight. Master Stanoje was overcome by an attack of hiccups. He lowered his head, breathing heavily and sitting there as serenely as if he were in church. But from time to time he still shook all over.

The pale moments before dawn came. Bodies cool off then, and grow tired; the eyesight becomes weak, consciousness dulls, and appetites fade. Only two things can excite one's numb and distracted consciousness: the prurient heat of thoughts about something strange and wonderful, like the body of this woman from another land up on the high wire, or the thought of anything at all that is painful, violent, or shameful.

But the manager, instead of waking up the acrobat, merely checked the lock on the wagon again. Then he headed to the police station, panting and stumbling over the cobblestones. The drunken men grew impatient. And then right at sunrise the gendarmes showed up.

On the following day news of the scandal spread. The shopkeepers were called to the mayor's office. They returned to their shops for money and paid their heavy fines. The circus pulled up its stakes and wound up its ropes. The town square reverberated with the sounds of trunks being nailed shut. And towards evening the tent in the middle of the green collapsed like a blister. Everything was then loaded onto carts, and at dawn the next day they set off.

Ćorkan was the only one they kept behind bars. They tied him up, and bony old Sergeant Ibrahim beat him with a vinegar-soaked ox whip. Ćorkan jerked his head at each blow, talking rapidly until he gagged. Tearfully, he implored the sergeant in his thin, high Gypsy voice: "Don't beat me! I'm not guilty. How could I even think of contradicting the mayor? What could this German tightrope walker possibly want with a Gypsy scoundrel like me?"

To each blow he responded with more and more screaming. Desperately rolling his one eye, his face was childlike: small, and covered with tears, and still sooty from the night before.

"I didn't do it, I didn't. I didn't. Have mercy! I want to kiss his feet. Help me, good sir, dear Mr. Mayor! You're killing me, wretch that I am. Never again! Don't, Sergeant Ibrahim, in the name of God!"

But Sergeant Ibrahim kept beating him—steadily, horribly, frightfully. He beat him as he was ordered to do: "until you drive all the love and foolishness out of him." He beat Ćorkan long enough to deprive him of his voice; he beat him until he could not scream any more, until only frothy spit gushed from the man's lips. That's how they left him.

Afterwards, he fell into a deep, long sleep, during which he moaned and whimpered like a little puppy. Sergeant Ibrahim's children climbed up to the prison window and looked in at him. When he awoke, he found bread by his side. There was also a pot of beans, the top layer of which had congealed and was now coated with a thin film.

At dusk they released him. He dragged himself off to the hayloft and fell asleep again. Several days passed in this way. Whenever he rolled over onto the places where they had beaten him, he would let out a sob, but he didn't wake up. His bruises and welts appeared to have grown to enormous proportions and they filled the vast night. It was a night that did not permit his eyes to open, a night without ending or waking; only his coughs and swallows, occurring at regular intervals, marked its passage.

Later he began coming down, with an empty gaze, numb, unthinking and unspeaking, but only for a short time. He would go to get bread and tobacco. Otherwise he just kept sleeping, day and night. Little by little, the aches disappeared and in his sleep he felt the sweet peace that follows torment. At time he stayed awake for hours, but there were no more desires or memories left to torture him. He watched as long streaks of sunlight broke through the empty knot-holes and cracks; he noticed the way dust danced all the harder in that light whenever he moved in the hay. He felt smaller than a child.

On the eighth day Ćorkan woke up feeling light and relieved. Descending the ladder, it seemed funny to him that he was putting his feet first on one rung and then on another. He was still laughing by the time he picked up cheese and a loaf of bread on credit in Suljko's shop; the debt was to be worked off later. Then, after coming down the ladder again the next day, he did not return to the hayloft. Instead, he made his way out of town.

He climbed up the hill to the old trenches and breastworks, where henbane grew now, along with low rows of wild lilac. The town was underneath him, so compact that it looked jumbled up in a heap; over it lay the huge, dark green roofs and a sheet of thin smoke. The clear light of day caressed Ćorkan; he ate, and from his belly a joyous energy spread throughout his entire body. He stuck out his chest, powerfully, and felt light and ready for anything. The sunlight hit his eye and sparkled, as if it were playing with him. Once more he remembered:

"Oh, they all put me through hell: the German girl and the mayor and the shopkeepers and Sergeant Ibrahim. All of them. Everybody!"

Happy that it was all over, Ćorkan laughed out loud. He laughed, too, because he was happy and free. He thought about the marketplace, about work, and about life as it had been for ages and ages. Satisfied, he began making his way back.

His feet capered along by themselves. Even if he had been so inclined, he wouldn't have been able to remember the pain and all the other things that had gone before. He entered the city at a brisk pace. The town square was empty. The familiar business district opened up before him as if in welcome.

The old game repeated itself. Ćorkan walked through the market area, dancing around. He spread out his empty arms as if he were holding an invisible *tamburitza*.

Stretching his left arm far out to the side, he strummed the fingers of his right hand playfully and tapped the buttons on his tunic as if they were the strings. Bending his knees and inclining his head first to one side and then to the other, he sang:

"Tralala! Tralala! Tweedle-dee-deedle-dee! Tralala!"

The shopkeepers leaned out of their double doors, laughed, and shouted out:

"Ah, did you sleep well, Mr. Ćorkan?"

"Has your tightrope walker written you a letter yet?"

"Every day is a holiday for a jackass!"

"Sergeant Ibrahim sends his regards!"

"You cured yourself from love, didn't you?"

But he just made little mincing steps, singing and hopping, as he had always done. He threaded his feet in and out of each other with considerable skill.

"Tralala! Tralala! ... Hip, hip, hooray!"

He only half noticed that they were shouting at him, and he didn't actually see anyone. For some reason his eyes glazed over; maybe it was tears, maybe it was joy. Everything was in its place, truly and invariably in its place. There was a great ringing in his ears, and the world swayed and swam before his eyes. Extending far and wide before him was something other than the marketplace: it was the radiant ocean.

Translated by John K. Cox

Byron in Sintra

Going to Sintra, Byron quarreled with his friends. They could not agree which was the way back. He was especially angry, as in these kinds of circumstances he could always see in his servants' eyes that they did not side with him but with his opponent.

As soon as they passed the gate of the park, he abandoned his friends. It was Sunday. He could hear the sound of music coming from somewhere. To rid himself of his anger, he ran up some steps, flapping his shorter, lame leg, forgetting how silly he looked when running. Before him new terraces, new roads and an ever wider and wider vista kept opening up: twelve miles of green fields engirdled by a belt of sea and an infinite sky. He didn't feel any fatigue. He felt as if he were not climbing, but growing taller. No one was in sight. Not even a bird. He thought: finally, here is a land where solitude is a delight!

Rushing through these pathways carved into the ramparts and with a wide view of the gardens in the distance and, beyond them, the sea, he suddenly encountered a girl of indeterminate age. She was standing on the edge of the ramparts beside a small, abandoned and empty guard house made of stone. There she emerged before him unexpectedly as if sent from some place, from someone, bearing tidings.

She wore a clean dress made of a white gauze-like material, her face dark brown, half-African, her nose small with wide nostrils, that had a certain look of candor, and her smart eyes full of vigor and joy. She quite shyly and quietly greeted this stranger with incomprehensible words, but in her voice and gestures was something more than an ordinary greeting, even though he couldn't tell what. He greeted her in return, then stopped. She stopped as well. She was rocking gently and smiling, looking him straight in the eye, licking her dry lips with her tongue. There's nothing more exciting than the lips of these Portuguese women! They contain something from the vegetable and mineral realms. Asymmetrical like an accidentally cracked fruit, they reveal a hint of the dark and sweet blood inside this small and ripe body from which they sprout. Only at the sides are they a little curved like the mouth of a Caucasian woman, but even those corners of the mouth are lost in an indistinct shadow, like the undersides of the leaves of plants. He thought: I must look awfully ridiculous and insecure, a man of unclear intentions. He was trying with all his might to look harmless and nonchalant. With all his might, that is whatever at his disposal. Because inside, he was aflame. It seemed to him that everything his whole being had been searching for, always—and much more than that—he had now discovered on this green hill. It was as if the unnamed evil which had forced him to flee England and had flung him across the world, had thrown him here with a plan.

Suspended over a double abyss, this one consisting of gray cliffs and green slopes and the other of everything forbidden and impossible, the source of his endless thirst, his imagination, excited by the high thin air and the proximity of this woman, soared with deadly speed. In lightning visions, sparked by this small creature, like a raging forest fire from a shepherd's ember, Byron tasted for the first time what dreams promise, what women never offer, what life constantly steals from us. All these thoughts raced through his mind, even as the blood surged through his veins.

But immediately afterwards he extinguished every desire, and enveloped this vibrant, smiling creature in a new, free, bright thought, a thought that filled him with eternal shame, hesitation and boundless respect for the human, the most sacred of all living beings.

And the entire time he was shifting from foot to foot, or moving slowly around the girl who turned steadily with him, never taking her eyes off of his gaze and watching his every move carefully. Byron kept mumbling some syllables incomprehensibly. It seemed to him as if she, too, were saying something. That's how they were watching and circling, like two wild beasts, one small, one big, sniffing each other and eying each other until they began a strange game in which they caresses and insulted each other by turns. And as he was encircling her in such a bewitched state, his every sense worked with intensified energy and speed. He saw the clear whites of her eyes which can only be found among primitive, quite young women, as well as her pupils sparkling as if made of topaz! Even from a distance he could sense, quite separately, the scent of her soft body and dry hair, and the odor of the cloth of her gauze dress whitewashed by the sun. It seemed as though the man were splitting into pieces, as though his every nerve lived on its own and with such intense life that it meant both his enrichment and his death as a human being. Now he could say he knew what a true moment of rapture and oblivion was! In hell, which is really life itself for every sensual being, such a moment is rare, an unexpected oasis where one can neither rest nor linger.

At that moment, from the dark bushes where the path disappeared, Byron heard voices from below. Roused as if awakened from sleep, he continued his interrupted run up the steep trail, leaving the astonished girl without so much as a wave farewell.

He wandered for a long time over the narrow trails and slopes. In the end those trails and abrupt downhill descents led him on their own back to the castle from where he had set out. His companions were already waiting on stone benches.

They all returned to Lisbon the way they had come, just as his companions had suggested but which Byron had so violently opposed. Now he did not utter a word. He was docile as a lamb and full of a gentle kindness not only toward people, but towards objects.

For the next few days he lived in the most serene and beautiful dream of his life. The barefoot Lisbon fisherwomen, who nudged each other and laughed, seeing how he talked to himself by the sea and thinking him a madman, were wrong. He was not alone, and he was not conversing with ghosts. He was talking to a human face who lived in Sintra, who had her own blood, her own heart, her own eyes, and of course her parents, her house, her name. But, that was the least important matter. He thought he might call her by the name of a fruit or a mineral, but he gave up, because it seemed that any name would diminish and confine her. In his thoughts he got used to calling her "Little Creature" which he did not pronounce as words, just a single short breath behind closed lips, which only touched the soft palate, and even so was enough to designate her whole. Here, on his palate, Byron jealously stopped that breath, guarding it there, relishing it.

After a time he left Lisbon, then Portugal. Visiting other countries, talking with people and joking with women, still he kept and cherished his secret, hid it beneath words, objects and faces where he could enjoy her without giving his pleasure away, not even a little. He connected some words in speech to her, and whenever someone uttered them in front of him, he was able to delight in her presence, unseen and undisturbed. In his own signature he included a small, barely noticeable line which designated the woman on the Sintra hill. Lemon, salt, oil and malmsey signified her being. Lunching with a dozen people, he could summon up green Sintra and its "Little Creature," as he played unnoticed with two grains of salt between his thumb and index finger. Where he found the least trace of her, there would he find her, in the faces, words and movements of women.

His contact with her, in his memory, healed him and protected him from all his encounters, from his women, from his very life. And in particularly happy moments, at twilight on the high seas, a miracle would occur, real, inexplicable and one that could not be described: the green hill in Sintra would be transformed into a celestial light without end, his limping run into a long silent, graceful flight, and all the sensual fever of that tryst into a clear triumph of the spirit beyond any painful consciousness or limits.

Such feelings lasted about a year. And then the "Little Creature" began to pale and fade like a vision in a dream at dawn, gradually losing its power. Byron felt impoverished, desperate, and helpless. Again he was swept up the evil currents that carried him through life, and again the meetings and confrontations became more frequent, followed, like a shadow, by disgust. And the world became even harsher and more painful than before the Sintra events, because it seemed to him now that the brutal laws of life had spread their power even into the kingdom of his imagination and that there was no escape or salvation.

Translated by Biljana Obradović and John Gery

Maltreatment

Everyone came out against Anica. Not only neighbors and acquaintances and friends, but with few exceptions, her family as well. Her father did not let her into the house the September night that she deserted her husband, and he later informed her that, in his house, there was no room for shrews—for runaways who "demand bread on top of their flat-cakes." (Proverbs, among our people, are the fastest and most unjust way to kill the living.)

And in truth, nobody could understand why one day Anica, wife of Andrija Zereković, abandoned her home and husband. There was no evident reason or reasonable justification for that kind of conduct, neither in her marriage, which was calm and exemplary, nor in the life of impoverished solitude she led after leaving home. Her husband conducted himself calmly and with dignity. He did everything he could to bring her back, and only when he saw that the woman truly would not, did he let the matter go its course and requested a divorce.

The religious court only confirmed general opinion. The union of Andrija Zereković and his wife Anica, nee Marković, was dissolved due to the fault of the afore-mentioned Anica.

Today she works as a saleswoman in a large store. She has grown thinner and pale. She lives the life of lonely, cast-off wives. She resides in one small room on the fifth floor, lunches at the counter, and on Sundays stays home to wash and mend.

When it is said what kind of marriage it was, it will be clear at once why general opinion was against the woman.

He was a man who had long passed his fortieth year, and owned a brush factory. 'Factory' is perhaps somewhat too grand a word. In fact, it was one well arranged and competently run workshop with about twelve workers, and with very diverse and solid business connections. Besides that, Master Andrija bought animal hair of every kind in bulk. His credit and reputation in the business world had been proven long ago. A village boy, he had, through his own labor, through frugality and modesty, won everything that he had: estate, shop, and status. It is true, he had never been a striking or handsome man, but neither was he without dignity or bearing appropriate to his rank. He was cautious and affable in speech, neat and particular in his dress. As a young journeyman, he had spent two or three years somewhere in Austria, where he had gained not only substantial knowledge, but also their polished way with customers.

She was a destitute girl. Her father was a minor clerk in an insurance group, precisely what is called a collector and designates not an ordinary employee, but a man of responsibility and a certain skill. There were three more sisters and a brother at home. Anica was the eldest.

Reticent, tall and ample, with white skin, luxurious dark hair and dark blue eyes, whose calm gaze betrayed nothing of what her large but regular and succulent lips implied. She was one of those shapely and strong girls who are always afraid of developing and revealing their beauty, and who are ashamed of their bodily shape; who drop their eyes before everyone's gaze and, in company, press one leg against the other, stiffly squeeze their chest with crossed arms, all from some pained need to make themselves appear smaller and weaker, if they cannot pass by unheard and unseen.

When their mother died, Anica ran the household, raised her younger sisters, and educated her brother. She was one of those rare women who know how to be useful without a word, who seek no incentive in acknowledgement, who do not assume a martyr's mask and bearing after every effort, and who in all things seem content.

It is not a rare thing among our provincial families, if the father is a widower with many children and little income, that the oldest sister, taking on the mother's role, sacrifices herself entirely, remains in the home as its benevolent ghost and 'buries herself' in the family's foundations. Such a girl is left without a personal life, outside of life entirely, astonishingly inexperienced and uninstructed in everything beyond the home. And while the younger sisters or brothers around her live and, with her help, develop, and all according to their own tendencies participate in everything—in good and evil, in the beautiful and the ugly that the life of that generation brings—she remains to the side, outside the stream of life from the very beginning. By necessity and by habit, such girls become characterless, dated beings, unresisting to the egoism of others, virtuosos of unselfishness, always ready for every sacrifice and always tormented by the feeling that they did not give or do enough. Because they have stifled in themselves, at its very inception, any natural female longing for personal happiness, they sacrifice themselves for everyone, and everyone can take advantage of them, but they are sufficient for nobody.

By her nature, Anica too would have forever run the household for her father, a man of grim and hasty temper, and married off all of her younger sisters. But her industry and her strong, hidden beauty caught the eye of Master Andrija. It was what he had been looking for, the reason he had gotten on in years and not wed, and what he could now allow himself: a beautiful, ample, modest and obedient girl. And so much the better that she was poor. To take a poor and hard-working girl into one's house—that means every day to feel additional satisfaction on top of hard-won prosperity, and every day to see it slightly increase. For acquisition is, in truth, flight from poverty. But if there were no poor, how could one measure the value and appreciate the success of those who acquire? And so far as beauty was concerned, that strong and lasting beauty that Master Andrija considered a second fortune and which was very, very important to him—beauty is a thing that sprouts and grows wherever it accidentally falls, among the poor as among the wealthy. Except that affluence attracts to itself the beauty of the poor as well, just as cold regions draw warm air. That was one of the all-powerful laws in our

societal relations; Master Andrija always had an exceptionally developed regard and sense for those laws, and
knowing them well, with their help as if by the help of
living forces, both ascended the social ladder and rose in
his own eyes.

It was one of those marriages talked about not only
among neighbors and acquaintances, but among unknown people, one of the rare examples of even hidden
virtues finding their recognition and reward.

From her pauper's home, in which deprivation and,
even more, her short-tempered father, animated sisters
and sickly brother created an atmosphere of constant
excitement and small but permanent tensions, Anica
moved suddenly into the bachelor's house, but spacious,
calm and well-arranged house of the husband unexpected luck had brought her.

For any one who knows how to read into things,
Master Andrija's home was in layout, furnishings and
unified décor a mute history of his ascent from poor,
hard-working and serious journeyman to respectable
businessman. As with many often used words, even today it is not precisely determined nor utterly clear what
that word, 'businessman,' means, but it spread in our
society somehow during the time of Master Andrija's
difficult apprenticeship; he made of it the goal of all his
suffering and effort, and now that he had achieved that
goal, he pronounced the word countless times daily with
a vengeful pleasure whose deeper meaning and true
sense only he knew.

It was an old-fashioned but beautiful two-story house.
According to an excellent old principle, it was near the

workshop, but not connected to it. He had lodged there in his youth as a bachelor, with a kindly widow who had held the entire first floor. When the widow died, he was still at the painful start of his craftsman's calling, but he bought from her relatives everything that the widow left behind, and so kept the entire first floor with three rooms. Later, when the shop was self-sufficient and Master Andrija began to turn money around with a deftness no one could have predicted and in which his modesty and humility played the largest role, he took advantage of the moment and bought the house for hard cash from the proprietor, an eccentric fellow and the last descendent of an old family, who lived on the second floor. Measured and reasonable in every respect, he let the former proprietor continue living on the top floor. Everything was as it had been before, except now he was the owner and the sometime owner became a tenant, but Master Andrija endeavored to make that change as little felt as possible. And so he awaited the death of the old eccentric. Then he took the top floor for himself as well, buying all the furniture, which was heavy and old but luxurious and tasteful. And so the different apartments, from bachelor's studio to the riches of one dilapidated family, found themselves in a single pair of hands but never quite came together.

Into this house Master Andrija brought his beautiful young wife. There they lived for two and a half years. That marriage stood apart from others in no way, other than by a quiet settledness and undisturbed harmony. It is true, they didn't have children, but not even that could disturb the perfection of this marriage. Everything went as God commands and as the world imagines and expects. He was well accepted and valued among people, a member of the Tradesmen's Chamber Committee and a benefactor of Youth in Commerce. She ran the large house in total accord with her husband, who knew everything that was necessary for a household, and she visited her father and her sisters, two of whom had married after her.

At first, Anica immediately grew less constricted and more beautiful in the new house. Her beauty now came to its real expression. The tightness that had restricted her entire lush body during girlhood relaxed. Her strength came unbound. Her gaze became gentler, her luxurious black hair gained a reflected dark blue shine. Reticent, modest and always the same, she moved calmly and freely around the house, which she transformed though her very presence as much as by constant care and attention. And whenever Master Andrija, according to his habits, began for sheer pleasure to calculate to himself what this wife meant as an asset and gain for all he represented and owned, his thoughts would halt, and his calculations grow confused. He would see that a good wife truly was priceless. It was the first time in his life that he could not calculate something accurately and completely. But he would sit a long time with his unfinished computation, filled with happiness and fear, like a man who does not even know the extent of what he has, and whose own wealth can always pleasantly surprise him.

For him, marriage fortified the joys he had hitherto known and which originated from work, speculation, societal position and acquisition; and besides that, satisfied also desires whose realization he had never dared to think of and had even doubted possible. In short, he had that complete and perfect feeling of happiness given to people of his caliber by a certain social order, when they consciously and devotedly serve it with all their might. Under his internal gaze, his earlier perspectives spread and opened to something like the unexpected paradise of an entirely successful civilian life, in which, in some wise and secret way, the desired and the realized met and were reconciled, the permitted with that which was not.

For it is hard even to understand and much less to express what this handsome woman meant to Master Andrija, this woman he had brought to his house one day, simply, without any effort or risk, and who in truth was the crown of all his many years of labor, humiliation and self-denial.

Now he could stroll on holidays with his fair-faced, quiet, well-dressed and very own wife; he could take her to the theater, to the cinema or to some celebration. Now he could speak freely about his wife in company, openly and with pride, instead of with shame and constraint ("I was walking so, the other day with my wife...," "I say to my wife: go on, wife, for God's sake..."). Those who heard him pronounce these harmless, ordinary phrases never even suspected what delight hid behind them, and how that word 'wife' provided his speech with a welcome crutch until now so sorely missing.

Now he could say much more to himself than he dared or could say to other people. Now in the darkness, he could lay both hands on the firm warm body of his sleeping wife, could place them wherever, where they accidentally landed, and say to himself: "All this is mine, from hair to toe, mine and no one else's!" From that feeling of happiness, the limits of one's personality spread into infinity. It is sweet to be awake because of that feeling, and sweet to fall asleep lulled by it.

For, one has to understand what a wife, or rather, the thought of a wife, had meant to this man during those long years of work, of suffering known only to himself, and of abnegation. Master Andrija was, as we have said already, the example of a conscientious worker: diligent and obedient while he was young, stern and, as he liked to say himself, just as a master. Everything about him was ideal, except for his outer appearance. Not even in the crib had he been good-looking, and later life bent him to a strange cast. In fact, he was a perfect example of an ugly man. On top of thin and short legs—a powerful torso and long arms; and on just such a thin and vanishing neck—a large head, tucked in and sunk between his shoulders. You are familiar with the kind of man, of whom it cannot quite be said that he is hunchbacked, but who has some flaw in the relation between his head, back and torso, so that in appearance and bearing he leaves a hunchback's impression. With years he gained weight and filled out, but his legs and face remained thin. On his face Andrija sported a thick, cropped mustache, which only nominally hid a large mouth with bad teeth in the lower jaw and with overly white and regular but false ones in the top. He had yellow, cloudy eyes with a professional smile in the wrinkles on the sides; eyes which, if he forgot himself a little, became tired and endlessly sad, somehow unpleasantly sad. His denuded scalp was only somewhat covered with tufts borrowed from either side. His feet and hands were disproportionally large, bent and calloused from years of labor and standing at the counter. But all that was softened by Master Andrija's manner of relating with people, in business as in every perfectly ordinary encounter. He was truly a man "who had a way about him," that is, who shows everyone a specific kind of submissiveness that flatters the collocutor without demeaning himself. He knew how to give advice to the poor and unfortunate, and to the wealthy and influential to say what interested them most at that instant. For years already, he held all the supplies for the army, railroads and many state institutions in his hands; he regularly remained the winner at auctions, and none of the competitors could say a thing.

That was the way of Master Andrija Zereković, and that way cloaked all his truly great bodily deficiencies. Because of that way of his, his ugliness did not manage even to reach most people's consciousness. He was skillful, courteous and obliging by nature, and through his effort only harvested the fruit of these natural characteristics.

And one of those precious fruits was this wife fate had given him as the fulfillment of his last and most hidden desire.

Only, such complete fulfillment of desire conceals great dangers; and the greatest lies in the new longing that appears to replace what was fulfilled. Who knows what that will be like, and where it can lead us? And who knows what our initial desire defended us from, while it resided in and tortured us, alive and unfulfilled?

In this new life, which denoted the fulfillment of all his desires and the zenith of perfection, Master Andrija began, for the first time in his conscious life, to be occupied with himself: to measure, evaluate, question and compare. The comforts of wealth, wedlock and home life give a man the time and opportunity for it. There are long and pleasant hours, evenings, afternoons and mornings when one's whole being expands and opens, as he had never thought he could or dared. It was no longer just mute thoughts and soundless wishes in the deaf silence of a bachelor's room, and in the eternal presence of one's own, always identical, plaguingly boring and familiar personality. No, now it was warmth and magnitude, the presence of a being who stayed silent or affirmed, and in front of whom one need neither hold back nor look small. For the first time in his life, he could speak freely, without calculation or deference, dream out loud, spread and examine everything he unearthed from within. And that was as sweet and intoxicating as if he were speaking to all of humanity, and as safe and confidential as if he were telling it to the mute black earth. Only with such a listener can a man really see himself: what and who he is; what he is like and worth; all that he knows and can do; what he can and dares do.

These were primarily short conversations apropos of everyday events at home and in town.

By chance, in conversation, Anica says that today she was in town and wanted to buy some item, but noticed that she had not brought enough money.

"Eh, my foolish one," Andrija reproves her gently and smilingly. In such situations, you go into the store, buy the things, then say: "I am Mrs. Zereković, Mrs. Andrija Zereković, I would like this sent home for me— yes, yes, 'sent home'!—and you just add: 'My husband will pay.'"

"It's unpleasant for me," says Anica.

"What about it is unpleasant? You don't realize who your husband is. Do you know that there isn't another man downtown who enjoys the credit and trust I do? Do you know banks give away hundreds of thousands of *dinars* at my signature? And you came home because you didn't have two hundred *dinars* on you! Don't do it a second time. There isn't a store that, hearing my name, won't send along merchandise in any quantity."

Master Andrija gets up and, spreading his arms with some gestures and grimaces that, during the day, in the store and in society, no one otherwise sees from him, explains the web of his business connections and credits to his calmly listening wife the way one explains a new planetary system.

Or it so happens that they bring Andrija a state attorney's file for the Tax Board, in which the lawyer complains about the Tax Committee's decision and proves that the Committee undervalued taxes for the firm of one A. Zereković. Master Andrija will later, in his reply, deny these accusations and prove that his store does not even make the returns or profit that the Tax Board had originally supposed, but now with a satisfied smirk shows his wife the text of the complaint.

"You see what they write about your husband. 'The tax was undervalued, for it is well known that the said firm enjoys a good reputation and that its yearly returns, and therefore its profits, far exceed the sum reached by the Committee in its valuation.'"

He holds out the paper with the official stamp and title to his wife.

"Therefore: 'good reputation,' '...far exceed,' that's how they express themselves about me on the Tax Board. And it's the same at the State Bank, and the same in the ministries. And then various private banks so often beg for my opinion and information about individuals and firms requesting credit. And if I say: 'Give it,' they give it, and if not—they don't give it. Eh, that already is responsibility. You understand? Then a man has to think. You understand?"

His wife affirms everything with easy movements of her head and in silence, and looks him directly in the face, not in the eyes but in the face, with cold dark blue eyes that he does not even see but continues to talk about business connections and successes, about his invisible but far-reaching influence in the business world, about his experiences, plans and bold intentions. At that he forgets about her entirely, and does not want or expect anything from her except that mute and passive participation, her living presence. And her constant silence enchants and intoxicates him, like the calm surface of the ocean does an excited swimmer; it inspires and goads him to find ever newer and more unusual things with which he might surprise or confuse her.

With each day, these conversations grow more unpleasant and difficult for her. She does not even admit to herself how much they torment and exhaust her. She

is taken aback by his new manner of speaking—
unrestrained, impetuous, ironic, strange and full of unhealthy imagination, and so dissonant with his speech and
behavior during the day, at work and in society. His constant "You understand?" offends her senses like an overly
bright light. She tries to look at him directly, without
blinking, but it is becoming an effort. And Master Andrija's conversations are growing and transforming into
ever new and ever bolder monologues, in which he allows
his imagination and language ever greater sway, and in
which his whole and even to himself previously unfamiliar personality, in ever stranger positions and newer gra-
dations, balloons and shines before the eyes of his astonished and slightly frightened but steadfastly calm wife.

It becomes a regular thing after dinner.

Anica takes her knitting and sits under the lamp, already trembling inside from his unavoidable speech.
Master Andrija lights a cigarette, unfolds the morning
papers and lounges into the armchair. (He only smokes
after meals and always unbuttoned like this, without a tie,
in a yellowish camelhair coat which reaches all the way
to his knees.) He reads some things to himself and some
things to his wife, aloud. And in connection with the
read material, he spins out his thought or expounds on
his memories, while his wife only gazes over the knitting
and rarely tosses out some word that inflames his elocu-
tion and leads his narrative onto roads unforeseen even
by him until now.

"By the order of His Highness the King…etc.,"
reads Master Andrija, "Mr. N. N. was appointed town
steward."

"You see, this is yet another mistake. I'm not going to say whose, but a mistake. He's another of those small and hungry clerks who prostrated himself in front of anybody and everybody, and begged the Jews not to protest his bank draft. And how can he now be what he really needs to be? Town steward of a metropolis? Do you know what that is?"

Anica looks at him. These stern and reproachful questions always bewilder her and she cannot get used to them, though she has long since learned that her calm gaze, full of suppliant ignorance and gentle curiosity, is all the answer required.

"Well that, my dear fellow, means receiving lofty characters, dignified businessmen, various foreigners. And for that you need style. You need to be impeccably dressed, measured, obliging but dignified. This is possible, thank you very much. But this, I'm very sorry, is impossible! And that's the end of it! And with clerks? That, even more, requires a confident and strong hand. Ah, if I were their steward!"

Master Andrija gets up from his armchair.

"There would be no tardiness with me, no disorder or excuses. You understand? It would go like clockwork, I tell you, like clockwork. Who doesn't want order, out! No favorites and no tolerance! Without mercy!"

He repeats his last words with relish. He fixes a tuft of hair that has fallen to the side and relights his cigarette, which has gone out, sits again in the armchair and continues in a soft, significant voice:

"Well, one has to go report to the king himself. And what can such a calamity of a clerk say to the king about the state of the town, about the people's frame of mind? He can bow, click his heels together, and amen everything they ask of him. But what's needed is precisely a man who will square his shoulder—at the right moment, you understand, at the right moment—and say: 'Your Highness, that is impossible.' 'What, how do you mean impossible?' 'It's impossible, Your Highness, like this and this, because of so and so.'"

Master Andrija is on his feet again, changing his voice and movements, acting the king one moment and town steward the next. In the moment he is being the king, he extinguishes his cigarette. Now it is the end of the scene. The newspapers are read on further. His wife's needles click rhythmically. And so on, until it is time to sleep.

Another evening, Master Andrija again tosses down the papers and lowers his glasses.

"There, please, see what it says there! 'The love affairs of a young merchant go before the court.' 'The son of a wealthy merchant fell into the hands of a crafty beauty.' You see these blind men and simpletons! God, God, how rational and unrelenting I always was about these things with myself and others! And it's not as if I didn't have the opportunity. Eh, hey!"

The brush-maker makes some grimace with his lips and cracks his thumb against the middle finger of his left hand, and his wife shudders inside and lowers her eyes, certain she was about to hear something ugly and painful. For there was nothing she fears and is disgusted by as much as talk of physical love and his allusions and jokes about it. But the man keeps silent with satisfaction and only smiles to himself loftily.

"There, I don't know how it was. I was never some kind of dandy or good-for-nothing. And there are so many better-looking men than me," says the brush-maker, seeking an answer in her eyes, "but somehow the women just stuck to me. And it'd boggle your mind, what kind of women, from what kind of society! But there's no weakness or relenting with me. I always knew what I wanted, where I could venture, and how far I could go. They were never the ones deciding that, but always me. And no exceptions, let her look like a nymph. You understand?"

And then come some pitiful, ambiguous and unclear stories, amorous experiences from his time abroad as a journeyman, which he tells without shame and in which he always triumphs as a great lover but as a rational and subtle man, a total master of his passions and others' appetites. After the landladies, some German women and their daughters, sailors' wives and jealous café owners, came a story about a countess from Pest, a real countess, who saw him working and cast her eye on him, sending her maid with messages countless times, but happily he escaped that older and lustful woman's trap.

"I was never foolish enough to squander my strength and youth just wherever, but at the time I had three women for every finger on my hand."

And the man shows his big, knotted fingers to the woman beside him. Beautiful, blooming, twenty years younger and two heads taller than him, she looks at them with cold astonishment inside.

And so on, until it is time for blessed sleep.

Then the young woman is free and can, awake and alone at last in the fresh and pleasant sheets, rest from everything she had to listen to that evening, and can finally think her own thoughts, in her own way. Andrija still needs a long time to get ready and prepare for bed. He removes the teeth from his upper jaw, cleans them with a special brush and leaves them in a glass of water. He rinses his mouth with special water, inserts wicks soaked with salve and Peruvian balsam into his nostrils, puts cotton wool in his left ear (only his left, because he sleeps on his right). Except in the summer months, he puts on special "Jeger" underwear for bed, and on top of that, a nightshirt: the shirt is the smallest male size they have, but it still reaches to the ground on the little man. On his bald scalp the brush-maker dons a special white wool cap.

When he finishes all that, he lies down in his bed, looks once more at his wife, who at that moment always closes her eyes as if sleeping, crosses himself, turns off the lamp, and, turning his back to his wife, falls asleep instantly like an animal.

Then Anica opens her eyes and exhales.

She begins to live—even if only the restless, tormented life of insomnia.

As the years of her married life passed, these hours in bed before sleep and on waking became more and more meaningful to her.

In the first few months of marriage, Master Andrija would cross over into his wife's bed at first every night, and then twice a week, and then once. But fairly soon even that stopped. After talking and giving orders about domestic matters and small social obligations, and after those long, exhausting stories about himself, Master Andrija would lie down in his own bed, satisfied with himself and with the entire world. And he would wake up early the next morning feeling the same way and prepare for daily life and work. (He had long stopped being aware that a young woman was lying awake or asleep next to him, did not think about whether she too might want something, or think or feel, and did not pay her any attention at all except as a domestic being and required interlocutor.)

His wife's slumber is broken in these nocturnal hours. She does not want her husband to come to her bed. Not for anything. Just the thought that he is sleeping makes her happy. But she herself can neither fall asleep nor remain calmly awake. It seems to her that the sheets are breathing beneath her, and that heat is radiating from her pillow. She tells herself that she only has to bear it a little and calm down for a moment, and then she'll see it's all an illusion. She lies on her back, closes her eyes and breathes deeply and rhythmically. If that doesn't help either, she gets up, goes quietly into the bathroom and dampens her throat and bosom with cold water. That usually helps and brings sleep.—And waking is also strange and difficult in its own way.

Usually at dawn already some unrest in her leg muscles wakes her, and a pain unfamiliar before now that tingles in her breasts, which feel as if numb. But there always awoke with her at that same time some hope, completely vague but infinitely rich and grander than the visible limits of reality.

They were not easy, those nocturnal hours the woman lay awake, often not knowing herself whether she could not fall asleep or wanted to stay awake. But still, they were dear to her, like those moments after waking, because they were hers alone, the only thing that was entirely and exclusively hers in her current life.

But the brush-maker had recently begun to take something for himself from her even in those hours. For his passion, to talk to his wife and to act in front of her—grew ever stronger, and the hours after dinner were no longer enough for him. More and more often Master Andrija, delighted and excited by his own talking, continued to speak even at his wife's bedside.

The thing begins, as always, in that low armchair. He reads aloud some article about necessary, wide-ranging reforms suggested by someone in the national industry, state government, school or army. And then he explains to his wife, with eloquent irony, how all those people are either hired scribblers or naïve professors who think they can transform public life with theories and articles.

"There is no manly hand there, my dear, I tell you. There's no manly hand to cut, with a surgeon's scalpel, without mercy! Without mercy, you understand?"

The brush-maker shouts that to his wife, as if she insisted on the opposite, and demonstrates with his long hand how that sort of thing is cut.

His wife follows the movement of his hand with her eyes, and then her unwavering gaze comes to rest again on his face.

"You see, it's the same thing on a large scale, as I have small scale in the shop. Prudence, resolve, perseverance! Everything's in that. And if, by some ill fate, the king were to call me and say to me, 'Mister Zereković, the thing is like so and so! You see how things are and how far we've gone. And I've heard about you as a businessman and industrious person who started from little, from nothing, and who today, thank God…I have called you, therefore, to entrust you with our industry, for you to reorganize it, to save everything at the last moment, and so on and so forth'—I would bow. 'May Your Highness forgive my candor and sincerity,' I would say, 'but I consider that I wouldn't be serving Your Highness or the national interests if I didn't tell you the full truth: half-measures won't help here. Everything has to change at the root. A surgeon's scalpel is what's needed. Only if you grant me unlimited power can I accept the task asigned to me. For, what's needed is this, then this, then that.'"

Master Andrija waves his hand, and his wife's gaze follows his movements, each of which represents some grand reform. For he has already accepted the mission entrusted him, reforming the national industry.

"I wouldn't know or recognize anybody. You understand? I'd receive and listen to everyone, but there'd be no compassion or scruples with me. I'm not familiar with any 'extenuating circumstances.' Whoever is lazy, corrupt, untrustworthy—I'd cut his head off without mercy. Someone comes and says, 'For God's sake, mister minister, don't, that is so-and-so—he has a wife, small children!' And I'd be cold as a mountain. Pitiless. And you'd see how things would take a new turn in no time. They'd remember and talk about how Andrija

Zereković took the steering wheel of the state into his own hands."

Before his wife's eyes, two knotted and hairy arms take and manfully steer that imaginary wheel.

At last that explosion too is finished. The moment of yawning and stretching arrives. His eyes grow smaller and teary. But, so it is, now more and more often not even bed brings his wife silence. After he finishes his long and complicated preparations, the brush-maker does not lie down immediately but sits on the edge of his wife's bed, curls one leg beneath himself and continues talking.

His wife's fine head stands out on the white Czech linen pillows, with luxurious black hair and dark blue eyes, and her bare neck and bosom bursting from the light covers give the impression of health, unspent strength and calm beauty. But Master Andrija sees nothing of all that, but looks through his wife and the objects around her into the far reaches of his own daydreams, with the gaze of vain people looking at themselves in the mirror.

In a quiet and significant voice, accompanying his words now with a sharp, penetrating stare, Andrija, undressed like that, continues the evening's conversation.

"Nobody knows just how stern and pitiless I could be. Yes, yes, many know me superficially. They think that if I'm obliging, polite and compliant like this, it's because of insufficient strength and daring, that I'm some kind of soft and compassionate person. Eh, you see, there they deceive themselves. A serpent, am I! An Albanian! I would, when state needs demanded it, fire people, send them to hard labor and kill them, if necessary. That's right, I would kill, kill! And my lips wouldn't tremble. I'd just check the thing, judge and condemn, then thwack, thwack, thwack!"

Here Master Andrija demonstrates how heads are chopped, slicing with the palm of his right hand above his clenched left fist. His elongated shadow stretches on the opposite wall like some antediluvian animal, and his hands, symbolically removing heads, look like the restless bridle-bit of that animal.

His wife looks at the tiny hairy man in his nightgown and warm underwear, with the white hat on his head. As he waves his arms, the foot of his bent leg peers from under the shirt with every swing. One moment his hard, large and bent toenail appears, and the next the gnarled heel, dry and bloodless like a mummy's. His wife closes her tired eyes just for a moment. Silver reflections from the small lamp on the night-table lie across her heavy eyelids. And at the same time, she hears the puffing man above her continue his state job.

"Thwack! thwack! thwack!" hisses his voice wildly and passionately.

When she opens her eyes again, she sees his suspicious and penetrating gaze, searching her features for approbation or denial. And then as proof that he is no man of weak will or timid heart, he tells her one of his early stories. There are only four or five of them and they are repeated frequently, but the brush-maker tells them each time as if they were completely new. The most frequent and convincing-sounding is the story of the general strike in Budapest, which Andrija lived through as a young journeyman. He had then, before the eyes of a frightened mass of workers that had crowded into some dead end, walked calmly across the entire square, gendarmes' bullets from the Danube's other shore flying overhead. And afterwards the entire world had wondered, who was that young man whom bullets, it seemed, did not hit; and they had wanted to carry him on their arms, to photograph him, and to bring him before journalists; but he withdrew, not being in the mood for that.

Anica knows the story well, but she follows it every time and checks with her sharp memory to see if the brush-maker is changing anything, taking away or adding. And miraculously, the narrative is always the same and faithful to every detail, as only stories about invented experiences can be.

"Yes, yes, my dear, Master Andrija isn't some soulful old woman," says the night-gowned man in an offended voice and with reproach, though his wife has not said a thing, and his upper lip begins to tremble lightly on one side.

His wife, embarrassed, lowers her eyes.

At last, the man decides to lie down, turns off the light, wraps himself in a comforter of pinkish silk, and with a gradually fading light grumble falls quickly asleep. And his roused wife widens her eyes and in the darkness stares steadily the irregular shapes of the little bundle the comforter and her sleeping husband make beside her. Sleep will not come to her.

The first year, she listened to her husband's bragging and to the petty stories in which he always figured as a grand personage; she listened without excitement, entirely without participation, restraining herself from yawning and pretending that the thing at least somewhat interested her. But his narratives grew, became ever longer and bolder, ever more presumptuous and strange. It began to disgust her. It seemed an affront that she had to listen to the boasts and fantasies of this man for hours, and to pay attention and participate sincerely. It offended her that he thought he could allow his fancy free sway in front of her, as if before an inanimate object or creature without reason, and did not consider it necessary to restrain his tongue or temper his lies and daydreams. She had heard as a girl from married women and friends that there exist wicked and peculiar men, with unhealthy desires, who demand offensive and unnatural things from their wives. She did not know any people like that nor their ways, but it seemed to her that this, what her husband was doing, could be that or something similar. In any case, she felt like a creature misused and maltreated in a soulless, insidious, but seemingly harmless and permissible manner. She was ashamed of all of it. It pained her and stung unbearably, more so every day, this profound feeling of degradation and shame; but rather than arousing a natural urge to protect herself, the pain took away her voice completely, hampered her movements, killed every decision at its inception. And that passivity and lack of resistance on her part stimulated the brush-maker to fly even more boldly and unscrupulously into boasting and false heroics. The healthy and intelligent woman, roused and displeased in her strong femininity, could have knocked the tiny man over with one motion of her able arm, could have wrapped him in his comforter like some deformed baby and threatened him to sleep; she could have silenced him and brought him down to earth with one word, and could have shown him how crazy he was to speak that way, and crazier still to think someone was crazy enough to listen and believe. She could have done it, and she wanted to with all her might, but she still could not find the strength. And as if cursed, she had to keep listening to what she despised, looking at what disgusted her, and enduring what she hated. And she allowed the brush-maker to perform in front of her every night, as if in front of a paid witness, his masquerade of lies and unhealthy prattle.

And when, sated and satisfied, he lies down and falls asleep just like now, only then does she really feel the exceptional weight and monstrous grief of her situation. She feels humiliated, crumpled and dirtied, as if some damp and filthy hands had wiped themselves on her and then thrown her into this dark abyss. She thinks she ought to defend and save herself, but she does not see how. Even misfortunes have their categories. To which does this belong? It seems impossible to define. And what cannot find a place in an existing category must be borne alone, for there is no cure for it. A person, especially a woman, in defending her rights and character must rely on other people and on her rights as formulated by the law, or at least by society's understanding and habits. And what can she complain about in this seemingly perfect marriage? How can she communicate that she is being abused in an exceptionally ugly and unbearable way, that she has to escape and save herself or go mad and die of boredom, shame and disgust, with him and with herself? How can she prove that life in this respectable, wealthy home, with an intelligent, courteous, happy man as a husband—is unbearable? And why? How can she do that when she does not even know how to express it to herself, when not even here between four walls, with this coward himself, can she find the strength to fight back and defend herself? She only knows she is suffering—and that she cannot endure it much longer. Maybe this is the essence of real, vast and complete human tragedy: when a person goes so mute with disgust and frozen with shame at what others have done to him, that he does not know how and cannot defend his rights, and on top of victimization has also to accept the blame.

It is in these moments that she most often thinks about running away from this house. Just as in childhood, like this in a warm bed and darkness, one dreams of fantastic adventures, great joys and wondrous successes, she now imagines how wonderful and frightening it would be to abandon this house and this man. With one decision and one move to free herself of everything, and forever. She knows full well how bold it would be, how mad and how frightening for her and incomprehensible in the eyes of her family and the world. She sees that it's impossible and unfeasible. But still, just one minute later, she catches herself fantasizing about her escape again to the last detail. At a moment when no one is home, to throw the most important things into her bridal suitcase, only what she brought, and to turn her back on everything. Just to return to her father's small house on the periphery! Aside from her father, her youngest sister and brother are still there. (Two sisters have married.) The girl studies philosophy and writes poetry, and he is sickly and doesn't like to work, but plays the guitar well and is so good-hearted that people nicknamed him 'angelic soul.' True, her father is rough, a man apart. True, it's hard at home. There's much work and something is always lacking. But what's all that compared to this? The poverty and labor of her previous life now seem like an unrealizable dream and unattainable happiness, like something that can't be bought for any price or ever found again once first abandoned. For she knows full well that her father wouldn't even let her in the house, that she would find herself alone, against the entire world, that flight would be an illogical and awful step, the same as suicide. And the woman closes her eyes tighter, and awake, still stubbornly dreams her dream of escaping to her father's house.

These sleepless hours grow more frequent and longer, as she lies next to the small burial mound of sleeping man—who will at the first opportunity, in conversation with guests, say modestly but confidently:

"A man who works doesn't know what insomnia is. Ever since I can remember, I've fallen asleep the instant I lay down, and I don't remember ever dreaming a thing."

She knows that sentence by heart, like all the others.

And while she is thinking that, the young woman feels a pain in her leaden breasts, a pain that grows,

grows and drives her to press her bosom with both hands, but then the pain spreads over her body, and she tearfully swallows her cries. The muscles on her thighs twitch so much her own legs urge her to stand. Her windpipe constricts towards her lips constantly and takes her breath away.

She remains awake like that, and like that at some hour falls asleep, when exhaustion assures her that it is hopeless to seek an escape where there is none, and that tomorrow, God knows how or from where, there will be something better, better, or at least different.

And tomorrow it is the same, and worse.

She feels more or less calm and protected until noon. Between her and last night stands a barrier of a little sleep and forgetfulness. She loses herself in giving orders and in petty domestic affairs. But the fear already starts around noon, of evening and what it can bring. And it can bring anything.

There were also nights when Master Andrija took his wife to the theater. Those were joyous hours for her. Even as a child she had loved the theater, especially opera. And apart from that, every moment she did not have to be alone with her husband was happiness, for then he was that calm, serious Master Andrija with his famous 'lovely way,' without a hint of the face only she knew.

When they returned from the theater, his wife always tried to go to bed as quickly as possible, avoiding conversation, to preserve that mood of light and warm excitement that lingered inside her after theatrical performances, especially after music and dance. But she succeeded less and less frequently. The brush-maker pursued her to her very bed. After lengthily and carefully completing his preparations, like some liturgy in his own honor, he would find himself in front of his wife, who was already trembling in advance, crushed into the bed from which there was neither escape nor refuge. At length and in detail, he would then explain to her that the National Theater ballet did not amount to anything, how everything was based on the wrong premise; it was unconscientious, incompetent, weak and slovenly. He leaned over her and proved that the renowned Russian dancer Krayevsky, whom they had seen that evening, enjoyed undeserved fame, that tonight he had danced lukewarmly and effeminately as the young knight around the sleeping princess.

"What does that pretty boy think, that skill consists of almond-shaped eyes and a little curled mustache? Is that how a man in love approaches the woman he longs for? I'm no dancer or an artist, nor is that my job, but I get the urge to get up there and show him how it's done. Ah, if I were their conductor or ballet-master! There'd be no evasion or shirking with me, that you can be sure of, nor that pretend skipping around, hop-hop! With me they'd have to stand on their toes and spin around until bloody blisters began to form. That one would fly like a bird if I only signaled with my eye—you understand?— And no grimacing and contorting, while here he is, receiving a large salary and calling himself an artist and dancer."

And, equipped for bed like that, in his long nightgown, without teeth, with cotton wool poking out of his nose and ear, the brush-maker bends over his wife in bed and conducts a mute orchestra and invisible dancers, sternly and pitilessly, and then he stretches mightily and demonstrates how, in his opinion, the renowned dancer should move around the princess on the stage.

And all that ends with his deep, unconcerned sleep, of which he is so proud, and with her painful insomnia. And tomorrow evening, the same game with different content.

She can no longer even explain it to herself, but just sees that her husband, after completing his work, when he is left alone with her after dinner, is quite simply turning into a monster. And every night there is some other role he plays in front of her, less logical and believable every time, ever more revolting and terrifying. She cannot find the strength to stop him or defend herself, and listens to him with vexation, with abhorrence, then with horror, for lately these conversations are beginning to inspire real fear in her. She knows it is all just the prattle of one powerless wretch, who at night, in the hours after a sober day of work and before a calm night's sleep, opens up his village-fair of monsters and reveals a face unfamiliar to the world—and only in front of her, the wife he feeds and clothes and before whom, it follows, he need have no shame or respect. She knows that, but is still overwhelmed with fear. For in his bragging and enumerating of everything he could do, were he at all like who or what he at that moment imagined himself to be, the brush-maker would have long ago crossed the line, not only of the believable and possible, but the permissible and natural.

The evenings now more and more often became veritable orgies of vanity, of his longing for power, craving for violence and fame and God knows what other urges he hides during the day or himself does not know he has—and for her, secret horror and ever longer sleeplessness. And anything can serve as provocation. A conversation started, for example, about a detailed report from the crime section. On an empty field, under a railroad bridge, a woman was found dead: a foreigner, stabbed many times with a knife. The woman was young, beautiful, noble, clearly from high society. The entire incident was inexplicable. All the papers wrote about it and everyone wondered: who was that mysterious beauty? Who were the killers, and what could the motive be for the evil deed?

Master Andrija at first reads the report of the crime aloud, then falls into his armchair and with a meaningful smile tells his wife:

"Fools! What's there to wonder about? Are secret societies and spy organizations so rare? And is there only one such beauty in their service? And with these societies it's like this: they recruit you and you join; you swear, you swear on a revolver that you'll execute all orders without discussion, and that you'll never give away the secret to anyone. Afterwards, you make a mistake or say something, and you're already sentenced. There's no saving you. When you least expect it: a knife in the back. And so it should be! No mercy and no hesitation. If it were my own sister, I still vote, Death. And the sentence is carried out automatically, with lightening speed. If necessary, I'd do it with my own hands. You understand?

And now these silly and soft-hearted police are running around and talking. Now it's a 'dark-complexioned powerfully-built man, tall in height,' now it could be this one, now that one is ruled out, and this one is unlikely. They don't know anything, I tell you. They're all blind men and weaklings, and they judge others by their own example."

Master Andrija gets up and moves closer to his wife.

"But maybe the killer is precisely a man who, according to our wise police, is 'totally ruled out,' someone no one even suspects. Maybe he's neither dark-complexioned nor tall. Maybe the chief of police passes him every day, and they greet each other like old friends. Maybe the killer watches with pleasure as they wander aimlessly, leading the investigation in a totally wrong direction, and laughs at them inside. Ha, ha, ha!"

Laughing loudly, the brush-maker circles the table once and again comes face to face with his wife.

"Whoever he is, he's a master of his work, a man who doesn't shudder when it's time to carry out a deed in the interest of higher goals, a man of sure eye and even surer hand."

The brush-maker raises a clenched fist and stares at his wife keenly, straight in the eye.

"I say this, because I'm like that myself. Everyone thinks: Master Andrija is courteous, a soft-hearted man, a real trump, but they don't even suspect just who and what Andrija Zereković is! Ha, ha! I'm no flea or lamb, but a lion, a lion, and the stealthy kind at that, the most dangerous kind. You understand? There, I know that even you think I could never even in my dreams kill some transgressor like that, like this woman on the field."

The brush-maker's face brims over, as if with light, with a smile full of pity and contempt from on high.

His wife lowers her eyes and the blood throbs in her cheeks; her lips move but cannot find words.

"There, you see you think so," the brush-maker leans like an inquisitor over her, "You see that I've guessed. And that's because not even you know me, just like the rest. Eh, you see, when it's a matter of principle, the interests of some sacred thing to which I've sworn an oath, killing one worldly wanderer in silk and furs like her is just like drinking a glass of water. 'You betrayed us— you know what's in store for you!' The first blow goes there under the neck, where the main artery passes— there!—and then three more blows, one in the back and two in the breast—there! there! there!—and it's done!"

His wife, frightened, watches him wield his short yellow pencil like a stiletto, panting: there! there! there! She knows that pencil well: he's already told her several times that it's the sixth year he's had it, because he can economize while writing and sharpening like nobody else—and losing a pencil or forgetting it somewhere, like other people do, that doesn't happen with him, and that's why his pencil lasts like nobody else's. "It can last six more with my way of economizing and saving. With me, all pencil factory owners would die of hunger;" that is how he put it, she remembers it well.

Still brandishing that pencil, Master Andrija continues:

"Like that, yes! Without a sound and without a cry. And afterwards, a man just washes his hands and returns to the market as though nothing had happened. And when talk about the incident starts up, he participates in the conversation, reads the papers, calmly, like every other citizen, and without the smallest muscle on his face twitching."

Master Andrija drinks the glass of water standing on the table and looks at his wife reproachfully, but with a mildness in which there is much contempt, as if forgiving her for not understanding and not knowing what was not easy to know, and what so many others, smarter than her, also did not know or suspect.

Next Master Andrija reads the newspapers a while longer, and then gets up and with a formal, calm step suitable to a much taller and stronger man, goes into the bathroom to prepare for bed.

And his wife lies in bed afterwards as if they had just brought her from the torture chamber. She is afraid of the dark but does not dare turn on the lamp, is revolted by thoughts of the evening's conversation but can think of nothing else. When she has the luck to fall asleep, the unknown woman's bloody corpse enters her dreams, so that she wakes with a choked scream. But the brushmaker does not hear her, because he is sleeping on his right ear and his left is stuffed with cottonwool.

On such nights, unable to sleep and choking with the desire to run from this stuffy room and from the even, mechanical breathing, more and more often, the woman got up and went to the bathroom. She washed her hands and face, splashed cold water on her swollen breasts. That brought only momentary relief. Back in the scorching sheets where her old thoughts awaited, the water's freshness changed right away into an intense heat that burned across her chest as if she was wearing flaming armor. She would jump up again, run to the bathroom and in just her shirt like that, unaware what she was doing, would throw herself on the cold stone tile floor and stay there, sobbing, until she felt her entire body go numb and tremble from the hard, cold berth; and alongside that painful cold, the thought permeated her that this would bring illness, or death—in any case, freedom.

Often half the night passed like that. And the next day brought calm everyday life, the evening her husband's stories, and night again unknown suffering.

In many a visibly ordered life there is an immense difference between day and night. There are many who, like this happily settled woman, walk with calm and composure by light of day, but at night endure such torment that even they do not recognize themselves in the scorching darkness of bed. But when the difference between day and night grows too great in a life like that, the capacity for hidden suffering and painful pretending becomes exhausted, and owing to unequal pressure between day and night—that entire life bursts into pieces.

Anica lived like that for more than two years. There was no reason a third year should not pass the same way, and a fourth, and the others all in sequence. In her mind she had long made peace with the fact that her torment could not be intimated to anyone, much less told, and that therefore there was also no cure. The years would pass; if she did not succumb, then she would bear them all in silence; she could bear the years, but she could not bear the hours and minutes.

One such insurmountable and fateful hour came halfway through the third year of her marriage. It was one of those moments that blaze in front of us and show, lucidly and without a doubt, that the life we lead is impossible, unworthy and unbearable. Our entire being then trembles from the root and braces itself for difficult, maybe tragic decisions. But since the world around us never rests, and we ourselves are always more likely to avoid fateful problems, some insignificant little thing usually happens—some facial expression, some conversation, some book or petty chore—draws our attention and tears our gaze away from the truth we just witnessed, and so allows us to deceive ourselves once more, to cravenly avoid making a real decision and continue our old way of life. But what happens so frequently did not happen this time.

That September afternoon Anica heard the girl opening the door for someone on the first floor. She thought it was her husband, returning home somewhat early, and she trembled. It turned out to be a young man from the shop, on some business. Had it been Master Andrija, she would have spent that evening like every other, and life in that house would have continued as before. But now she had to wait for her husband to come home. It was unbearable and, at that moment, became impossible. Sharp, restless thorns came alive in that strong, still girlish body, all pointing in the same direction in panic, pulling at her and driving her irresistibly out of this house. Her thoughts were full of fear, uncertainty, and

just one question: what scenes and stories was this evening bringing, and what kind of night awaited? If only
the girl were there. A few meaningless words exchanged
with her would redirect the woman's thoughts and restrain her. But by chance the girl had also that moment
gone somewhere across the street. The woman suddenly
found herself by her wardrobe in the bedroom. Her
small and cheap bridal suitcase of false leather was already open before her. As she had done so often in her
dreams and in delirious thought next to her sleeping
husband, she now quickly folded the most important of
her things and clothes (only what she had brought herself) and with suitcase in hand descended the stairs. And
again, did not hear or run into anyone. Thought ceased
entirely. And the powerful unrest in her body grew ever
stronger and so forceful it could have broken through
chains. That unrest swept her along like a straw up the
steep street and led her straight to her father's house.

Translated by Marijeta Božović

The Surveyor and Julka

The surveyor P. from S. paid me a visit this morning. That was how he had introduced himself on my doorstep. He was one of those visitors who did not barge his way in and did not come wandering into my house by virtue of his intrusiveness or persistence; instead, he just suddenly found himself in the spacious ground floor room, which may be rightly attributable to his restraint and calm. I still hadn't come to my senses when I found myself sitting opposite that meek intruder, a middle-aged man, diminutive in stature, who looked miserable. We were silent. He was looking at the floor, and I was looking at him. Everything about him is average and ordinary, but at the same time he was clean, groomed and rigid, as if he were going to a county fair.

"I am Surveyor P. from S.", he repeated, emphasizing every single word.

"?"

I was looking at him exerting my memory to no avail. I did not recognize any such name or face among my acquaintances, either past or present. My guest was not only waiting patiently, he was also discretely trying to help me. He was mentioning something about an encounter on a train during a trip from Belgrade to Novi Sad. It was a long time ago...many years ago.

It required some effort on my part, and some time passed before I remembered. The post-war years (I mean after the "other war," that is to say the 1920s) slowly emerged from my memory by degrees.

It was summer, and we were suffering through one of those scorching hot July days that only the plains along the Danube could produce. The afternoon was slipping away. The Belgrade train station was just as it is today, continually being demolished and rebuilt, but now even more paralyzed by the heat.

I was traveling to Novi Sad. The Subotica train was about to depart. I entered a third-class passenger car that appeared to be empty. The coaches were spacious with thirty-two numbered seats that were well arranged and not divided by partitions; the seats were sunny and cheerful, as if the seating had been designed for excursion groups or wedding parties; the passengers could move freely around, and go visiting from one bench to another to chat, to embrace one another and to sing.

Fiddling with the lock on a small suitcase right at the entrance of the passenger car, a little man was shielded by the open doors. He rose from his seat, as if he wanted to clear some space for me. I stopped just for a moment, and then decided to find an isolated seat a little farther down the aisle where I could be left in peace to read without having to hear the conversations of the other passengers or even participate in them. Taking advantage of the opportunity, the small man hastily introduced himself with some ceremony, as if he had been waiting for me a long time; no doubt he wanted to detain me.

"I am Surveyor P. from S."

Instead of saying my own name, I replied that I was delighted to make his acquaintance and I quickly left, and went to the far end of the car.

The surveyor remained standing indecisively for another moment as if he were disappointed, and then he lifted his small suitcase into the netting of the luggage rack above, sat down in his spot in the corner and remained there with his hands folded in his lap, hunched over, as small as if he were some lost thing. He was a man of woeful appearance; he had an undersized head and bright eyes; he was visibly struggling with some inner turmoil, yet his outward appearance was stonefaced.

I remained seated and read, but from time to time when I lifted my head, I would always make eye contact with the timid gaze of the man sitting in the far corner of the passenger car. I had the impression that his eyes were calling, begging, searching for a closer acquaintance, and perhaps even a conversation. I was not up to it, so I kept lowering my eyes and I continued reading.

Only two or three passengers boarded in Zemun and they dispersed themselves throughout the car farther away from me. It was the same with the other passengers who boarded later at whistle stops.

This was an ordinary passenger train that made its way very slowly. In any case, our old, rickety, weather-beaten passenger car shook and jolted, thundered and clanged so much that it was rather hard for me to read, but I clamped the text before my eyes as I was being jostled, even though the printed words kept snapping apart and jumbling together.

We finally arrived in Novi Sad. I got up, put my book in my traveling bag and got off the train, deliberately avoiding looking in the direction of the far corner of the coach where my fellow traveler, the surveyor, remained staring at me, which I found disturbing.

And when I stepped off the train and headed toward the platform, something urged me to turn my head to look once more into the windows of the car that I had just left, but I kept my composure and did not do so.

And now, he was sitting right in front of me in my own home, looking just as he did on that summer day in the train, but he was somehow closer, clearer and more certain of his sense of being lost. His voice was low and monotonous, as if he were speaking of a third person.

I was able to gather this much. His grave had been in the cemetery of S. for the last quarter century. He had been buried there one November afternoon in the same year we had met on the train. Three days earlier, his body had been found in the muddy shallows of a branch in the river.

A funeral was held and nearly all of the townspeople of S. attended. Even a priest chanted the graveside prayers, although the mourners were firmly convinced that he had committed suicide. (A commission composed of a physician and a judge did not render a definitive opinion on the cause of death.) But people had considered him to be a lost cause long before he lost his life in the turgid waters of a nameless and muddy branch of a river, and most people thought that it was neither right nor just to punish him for it once again in death.

He had come, he said, to hold the conversation that I had owed him ever since that summer afternoon when we met on the train so many years ago.

(The years swirled together in a confused whirlpool in my mind, accompanied by all sorts of obligations, formal and informal, fulfilled and unfulfilled. I felt something like a pang of conscience for that long forgotten encounter on the train. All at once, it was clear to me that it was not a good idea to avoid such meetings with people to whom they are necessary, no matter how nonsensical or how unpleasant they may appear to be. Such conduct is neither nice nor wise. Because, even if we avoid having to listen to such a person out of selfishness or regard for our own comfort, one day we may be shamed into doing it, in a troubling memory or a dream, which only makes it harder and more unpleasant.)

My guest's voice startled me and roused from of my musings.

"I just came to see you," continued the surveyor somewhat more clearly and with greater animation, "I came to ask you something. Look…"

As soon as he had said the word "look," my guest room was flooded by luminous fog, which kept getting thicker until the room was immersed in it; and then, having been thus transformed, an old-fashioned third class passenger car immediately emerged, and it was barreling down the railroad tracks, shaking and jolting its way from Belgrade to Novi Sad.

We were alone in the car. My fellow passenger, the surveyor from a town on this railroad line, and myself. This time I was sitting next to him. After a short introduction and some hesitation, he began his rather long and unusual story. He spoke in a confessional tone of voice; he spoke without interruption and did not lift his eyes from his hands that were folded in his lap. At first, I listened with astonishment and disbelief, and then with a sense of reconciliation, yielding as much to the suggestion made by his narration as to my own curiosity, which, privately, I was a little ashamed of. An unopened book, which I had brought along to read, lay in my lap.

The surveyor lived with his young and unusually beautiful wife in a solid, bustling community. There were many relatives and merry company, and he made very good money. There was only one problem—he didn't know how to put it—well, because he was married, and he frequently had to go looking for his wife, Julka, who, when she left him, was accustomed to go off wandering in different places both near and far. (*Voilà*, he was now returning from one such trip, and he still has unfinished business on his hands.)

"And that's not all. From the very beginning, you know, Julka liked having guests, and people are sociable in our town. The army have officers there. But you know, the army in peacetime is like an open furnace in summer. And you know how officers like to have fun; they've got plenty of free time on their hands, and once they sit down somewhere, it's hard to pry them out of their seat. And sometimes they go past midnight. There was a certain blond captain—a Serb from Serbia. I didn't like him right from the start. You know, I don't dance, but they crank up the gramophone and start dancing. And Julka and the captain did most of the dancing. There were others who were dancing, too, but little by little, the two of them slipped into another room where it was dark; there was only a small lamp with an orange-colored silk lampshade on a night stand. People say that this is how these dances are best danced, and that's how Julka likes it. At one point, I was going down the hallway, and then I entered that same room through another door, where I stumbled upon them: the captain was in the act of kissing her hand, and they were standing completely still, as if they had been petrified. Now what kind of dancing is that, that involves kissing? I at once approached the captain, and addressed him very seriously:

"Please, I kindly ask you, please!"

I turned my back on Julka. But later, after the guests had all left, she heard the things she needed to hear. I gave her a piece of my mind, and I told her that I had but one single honor, and that it was her duty to protect it, and I made a serious threat.

"Julka, restrain yourself!", I said.

That was all I said. And she knows well what those words mean when I say them. She ought to know. But, in any case, it seems as though she doesn't know or doesn't really care one way or the other. But the devil knows a thing or two about it. We sat down and had a conversation like a husband and wife about everything that needed to be talked about, and we squabbled a bit and there was reason for it; we didn't agree on anything.

I was always right, and in the end, it turned out as if we had not talked about anything at all.

Not a week passed before she took up with another guy, either an officer or a civilian, it doesn't matter, and then came some discrete conversations and whispers. "He is a kindered spirit," is what she said when I reproached her. "And what am I?" "You are—you," she said. And you couldn't tell what she was looking at any more than you could tell what she was thinking about. And you couldn't figure her out or her reasons for doing what she did.

Work was going well and I was often away from home, out in the field surveying land. When I returned home, I received some anonymous letters and even relatives started coming by to tell me about the visitors Julka was entertaining. When I confronted her about these accusations and told her that it was no good and that things couldn't go on like this, she agreed with me. She pretended to agree with everything I said but she kept doing whatever she wanted to do. She had no recollection of anything at all. It was a real phenomenon, Sir. At first I thought she was just pretending, but then later I was able to confirm that everything we talked about really did go in one ear and out the other.

And this has been going on now for three years straight. I prove things to her point by point, like a man, everything, so that it couldn't be plainer or clearer, and she calmly listens and looks at me without uttering a word, looking at me, but when I make a fair appraisal by studying the expression on her face, and I know how to do that, I can plainly see that she is not looking into my eyes but somehow past me as if somewhere far behind my back, somewhere far away, there was a tent in a village fair, wide open, brightly lit, and full of clowns and circus performers.

I seize her hand firmly and force her to look me in the eye and pay attention to what I have to say. She comes to her senses and she even feels a little ashamed of herself and she pulls herself together. "Well, look, I'm listening," she say. But what good is there in her saying so when not a half a minute later such belief and its own proper concerns do not take root, do not enable her to listen to someone who is talking to her about something she's not interested in. And what is she interested in? No living soul knows what that is. She doesn't even know herself. She knows what she is not interested in. Anything that's related to me, the house, the family, serious matters.

Not two minutes pass since she said that she was, apparently, listening to me closely, and once again I see that expression on her face that is looking past me, fixed on something far behind me where the devil himself is dancing in a circus arena. I can see it in the radiance of her eyes.

How can you force her to look at you when she doesn't want to, and she won't even say: I won't! On the contrary, she keeps confirming it all the time: "I'm looking at you," but it is obvious that she is seeing something else and that she isn't thinking about what she's talking about. And then, her face assumes an expression of martyrdom.

And the same goes for her sense of hearing.

"Restrain yourself, Julka," I said again on some other occasion, but she didn't say a thing and shut her eyes with undisguised boredom. As if that, I beg of you, meant something, as if that were some kind of answer. And even if she does say something sometimes, she only says it in a low, absent-minded voice: "Yes, yes" or "yeah, yeah." And it sounds like an echo of other conversations involving other people. You don't notice it at first, but little by little it becomes clear that her various approving statements come automatically, above and beyond what you're actually talking about, just as her expression looks past you. It starts to drive you mad, then madder, and finally, it can lead a man to, to…rage.

As I was thinking this over, I came to the conclusion that she doesn't even hear the better part of what I say—no matter what it's about. She doesn't want to pay attention, she doesn't want to make the effort or expend the energy required to hear something. She only pretends to be listening, but she doesn't even make enough of an effort to make the pretending look natural and convincing. That's enough to enrage even the most docile of men and make him lose his tact. In any case, I'm not like that; I value tact above all other things. But…

That's what I was saying to her, as a husband would to his wife. That's my right—isn't that so?—just as it's her duty to listen. But she does everything her way: she's scatterbrained. That's what it's all about. She physically present, but she pulled the plug on the machine, shut down her sense of sight and her sense of hearing, and her soul left and went who knows where and who knows with whom? And she left behind instead some phonograph that just keeps repeating: "Yes, yes," "yeah, yeah." It is all so mechanical and disconnected from what I'm talking about; she acknowledges and agrees, but she doesn't even wait for me to complete my sentence to see what I was getting at. It's just plain insulting!

You know, a man can have a good upbringing and be peaceable by nature, but situations exist in which none of this is helpful. When you get the feeling that someone who lives with you holds you in such contempt that she does not even take notice of your presence, pays no attention to what you say and refuses to answer your questions, as if she were dealing with a child or a dim-wit—the blood starts pounding in your head and you feel that you had better start defending yourself to prove that you're still there, still alive, and that you haven't lost your mind.

Sometimes she cuts loose with one of her *yeah, yeah*s at just such a moment. I flinch and take a closer look at the face of the sleeping beauty next to me:

"What? What do you mean by *yeah*?"

A moment of silence. She comes to her senses only to the extent necessary, then a bit of confusion follows with a wounded expression on her face, and some mumbling:

"Well, yeah, it's true…what you said…"

"What am I saying? What did I say, for heaven's sake!"

I leap from my chair shouting those very words. She is apparently insulted, and starts crying. That's all I need!

Now that, that's a chapter all by itself, Sir. What can I tell you about her tears, the way she cries, and the groaning and the catch in her throat, her swollen lips and red-dening eyes? Ah, her deep sobbing, so baseless and un-justified, is a genuine misfortune that unexpectedly be-falls us from time to time, and it disturbs and upsets the household. Our cat bristles and wanders through the rooms of the house. Julka's lap-dog keeps running around us in circles, barking continuously. Then our neighbors open their windows because they want to hear our domestic music. The worst thing about it is that her crying seems staged and I wouldn't believe its sincerity even if you had threatened my life. But a blonde like Julka is completely transformed by her bouts of crying; her face turns red, her shoulders look as though they have been flayed, and she looks like a genu-inely unfortunate creature.

And when you start hoping that she might pipe down a little and come to her senses, and as soon as you open your mouth to say something nice, she bursts into tears once again. Her crying pours out of her and gives you the impression that it will never stop: instead it makes you feel that she, as pale and small-boned and plump as she is, will dissolve into weeping and tears.

I tell you, Sir, it's not the kind of crying you hear when women cry; instead, it's an earthquake, and the sky comes toppling down. I don't know if you've ever seen a forest fire, because that's what it's like: it spares noth-ing and cannot be stopped. Her weeping doesn't let you get close to her, it prevents any conversation, and ig-nores moderation and reason. As she weeps, this world we live in vanishes, and along with it the house, the fam-ily, and me, too. Everything vanishes in her convulsions and eruptions. And it looks to me like she's doing it all on purpose and that she is secretly reveling in her convulsive sobs.

"Restrain yourself, Julka," I say, trying to calm her down, but she bursts into tears again, as if I were emptying a jerry can of benzine onto a dying flame.

Her crying bouts are strange, Sir, really strange. They appear suddenly, and they end just as suddenly. It's hard living with them, and it's harder living without them. You must know that my wife feels mortally insulted like this at least once a month. And the precise moment when such fits occur? It is difficult to know in advance. And if it doesn't wind up in an outburst of tears and weeping, then something much worse starts. Julka gets up, rushes around like a madwoman packing her personal belongings and, without explanation, leaves and goes off somewhere to anyone at all: to her mother's, to some relative's home, to someone's farm or to some nearby hotel. And she waits for me there to come and get her. And when we meet and make up, there is not one word of explanation, not one word of apology or anything like it. And I don't dare ask too many questions because I'm afraid of provoking a new explosion. Now, who's going to find his way out of a situation like this? What can you do about it?

When a man starts wondering—and I am always wondering—about what really interests her, I can only draw an approximate conclusion: games, nonsense and mindless behavior. Once, when I put a little pressure on her, she admitted that she wanted more than anything else to swing naked on a flying trapeze in a brightly lit circus ring before a packed house. She was happy, even inspired as she spoke about it, as if for a moment she were not talking to me but to someone else, a stranger.

Then she immediately retracted her statement. No, she says, that's not what she really wants. She never really said such a thing to begin with, after all.

Therefore, she did not say it. She says that to me, right to my face. Look, that's what this woman is like and that is how I live. Now what? Look, two years have passed, and she's not getting any better. It's not easy, Sir. I had a good upbringing and I'm a man who has a soft spot in his heart. I can't bear to see chicks slaughtered, but I'm afraid that I might do something crazy or evil one of these days. I will.

There the surveyor fell silent. He appeared even more frail and more stooped than he did before and his face had grown darker than it had been when he began speaking. I took advantage of the opportunity to detach myself from the magical power of his narration, and I rose to get off the train. The train was approaching Novi Sad. The train rattled over the bridge spanning the Danube and blew its deafening whistle. The passenger car filled with smoke from the locomotive, and with some dust and the dark red gleams of the onrushing evening, as if we were in a blacksmith's shop.

I got up to go before we pulled into the station, and I paused to say good-bye to the surveyor, who looked as though he were carrying the weight of the world on his shoulders. His weak, spastic hand clenched my fingertips, and he added with some concern in a businesslike manner:

"You know, I would never do something like that."

That was how we said good-bye.

I took my leather traveling bag and headed for the exit, but I never reached it because at that very moment the third class passenger car vanished, and it occurred without fogging, without any transition, all at once.

Once again, we were sitting in my guest room. Everything was in its place, but the surveyor, who was as light as a shadow yet powerful and irrepressible, had already stood up and headed for the door.

I wanted to ask him to stay a bit longer, to ask him about some details, to look for some explanation. Now I wanted to talk to him, but the surveyor, like a man who was in a hurry, avoided any further conversation because we had the conversation that we were supposed to have had at its appointed time on the train from Belgrade to Novi Sad, which we had subsequently conducted and completed. And he vanished just as he had appeared, strangely and silently. And now I became the one who was absorbed in thought, confused and dissatisfied.

Translated by Milo Yelesiyevich

Olujaci[1]

I<sup>t is said that a traveler of saintly demeanor once remarked about Olujaci: "God has given them wealth
and every sort of misery." If there was some truth
in that comment a long time ago, certainly nothing has
changed since then to contradict the words of the holy
man.

Olujaci is a mountain village, but it is not located on
a plateau. In fact, it is built in a steep cleft high up, as if
it were in a mountain ravine piercing a mountain plateau.
The houses are for the most part two-storied, less
spread out than houses in other villages and mostly built
along Black Brook, which cuts straight through the
middle of the settlement. Due to the steep terrain, they
are perched one on top of the other. The village tapers a
bit at both ends of the cleft and thus, from a distance,
resembles an ark that some enormous flood had cast up
and grounded on this mountain peak long ago.

From the center of the village runs a path which
drops off suddenly, twisting and descending down the
cliffs and steep slopes toward the bed of the Drina,

[1] "Olujaci" is the name of a village in the eastern Bosnian district of Višegrad.

151

which is painfully pinned between stony walls. It takes two hours to go down this path, but more than three to climb up it. Winding and diving, Black Brook rushes alongside the path, leaping at times headlong off the rocks in falls so high that its scanty waters turn into rain and mist before they reach the ground again. Every rock that is splashed gets covered with a lichen-like black film. The water is not drinkable and even children who can barely walk know that.

That remote and isolated village differs from the other villages not only because of its location but for many other reasons too, most especially its fertility. Although the grain crops, except for oats, are rather thin because of the high altitude, everything else grows and flourishes in this shaded and secluded region bigger, better and more lushly than in any other village in the Višegrad valley. Especially fruit, and most of all nuts. Olujaci is surrounded by a wreath of nut trees both young and old. There are years when Olujaci brings to the Višegrad market more nuts than all the other villages put together.

Everything in Olujaci grows well except the people. The locals are on the short side, bow-legged, with broad but crooked backs, exceptionally long arms, broad cheeks with flattened noses and small black eyes with an unexpressive but insistent look in them, and wide necks that at the base broaden so as to form one indistinguishable unit with their torsos. It is easy to spot them in the town bazaar among hundreds of other villagers. As the location of their village makes them constantly climb up and down the mountain, they carry themselves in a particular way—when they walk, the entire upper half of their body is tilted backwards.

They are known as hard, mistrustful people who speak little, rarely sing, always work, and regularly profit. There is also a belief that everyone born in Olujaci must bear a mark. It seems that there is not a single villager who is not goitrous, crippled, or branded in some other way.

But these little powerful people from the high village excel in their cunning, animal-like taciturn energy, and stamina at work. Their farming is cleverer and more diverse than in other villages, their fruit is better not only by growth and kind but also in the manner in which it is harvested and prepared. They do not haggle in the market or sue in court, but they get their price and, when they do sue, they sue to the full and regularly prevail. Most often they marry among themselves. Therefore, when someone is related to someone else so that it is difficult to determine the precise relationship, they say in that entire region that they are "Olujaci relatives."

The old people used to joke saying that the Austrians conquered all of Bosnia except Olujaci. There is some truth in that since Olujaci almost did not exist during the occupation, for it had burned down just before the Austrians arrived. Here is how it happened.

There was a rather prominent family in Olujaci called the Muderizovićes. Some time before one of them had left for Sarajevo, gone to school, and risen to become a *muderiz*.[2] That was a rare and exceptional thing for Olujaci. That *muderiz*'s son was also an educated man who

---

[2] Muderiz: instructor in an Islamic high school.

eventually became a judge in Mostar. He maintained closer contacts with his relatives from the distant Višegrad village than his father had. One hot summer the judge came back to his home village with his entire family. Thus it happened that he and his wife decided they would marry off the most prominent Muderizović boy to a beautiful and wealthy girl from the vicinity of Mostar. This was something new and unheard of. Neither the older villagers nor the family members approved of a bride from a distant, alien world, but the ambitious judge nonetheless concluded the matter that fall.

The beautiful girl from Mostar was brought one early evening. The groom's younger brother and one of her relatives accompanied her to Olujaci. The girl was weary from the trip. Earlier that afternoon, as they passed along the stony and sharply incised bed of the Drina, with its deep, green, terrifying waters and a horse's desiccated and scrubbed skeleton bleaching on a narrow sandy spit, she felt as if she were facing horrors from fairy tales which one has to overcome in order to get to beautiful places and experience great joys. But when they finally left the Drina behind and began to climb to Olujaci following the red, almost vertical path of hard-baked earth, the bride began to worry that the end of this inhuman road would be the same. She was wrong. The end was such that the very next day she longed for the bed of the gall-green Drina and the steep path. The house, the groom, and the household—everything was horrible, impossible, and indescribable.

As she bade farewell to her relative who was returning to Mostar and kissed his hand, she sobbed without tears but despairingly: "Give ... my *selam*,[3] my *selam* to everyone."

And she watched as he and his horse sank into that gloomy depth that separated Olujaci from the rest of the world.

It did not take her long to realize that she could not live there. She could not force herself to die, yet she could not live there. Lost and crushed with pain, she did not know what would happen; and yet, she clearly felt that something would have to happen.

Whatever was the Mostar judge thinking when he married that girl into this village? She towered two heads above the groom, and three above the tallest woman in Olujaci. She was slender but ample, while they were all without exception stocky or wiry; she was lively and happy, they gloomy and grim; she loved song and dance, and they loved work and dark brooding, the point of which was difficult to perceive; she loved to dress up and pamper herself, which her sisters-in-law and other relatives looked upon with amazement and condemnation...

All those differences constantly dogged her life and estranged her even more from the entire village and her husband's numerous family. Her husband would appear at night. He was a powerful man, with premature wrinkles on his swarthy face, a neck that widened at the base towards the shoulders, and dim, suspicious eyes. She would tremble sensing his odor approaching from afar. He smelled of the earth, the sheepfold, and soured milk.

[3] Selam: greeting.

He would come to her mutely and brutally and then leave in the same way. Only woman's unhappy fate and the dead of night know what happened between them in those moments. But fate's lips are sealed.

The windows of her house looked into the hillside. The yard was steep, like everything else in and around Olujaci. But when she raised her head and looked at the blue autumnal sky and the slow flight of the wild doves, she recalled her own village on the lush plane near Mostar, and suddenly she would begin to cry noiselessly, swallowing her tears.

The fruit ripened and there was much work to do. At that time of year Olujaci resembled a busy hive. Without many words, following the rules they knew from birth, all villagers were at work, from children to the elderly. This small and ugly breed of people did every kind of job from the grossest to the finest without measuring time or sparing effort. They kept working by torch-light till late. Even two-year old toddlers in their little shirts, which looked shorter in front because of their protruding, rounded little bellies, would bring in a smashed apple and, following a primal instinct of their clan, throw it into the press lest it be lost. As if the orchards were innumerable, load after load of fruit kept arriving on horses, oxcarts, or simply on people's backs. The great beach-wood press in which tiny apples were smashed for jam resounded, plum jam was boiling hot in the copper pots on the fires burning in the courtyards, the drying racks smoked. For nothing of the harvest could be wasted. Everything was carefully garnered and had to be wisely utilized and handsomely profited from.

Although the entire village smelled of fruit and fermenting juices, it was nuts that were particularly abundant. They were the main source of income and therefore received the greatest attention. This was women's work. The women dried, shelled, mixed, and separated great heaps of nuts on spreading sheets made of goat's hair. They shelled them expertly and fashioned them painstakingly into the famous Olujaci "chains": long arrangements of shelled or whole nuts and prunes, one strung after another.

Bent over her work, the young woman from Mostar was in a group of these cramped, silent women. Their broad hands with cracked skin and short thick fingers blackened from the nuts and juices touched and mixed with her shapely hands on which the oval nails had recently been polished. Though they did not talk—in Olujaci even the women spoke but rarely—their hands did the hating while their deadened eyes clashed with the bride's large amber eyes. In addition to that innate hatred and envy, the young woman brought down upon herself their contempt as well, as she was not used to the work and performed it absentmindedly. Over a sea of rustling nuts she gazed all day long at her misery and the ultimate downfall that somehow appeared to her inevitable. And at night, in place of the green, merry fields of Mostar, she dreamed of an endless desert where instead of grains of sand black nuts rolled and rattled ominously.

So passed that autumn and the difficult winter after it. Spring came. Back in Mostar her family realized that in Olujaci they would not even consider sending their daughter-in-law off for a while to visit with her kin, as was the custom. So they decided that her younger brother, who was traveling around Bosnia on business, should visit her instead and see how she was. She loved that brother more than all her other siblings; he was her mirror image, tall, handsome, with thick blond hair, and dark eyes. He was special to her even before, but now, when he showed up unexpectedly, like some saving angel, she saw him as the embodiment of all that she had lost down in Mostar and all that she had not found in Olujaci.

She grew faint with joy when a horseman appeared against a bright sky on the Olujaci slope; through the falling dusk and her tears, she realized it was her brother. Not knowing what she was doing, she stroked his horse's red harness, the likes of which did not exist in Olujaci. Not even after dinner did she want to part from him. Her husband stood next to her and waited like a patient executioner.

Later on that night, when her husband appeared to be asleep, she snuck to the front room where her brother was spending the night. Although he urged her to return to her room and go back to bed, she sat down next to his mattress and spoke to him at length and in muffled tones. She told him how unbearable it was in this backwater, among the insensitive and evil brood of monstrous dwarves and trolls. She revealed to him that they had married her off to a man who looked healthy and normal at work, but who was insane, who had visions at night and could not free himself of the thought that he and all he owned were in peril. He had decided to separate himself from everyone else and now he slept with her not in the large family house of the Muderizovićes but in this remote wooden shack. From their first night in the marriage bed, he had kept a loaded gun ready by his head and had placed a long knife between himself and his wife. He was pathologically jealous from the start, without any real cause. Jealousy without love. Nothing but the pathological need to torture and destroy. She had done everything to drive such sick thoughts from his head and tried to remove the weapons, but that just prompted him to further suspicions and fears. He threatened that he would burn her alive if she tried to do that again. And so, after a day of hard work, she lay in bed with a large knife and a wretched madman who pretended to be normal next to her. And she cried day and night. When she could not manage to hide her tears, her husband's relatives told her dully and coldly that she was just being a bride and would keep crying until she heard her own baby cry.

Her brother started a few times during her long and agitated tale. It seemed to him that he heard strange sounds and a knocking, but she calmed him, stroking his hair and pressing to her cheeks his large lovely hands which so completely resembled hers. And she just whispered:

"My dear, my only one, take me away or kill me. Save me any way you can."

The young man tried to fend off her ardent words and hugs. He wanted to collect his thoughts, to make a decision.

"Wait a minute, stop it, let's see, let's think this over till tomorrow. I'll speak with him. Wait! Don't cry, don't be afraid!"

But the woman would not let him go. She clung to him as if she were drowning.

"My dear, my only one!"

Nonetheless, it was she who first smelled the smoke and the burning. She tore herself away from her brother and tiptoed toward her room. Carefully and noiselessly she pressed on the latch but the door did not open. She pressed again, quietly but firmly. In vain. The room had been locked from the outside. Her knees buckled. She barely made it back to her brother and told him in a terrified whisper what was going on. The young man got up quickly. They stood thus in the dark, holding each other's hands. They could hear their own blood rushing in their ears.

Who can understand those incredible moments at night, when it is difficult to restore the sense of vanished reality and reclaim the supremacy of reason, when things happen which are impossible to understand and explain in broad daylight, only to remain forever in the darkness that had given them birth!

From outside came the sound of someone doing something around the shutter on the single window. The young man approached it. The window was shut— something heavy was rolled against it from the outside. He pushed in vain. There he caught a sharp whiff of smoke. He crossed the room quickly and unlocked the door that led to the low porch, but it too was blocked by something heavy and would open only a crack. Through the narrow opening wafted sharp and choking smoke from lamp oil and burning hay. In a frenzy, the young man threw his whole body against the small opening, trying to widen it enough so that he could crawl through. At that moment, from the outside darkness someone struck him on the head with something sharp and heavy like a dark, silent bolt of lightning. He staggered back and collapsed in the middle of the room. The woman screamed and fell on her knees. And from that narrow opening through which the young man from Mostar had tried to squeeze in vain, the small and wiry Muderizović crawled in, with a long knife hidden behind his back. He locked the door through which smoke was already pouring in, pushed the key into his pocket, and approached his wife, who, mute with horror, spread out her arms in despair over her unconscious brother.

Less than an hour later an old Olujaci woman who could not sleep noticed the fire and woke the household. The isolated wooden shack where wealthy Muderizović spent the nights with his beautiful Mostar wife was burning from several sides. While the numerous Muderizović clan came running with hooks and buckets of water, the house was already engulfed in flame. The door and all the windows were locked from within. Those who tried to break through had to retreat before the flames because stacks of hay placed short distances apart were burning in and around the house. They called Muderizović, his wife, and his brother-in-law by name. No one answered. The fire crackled violently, drowning the house more and more in the flames. The frightened people stood back.

A heavy warm southern wind arose and began to blow harder and harder. Burning shingles and sparks started to fly off the roof as if winged, borne by the wind toward the village. Now everyone had to take care of his own house. Men climbed up on the roofs, and women and children with desperate cries and gestures from below indicated to them where they needed to put out the flames. But the sparks were many and flew fast. The wind picked up as dawn was about to break.

More than a half of the village burned down that night, the part on the right bank of Black Brook. Several people were injured attempting to salvage things and put out the flames, but no one had perished. They managed to save the women, children, elderly, and disabled and get them to the other side of the stream. Valuable things were rescued for the most part. They were all piled up in one large garden, wet and in disorder: copper pots, carpets, furniture, tools, weapons. Only the threesome from the Muderizović shack were awaited in vain. Among the charred beams they found their remains. A small, burnt out, black corpse was all that was left of Muderizović, while only featureless, scattered, and scorched bits remained of the brother and sister.

Right after the disaster, without ever trying to find a plausible, convincing explanation for everything that had occurred, the Olujaci villagers threw themselves upon the charred ruins, clearing the ground and preparing the material for building. That same summer they would have rebuilt at least some of the houses had not the war begun and the Austrian army arrived, which upset the whole world, including Olujaci. But the very next spring, after the situation in Bosnia had calmed down a bit, they restored the village like ants repairing a trodden down anthill.

They rebuilt all the houses, stables, and stalls as they had been earlier and on their original sites. Only Muder-izović's shack, in which the inexplicable accident had occurred, was not rebuilt. The level plot on which it had stood earlier, insomuch as one could speak of a level plot in steep Olujaci, remained empty like a nameless clearing. On sunny days the women of Olujaci would spread out canvas there to dry their nuts.

Translated by Henry R. Cooper, Jr. and Bogdan Rakić

Thirst

S oon after the Austrian occupation of Bosnia, a post of the *gendarmerie* was opened high up in the mountain village of Sokolac. The commanding officer brought with him, from somewhere abroad, a lovely fair-haired wife with big blue eyes that looked as if they were made of glass. With her brittle beauty, her Western dress and outfit, she was like a precious and frail thing mislaid on the mountain heights by some travelers en route from one great city to another.

The village had hardly gotten over its first shock of astonishment, and the young woman was still busy furnishing her new married quarters, filling the rooms with little cushions, embroidery, and ribbons, when bandits were reported in the vicinity. A company of special scouts arrived at the post, doubling the barracks population. The commandant spent his days out in the field, deploying and supervising his patrols. His young wife was left, bewildered and fearful, in the company of village women, so that, nominally at least, she would not find herself completely alone. Her time was spent in waiting. Even her sleep and meals took on an aspect of waiting and no longer refreshed and nourished her. The village women coaxed and begged her to eat, until in their nudging and wheedling they themselves ate up all the food and drank all the milk. At night they sat by her bedside and told her tales of village life to lull her to sleep. In the end, exhausted by their talking, they would doze off on the red carpet while she, from her bedstead, would gaze at them with her wide-awake eyes, sickened by the heavy smell of milk and coarse wool that came from their peasant skirts. And even when, after several days of such waiting, the commanding officer would return, she had little cause to feel joyous and relieved.

The man came back dead-tired from marching and lack of sleep, his face hidden behind a thick stubble, his clothes dirty and soaked through. His boots, which he had not taken off in several days, bulged with mud and water and it took a pair of orderlies to pull them off; and with the woolen putties bits of skin came off his sore and swollen feet. His lips were chapped, his face weathered by the sun, wind, and mountain air. He was worried and distracted by his lack of success, and in his mind would already be plotting his next expedition. Tense and wound up, he literally burned with zeal and anxiety. In those short intervals of rest at home his wife nursed him like a wounded man, only to send him off again two or three days later, at the crack of dawn, into the mountains. And so all her thoughts and prayers were animated by a single wish, that the wretched brigands be rounded up as soon as possible and that this dreadful way of life might finally be brought to an end.

And then one day her greatest wish came true. They caught the chief bandit, Lazar Zelenović, the most cunning of them all. After him, according to the barracks talk and village gossip, it would be easier to catch or scatter the other petty bandits who were less skillful and experienced.

It was by a fluke that Lazar was caught. A patrol that was on the trail of another, younger bandit stumbled on him accidentally. Some two months previously, when he had moved into this region from Herzegovina, Lazar had been wounded in the chest by a bullet. This no one knew. In order to tend his wound, Lazar, with the help of younger bandits, had built himself a shelter beside a mountain stream; it was made up of dry branches and driftwood and washed-up silt. He lived in that hole out of sight of the paths that traversed the hillside high above the stream, yet was able to reach water by stretching out his hand. In this way he could bathe his wound all day long while the patrols looked for him everywhere, scrambling up the crags and mountaintops. And he might have recovered had he dared to look for a more comfortable shelter and had the weather just then not turned unseasonably warm, which made his wound much worse. He did his best to ward off mosquitoes and flies, but the wound grew bigger and, deep down under the skin where the water could not reach, it was beginning to fester more and more. And his fever rose.

Such was the condition of the bandit when one of his younger companions decided to bring him some wax and brandy to use as medication. A patrol spotted the young man as he was leaving a shepherd's hut on his way down to the stream. Noticing them only at the last moment, the boy scampered down the stream bed and vanished without a trace.

The commandant who had left his horse in a meadow below and was running at the head of the patrol after the young bandit, stumbled into a patch of soft mud and grazed his feet against something soft and lifeless, before sinking up to his waist in the silt. And he might have gone on ahead, after extricating himself with difficulty, and might not have discovered Lazar's small and deftly camouflaged hideout, had he not smelled the terrible stench of the bandit's wound. After pulling his legs out of the mud, the commandant glanced through the parted branches and saw a sheepskin. Sensing that a live man was hiding in the burrow underneath, he never even dreamed that it might be Lazar himself; he thought that it was the younger bandit or some accomplice of his. To hoodwink the concealed man, the commandant gave loud orders to his patrol:

"He must have run ahead. Go after him and I'll follow you slowly. I've gashed my leg on these thorns."

As he was shouting this, he cautioned them with one hand to keep quiet and with the other signaled them to form a circle around him. When three of the men came near, they threw themselves all at once at the shelter and pinned the bandit down by the shoulders, like a badger. Since his only weapons were an old long-barreled rifle and a big knife, he had no time either to fire or reach for the knife. They tied his hands with a chain and his feet with a rope and carried him thus, like a log of wood, down the hill and to the meadow where the commandant's horse was waiting. All the way down they were aware of the heavy stench, but it was only when they put him down that they saw the ugly wound on his bared chest. A certain Živan from the village of Goražde, who had joined the patrol as a guide and scout, recognized Lazar right away. They were from the same village; both their families honored the same patron saint, St. John.

The bandit rolled his big gray eyes, which had grown clear through his living out in the open and beside the water but which now were aglow with fever. The commandant asked Živan to confirm once more that this really was Lazar. They were all leaning over the bandit. Živan addressed him for a second time.

"It's you, Lazar!"

"I can see you know me better than I know you."

"You know me, Lazar. Sure you know me."

"And if I hadn't known you before, I'd sure know you now. I would know who you are and what you are. And so would every last village from here to Goražde...every man who calls himself a Serb or a Turk would know you. If you came with a stupid child who'd never seen us, and he saw us now just the way we are, he'd say, 'The one lying tied up on the ground, that's Lazar, and the bastard that's bending over him, he's Živan.'"

The bandit had a fevered need to talk and mark time, while Živan wanted to assert his authority and buttress his reputation before the company, and who knows how long the two of them might have dickered in this fashion if the commandant had not interrupted them. But the bandit met all further questions with silence. He would say nothing about his accomplices and contacts, using the excuse that he was wounded and in pain. After consulting with the patrol sergeant, a strapping man from the province of Lika, the commandant issued strict orders that the bandit was not to be given a single drop of water no matter how much he begged for it, but was to be referred to the commandant.

While they were readying a stretcher on which to carry the wounded bandit, the young commandant sat down some distance away to rest and collect himself. Planting an elbow on his knee, he leaned his chin on the palm of his hand and gazed at the mountain, which had only just turned green and seemed as endless as the sea. He wanted to think about his success, about the citation that awaited him, and about resting up in the company of his wife. But he could not concentrate on anything. All he felt was a leaden exhaustion, which he resisted and fought as a man caught in the snow at night fights against sleep and freezing. Wrenching himself up from the ground, he stood erect and ordered his men to move on. A second patrol overtook and joined them. Now there were nine men in all. The litter they had improvised for the bandit was rough and made of gnarled branches. One of the gendarmes threw his tunic over it, averting his face as he did so, almost as if he were abandoning his coat forever.

They traveled by slow marches. The sun was beginning to burn in earnest. The commandant, who rode in the rear of the litter, was forced to move to the head of the column because the stench from the wounded man had become unbearable. It was only after midday, when they had climbed down to the Glasinac Plain, that they managed to commandeer a cart and oxen from a peasant. In this way, shortly before sundown, they reached the broad valley that stretched out before the village of Sokolac. They looked like a party returning from a hunt, save that these huntsmen were lost in thought and their game was extraordinary.

In the meadow in front of the barracks the women and children of the village had gathered. Among them, too, was the wife of the commandant. At first she gave no thought to the bandit, and was simply waiting for her husband, as always. But as the women began to chatter more excitedly about the man on the litter and their tales grew more and more lurid, and as the procession came nearer, slow and drawn out like a funeral, she too was filled with a sense of misgiving and suspense. At last they arrived. The men noisily threw open the left wing of the barrack gate, which ordinarily was done only when a cart-load of wood and hay had to be taken in. Here the commandant dismounted, hitting the ground with a thud, as exhausted riders are wont to do. The young woman felt the scratch of his sharp stubble on her cheeks and smelled the odor of sweat, earth, and rain which he always brought with him from these official raids.

While he gave his orders, she stole a glance at the bandit who lay bound and motionless. Only his head was raised a little on an improvised cushion of straw. His eyes didn't seem to see anyone. The acrid stench of a wounded animal spread out around him.

Having ordered all that was necessary, the commandant took his wife's hand and led her into the house, for he didn't want her to witness the unloading and untying of the bandit. After he had washed himself and changed, he went out once more to see how they had settled and

171

secured the man. Lazar was locked in the cellar under the commandant's apartment, which was to serve as a temporary jail. The door was not a strong one; the upper half had iron bars, and the lock on it was the usual kind. Thus a man had to be detailed to stand guard in front of it all through the night.

The commandant ate sparingly, but talked a great deal with his wife. He chatted about trifles and was as lively and cheerful as a boy. He was well satisfied. He had caught the leading and most dangerous bandit, after five months of strenuous traipsing up and down the mountains and after undeserved reprimands from his superior officer at Rogatica and from the headquarters at Sarajevo. He would find out from Lazar about the hiding places of his accomplices and so earn a respite and an official commendation.

"What if he doesn't give them away?" asked his wife timidly.

"He will; he'll have to," replied the commandant, unwilling to discuss it further with his wife.

Presently he grew sleepy. Exhaustion weighed on him heavily, overcoming his joy, his hunger, his desire for his wife. The freshness of the bed linen went to his head like wine. He made an effort to speak, to show that he was not sleepy, but the words became raveled on his tongue and the pauses between them grew longer. He fell asleep in the middle of a sentence, the fingers of his left hand still resting on his wife's small white and rounded shoulder.

The woman didn't feel like sleeping. She was contented and thrilled, and also frightened and sad. She gazed long at the man sleeping beside her, his right cheek sunk in the softness of the down, his lips slightly parted as though he were greedily drinking in the pillow. Between a person who is wide awake and his sleeping mate there is always a great and chilly chasm that grows wider with each new minute and becomes filled with mystery and a strange sense of desolation and tomblike loneliness. The woman tried to fall asleep. She closed her eyes and breathed evenly, but was startled out of her first light sleep by the changing of the guard in front of the cellar door. As if she had never slept or thought of anything else, her mind returned to the bandit.

The new guard was Živan, Lazar's countryman. Now she realized that she had not been awakened so much by the change of sentries as by Lazar's crying and calling. The prisoner was asking for water.

"Which of you is out there now?"

There was no answer.

"Is it you, Živan?"

"That's right. Shut up!"

"How can I shut up, you infidel, when I'm dying of thirst and fever. Give me a little water, Živan, for the love of St. John, our common saint. Don't let me die like a beast!"

Živan made as if he didn't hear and gave no answer, in the hope that Lazar would get tired of begging. But the man called him again in a low, hoarse voice.

"If you know what suffering is about, and prison, don't play deaf with me, Živan, in the name of your children!"

"Leave my children out of it! You know I've got my orders and I'm on duty. Keep quiet! You'll wake up the commandant."

"Let him wake up. He has no right to sleep. He's worse than a Turk…letting me die from thirst, on top of all my troubles. I beg you, in God's name, hand me a little water through the bars."

As they went on talking in muffled voices, the woman learned that he was being kept off water on the orders of her husband, who was determined to force him to betray his fellow bandits and helpers. And Lazar, racked by unbearable thirst and the fire in his blood, apparently found a certain relief in obstinately repeating the word: Water. He would lie still for a few minutes, only to heave a long and deep sigh immediately afterwards and follow it up by a spate of words.

"Ah, Živan, Živan… May you never taste my salt and bread again, that you make me suffer like this, worse than a Gypsy. Give me a jigger of water and then you can make short work of me…and no one will be the wiser in this world or the next. Oh-h-h-h!"

But Živan had stopped answering him.

"Živan… Živan! I beg you… I'm burning up!"

Silence. Afterwards, a ragged last-quarter moon bobbed up in the sky. Živan had backed away into the shadows and when he spoke his voice was an indistinct mumble. The bandit was now loudly addressing the commandant.

"Oh, Captain, don't torture me needlessly! May the Emperor's bread rot in your mouth!"

After each of his imprecations the silence closed in more thickly. In that silence the bandit growled and moaned heavily, no longer bothering to lower his voice and heedless of what he was saying.

"Oh-o-oh! Heathen sons of bitches! May you drink blood through all eternity and never slake your thirst! I hope you choke on our blood. Where are you, Captain, you son of a werewolf?"

He shouted the last few words in a smothered, helpless voice that peeled strenuously off his parched palate. Once again Živan tried to silence him, promising that he would call the commandant first thing in the morning and that they were sure to give him water, if only he would tell them what they asked; till then he would have to be patient. But Lazar, in his fever, forgot everything after a few moments and started wailing again.

"Živan, I beseech you, in the name of God … I'm burning! Water!" And like a child he repeated the word a hundred times, his voice and speech waxing and falling with his uneven, fevered breath.

Wide awake and trembling, sitting on the edge of the bed, scarcely aware of her body and of the room around her, the woman heard it all. She was overwhelmed by a new terror, a kind she had not known till then, touched off by the prisoner's groans and by Živan's hissed warnings and by the deep, exhausted sleep of the man beside her.

When she was still a child in her parents' home, sometimes during the nights when she could not sleep, in the spring or in the autumn, she had spent the whole night listening to such monotonous and frightening sounds from outside: the wind rattling the metal vent at the top of the chimney, or the banging of the garden gate which someone had forgotten to latch. As a child, she had endowed those noises with a special meaning, she had imagined that they were living creatures who were struggling, rasping, and sobbing. Life often transmutes on a larger plane the imaginings and terrors of our childhood, and out of petty fancied fears weaves some real and potent ones. She thought how wonderful it would be if the innocent horrors that once had disturbed the sleep of her girlhood were true and the reality of this night, in this godforsaken village, in her marriage bed, and the dreadful talk and moans of the bandit down below, were nothing more than a dream and will-o'-the-wisp.

And during all this time—just like the soughing of the wind in a tinny chimney vent or in a crack of the attic trap door—there could be heard, almost at regular intervals, the steady, labored breath of a man in high fever and a weary human voice as it gasped in fits and starts through a parched, wide-open mouth over a thick and coated tongue.

"Water, water! A-a-ah!"

Živan's watch presently came to an end and he was relieved by another gendarme, yet the bandit's appeals for water did not cease; they merely grew feebler and more tired. The woman continued to sit up stiffly, listening to every sound from below and thinking the same thought over and over, endlessly and inconclusively. How was she to fathom and understand this life and these people? All she could see was that on the one side were the gendarmes and on the other bandits (two aspects of the same misfortune), that they both pursued each other without mercy and that here, caught between the two, a person was certain to pine to death from sorrow and pity.

For months past there had been a lot of talk in Sokolac about this man Lazar. She had heard awful tales of his cruelty, how he tortured in the most brutal ways the peasants who wouldn't yield to him, and shot gendarmes from ambush, stripped their bodies to the skin, and left them naked on the road. And now she was witnessing how the gendarmes repaid him in kind. Could this possibly go on forever? It seemed to her that they were all rushing toward some kind of abyss and that they would all perish together in a night just like this, destined never to see the light of dawn, in blood, in thirst, among unspeakable horrors.

She thought now and then of waking her husband and begging him to dispel, with a word or a smile, all of this horror as though it were a hideous dream. But she could not bring herself to move nor to arouse her husband, and remained stock-still on the edge of the bed almost as if the body beside her were that of a dead man, and listened to the voice in the cellar, alone with her terror and her questions. She even thought of saying the prayers they had taught her in childhood, but those were the prayers of another, forgotten and vanished life, and they gave her no clue or comfort. As if making peace with her own death, she resigned herself to the thought that the wailing man would go on wailing and imploring forever, and the man sleeping and breathing beside her would thus sleep and remain still forever.

The night kept pressing in from all sides, growing thicker and more ominous. This was no longer an ordinary night, one of the countless ones in the string of days and nights, but a long drawn-out and perpetual desert of gloom in which the last man alive was moaning and crying for help, begging hopelessly and in vain for a drop of water. Yet in the whole of God's wide world with its waters, rains and dew there was not a single tear of water, and among all living creatures not a single hand to offer it. All the waters had run dry, all mankind pined away. Only the frail rush-light of her consciousness still flickered, like a solitary witness to it all.

At last came the dawn. Not daring to trust her own eyes, the woman watched the slow paling of the wall, at the same spot where it always paled at daybreak, and saw how the morning twilight, first pearly and then pink, spread through the room bringing shape and life to all the objects in it.

If she strained hard she could still make out the bandit's voice, but from a great distance as it were. The cursing and oaths had stopped. There was only an occasional dull "A-a-ah!" And she inferred that rather than actually heard it.

Although the daylight was growing brighter, the woman had no strength to move. Doubled and rigid all over, with her chin cupped in her hands, she was crouching on the edge of the bed and never even noticed that her husband had woken up.

He opened his rested eyes and his gaze fell on his wife's curved back and on the milky white nape of her neck. At that moment, when the haze of sleep first cleared from his eyes, a sense of joyful reality flooded back into him, washing over him like a warm, luxuriant wave. He wanted to call to his wife, to sing out her name, but changed his mind. Smiling, he raised himself a little, making no sound, then propping himself on his left elbow reached out with his free right hand, and without a word, suddenly took her shoulders, pulled her over, and brought her down under him.

The woman struggled briefly and in vain. The unexpected and irresistible embrace was dreadful to her. It seemed blasphemous and unthinkable that she should betray so quickly and easily, and without any explanation, the world of night in which up to that moment she had existed and suffered alone with her anguish. She wanted to hold him back and convince him that it was not possible, that there were grave and painful things which she had to tell him first and over which one could not pass so lightly into everyday life. Bitter words rose to her tongue, but she could not speak a single one. Her husband never even noticed this sign of her resistance, this fragmentary sound that never hardened into a word. She would have pushed him away, but her movements were not nearly as strong as her bitterness, or as swift as her thoughts. The very heat of that awakened and vigorous body crushed her like a great weight. The bones and muscles of her young body gave way like an obedient machine. Her mouth was sealed by his lips. She felt him on her like a huge rock to which she was lashed, and together with which she was plunging downward, irresistibly and fast.

Losing all recollection not only of last night but of all life, she sank into the deaf and twilit sea of familiar and ever-new pleasure. Above her floated the last traces of her nighttime thoughts and resolutions and of all human compassion, dissolving into air one after another like watery bubbles over a drowning person.

The white, gaily draped room quickly filled with the vivid light of day.

Translated by Joseph Hitrec

Miracle at Olovo

Everything that was born or lived in the Bademlić house was cheerful, feckless, and gay. The only exception was Kata Bademlić, the wife of the eldest of the Bademlić brothers. She was tall, bony and blonde with blue eyes and a cold, penetrating regard. Brought to this rich and spacious house twenty-six years before, she had grown gloomier, duller, and more silent from year to year. She had not been happy with her husband, and she had had no luck with her children.

Her husband, Peter Bademlić, the eldest brother of this wealthy family, had married very late. All manner of stories were told of his younger days. Even when he had brought Kata home, although he was by then played out, there still remained in his way of talking and moving, and particularly in his way of smiling, something of his old wildness and dissoluteness. It was a broad, stupid, sensual smile that was stamped on all the swarthy Bademlić faces like a hallmark, impossible to conceal. There was something about that smile that during all these years had Kata, coming as she did from a fresh and healthy family in Livno, with terror and repulsion.

With her children it had been still worse. In the first twelve years she had borne nine children, and all had

181

died, one after the other, just as they were entering their best years. The birth of the tenth child she barely survived. From then on she ceased to have children. This last child was a girl, and it lived. Up to her sixth year the child throve; she was small, but she was fair-haired and so pretty that people in church turned to look as she went by. In everything she took after her mother and her healthy Livno kinsmen.

But when she was about six, she began to waste away and grow ugly. She suddenly began to bend at the knees and to hunch over at the waist; her face coarsened and her eyelids grew puffy. In this condition, huddled up and with her mouth always half open, she crept from one divan to another and lay for years in the cold gloomy rooms of the Bademlićes like a curse on the house and a judgment of God. Now she was nearing fifteen, but her bodily development was feeble, and her mental development even feebler. She was unable to straighten up, nor could she walk without someone to support her. She said little, only the most ordinary things, and then hoarsely and indistinctly. She got on best with her mother, and the old woman devotedly nursed the child; she would not let a single servant near her, but herself carried the girl from place to place, fed her, washed her, and changed her clothes.

She did everything she could to cure her daughter. After she had been the round of all the doctors and wise women with cures, and had tried all the medicines and everything anyone had ever mentioned to her, and had paid in vain for masses and prayers, she took a vow one day before the altar of the Virgin Mary that on the

Blessed Virgin's Nativity she would go barefoot to Olovo and take her sick daughter to the monastery of Our Lady of the Springs.

Like all people who have suffered much misfortune and seen many deaths around them and who live apart and wholly within themselves, she took account, in all her affairs, of the forces of the invisible world and was closer and more intimate with them than she was with the real world. When she had made her vow, she continued praying for some time, and when she rose to her feet, she repeated her prayer and her appeal to the Virgin Mary.

"I can bear it no longer. But grant that one of two things may happen: either cure her for me or take her to Thyself, to heaven, like the other nine."

A few days after this vow, the travelers set off before dawn from the Bademlić house. The old woman took her sister-in-law, a pockmarked old maid, and with them went two menservants to carry the girl, since she was unable to stay on a horse. They led two horses in halters for the return journey. It was light when they came out on the first heights above Sarajevo. The girl, who up to that point had complained, protested, and cried a good deal, was now resting in a specially constructed shallow wicker basket, which the menservants carried on two pitchforks passed through the sides. Exhausted by the fresh air, she was sleeping with her head on her right shoulder. Every now and then, when jolted, she would open her eyes, but seeing green branches, the sky, and a rosy glow overhead, she would shut them again, thinking it was a dream, and smile, with that wan smile that sick children have when they are beginning to get better.

After a while they ceased to climb. They passed through thick woods and the road became broader and easier. At this point they began to meet people from other places. There were some who were seriously ill, loaded onto horses like sacks, and moaning hoarsely and rolling their eyes. There were crazy and possessed people, whom their relatives tried to restrain and calm down.

The old Bademlić woman went ahead of her party, thrust her way through the crowd, paying no heed to anyone, and told her beads in a whisper. The bearers could hardly keep up with her. Twice they rested in a beech wood beside the road. At lunchtime they spread a dark-colored rug on the grass and laid the invalid on it. She stretched out her wasted legs and crumpled frame as much as she could. She was frightened when she saw her mother's feet beside her, bare, bruised, blue, and all bloody from their unaccustomed journey. The elder woman quickly drew her feet under her Turkish trousers, and the girl, joyful and excited by so many new sights around her, forgot at once. Everything was new, unusual, and cause for joy—the thick, dark forest grass, the heavy beeches with growths like shelves on their silvery bark, the birds that dived at the horses' nosebags, and the wide horizon with its bright sky and streaks of cloud drifting slowly along. Whenever a horse tossed its head and the birds fluttered around in alarm, the girl, tired and sleepy as she was, felt she had to laugh, long and quietly. She watched the servants eating slowly and seriously, and in that, too, there was something funny and amusing. She herself ate some preserves, then

stretched out on the rug as far as she was able. Parting
the cool grass with her hand, she looked at a flower
called Grannie's Ear, a tiny bright red flower clinging
close to the black earth as if lost. She gave a little cry of
excitement. The old woman, who had dozed off from
fatigue, started up and picked it for her. For a long while
the girl looked at it and smelled it, holding it in her
palm; then she pressed it to her cheek and closed her
eyes in rapture when she felt how velvety and cool it
was.

They reached Olovo at dusk. Around the ruins of the
monastery and the vaulted pool, from which could be
heard the muffled fall of the hot springs of Our Lady, it
was as crowded as a fairground. Fires were burning and
people roasted food and ate. Most of them slept on the
ground, but there were places in a wooden hut for the
wealthier and better class. Here the Bademlić family installed themselves. Both women quickly fell fast asleep,
but the girl spent the whole night in a kind of reverie
and gazed through the window at the stars over the
black woods. She had never before in her life seen so
many stars. She listened to voices, which murmured
around the fires all night long, and in this way glided off
to sleep. At times she would be awakened by the neighing of a horse or the fresh night air; and listening once
again to the murmuring voices, she could not determine
when she was asleep and when awake.

Early the next morning they went to the springs.
First there was a low, almost dark room where one undressed. The floors were damp and slimy. Around the
walls stood wooden benches on which the clothes were

left. From there three wooden steps led down into a bigger and somewhat lighter chamber containing the pool. Everything was made of stone. The roof was of stone and vaulted, and high up at the top were small, round apertures through which shone beams of strange light. Footsteps made echoes, and the stone vault magnified and returned the slightest sound. The noise of water rebounded from the vaults, and, thus multiplied and magnified, filled the whole place, so that it was necessary to shout when speaking. And this shouting in its turn broke and redoubled beneath the vaults. The steam made it hard to breathe. Water streamed from the walls and roof beams, to which green stalactites clung as in caves. The water fell in a thick jet from a stone conduit. It was warm, clear, and full of silvery bubbles; it spread out over the stone pool and there took on a greenish tinge from the gray slabs of stone.

Men and women took turns bathing. When it came to the women's turn, there was pushing, quarreling, and yelling. Some wore clothes and merely took off their shoes and paddled in the water, which came up above their knees; others had stripped down to their shifts. Childless women squatted up to their necks in water and prayed with eyes closed. Some caught water from the spout in their palms and rinsed their throats, ears, and nostrils. And all were so taken up with praying and thinking about a cure that no one felt shy of anyone else; it was as if they did not see one another. They pushed and squabbled a little for more room, but a moment later they had again forgotten both their squabbles and one another.

Old Mrs. Bademlić and her sister-in-law led the girl into the water. Although all the women were in a state of transport and each was preoccupied with herself, they made way for the Bademlićes, since people of wealth and standing never lose their pre-eminence anywhere.

Huddled up as she was, the girl trembled and was afraid of the water and the people. But little by little she lowered herself deeper and deeper into the pool, as if wishing to hide. If they had not supported her under her arms, she would have gone to the bottom. Even so, the water came up to her chin. Never in her life had she seen so much water or heard so many voices or strange cries. Only now and then, when she had dreamed that she was well and that she could walk and run, had she imagined herself bathing with other children in water with countless tiny shining bubbles playing about her body, just as they were doing now. She was carried away. She shut her eyes and quickly breathed in the hot steam. She heard the voices of the women around her from farther and farther away. She felt a kind of tickling in her eyes. She drew her brows down harder, but the tickling did not stop. Finally, with an effort, she opened her eyes. A beam of sunlight came down through one of the holes in the vault and fell on her face. Into the light, steam from the pool soared and hovered like fine dust, green, blue, and gold. The sick girl followed it with her eyes. Suddenly she began to shudder and twitch, and then started with an effort to rise from the water. Astounded, the mother and aunt began to let go of her, loosening their hold little by little. And all at once the huddled, crippled girl straightened up, as she had never

187

done before, letting go of the hand that had supported her from either side, and, although still stooping a little, she began slowly and unsteadily to walk, like a small child. She spread out her hands. Through her thin, wet shift her little breasts showed their dark rosy nipples. Drops of water sparkled on her heavy eyelashes. Her full lips parted in an oddly stupid, sensual smile. She raised her head and, looking up, high up, into that beam of light, she suddenly cried out in an unexpectedly clear and piercing voice: "There He is, coming down on the clouds Jesus! Jesus! A-a-ah!"

There was something awesome and triumphant in that voice. All the women cowered beneath it. No one dared to raise her head and look at the sick girl or at her vision, but they all felt it above them. Some began to pray at the tops of their voices, and some started to cry, and their praying turned to weeping and loud sobbing. They could be heard beating their hands on their wet breasts. All their cries were strange and weird, like those that people utter only when they are in transports of pain or joy and when they forget human measure and shame. The ringing echoes magnified and prolonged their cries, and everything was mingled with the din of the water that fell with a continuous roar from above.

The only one who did not bow her head was old Mrs. Bademlić. She climbed onto the second step so that she was only ankle-deep in the water and from there sternly and intently looked at her daughter, her dreamlike movements, and the new smile on her face. Then suddenly, pushing her sister-in-law aside, she went up to the girl, seized her around the waist, gripped her beneath the knees with her other hand, and with great, angry strides, as if hiding something shameful, carried her out into the room where the clothes were.

Here it was dim and quiet. She put the child down. She looked around her. No one was there. The girl shivered from the sudden change and, bent once more, lay on the bare earth; but still there remained on her face that broad, unhealthy smile of sensual bliss.

From the pool came the sound of voices in prayer and exclamations at the miraculous cure. But the old woman stood motionless, thunderstruck, even sterner and grimmer than usual. For she alone knew that this was the Bademlić smile, that there was no healing here, and that it had all been in vain. It was as if she could hardly wait to flee the world and be alone with the Virgin Mary, with whom she had a pact still unfulfilled. She did not even heed the girl who was shivering at her feet, but turned toward a dark corner and exclaimed several times in a sharp whisper: "Take her to Thyself! Take her to Thyself!"

Translated by Michael Scammell

In the Camp

etachments of hard-breathing Tartars began to arrive more frequently, billets were multiplying, and now every townsman took it for granted that the Pasha would also come and the army would be mustered here. The district judge of Višegrad, Abdurahman Effendi Pozderac, a dour and unusually fat man, thoughtfully fingered the latest official order from Travnik, the provincial capital. The Pasha had written to "all district officers, school principals, the mayor of Sarajevo, the commanding officer of the janissaries, the agas of the reserves, standard-bearers, big landowners, and all men of action and decision":

In accordance with the resolve of the Leader of our Faith, I have received two firmans from Istanbul ordering me to make known that the brave warriors and Muslims of Bosnia, who wish to do so voluntarily and thus receive Imperial Blessing, should make ready for war and put in a supply of food and biscuit and wait for me. With the help of Allah, I plan to set out from Travnik on the second day of Bairam, on Thursday, with my escort and bodyguard, and proceed through Sarajevo to Višegrad and beyond.

191

O you leaders and effendis, take note of my departure. I don't ask of you any provisions or expenses for myself or for my escort, except that in each district where I shall spend the night you prepare a thousand pounds of bread and five hundred sacks of barley. Let this be ready and waiting for me and I shall not demand that you prepare any other viands. And take good care that you do not requisition in my name even a single grain from the poor peasants, or trouble them. Therefore this order is forwarded to you through the office of the governor of Bosnia, and when it reaches you be guided by the content thereof and act upon it.

As he stood by a window full of flowers, the Više-grad judge muttered to himself:

"Splendid, upon my faith! For one night he asks nothing but one thousand pounds of bread and five hundred sacks of barley. If he stays here ten days—and he might stay longer—merciful Allah, he'll eat up the ground from under me!"

Worry and anger sent the judge into a coughing fit and he flushed deeply; it took him some time to regain his breath.

The town was overflowing with refugees from Užice, Novi-Pazar, and Senica. Everyone who had fled before the Serbian rebel Karageorge sought haven here, terror-stricken, half naked, and barefoot, without food or money. And now the governor himself was to come with his whole entourage and army, to make camp here.

"Oh, oh, oh, spare me, you devil! Oh you blight, get off my neck!"

He was as well known for his stinginess as for his wealth. He did not smoke or drink, he dressed and ate

192

frugally, and penny-pinched with everyone, even his own family. Like all true misers, he loathed all giving and was appalled at any expense, no matter where in the world, or for what. The thought of the oil burning for nothing in the mosque lamps kept him awake some nights. His favorite dream, one that seemed to him the ultimate in happiness, was of a cash sum of money deposited somewhere in a safe place and growing without ever being touched, without risk, multiplying on and on. And because in this world such a thing is out of the question, he hated the whole world and all its regulations, which made it possible for capital to change hands, to fluctuate in value, and become spent. A diabetic who suffered from coughing fits and breathlessness, he lived his days wheezing, rasping, scolding, and counting. Now he summoned several town clerks and gave them his orders. With tears in his eyes, he exhorted them to save—save time, money, and their own town.

"No, no, no, we simply do not have it! In God's name, where would we get it from? Where from—when this town isn't like other towns? Here we have nothing but misery and calamities. Flood, drought, rebellion, war! Ah, all we need is a pestilence and cholera to wipe us all out at one stroke!"

With difficulty they came to an agreement on where to billet the Pasha with his retinue and where to accommodate the army, how to collect the grain store and divide up the food. The judge kept throwing up his arms, moaning, clapping a hand to the sallow, fat, creased nape of his neck.

"Go on, climb up here, why don't you! Give them everything! Here are the keys! Take the courthouse, distribute all there is!"

Then word came that the Pasha was traveling slowly because his entourage and baggage were enormous, and people began to talk about his luxuries and the marvels he carried with him. Rumor had it that he was unable to sit down to supper until a dozen candles "as thick as your arm" were lighted, that he had with him a pair of Arabs, monkeys, and a talking bird, and also the half-wit Sheh Dedije, who could eat thirty boiled eggs for a snack. The judge fell ill at this intelligence. He ordered his sitting cushion moved from the window to the far side of the room so as not to have to look out on the street or see anyone. He moaned like a wounded man.

But the tales were exaggerated. On the eve of Friday, the Pasha arrived; with a large retinue, it was true, and a big load of field trunks, but without monkeys, birds, or Arabs. Behind him rode only Sheh Dedije, gross and red-faced, on a longhaired horse. Both the Pasha and his men took up quarters at the huge Suleiman Bey blockhouse; and the latter still had the hollow sound of near-emptiness. Cheerful columns of smoke rose skyward, marking the end of the day's fast.

As the army trickled in, the troops struck camp on the slopes around the town. They came late and in disorder. The best disciplined contingent was the one from Prozor; it numbered an even hundred and was led by Salih Aga Ramljak, a tall man with a pock-marked face, a passionate hunter, known far and wide for his bravery and integrity. These men occupied the bridge and its watchtower. The troops from Travnik, mounted for the most part, were disgruntled with their food rations and billets. The last to arrive was the Sarajevo contingent, tardy and quarrelsome as always. To spite the Pasha, who had reprimanded them for their sluggishness as he overtook them on the road, they had recruited one whole company over and above the stipulated number.

Promptly on the morning after his arrival, the Pasha received the district judge and the town elders on a sofa in front of the blockhouse. With an air of careworn dignity, he consulted with them and smartly tossed rolled-up cigarettes to each as they sat in a semi-circle around him. He asked them what they had heard about the rebel Karageorge and about the attitude of the Christian peasants in the villages, and how well the Turks were armed, how many refugees there were, and what they were saying. He told them of his intention, the moment his supplies arrived, to continue marching on Srebrnica to join up with Ibrahim Bey, whom the Serbian rebels had surrounded, and from there to cross into Serbia itself. They either kept silent, or nodded their agreement, and the meeting broke up amid deep bows, scraping, and polite mutters typical of old people.

Toward the end of the meeting, the judge nevertheless managed to broach the difficulty of feeding both the refugees and the army. Seeing that the Pasha was willing to listen, and prompted by his own concern, he hastened to mention some other troubles and expenses; he wound up his itemization with the remark that for over a month now he had been sheltering and feeding, at his expense and in his house, a certain unfortunate refugee girl, daughter of a leading Turk in Trebinje. The Pasha reassured him that he would move the army in a few days and that all levies would be reduced as soon as, God willing, he was successful in routing the Serbs; as for the girl refugee, he advised him to send her back to her father in Trebinje. The judge protested that in these dangerous times, with the cost of living so inflated, he could not afford to do it. At length, the Pasha promised that he would personally see to it that the girl was sent back; whereupon the judge took his leave. In his excitement and effusive politeness he even forgot to cough.

The Pasha and his imam, Mullah Jusuf, had a good long laugh after supper, talking about the judge.

In moments such as these, the Pasha did not conceal his loathing for Bosnia and Bosnian men. Born in Istanbul and a courtier of long standing, he saw in his appointment as governor of Bosnia a successful intrigue of his opponents at the High Porte, a misfortune which one should endure wisely.

He had nothing but contempt for these unlettered, boorish, unbelievably narrow-minded Bosnian Muslims, who spoke their inanities with so much solemnity and importance. He was also contemptuous of the Serbs, that glum, shaggy, fanatical mob of Christian nobodies, who fought with such single-minded obsession against great and ancient institutions and blindly rushed to their deaths, thus losing, in the name of foolish dreams and lies, the "good life," as he called it. And he looked down his nose on the meek Bosnian Jews, on the whiskered Orthodox priests and wily Franciscan monks, regarding them as people without honor and dignity. Once, after receiving a deputation of Franciscans, he had said to his police chief:

"When the whole world and all the states have sank and perished, these friars will be floating on top like oil on water."

He abominated the whole gloomy and mountainous country with its tortured landscape and insane climate, as he did its eternally wrangling and restless inhabitants, for he shrank from everything that was loud, shrill, and intemperate. He loved quiet work in a settled groove and moderate delights and pleasures. At times he would dream all night of the sea, dotted with white sails, and next morning he would feel a double hatred for the bearded and wide-shouldered Bosnians around him, and for the violent line of mountains that shut off the view above Travnik, his capital. He was secretly working through friends in Istanbul to regain his old post there. While he had no clear idea of the scope and extent of the present rebellion, he knew that nothing much could be accomplished with this Bosnian "army." So he planned to disperse the Serbs in quick order, or else, by delaying his punitive expedition, to wait for autumn when the contingents would disband and return to their homes. He had hopes that during the winter his scheme in Istanbul would bear fruit and he would be happily rid of Bosnia and war.

His advisers and intimates were all non-Bosnians. He had left Travnik in charge of his deputy vizier, Ibrahim Effendi, a tall and methodical man from Istanbul, and Tahir Bey, a trusted Muslim convert. With him he had taken only this Sheh Dedije, who under the mask of an amiable harebrain concealed quite a treasure of healthy sense and artfulness—and his imam, Mullah Jusuf.

Until recently this Mullah Jusuf had been principal of the Muslim school at Sarajevo. During a controversy between him and the Sarajevo elders, the Pasha had interceded on his behalf, and afterwards, when Jusuf was relieved of his post anyway, he had brought him to his court at Travnik to spite the old men of Sarajevo and his own enemies at the Porte in Istanbul. The man was now part of his retinue as an official imam of the army.

This wiry and brisk mullah, with a sparse beard and mustaches of uneven length, swarthy and flushed as if scorched by the sun, had been a well-known personality in Sarajevo.

Born at Edirne, he had moved to Istanbul while still a boy and there very soon won himself a reputation for learning and debauchery. Later he had lived at Brusa, spending several years as military imam in various expeditions in Armenia and Transylvania. After he came to Sarajevo, he taught grammar and speech at the high school on Čobanija. He knew many languages, and learned new ones very quickly. With great skill and accuracy, he determined the lunar periods and holidays, and forecast the eclipses and seasonal changes. Handy with writing and things mechanical, he was clever at repairing any type of clock and dismantling and reassembling guns and coffee grinders. He composed verses, instructive and easy to read, for his senior students; he also wrote (but read only to his colleagues) humorous and extremely bawdy doggerel, some of it in the "Bosnian language, for Bosnians"; and epitaphs for the cemetery

monuments as well. He had no peer in this kind of thing.
There was only one type of writing he refused to touch:
the customary sick records of ailing citizens—which
they also held against him. He had a fine voice, clear and
strong, that could easily be picked out among a hundred
other muezzins, and he called the faithful to prayer from
the Sultan's mosque, and that only during the sacred
month of Ramadan; and occasionally to mourn a dead
person. He was unkempt and a careless dresser. The one
piece of clothing on him that was always neat was the
chalk-white hadji band, deftly and meticulously wound
around his red fez, under which his narrow and swarthy
face all but disappeared.

In the complaint of "Sarajevo dignitaries," in which
they had demanded his removal, all the bad things that
were known about him were listed in malicious and ex-
haustive detail. The petition alleged that he was of
Gypsy origin, that he had been obliged to flee Istanbul
as well as Brusa on account of some incidents which,
though not fully known, were most disgusting and rep-
rehensible. It was said that in Transylvania he had been
found bending over a woman whose throat had been slit;
and it was only thanks to the sudden withdrawal of the
army ordered that day that the matter had been forgotten. There was also mention of a Christian female domestic who had disappeared the year before; the investigation about her had dragged on and then ground to a
stop, but while it was in progress it had revolved unmis-
takably around the school. All in all, the mullah's manner
of life was disorderly and invited derision unbecoming
to a learned person and a cleric. The list of his misde-

meanors included many other incidents, some hard to believe, others plainly absurd, and for all that "furor and dissatisfaction" he was finally relieved of his post.

The Pasha kept the mullah because he needed him and because he wished to spite the Sarajevo faction, but he did not like the man. Even though at Travnik Mullah Jusuf had not been guilty of any conspicuous indiscretion, the Pasha found him unpleasant and at times detestable. When he was alone with Sheh Dedije, and in a bad mood, he would call the mullah "a pig above all pigs."

Now, during the mobilization, the mullah made himself indispensable. He kept accounts and records. In this sultry and airless valley, the mullah was unable to sleep at night, or, for that matter, stay put in the daytime. He made the rounds of the camp, received and escorted the mounted couriers; and on many an afternoon he would go down to town and, like once in Sarajevo, tear through the streets as if chased by someone, his dusty and scuffed boots creaking, the folds of his black cape gusting behind him. Women rushed to close their window shutters, and children, squatting on the door steps with large chunks of bread in their hands, simply tumbled back into the doorways. He asked to substitute for old Alihodja, the local mullah, so that he might announce the time of the night prayer. With an oil-spattered lantern in his hand, he scraped his shoulders and knees against the narrow walls as he climbed the spiral stairway to the top of the minaret. Once up there, he would cry out through his cupped palms and thrust his chin out fiercely at the invisible sky and the new moon that was melting softly in pools of murky crimson vapors. And his voice rose steadily, lashing and cutting through the darkness above the town like cold, thin, but irresistible steel, so that children awoke and whimpered and seamstresses lifted their heads from their work. Afterwards he could not sleep again.

The end of that poor, flood-ravaged spring was drawing near. At the confluence of two rivers just north of the town, naked trees poked up from the muddy banks; crows flocked in the silted fields. The days were humid and full of a trembling gray light that wearied the eye. An acrid smell of burning lay heavily on one's breath. From the ashen sky a sweltering heat continued to seep down. The seed in the earth molded and failed to germinate. The tongue grew dry in one's mouth; the eye corners smarted. There was no freshness even at night. Rain clouds would pile up in the distance, but as soon as they drew over the Višegrad valley they thinned and shrank and dissipated in a tepid mist. As for the air streams that swept down from the mountain passes, no sooner did they pour into the valley than they slackened, grew lukewarm, began to swirl dizzily in a flagging spiral, only to settle, exhausted, on the layers of humidity already stacked there.

The slopes on both sides of the river had become encampments. The army had shaken down, though latecomers were still arriving. Bakers, who were Christians for the most part, were building clay ovens and kneading bread dough. There were fires all round. Pickets began to disappear from the fences, haystacks to lose their hay. Paths were trodden in places that had never had them.

Drinking fountains clogged and spoiled. Drums sounded, interspersed with loud cries and swearing. Loudest and most numerous were the reed pipes of the Sarajevo contingent; but the men from Travnik were better singers. And on an evening such as this, most of the others fell silent and came to listen to them, even though ordinarily they disliked them.

Time passed and the supplies did not come. The army was bored and grumbling over the bread-and-flour-soup rations. Chickens and spring lambs began to disappear from private courtyards. Soldiers banded in groups and went down to town, to loiter in front of shops and quarrel over prices and portions at the various inns. They roamed through the streets and peeped through fences and house gates, they ran after girls, jabbered, guffawed, and whooped. There came a rumor that a detachment of insurgents was at Staniševac. A strong column went out to reconnoiter, but they found nothing; all they brought back with them were the heads of a Serbian Orthodox priest and his brother, and those, already quite wizened, were now hoisted on stakes on the bridge.

Of the Christian inhabitants, very few ventured outdoors. At the first sign of dusk they padlocked themselves and went to bed to avoid having to burn lamps. In the big squat house at the bottom of the hill, the Orthodox priest Jovo sat uneasily, pale and with cataracts in both eyes, dressed in a dark-blue soutane and a greasy cap, waiting till they came for him. Beside him sat his wife, a portly and simple-minded woman, trying to recall a prayer that might help them, but, unable to remember it, sniveling and cowering instead. Not a soul dared to visit them. Their servant girl Ikonia had had a miscarriage and was lying in bed with fever.

All through the encampment the kneading of dough, slaughtering, cooking, and eating went on without a pause. It looked as if the Turks, through sheer idleness and long boredom, had become transformed into mere stomachs and mouths; their lapping of food, their clattering and scraping of pots could be heard long into the night. The camp stank from afar with the gluttony and loafing of the multitude. The damp and stuffy air made it seem as if the very ground under them were rotting and smelling.

Puffy, yellow-skinned conscripts from Asia, who were without equipment and money, roved through all the nooks and alleys, picking up and scrutinizing every rag they could find, after first rubbing it against their hips. They gaped with dull, inhuman eyes at the children and women, and shunned military patrols. One morning a little boy was found dead under the bridge, hideously mangled. There was a hue and cry, and the Pasha sent another courier to Sarajevo to expedite the supplies.

The judge despaired over the mounting costs and the loafing. After a vexing and exasperating day at the courthouse, he would shut himself in his home and threaten not to come out again until the camp was moved; but next morning fear and impatience would drive him out once again. His house was in the center of the little town; the only occupants of the large dwelling were he and his wife and the servants, whom they changed frequently. The old curmudgeon's home was crammed to the rafters; the cellars, granaries, and barns were piled high with stores. The rooms, in which a wintry silence always reigned, were smothered in carpets, spreads, embroideries, boxes and chests of aromatic wood. But everywhere and over everything there lay that chilly spotlessness so often found in Bosnian homes that was intimidating and forbidding, that neither cheered nor served anyone. This wealth and cleanliness were guarded and protected all day long by the judge's wife, a flat-chested woman with missing teeth, contorted and rumpled from so much fussing around the rooms, from bickering with the servants, and from her excessive thrift. It was in this house that the girl refugee from Trebinje was sheltered.

She had been kidnapped from her father's estate by the rebel-brigand Špaljo Montenegrin, who then took her to the Tara monastery with the idea of having her baptized so that he could marry her. As the Turkish police were close on his heels, he had to flee with her from monastery to monastery, from accomplice to accomplice; he would leave her in hiding for a few days and go away to do his raiding, and then, without warning, in the middle of the day or in the dead of night, come back and drag her away again. Eventually, a superior Turkish force had routed him on the highway between Goražde and Sokolac, and retaken the girl. They brought her to Višegrad, where the town elders decided to send her back to her father at the first opportunity and until then to put her up in a home where there were no children. And so she was allotted to the judge.

This tall girl was quite deranged by her terrible and disastrous experiences. She had lost her power of speech and now stared dully and fixedly in front of her, incapable of recognizing or comprehending anything.

The dreadful Spaljo, who had swooped down on her family's manor like lightning and killed everyone and dragged her away with him, had been all skin and gristle, cold and hard. Then there had been those peasant huts full of smoke and goat droppings. Then the icy monasteries that smelled of pork fat and incense, and gray-haired monks with sepulchral voices and beards yellowed by tobacco. And betweentimes, those headlong night flights when under the blackness of the mountains one's will and wits crumbled and tree branches whipped one's eyes. In that terror, hardness, and cold, she had lost all sense of herself. Since they had brought her to the judge's house, she had calmed down a little. She still did not open her mouth but did not weep either, and spent the whole day sitting in the small garden that was enclosed by high walls; it was damp there and full of fiercely tangled undergrowth. As soon as they led her indoors, she would back into a corner of a room and crouch there with her hands pressed between her knees. Days passed and the judge waited in vain till the Pasha sent for her as he had promised. Supplies had still not arrived. The army camped on.

It was only toward the end of the second week that everything suddenly took a turn for the better. To begin with, the temperature dropped sharply on Friday evening and streams of cold air soughed loudly into the valley and broke the stagnation. The sky shook with thunderclaps;

bolts of lightning vaulted across the slopes one after another. When night fell, there was a heavy cloudburst.
Sheets of water hit the ground with such force that they
turned to vapor, swept this way and that by the wind. All
things vanished and lost their voice, save for the down-
pour that fell all night like a dream and a respite.

Next morning, the greater part of the supplies arrived
in town. The day was damp and clean-washed; the views
acquired new depth, the horizons were clear. The forests
on the high slopes looked like new. It was decided to
break camp at dawn next morning, to move out and
send a detachment for the balance of the supply train,
which was then to proceed directly to Srebrnica. The
Pasha summoned the judge again; the girl was moved
from the latter's house to a furnished inner room at the
Suleiman Bey blockhouse. Mullah Jusuf took upon himself the responsibility of sending her that evening to Sarajevo in the company of old Avdaga and some
mounted men, and from there, through his friend Munir
Effendi, who was a dispatcher of mails, to deliver her to
her father at Trebinje.

The camp echoed with noise, preparations, and live-
lier singing. After a brilliant day the dusk was gathering
fast, with only a fleeting afterglow, when Mullah Jusuf
came down to the blockhouse to see the girl.

The old woman Fatima had gone home. The girl sat
in a corner, wrapped in a shawl. He addressed her gently,
hastening to assure her that he would say a prayer over
her in order to cure her and send her home; but for that
she would have to take off the wrap. She rose for a
moment, as if wavering.

"Better take it off, daughter. Go on."

She threw off the shawl and stood tall and motionless before him, somehow bigger and handsomer now that she was set fully against the small, low-ceilinged room; surprising and dumbfounding him with her good looks and well-shaped body. Her neck shone palely; darkened neither by hair nor shadows, it looked extraordinarily smooth and white.

"You must take off the jacket too. Yes, the jacket. Otherwise it can't be done."

His voice quavered and he smiled fixedly.

With a meek air of helplessness, the girl raised her arms (as if about to be crucified) and peeled off her short sleeveless jacket. The movements of those arms, white and ample and yet drained of all strength and will, overpowered and shattered the trembling mullah, and he came up to her to untie the sash of her pantaloons.

"This, too, daughter. Off with everything, everything!"

She resisted weakly, with gestures that were stunted and mechanical as in a dream.

Here the hand could wander at leisure, over those thighs and hips. No end to it, ever! It was warm there, and smooth like ice. His mouth twisted and gathered in a pucker, as if from raspberries; he felt weak-kneed and the muscles of his left cheek twitched visibly. The girl stood there absently and permitted everything with an air of grave, dull apathy that brought the lecher back to his senses and spurred a desire to prolong and sharpen the thrill, to draw forth some protest and movement. He reached up to a low shelf for a barber's razor. He was

207

breathing hard and felt chilly from head to heels; yet kept slavering and using his hands.

"I have to shave you."

At that point, however, the girl unexpectedly slipped away, gave a stifled shriek, and began to dash around the room. She was only in her shirt, and now that she was in motion it seemed as if every part of her had swelled and was brimming and spilling. She fought back, stumbled and fluttered across the room like an unfurled banner, while the mullah, thin and darkly flushed, lunged at her and sprang after her, keeping up a disjointed mutter and brandishing the razor.

"Stop! A shave first, stop …!"

Her shirt split on the right side and the shoulder gleamed up, once more white, round and plump beyond belief. In the tussle and struggle, he accidentally grazed the naked shoulder with the razor, and the shallow cut filled with blood.

The mullah stopped short, his head lolling, the face ashen; his dark-blue lids came down low. A pair of teeth flashed through his parted lips. He remained like this for a second, then shivered and hurled himself furiously at the girl. She screamed, but in a choked and thin voice (a mute animal), waiting for him and repulsing him like a battlement, hard, white, and naked. She pounded the walls and rattled the locked door. And through the stampede of their feet and through their panting this sound of her big strong body could still be heard—clear, resonant, almost metallic. Disfigured beyond recognition, the mullah raged on. His turban slipped all the way to the back of his head and his breath came in an exultant rasp.

"Kh-kh-kh!"

There was blood on her again, now on the other shoulder, and presently it gushed out of her throat in a spate. She doubled over, slipped to the floor and filled the corner of the room, while the mullah dropped alongside and mingled with her indistinguishably.

Translated by Joseph Hitrec

The Slave Girl

It was one of those encounters, which no man could ever wish to experience, but it was one which could not be avoided either. And its story was told me not by the slave girl herself, but by the heavy and monotonous thudding of the southern sea waves, which break against the foundations of the ancient and dark citadel of Novi Grad. The sound reached me one night in my Sarajevo solitude; it woke me from my first sleep and forced me to listen to its tale.

After the expedition to Herzegovina, which lasted a long time and gave rise to much talk, the town was expecting the arrival of Herzegovinian slaves. But when they finally arrived, there was a great disappointment even among the children who had, as was their custom, run out to stand by the side of the road. The slaves were few and of miserable appearance. Most of them were immediately taken to the Albanian ship which was riding at anchor in the harbor. The rest of them had stayed in the town and appeared in the marketplace only two days later. That was how long it took for the slaves to rest, wash and put on somewhat more decent clothes.

The small marketplace, paved with fine cobblestones, was in the shadow of the cliff and of the citadel which stood upon it. Here, cages were cobbled together with laths and sticks to accommodate the slaves during the sale. In them, the slaves sat or lay about, for everyone to see, and were taken out only at the request of serious buyers who wanted to inspect and evaluate them more closely.

In a largish cage were crammed five male slaves—all peasants, all past their prime—in another cage, smaller in size, was a beautiful, strong, well-built young girl. She looked like a wild beast, always cleaving to the wooden bars, as if wanting to squeeze her way through them.

Close to her cage, one of the two guards sat on a low three-legged stool, while the other sauntered up and down the quayside. Each had a short gun stuck in his belt and a short whip hanging from it.

Some ten paces further up the hill there was a rocky hummock with a little garden. There sat the slave trader and talked with the buyers. He was a foreigner but well known along this coast, spare but tough, sharp-eyed and free in demeanor. His name was Uzun Ali. The guards would bring some of the male and female slaves from down below for viewing and take them down again to their cages. And the owner and the buyer would continue their conversation about individual slaves, haggling about the price and the value.

The first one to be brought there on that morning was the tall girl from the smaller cage. Her name was Jagoda; she was from the village of Pribilovići. The buyer was sitting in the shade next to Uzun Ali. Long chibouks lay in front of them wreathed in wisps of smoke. The slave girl held herself stiffly. Her feverish

eyes darted from side to side, avoiding everyone's gaze.
The guards ordered her to spread out her arms, take a
few steps, show her teeth and her gums. Everything was
fine and in perfect order. She was tall, fresh, strong.
Nineteen years of age. True, her demeanor was wild and
surley, but one should chalk that up to her present situation and state of mind. Then she was taken back to her
cage.

The buyer who had inspected the slave girl was a
townsman Hasan Ibiš, one of the foremost agas of this
coastal town, if not by distinction then certainly by
wealth. Thin, concave-chested and hollow-faced, he
pulled on his chibouk quietly, showing no sign of emotion as he watched the big and lush body of the village
girl turning and spreading before him. Later, with equal
indifference, puffing lazily he spoke with Uzun Ali
about the price of the slave girl.

In his hoarse voice he told the trader that the price of
twenty-one ducats was unheard-of in its exorbitance and
designed to trick the buyer into "rounding it off" and
offering twenty ducats. But so stupid a customer would
be hard to find. If the trader were offered fifteen, maxi-
mum sixteen, ducats he should consider himself lucky.
And that would be in some distant place, after a long
journey undertaken at great expense, because a customer
willing to buy even at that price would not be found
here. Merchandise was ordinary. Ransom was not to be
hoped for as the village from which she came was razed
to the ground leaving nothing standing and no one alive.
And, finally, a slave from Herzegovina was hard to keep
here as escape was easy.

The trader answered in a somewhat more animated manner but with the same calculated indifference and asked Hasan Aga whether he had ever seen such a female slave brought to this small town. Hasan Aga silently waved his hand dismissively as the trader continued.

"This is not a girl but a fortified city. You saw for yourself. This is not a piece of merchandise dragged from one marketplace to another or left to gather dust in shops. And for ransom, this merchandise is not to be ransomed. Whoever buys this, mark my words, will never sell it again. And if he really wanted to sell, he could always get his money back with an additional ducat or two to boot. And as far as escaping is concerned, any slave can escape. But what's the point of talking about it! Merchandise speaks for itself! It's a real find!"

He said something else under his breath, assuming a warm tone of voice which was both sad and confidential, wanting to convey that he was accidentally and to his own detriment revealing a business secret.

Hasan Aga listened absentmindedly. He knew well that the trader's words contained both falsehood and truth in approximately, he guessed, equal parts, but that was not what lent his face the somewhat worried and tense expression, which was so at odds with his feigned indifference. His thoughts were moving in a different direction.

He himself was from a family which had recently arrived in this town. He was a rich and an influential man, but an upstart. So much an upstart that he could never, not even while he slept, forget about his lowly origins which blighted all his efforts and all his successes. His wife was an Alajbegović. The Alajbegovićes were the oldest and the most distinguished family in Novi. He married her six years earlier. Within a year they had a little girl. They barely managed to keep her alive. Even now she was weak and small for her age. His wife had no more children and looked as if she would not have any more. Hasan Aga, who was always known as lascivious and unrestrained in his lust, had never limited himself to the pleasures his wife could offer—not even in the first year of their marriage, much less now. He always arranged to have someone young and comely among the servants of his household. Not in order to indulge his lust—a member of one's household, albeit a slave, was not to be touched—but he wanted to look at some strength and beauty besides his cold and thin wife and his sickly daughter. So he sought love for money outside his home, and did everything he could to keep even that hidden from the world and, particularly, from his wife. That thin, clever, decisive and, above all, proud member of the Alajbegović family, whose strong matriarchal hand guided everything in the household, found it hard to reconcile herself to his excesses. For his part, Hasan Aga himself did not want to offend her and turn her completely against him out of consideration for herself and for her distinguished brothers. (He had grown up with her brothers, went to war with them, hunted with them and with them shared every sort of youthful mischief.) She spoke little, did not complain and did not threaten, but he found it hard to bear the gaze of her dark blue Alajbegović eyes.

The day before, after Uzun Ali had made his offer, he mentioned to his wife in a round about way that an opportunity had arisen to buy a cheap female slave to help in the house or work in the garden. His wife looked at him reproachfully and he immediately lowered his eyes. Then she went on to say that she had enough servants, that *she* did not need a slave girl and would not tolerate one in the house. She said this softly but firmly, with barely concealed disgust in her voice. Whenever he was confronted with this voice and this gaze Hasan Aga would feel ashamed and impotent and invariably retreated renouncing his intentions, or at least seemed to do so, only to carry them out secretly and deviously sometime later. Occasionally, he would indeed renounce them.

And now, while talking with the trader about the value and price of this slave girl, he remembered the voice and the gaze of his wife and simply could not work out in his mind what, if anything, could be done to buy this slave and keep her in his service. And yet, he continued to bargain over the long-stemmed chibouk, deriving pleasure and almost sensuous gratification from the skill with which Uzun Ali praised his merchandise.

And down below, a few paces from them, the slave girl sat in her cage with her legs folded under her, her eyes closed and the nape of her head wedged between two rough-hewn laths.

She tried to think and with her thought to encompass her situation, to find a way out of it or, at least, to gauge the degree of its hopelessness. She tried, but in vain. She

216

remembered that there had been a time when she could think about everything which was happening around her, not only about pleasant things, but also about such things as a lost kid, or some other damage done, about sickness or discord in the house or in the extended family. Even then she had not always been able to complete her thought or find a way out. Nevertheless she could think and seek a way out in her thoughts. But that was before that black day, before the disappearance of her village and of her family in it. And now she could not even think.

There was no point in thinking, nor was she capable of the effort. Her village, the village of Pribilivići was no more. As soon as some thirty houses which constituted the village had burned to the ground, at that very instant there arose in her soul of its own accord a new village of Pribilivići—black, heavy and dead. And now it lay in her chest and prevented her from taking a deep breath, and the people of Pribilovići, her people, those of them who had not been killed, became slaves and were dispersed all over the world. She herself was a slave, and nothing but a slave. This was the way of her life now. This was the only way she could see the world and people around her, because the image of the world within her had gone dark and become distorted. Every man was a slave. Slaves were women and children because from birth to death they lived enslaved by something or someone. Every tree was a slave, every stone, and the sky with its clouds, its sun and its stars were slaves. Water, forest and wheat, which somewhere—somewhere where it had not been burned or trampled into the ground—must be forming ears now, were slaves. Its grain would rather not go under the millstone but it must because it was a slave. The speech with which people around her communicated was the speech of slaves, regardless in which language they spoke, and all of it could be reduced to five letters: slave. Every life was slavery, the one which was eking out its duration and the one which, invisible and inaudible, was just beginning to germinate. Man's dreams were slaves, so were his sighs, the mouthfuls he ate, the tears he shed, the thoughts he thought were slaves. Men were born in order to be enslaved by a life of slavery and they died as slaves to sickness and death. There was nothing but slaves slaving away in service to other slaves. Because slave was not only he who was sold, all trussed up, in the marketplace; slave was also he who sold and he who bought a slave. Yes, everyone who did not live and breathe in Pribilovići was a slave. And Pribilovići had ceased to exist a long time ago.

Pribilovići no longer existed; her house, her family no longer existed. Well then, let her not exist either! That was the only remedy, the shortest way to salvation: to renounce life for the sake of life. She kept having visions of flames, and from them came the desire to be consumed by these flames! To disappear, but completely and forever, as everything she had ever known had disappeared. Yes, but how?

As she opened her eyes she caught sight of her hands, pink and strong. Then she saw her bare feet in thin peasant *opanci*. Her feet were full of blood and heavy. They did not exist for her. She had no use for them, but here they were, alive and warm in spite of her will. And all of that, together with her seeing eyes should be consumed in flames and disappear so that she could free herself from this disaster, this nightmare which she had lived, asleep and awake, for the past several weeks. If only that could be erased, she would be with those who belonged to her again. She would be there where everything belonged to her.

But the world continued to exist, the world without Pribilovići, which was the same as slavery, disgrace and perpetual pain, and in that world her body, full of blood, and fire, and strength—indestructible—continued to breathe and to exist. If that was so, then let the world disappear, the whole world, together with her body. Then the slate would be clean, all accounts settled. Nothing would exist, which meant all would be well, or at least bearable because there would be nothing to bear.

That was what she thought, but at the same time she realized that her weak and erratic thought could do nothing. It could not break the lock on her cage, much less destroy the sight, the blood, the hot breath within her, let alone the entire dreadful, invisible world without her. It could not do that, and yet she kept listening to this thought and stalking this one desire she had.

With her back against the wooden bars of her cage she braced her feet against the fine cobblestones. Her arms were folded over her breast; her eyes were closed. From time to time she would open them briefly and then her gaze would move from the cobblestones under her feet, over the dead-looking front of a huge and ugly house, to the walls of the black citadel and the narrow band of the clear sky above them. Then she would immediately close her eyes again, squeeze them tightly shut, more tightly still, as if she had never opened them at all, never seen anything at all. There were no more houses, neither small nor large. They were all burned down. This was just an evil apparition. The sky no longer existed since it had disappeared forever in smoke and flames.

One should not look. One should not breathe. To breathe would be the same as to remember, and that would mean that one was seeing not what one was looking at, but what one had seen in the light of the conflagration, in the whirlwind of the massacre. It would mean to know only one thing: that none of one's kith and kin was living; that one's life was something monstrous, a curse, a disgrace. That was what breathing would mean. She jumped up and began to measure the space in her cage like a wild beast.

"I shall not breathe. I shan't!"

She spoke this under her breath hissing in her fury.

Pacing from one corner to the other she noticed that the guard, who had absented himself from his post for a moment, had left his folding chair quite close to the door. She looked at the chair, squatted down, put her hand through the bars, grabbed the chair by one foot and began to turn it around and fiddle with it until she managed to fold it and pull it into the cage. Not even trying to think coherently, not explaining her actions to herself, she went to the other end of the cage, unfolded the chair and placed it against the bars. Then she climbed on it, as might a child who is left alone and starts inventing unusual games.

She pressed harder and harder against the bars wedging the nape of her head ever more tightly between them. At the same time she braced herself against the stool under her feet.

Occasionally, but that was a long time ago, in her childhood, she would climb into a three-legged wooden armchair, in which only her father sat, and using the weight of her entire small body she would begin to rock. She would rock on only two feet of the large three-legged chair. She would rock and rock, finding painful enjoyment in the fear of losing her balance and falling down together with the chair. That was what she did now. She rocked and rocked, teetered on the verge of falling and fell, only to return to the point of balance. But these returns to the point of balance became less frequent, the rocking motion became stronger and her head more tightly wedged between the bars. The pain was terrible and seared her like a flame. Yes, a flame, that was what she wanted at this moment when, making use of the same urge, which every young body has to defend itself and ensure survival, she sought her self-destruction. She would disappear so that the world could disappear.

Let it be so. Let everything disappear, everything which lived and breathed and was real and tangible and had connection with human beings, with fire, battle, pestilence or slavery. Let the world disappear! Or let it be something that had never been. Never, never! That was better. That would mean that there never was and

221

never could be either bloodshed, or arson, or enslavement, or sorrow, or parting from those one loved. Nothing!

She had only two points of contact with firm ground—the nape of her head and her feet—and between these to points her body was curved in a convulsive arc like the body of a dead fish. She whimpered, barely audibly, clenching her teeth and tensing her muscles. It seemed to her that in this way she could also make her heart stop; the spasm would end and, finally, the heart would stop beating, the darkness, which, could never be lifted, would fall and she would disappear and so would the world.

She pressed back harder and harder. The pain in her nape, wedged between two knotty sticks, became sharper and sharper and finally began to dissolve into a dull ache. Of course! It suddenly became clear to her that she, together with her father's large chair, with which she had played in her childhood, had flipped and was now floating in the air in an unnatural position. Her feet were no longer touching the surface of the little chair, nor were they touching the fine cobblestones, and her body, pulled by all of its weight, was hanging down the wooden sticks with her neck caught between them.

It was as if the world were standing upside down now. As if the weight of the entire earth had come to rest on the soles of her feet, which were now unsupported. And that weight was now pressing her head deeper and deeper into the cleft between two hard sticks, which have turned into a noose, into a narrow gorge through which one must pass to reach some place on the other side as one did in the moment of one's birth. Dully and feebly, but surprisingly painfully, she heard something break in her neck and with that sound a wave of darkness began to flow through her body.

Before this dark but burning wave had time to engulf her completely, instinct and fear flared up in her once again. She suddenly thought of saving herself and returning to the original position. Like a streak of lightning, a new and intense desire to resist, to defend herself against the pressure and strangulation filled her. No, not this! Not death! Let there be pain, let there be torture, but not killing. To live, just to live, no matter how, no matter where, even without anyone of one's own, even as a slave. But all this lasted as last streaks of lightning. There was just one last convulsion, the blunt sound of her body hitting the bars and then she stayed motionless.

When one of the two guards passed that way and cast an indifferent glance at the cage, he noticed with horror that the large body of the beautiful slave girl was hanging low, with her head clamped between the bars. He began to call the other one, who had the keys.

The two of them fell into the cage at the same moments. They saw that the girl was still warm. Her face was bloodless and already somewhat altered. Surprised and troubled, they managed with difficulty to lift her up a little and pull her head clear of the bars. As though sinking into itself, the dead body slipped onto the ground and lay there, bent double. They straightened her, knelt beside her and tried every way they could think of to bring her back to life, but in vain.

This lasted a long time. And when they stood up, the guards remained stranding beside her head and her helplessly limp arms, one of her left and the other on the right. They looked at each other without blinking, wordlessly wondering: who will be the first to dare go to the master, look him in the eye and inform him of his loss and the great damage that had been done.

Translated by Kosara Gavrilović

Zuja

———

When a person is referred to for all time by a childhood nickname, and they spend their life that way, this already speaks enough of them and their place among people. This elderly woman, alive only in my overcrowded memory, hunched over at the waist, always wearing a gray kerchief, was called Zuja. That and nothing more. She was connected to the large and prosperous Aleksić family. Their houses were a half hour's walk from town, among the hills, above a rapid mountain river that was diverted into conduits, with a big saw mill and textile mill and a number of auxiliary buildings. This was a whole little hamlet that everyone called the Aleksić Conduits.

This woman with her broad, good-natured face, with her shallow, flat little nose and light, colorless eyes, which always had a slightly startled or frightened expression—but only a little, as if she were joking—was a voluntary slave and lifelong servant here, and the most beloved member of the family. Wrinkled, yet ruddy, small and spare, but sturdy and vigorous, Zuja did all jobs, and lived only as defined by them. She worked mostly with the children in the family. She nursed two younger generations. As soon as one of them was born, whether a boy or a girl, she would take charge of the child, raise it, guide it and follow it, if it did not die in infancy, all the way to the child's wedding day. The family was large and lived as a commune, and there were sons-in-law and daughters-in-law, and Zuja was never without work to do, and she never tired of greeting each newborn with her bony, perpetually reddened hands, as if the babies were little unleavened loaves of bread.

For the Aleksić sons and daughters, and then the grandchildren, and even great grandchildren, as each one would tumble to the ground, Zuja was always there, being as she was, understandable and indispensable right at the side of the child's own mother, and sometimes even dearer and closer than she. Everyone knew it and this was the only way they could imagine their life. With Zuja the world was discovered, with her they played and ached, sobbed and sang. Zuja was ingested with the bread, like *kajmak* cheese and honey; the seasons and holidays were celebrated with her, the early cherries joyously picked, watermelons sliced open or the first snowfall anticipated; with her they peed and shat; they swallowed bitter medicine, their first teeth came out; she was entrusted with the little hurts and guilt, the first trouble or joy.

No one remembered when or how she came to the Aleksićes and no one wondered what she was to them or they to her. Zuja. Always at hand, a burden to no one, useful to all. In the hamlet she was everywhere to be found wherever there were Aleksićes and their brood with their needs.

There were actually three houses, raised over half a century, interconnected and crowded in close together, as if they had collided in the ravine. Spreading with new additions, in time they formed a bridge and enslaved the water and conduits underneath them. And Zuja served all three houses in such a way that it looked to everyone as if she, like a good fairy, was present every moment in every one of them, serving them all. That was what she lived for, her whole world. She could speak of nothing but the Aleksić clan, their children and anything having to do with them. She grew older, and no one ever heard her say anything about herself, nor did she ever ask for anything for herself. She was deaf and blind to empty prattle and women's gossip, and as soon as she was left alone, engaged in work of some sort, she would begin whispering, mumbling and singing something to herself that was not speech and it was not song; it was a toothless hum most like the monotonous melody of the cricket chirping in the wall by the hearth. Zuja's strange singing frightened and drew the children and we often sneaked over to listen, mastering our fear and choking back laughter, to how Zuja was "singing" or talking about something to herself.

That was how she was known and remembered not only by all the members of the household, but by all of us who, as schoolchildren, used to come out from town to play with our friends, the Aleksić grandsons, and to catch sight, just for a minute, of his pretty granddaughters, who were our age.

Zuja spent more than fifty years in the shady ravine over the water, in silent, devoted service to the Aleksićes.

She buried her first masters, Master Manojlo and his wife, and kept on serving. Here, after many years, tending to his great grandchildren, she met her death. She fell asleep one night in her little room, and the next morning she did not come down to work. She crept out of life and out of the family circle as unobtrusively and quietly as she had entered it. The Aleksićes did not even have time to be surprised or to wonder, it was so hard imagining their life without Zuja.

In strong, wealthy families like this, the nearest and dearest are never spoken of once they die, especially not in front of people from beyond the family community. They seem to be grieved for hastily, with a weighty and costly sorrow, once for all time. It is not that they have been forgotten—by no means—but rather they are buried as if embalmed, in the depths of a tacitly embraced, implacable silence. The family showed this same honor to Zuja.

After Zuja's death, and even in the last years of her life, there had been changes happening to the destiny of the Aleksić household. Their sudden ascent lost momentum and their growth slowed. That little clan, which had become affluent, then rich, started, for that very reason, to disperse. The boys, then the girls, went off into the world and few of them returned to these houses by the Aleksić Conduits, and fewer stayed behind to live, work and earn, as their elders had done. Then the wars came, small and large, and with them bloodshed which in these parts was the fiercest and most gory. The population dwindled and moved away. And so it is that today there are Aleksićes in parts of

Bosnia and Yugoslavia, and even far off around the world, but in town there is not a single one of them left. Since the last war even their houses and the other structures over the water have gone. All that is left now is a mound of charred ruins among the smashed conduits that are gradually reverting to marshland. Everything that was once Aleksići, that was called theirs, lives on only in the frail memory of the occasional surviving person in the town. And so it is with Zuja, their maidservant.

This afternoon, unexpectedly and without any reason in particular, she showed up in my yard, alive and unchanged, just as she was back in my childhood. When I caught sight of her at the entranceway with her large bundle, she reminded me of the elderly women in the old days who, whenever they set out to visit someone, would stay for a day or two. She stepped into the house so naturally, with such ease, that she would certainly be staying for dinner and the night.

We sat and tallked for a long time about the Aleksićes. She knew all their fates and lives down to the smallest detail. From old Manojlo Aleksić "Grandad", a remarkable man who stood out from the gray crowds of the town and was the black, silent root from which the Aleksićes and everything that was theirs sprung, down to the great grandchildren who scattered worldwide and were lost without a sound. As we spoke I tried several times to get Zuja to tell me something of herself, her personal life, her background, but with no success. She could speak only of the Aleksićes and their circle in which she counted as the world she knew all the things that were tied to them in some way—their relatives and friends, partners and serfs, competitors and enemies.

The room began to grow dark, but Zuja did not cease talking. I was the one who got tired of asking new questions, seeing that she was truly unable or refused to say anything of herself. So we sat for a time without a word. Then, in the gloom and quiet, first, as if from afar, unarticulated, and then more clearly, I heard the familiar hum and drawling mumble that we used to giggle at so long ago, in our childhood, as Old Lady Zuja's peculiar habit and innocent weakness. The room got darker and I strained my hearing and picked up a monotonous and persistant melody that Zuja was repeating like a cricket in a warm wall. Now it seemed that what had sounded long ago like the mechanical dance of aged lips was nearing human speech, it was not bereft of meaning and it was saying something new and unfamiliar to me. I listened with bated breath, forgetting myself and the time and where I was.

Before me flowed a garbled yet vital story about how Zuja moved in with the Aleksićes, remained with them and became what she was.

It was long ago, when Serbia went to war with the Turks and when the border area passing right above the town was stirred by rebellion. Zuja's father's house was right there on the border. She only vaguely remembered her mother, a tall, blonde and angular woman, but she remembered her father clearly. A dark-haired, stocky and steadfast man with a squeaky voice and wolf-like movements. His wife died early and he was left alone with two small children. An elderly relative, a widow, steppped in, ran his home and raised the children, and then somehow right before the war she, too, died of some sort of an epidemic. Again he was alone, with his fifteen-year-old son and fourteen-year-old daughter whom he called Zuja out of tenderness. The war and rebellion apparently had an irresistible pull for him. That is when he resolved to take his son with him and place his daughter in a good and safe home.

Manojlo Aleksić, known as "Grandad", was at the beginning of his ascent at that time, a husbandman in his best years, with an ailing wife and three children who were still small. The first of their houses over the mountain river had just been raised. Zuja's father brought his little girl to that house, handed her over to Master Manojlo and made him swear to God and St. John that he would take her into service, that he would feed and defend her, because he had no one else to leave her with. Then, without so much as a farewell, that same night he set off up the steep road of baked red mud and vanished into the dark woods that covered the mountain peak.

The children in the Aleksić household, lisping, called her Zuja. She was blonde and pale, skinny but sturdy. Her light, sharp hair, cut close like a boy's, looked as if it had never known a comb, it stuck out every which way. They were barely able to convince her to discard her worn-out village skirt and vest and don an old dress that had belonged to her mistress, a city dress which did not have to be remade. The girl had grown so and Master Manojlo's wife was thin and petite. Zuja helped around the house, but silent and frowning, avoiding encounters and conversations, and lowering her eyes before everyone.

Whenever she was without a task or supervision for a moment, she would go up above the house and vanish into the tall piles of pine boards. Here a walled tributary of the river branched off, creating a powerful sluice and, a little further, it flowed downhill toward the saw mill in the valley. On that spot there was a big water dam and over it a short, covered bridge which crossed to the steep and always dry path that led up into the mountain. Shielded from everybody's eyes, draped over the rafters on the bridge's railing, she loved staring at the broad sluice below her, wide, framed by boards, and the shallow water in it which, captured here, swirled and cascaded down the slope. Here she would stay as long as she could. This was the only thing the Aleksićes could say against her. They warned her not to go out, that she should not be off lurking in the corners, because the times were troubled and more than ever a maidservant's place was in the home. Silently she seemed to acquiesce, but the first chance she got she would vanish again and off she would go, leaning over the railing on the wooden bridge, watching the dark water of the great sluice, as it swelled, shrank, like taut broadcloth on a loom, before it gushed noisily down. She followed the restless hues and play of light and shadow on that cloth and she never tired of watching. And while she watched, her mouth open, she would hum something that was not a song or intelligible human speech and which was lost in the noise of the falling water.

When it became clear that warnings and scoldings did not help, they threatened to whip her if they caught her so far from the house. But still she would go. Once it happened that she slipped away right before nightfall, and, leaning over the railing, she stayed there, transfixed by the sound of the water and the rapid sequence of newer and newer images that moved by her. The damp settled in and the first shadows spread. The sun went down and created a ragged band of orange light behind the dense net of black pines at the top of the mountains. Zuja felt she should leave all that as quickly as possible and return with all haste to the house, and she said so to herself and she repeated it in a soft voice, but it was hard to wrench herself away from those smooth, warm boards that pressed and carressed her breasts, and to part with that moment and that place, to sacrifice her one and only wish: to see what would happen next, what came after this.

And come it did. Along the steep path of baked, red earth, that came straight down to the bridge from the woods.

She was staring downstream, and then up at the sky at the last traces of light. To the left, in the corner of her field of vision, a little shadow suddenly appeared like a bug floating in flight, more sensed than seen. The shadow neared and soon turned into the blurred features of a large man in a broad cloak who was making his way downhill. He disappeared from sight for a while because he was going around a curve, but the girl felt him approaching at his slow pace, invisible, and that the reddish path, which was darker and darker, would bring him to the bridge. Then he would have to cross it behind her back, and the bridge was so narrow that the unknown traveler, in passing, would inevitably brush her with his cloak of a strange cut, its color indeterminate. In advance she could feel the touch and she quaked at the thought of it. She still had time to leave the bridge and get away, but she did not budge. She could have turned to face him at least while he passed her by. But instead she stayed there, standing still as she had been: leaning over the railing and staring into the already darkened water that noisily splashed in the conduit and coursed past.

So it was that she was anticipating what was coming down from the hill, dark, heavy, and inevitable. It moved toward her slowly, strange: as if it both was and it was not, it would and it would not.

"It is and it will!"—as she said those words to herself, it got colder and darker around her. The traveler from the hills was standing at her back and blocking her with his body and his great cloak from which spread the chill of the mountain. He stood there without words and without visible movement, but she felt he was moving closer, that, like the darkness and the damp, he was enveloping all of her and that he was pushing her harder and harder against the railing of the bridge. Bent over and facing the water, she could not see his face, but she felt him all around her and on her. The thought went through her head that she should have run from there earlier, that at least she ought to be resisting now, but it was too late for everything. His chin was already crushing the back of her head, and his hard and cold hands slid along her haunches. Her bared skin shivered from the chill that came up off the water, from fear, from shame at her nakedness. She would cover herself, she did want to, but she could not. She was out of breath, and the crush got worse, it was all in one place, and turned to sharp pain. Those two hands, which were bigger, were bending her at the waist and at the same time they were breaking her all down her spine; they were breaking her apart the way a loaf of bread is broken into four chunks, lengthwise and crosswise. What was he doing to her and what did he want? she wondered with helpless hatred, gulping tears, gushing and bitter. A terrible force wanted to break her down the middle, to tear her and rend her asunder. That is certainly what he would do if he kept twisting and crushing her. This must be the way they kill a man. How could a person bear it? How could she defend herself and with what? How could she shove back at least a little from the railing, pull away from the invisible man above her and push him off with a blow or at least a scream, but there was nothing left she could do. The pain and the weight were on her and in her. She could not resist or adjust. Here is the end. She felt her consciousness darkening and all of her was sinking into that darkness.

Night had come by the time the concerned members of the houshold called the boys from the saw mill and sent them off with blazing torches to look for Zuja. They called to her, lit all the corners where darkness had gathered, until finally the first who set foot on the bridge came across the unconscious girl and called out hoarsely to the others.

She was lying by the railing, doubled over, deflated, diminished, like a little heap of torn and discarded woman's clothing. They collected her up and carried her on a reed mat down the hill to the house.

She did not regain consciousness for several days. They even lit a deathbed candle for her. But she stayed alive. They called Father Joca to read her the Great Prayer. But what seemed to help her the most was an old woman from Dobrun with her herbs. Zuja was bedridden for five weeks. And then one day she got up, got dressed, and with no questions or explanations started to work around the house, and to do all those things that she would do for the rest of her days.

I listened to Zuja's mumbling speech for a long time. She talked about the years of her service, and this meant that again she was speaking only of the Aleksićes and their family life, and of how they went out into the world, grew up, married, and had their own children, got sick and died. She remembered every single detail, and all of it was equally grand and important, and she wanted me to hear about every last one of them.

The monotonous talk started wearing me down, making me sleepy, but I could not muster the courage or strength to interrupt it. At moments I lost the thread of the long story about the Aleksićes; their names mingled with the names of cousins and business partners. My eyelids drooped and the need to doze overwhelmed me. Finally I succumbed and sank into the milky cloud of easy sleep.

Something thumped and woke me up. I started like a culprit and lifted my head with my right arm that had gone numb.

It was dark in the room and the silence was total. Confused, almost fearful, I could barely find the light switch and when the light shone I saw there was no one in the room there but me. Zuja and her bundle were gone.

Since I have been living in this house, I have grown accustomed to guests who show up unexpectedly, behave oddly, and then disappear like phantoms, but that woman with her sudden appearance, and even more, with her disappearance, so disturbed me that I stood there for a time in the middle of the room, blinking at the glaring light. And I needed a bit of time to pull myself together and find my way back to my real evening and my evening habits and tasks.

Translated by Ellen Elias-Bursać

Loves

Not only do individuals or groups of people come in front of my house and drop by my room, asking something of me, taking up my time, changing the direction of my thoughts and my mood, according to their will. Entire regions or cities, streets or people's dwellings fly in like light airy visions carried by memories in a desire to find here, on my paper, their final shape and true meaning and explanation.

In fact, it was always like this. Only now, in the summer silence and great solitude, this happens even more frequently and more vividly. Inside me, I am constantly settling accounts not only with cities but with small, even the smallest of settlements. Voices and smells around me, signs and apparitions in the sky, changes and movements within me, light patterns of my own blood vessels behind my closed eyes, unexpected memories, even people and events from my dreams—all this can conjure in me images of towns and places in which I stayed, through which I passed or which I saw only from a distance like a sharp silhouette at the edge of the horizon. I daresay, I have not succeeded in completely forgetting a single town. They do not appear often, and never more than one at a time, but I know that they all live within me and that, after many years, each can always appear in my memory, larger or smaller, but always transformed like an unexpected and unbelievable apparition. That often tires me and sometimes torments me but I can do nothing against that capricious and stubborn game. Thus, towns, streets and houses, or only parts of streets and houses crop up in my mind posing new questions, or asking of me, like an outstanding debt, the answer to old questions I never knew how to answer. They block the world from me so that suddenly I cannot see anything that is there around me, real and living, but only that which has risen from somewhere within me and does not want to get out of my way or budge from my line of vision. And I abandon all my thoughts and concerns, neglect my work, miss opportunities and define myself by the fog and mirage of far away lands and other people's destinies.

The South of France. I arrived in a sea-side town at dusk. The streets were throbbing with life. It was the eve of a big holiday. The windows of cafes and restaurants were decorated with multicolored streamers. Signs in the windows invited citizens to spend the evening there. I checked in an old-fashioned hotel in the center of the town but left immediately for a stroll. After a long walk, I found a small bar in an old back street untouched by the holiday atmosphere. I had my dinner there. The bar, like the entire street, was dusky, unpleasantly quiet, almost deserted. There were only an ill-tempered owner and a young boy helping him. A few customers would quickly leave after drinking and eating what they ordered.

At the next table sat a simply dressed woman. She was pale and well built, large, with a full and firm figure, but on her face and clothing there was something of the uneasiness and silence of the bar and street. It was not hard to guess her profession. She started the conversation first. Was I a traveler, a passer by? Surely, a foreigner? I answered vaguely and offered her something to eat and drink. We ate for a long time and drank red wine. We also had coffee and smoked cigarettes and then she invited me to her house for an after dinner drink.

Her apartment was nearby and consisted of a spacious room, cluttered with cheap, sooty and worn-out furniture, and a kitchen in which obviously one cooked rarely and little. A dense, heavy and cold desolation reigned in the apartment, just like that flooding the street from which we came and the bar in which we ate.

The woman had already been a bit tipsy. Now she hastily drank two or three glasses of liquor offering me some as well. It was clear that she was becoming absorbed in her thoughts. She told me, looking absentmindedly through the curtained window, that she was glad she could sit like this with someone tonight, and then she drank another drink, followed by another. Then she started to talk. Suddenly. And in an unexpected and unusual way.

No one knew and no one could understand her suffering. She lived quite well, as well as a women of her kind can live. She had several steady clients, among them two or three serious and indeed wealthy, well respected citizens. All had been going well until he, that man of hers appeared. He worked in the Navy Command, a sergeant, tall and strong, and good looking, but…

"An animal, mister! What am I saying? Even an animal can be tamed but not he, no way, not at all, never. He is a torturer of the kind that does not exist among baptized beings. What exists between us I cannot say, nor can anyone understand. We cannot be without one another but we live…"

She stopped for a moment, waving her hand weakly as though she did not wish to talk any more but quickly changed her mind and continued:

"But we live, if this could be called living, like nobody else. The moment we meet, the same game always begins between us. I say a tender word—he curses; I caress—he hits. This often lasts for a very long time. And strangely, the longer it lasts, the less his blows hurt me; it seems that each one of them raises me higher so that I soar on them as though on waves of fire, and that I can soar like this for I don't know how long, how far and how high. It is he who tires first and stops. Only afterwards do I see that my body is purple and battered, and only then do I feel how each separate blow truly hurts me. Then I hate him just as I hate my sins. Sometimes, I become frightened at the very beginning that he might kill me and I immediately run into the kitchen and lock myself in. And again, at times, he gets bored and stops quickly, turning his back on me in disgust.

'Why do you beat me?' I ask him at such moments, trying in vain to see his face and catch his eyes. 'Why?'

There is no answer. If he would at least look at me, perhaps then I would be able to read something in his

242

eyes, but he won't. He won't, damn him, he only turns his head away and is silent. But he does not want to leave me either and stays, then at the first opportunity he beats me again.

Oh! All this seems like a mad house or even worse. I must say that there are rare, very rare moments of calm. Then he is the most pleasant and decent man in the world. (I know he'll never be that, he just seems so to me.) He does not say anything, just sits and stares but in such a way that I am beside myself with happiness that he is there. I cover my face with his white, lightweight visor cap as though with a mask. Inside the cap is the smell of his hair and, believe it or not, the smell of wild strawberries. Not of some perfume or toilet water but indeed of the forest and strawberries on a warm peaceful summer day. I grew up in the country and I know that smell well. That is all I can have from him. Nevertheless, at such moments I think I am living in heaven. Only that happens less and less frequently and does not last long. It seems as though I just dreamed it. Soon after that he is back to his old self. A monster! Nothing attracts him, he doesn't love or value anything. He doesn't go to the movies, he doesn't play cards, he is not interested in sports, he doesn't read newspapers. All that, he says, is shit. You see that there is nothing he cares about. I prepare some food, something nice and special; if he is hungry he eats it without a word, if not he overturns the plate and turns his back on me. The man has no smile on his face and does not utter a human word. He will not respond to my words with so much as a glance. It appears indeed as though he does not hear.

I think that he even does not know my name, at least he never pronounces it. We live like animals. When I tell him that he turns his head away from me. I muster all my strength and ask him how come he is so often with me and I do not exist for him. He is not even jealous of me. How is that possible? He jumps up immediately: 'Shut up,' he says, 'or you will get another beating! I am sick of beating you.' And he slams the door behind him. Then the next day or the day after that he comes again. And it is all the same. Exactly the same! See, mister, if you do not believe me."

The woman stood up briskly, moved away a little and lifted her skirt easily and naturally as peasant women do when they have to cross a brook. Before my eyes appeared the white expanse of her thick thigh and on it, diagonally, a dark bruise in the shape and size of a navy boot.

I flinched with heavy shame and great confusion: as if in front of me was suddenly opened a new and destructive face of nature, in which we all live and in which I also lived until that moment. I did not know where to look or what to say. The woman rescued me from this predicament. "I'm sorry," she whispered in a deep, muffled voice, lowering her skirt as easily as she had lifted it then sat down and continued the conversation.

"That's what he left me yesterday. On the eve of the holiday. He went somewhere for two days. Most likely to visit his parents. I didn't dare ask him. He will come back the day after tomorrow. That's for sure. But why? To be silent, to curse and beat me without mercy. And so it goes from day to day, from month to month.

I have grown attached to him and I won't be able to detach myself alive. We live like beasts. I endure what no one can endure. If I were a dog at his side he would pay more attention to me and treat me better. I see that this can't last much longer. And yet it does and I live in pain and in constant fear. I am afraid, I am afraid mister! Because I know that I'll kill him one day, for sure I'll kill him. I'll knock him down with five bullets, I swear by the the blood of Christ, just like an animal."

The woman got up again and took a small revolver from the drawer of the night table. She showed it to me on her outstretched palms as on a china plate, and as though she were taking an oath or casting a spell over it, she kept on talking.

"See, I've prepared everything. And now, I only fear and wait. I'll kill him at an evil moment. For sure. I'll kill him yet I love him. May God forgive me. I love, I love, I love! I'll lose him and I'll destroy myself. To tell the truth, I do not have him even now and I am already destroyed. But what is left to me and what can I do? Fear and to wait. This is how my life passes by. And I feel, I clearly feel, that all of this cannot end well."

That evening at least all ended well. At a given moment, I found the strength to interrupt her talk which was becoming slower and slower, stand up and take my leave. The big woman saw me to the gate, thanking me for the honor I had done her, attention and patience.

The little bar at the corner was already closed. The old-fashioned street was full of shadows and heavy silence. It was late. After a long walk I reached the center of the town. Everything was still lively. All the restaurants were open and brightly lit. I was tired and thirsty but that very liveliness and illumination deterred me from stopping somewhere and having a drink. The door of my hotel was locked. I had to ring the bell. I did it fearfully, with a vague sense of guilt. It seemed to me that it was very late and that I was coming from far away.

Translated by Radmila Gorup

Woman on the Rock

Hotel Marina, built only a few years before the last war, small and hidden away on a green island, is bound to be remembered by those who had known it. (Alas, it was gutted completely during the war and today only a charred ruin marks the site.) Its beach, enclosed by greenery, consisted almost entirely of pale-yellow and reddish rock tumbling unevenly into the sea.

The guests took their sunbaths on the flat slabs of these giant cliffs, as if they were specially devised beds of stone. Off these rocks they dived into the sea, which was deep at that spot, and rose out of it on cement steps or by climbing an iron ladder built into the steep rock. Around most of the bathers, especially the women, the stone was littered with colorful odds and ends that they had brought with them for the swim. Large, gaudy beach towels, jars and *flacons* of lotions, balls, newspapers, books, cigarette packs, and a motley of Sunday magazines in various languages. The guests left each other alone. The majority had their steady places and occupied them day after day as if by unspoken agreement.

Each lowered himself on the seething stone in a posture that answered his body's needs, much as a drop of liquid takes the shape dictated by the laws of its physical composition.

For the most part the guests didn't know each other, and when occasionally there was laughter among the younger couples and friends, this occurred without noise and without noticeable commotion. Only now and then, usually on a Sunday or holiday, bathers from the big nearby strands would arrive in their motorboats and ketches and step ashore for a while, disturbing the quiet and upsetting the established tine. But as soon as they had left, the beach would lapse into its usual quiet. Occupied each with himself, the bathers read on their stony bedsteads, gazed through their sunglasses at the blue horizon of the sea, or else, with their eyes firmly closed, gave themselves up to the glare and fire of the searing sun in the high blue dome, each relaxed in the knowledge that no one paid him the slightest attention, just as he wasn't expected to pay any to the others. From time to time one of the bathers would get up like a sleepwalker and descend the steps, or jump from his perch into the sea, only to hasten back afterwards and take up his old position.

On the craggy shore that was raised above the water and completely exposed to the sun, peace was a thing of dazzling incandescence, bruised only fleetingly, peripherally, by a lone cricket in the hotel garden and by an occasional broken-off cry from the water. In that torrid, brilliant, and blue calm of the land, the sky, and the sea lay the motionless, fakir-like bodies of the bathers as if stilled by an unknown drug, surrendering their pores to the sun.

One of the slabs—the same one day in and day out—was occupied by a middle-aged woman; she may have been closer to the upper limit of that age than to its uncertain beginning. Without the radiance and freshness that only youth can give, yet well-formed and preserved, she invariably came at the same hour of the day, always alone and unobtrusive, spread a large towel of a fluffy orange fabric under her, arranged her colorful trifles around her, and lay there for hours, now on her back, now with her face on the towel, offering every side of her body to the sun like a person submitting to a sacrifice. Now and then she rose and jumped into the sea in a smooth but unspectacular dive, then returned to her place after a short swim. She was among the last to leave. She made herself quite inconspicuous, save perhaps with this marked eagerness to remain unnoticed. Still, her swim suits, towels, scarves, and toiletries gave one an idea of her tastes and sense of color.

There are those women, like this one, in whom the feeling for color and chromatic harmony is highly developed, as if inborn. Like plants, they live and talk in color. Around such women colors sing, as it were, inaudibly and yet in such unison that they seem to be part of cosmic harmony scaled down to a woman's being and the power of human senses. Women like this seem to gather new colors from nature, and to create new relationships between them, and new iridescences; actually, all they do is to uncover them to our eyes, which otherwise wouldn't know how to see them. Slowly and calmly, as unerringly as nature herself, they spread about them, according to their age and possibilities and the circumstances in which they live, their *own* colors, as if that were all they had to communicate about themselves to other people.

Very little more could be said about this woman who lay at some distance from the rest of the bathers, her hands clasped on her breasts, stretched out and slender, with her eyes shut, like one of the stone duchesses on a sarcophagus.

We know next to nothing about people who pass by us or lie next to us. Was there anything more one might have added about this woman, laid out like a statue, Martha L., an opera singer on her vacation, in her forty-eighth year? She herself was trying to forget who and what she was, and how long she had been around. Drowsily she gave herself to the sun's fire and to the dim memories and daydreams that welled in her aimlessly and against her will. Vague stirrings, words clearly spoken and yet unintelligible, silences of an unknown meaning, all this mingled inside her, ebbed swiftly and came back again, refusing to fade into limbo. Though not asleep, she was dreaming. And now she saw clearly: a strange image out of her past life, one that she had never suspected was still alive in her memory. She was sitting on a garden wall.

It was the high wall that enclosed their rambling garden. It was built of a hard stone, thick, some six or seven feet high; almost a rampart, that gave the passer-by a fair idea of the size and richness of the garden hidden behind it, and of the substance of its owners. Along the wall ran an alley strewn with the needles of big old pines. In the distance was the sea, with two small islands floating on it. When she was still a moppet, not allowed to leave the garden, she had got into the habit of secretly climbing the high wall and, from up there, watching the sea or the occasional passers-by in the alley below her. The habit stayed with her even later when she was already free to come out, when such infantile squatting on the wall, always in the same spot and position, was no longer becoming to her.

She was fifteen, if not older, when one day she again settled down in that favorite spot of hers. Letting one leg dangle over the wall, she raised the other and folded it until her heel rested on the very edge. A strong wind was blowing. She felt the cold stream of air wash her naked thigh above the stocking on the crooked leg and seep through her body with the same shivery chill that also filled her eyes, which were glued to the dark-blue and furrowed sea. She tingled all over, in a gooseflesh that was both aching and pleasant; she barely stirred. It was much like the moment at night when, after she had uncovered herself in her sleep, the chill would grow stronger and threaten to grip her completely; she would want to reach for cover but couldn't part from the lovely dream, and so kept putting off the actual movement, which unconsciously she had already made. She endured the cold with pleasure. Entranced, as if soaring on the bright crest of a wave at great and exhilarating speed, she never even noticed whether anyone had come down the alley or was looking at her. Only belatedly, and with a start, did she see old Matthew down on the ground below her.

The man was about fifty, homeless and without a wife, a good-natured eccentric. A part-time day laborer, part-time beggar, he worked for the wealthier families. Because he was valuable and utterly indifferent to money, everyone was fond of him and wanted him, especially for garden work. He did his chores as though he were bound to the soil, talking very little, his mouth set in a small fixed smile whether he dealt with people, animals, or the plants he hoed. Afterwards he would wander around for days, at loose ends, along the shore or down the paths between garden walls.

For a moment the girl looked at this man as if she had never seen him, her eyes batting as though she'd been caught in some light mischief, recalling with difficulty which side he had come from and how long he had stood there by the wall, his head lifted up like someone whose name had been called. As soon as she'd collected herself and realized that it was only the harmless "old Matthew," she grew quiet and reassured. But when she saw the direction of his stare, she dropped her raised leg in instinctive haste, only to pull it up again a second later, a little uncertainly, to its original position.

Rooted to the spot and gaping at her, Matthew furtively snatched off his cap, as though he were standing before a roadside shrine. She then saw that his eyes had opened wide and that they were unusually shiny. It was a new kind of stare, hard and unabashed. Overcoming her shyness and ignoring the chilly airstream, she lifted her leg a little higher. He thrust his head out and echoed her movement with his whole body. His eyes were round, clear; on the burnished, unshaven face their gleam seemed to be all of a rich and precious fire that was quite unconnected with his workman's bent body and his shabby clothes. (What is it they see, the eyes with that kind of look?) Again she moved her leg a little higher, feeling a vague sense of numbness and dizziness. Matthew leaned still closer to her, as if tied to her movements. It didn't seem possible that he could hold that position for long; he was bound to lose his balance. By now chilled to the bone, she pulled her leg higher yet, pressing it to her chest and tucking the knee under her chin, and he, in turn, tilted forward even more, pressing the cap to his body, frozen in his unnatural pose, deep in a rapture that seemed to overcome the very laws of physics.

Everything was changed. Her posture, the expression of her face and her whole bearing were no longer those of a little girl from a good home, nor was Matthew a day laborer and a crackpot. The wall, too, had ceased to be a wall and the wind was no longer what it usually was. Everything became nameless, unimportant, and weightless; it floated about like some kind of thistledown, neither rising nor falling, boundless and measureless, without a destination, swept by an anonymous, inexplicable force. And whether all of it happened in that precise way, or how long it actually lasted, she could not have accounted to herself even then, let alone today, some thirty or more years afterwards. But she knew today, just as she had known then, that she made a sudden end to that exceptional moment which had seemed utterly unbelievable while it lasted, and remained so forever afterwards, but which all the same, between those two implausibilities, must have taken place and existed as vividly and surely as any other public and acknowledged event of her life. With a swift and fluid move of her body she pivoted around and shifted abruptly to the other side of the wall. (The skirt fluttered brightly. The two silk stockings rubbed together, producing a low but sharp hissing sound, like two wires passed quickly one over the other. Once more, around her naked thighs and into her very groin, she felt the spurt of the cold wind from the sea.) And now everything was changed again and restored to its erstwhile, everyday place. She already stood with both her feet on the middle rung of the wooden ladder in the garden. Not climbing down right away, she turned her head and, hidden up to her neck behind the wall, studied the man in the alley a while longer. He stumbled at first, as if her sudden movement had deprived him of a foothold, but remained on his feet. Then all at once he shambled, away, in his gait and appearance once again the old, commonplace Matthew. The only other thing he did was to mutter:

"Thanks, *signorina.*"

His voice faded. He turned once more.

"And—well—thanks!"

And he vanished behind the greenery. She sprang from the ladder and landed on both feet with all her weight, so that her teeth chattered and from the parched earth, which now appeared unexpectedly hard and unbelievably close, a painful tingle shot up her legs and all the way to her hips.

Some years later (soon after she got married), she learned accidentally one day in February that old Matthew had died in his drab room in an attic, in such monastic poverty and want that they had to get up a collection for his funeral. The young man and the girl who came to ask her contribution told her that the dead man did not have a shirt in which they could bury him. She gave them money and, as they thanked her and were about to leave, asked them to wait and then hurried into the bedroom. From there she brought one of her husband's fine new white shirts and gave it to them, so that poor Matthew might be laid to rest.

And now, with cap in hand, elongated and huge, he was drifting slowly, ghostlike, over the rocks and the blue sheet of the sea and across the sky; hovering, indeed, like a giant shadow rather than moving. And as he turned over his shoulder, he spoke his parting words over and over with an ambiguous smile on his face.

"Thanks, *signorina*, thanks!"

She twitched angrily and made an effort to shake off the distressing vision. Still oppressed by the daydream, she struggled against it with the alert part of her mind. Where did this sudden memory, twisted into a nightmare, come from? Was the curse of growing old so strong that it not only warped the present and darkened the future but also dominated the reveries of the past? Where did this apparition come from, and why—this image of more than thirty years ago, absurd, tarnished, splayed, and yet so morbidly fascinating?

Aware that she must resist it, and bracing herself for the effort, the woman half-rose and quickly turned. Now she lay with her face in her palms, as on an open book. But what she might read in the russet twilight behind her lids was again the same thing, one and the same thing always: the tortuous, appalling, and secret course of her battle with the advancing years, a futile and never-ending strife without allies, without a moment's rest, and without any hope of success.

Everything that had happened to her lately was opposed to her whole nature, to all that she had ever been; it was completely contrary not only to her wishes, her feelings, strength, independence, and personal dignity, but also to her whole understanding, her sensibilities and, in a way, to her familial tradition.

At this point she thought of her father—and only of the father—for she never thought of her mother, a soft, pale, colorless woman with that passive sweetness of people who are good because they could not exist in any other way. She thought of Father, who had loved more in her than an only daughter; in whom she had always, in all things, had not only a parent but also the best and most trusty of friends, to whom ineffable ties had bound her, ties that did not depend on tender words and sweet nothings (or on words altogether), nor on wistful parental caresses, for those things would never have expressed adequately what the father and daughter felt and thought about each other.

A man of great physical strength and a well-rounded mind, simple to the point of apparent coarseness, he had loved this daughter of his ("an engineer's child") especially for her strong will, her uncomplicated spirit and resoluteness of thought and conduct, and also because she seemed to temper her rich zest for life with an inborn restraint. While still a child, she once overheard one of his crude though amused and good-natured "engineer's" quips. Somewhere in the gathering dusk of the terrace, speaking not to her but to one of his companions he had observed as if in an afterthought: "A woman's machine is always in repair." (His taste had never been too fine and his tone never particularly delicate, just as those playfully caustic and overemphatic opinions seldom were actually and wholly accurate; but they were marked by a naturally bold and cheerful brightness that helped the listener to get the point sooner and grasp it better.) She overheard, but didn't dwell overly on the meaning of the words. The world of her senses was then still intact and of a piece, not yet open to outside influences, and her body, womanly and frail, was still without a trace of dull weight and softness, of excessive juices, unburdened by tears and the need of support; in short, without any of those signs of weakness that so often hamper the bodies of even the most beautiful women. It was and remained for years harmonious, strong, and marmoreally pure, nimble as a light and finely built sailing boat. While not conscious of it, she used it and controlled it like a vast and immensely varied fortune; she never felt the need to think about it, much less talk. She lived its life, which was luxuriant, free, consistent, unclouded, sufficient unto itself, and seemingly incapable of being anything else, free of petty scruples and vulgar reckoning.

And now for some time past everything had been changing for the worse, grading into something unlovely and shameful, quite unfamiliar and fiendishly alien to her.

It had started about three or four years ago. "About"—because when it comes to big and difficult changes in one's life, one can never say exactly when they had started. Sometimes it seems as if they had always been present, and then again as if they had only just come to light and become visible to one's eyes. Moreover, they are deceptive and treacherous. This anguish seems at times to be hard and palpable, a single overmastering one, like some dark mountain that hides the world and will not change or budge from the spot. Afterwards, there are days and whole weeks when the mountain seems not to be there, seems never to have existed, when it is altogether unimaginable that it might exist. Until one day, at a certain moment, it springs back to life and looms before us, real, larger than life, darker than it had been before that short and illusory truce and respite.

That was how several years ago she had begun to notice the first outward and inner changes and signs of age, and, after each discovery, to debate with herself the hellish question: Is it—or not—is it? She took pains not to answer either yes or no, and to silence her questions, to forget them. But they came back again, now sooner, now later, when least expected. And the sea which had always been the greatest joy of her life became now her main and foremost antagonist and tormentor.

Born and reared by the sea, she had abandoned it soon after her first marriage; since then she had always lived far away from it, except during the summer months. Lived! What did that word contain? Two marriages, both rather brief and without any real meaning, and not in the least memorable.

Next: ten years of a great love for a real man in which everything, even the unavoidable end, was good and fitting. And finally, the twenty years of her career as an opera singer, a quiet and secure career, free of the bluster and humiliations that often accompany this kind of success. Even now she was still in good voice and her interpretations were subtler and profounder than ever.

Throughout those twenty years she had never failed to spend the summer on some beach or other. It was her best time, the glorious climax of each year, one that promised still better things for the next; carefree, poised, harboring no misgivings, she accepted the crowd of people around her in no way different than she did the sand and the sky and the sea that were necessary to her summer vacation.

And this went on from year to year. To others and to herself it appeared as if the laws of nature had no power over this body. People talked about it as about a small miracle; they talked too much. She herself hardly ever gave it a thought, accepting it all as if it were the most natural thing in the world. And it was only now, it seemed to her, that she saw herself as she must have appeared in the eyes of others during the many years of her exceptionally long youth. For doubt and worry can see what happiness and confidence never can.

Until that summer four years ago, everything had gone passably well. But then, unexpected and unbelievable, the thought of change appeared for the first time: a faint cloud between her and her summer at the seaside, a portent that accompanied her home and stayed with her all through the winter. And having invaded

259

her, it smoldered there like a hidden sickness. What at the outset had seemed like a horror that was hard to believe, a hideous dream bound to scatter itself, awaited her at the beginning of the next summer already as a part of reality and a festering dread. And it kept growing and taking hold of her with each new year. She found it almost impossible to face. Sickened by her own question, she would ask herself: Could it be, dear God? Is it possible?

There was no answer—there couldn't be—to that question of hers; nor did she expect it, knowing that she was addressing a hopeless void. All the same, she knew perfectly well that these questions meant: Was it possible that she was aging and losing her looks visibly and irrevocably, that soon there would be no more blithe summers for her, no more sun and murmuring voices and bright hues of the seashore? Was it possible that this wretched body, having betrayed her and become her enemy, had reached the point where it was no longer fit to be exposed on a beach, where she herself could no longer look at it without a pang, let alone take it into the sun, into the gay and sham dazzle of the world?

This was why in the last few years, starting in the early spring, she had begun to query and observe herself, to study her complexion feverishly, as a lost traveler studies his map, to preen herself naked between long mirrors, scrutinizing every movement and asking herself uneasily whether this one more summer, at least, she might show herself on some modest beach, quietly, without any flashiness or real joy, yet also without shame. At least without shame! For weeks and months on end she would busy herself with the question of an appropriate swim suit, a problem that once she used to settle in the manner of a youthful athlete—simply, quickly, casually, but always with the happiest results.

Such had been her life in recent years. Indeed, one could hardly call it life; it was a madness that hung between her and the world and life and made of her a solitary being, racked by insane thoughts which she had not known before, and by an endless, muddled dialogue with age and aging. Even now, here in the sun and air, these thoughts and the awful, witless reproaches coursed inside her like some dark and sour juices. She carried on a wordless private debate with herself. Every word burned and hurt her, but there was no way of stopping them. She talked with herself as if dickering with another, invisible person.

No, there's no goodness or grace in old age! Not in any part of it. It's not even clean! It's not only that one's attention wanders, consideration becomes blunted, interest dulls, so that one tends to neglect one's dress and posture, but it's as if the body itself were harder to keep clean and were more easily dirtied. It gets dirty by itself, from inside. And even when a person who is getting old manages with the utmost effort to keep himself neat and clean, it is the sterile cleanliness of a pharmacy, not of a flower. Youth is clean because her sap renews itself, but the fluids of advancing age are stale even when they hadn't yet dried out. And what was so venerable about gray hair if one had to hide it like a shame, yet could not? It was the same thing with the wrinkles on one's face. Wrinkles inspired respect in most people and lent a certain charm and warmth to modest old women and dignity to a thinker's forehead, but those same creases on the face of a lovely woman who is beginning to age are like a brand of defeat, something misshapen and almost disgraceful, since in the eyes of the beholder they evoke the same feelings as those in the woman who bears them. Cosmetics can't gloss them, massage can't erase them; sometimes, in fact—damn them!—it is as if one can't even wash them properly. The shadow of age seems to have settled in them for good and ever, just as on those marble and bronze busts in the provincial museums there always remains some dust in the wrinkles of the faces and the folds of the dresses. And from these barely perceptible but always visible—above all, visible!—lines on the face of a beautiful woman who is beginning to fade there wafts a bleakness and chill as from deep-sea weed and mountain gullies.

And what was she to think of her eyes? There is nothing harder and more painful than to look at the world around you with the eyes of a former beauty. The glance of such a woman grows more and more restless, hard, distrustful, and vindictive, for she wants to see only one thing in the eyes of others: the impression which her appearance makes. Even in a mirror she timidly catches this new glimpse of herself, smiles at it, trying to iron it away or at least soften it, but the visage slips even through the smile, wretched, full of misgiving about other people and its own diffidence, hesitant and at the same time keen as an inquisitor's. (Never again the old carefree sparkle!) And if at times it manages to recapture a little of that youthful dazzle, this gives the whole face an expression of something giddy and frivolous, almost indecent, and to herself so repulsive that she would best like to snatch the nearest lotion jar and smash the big mirror together with its vision.

Such is the horror of old age that all things turn against the person who is already at odds with everything because she is growing old.

She no longer simply mused about old age; she conjured it up, magnified it; and reviled it. Her warped, poisoned thoughts gave no quarter to anything: not to the weakness, or wisdom, or dignity of old age. These struck her as self-delusion and a cheap comfort, and she didn't want them because her eyes had been opened at last to what is called the truth of growing old, and she refused to deceive herself, could not be satisfied with her own deceptions. She wanted no part of it, and cared not the slightest about anything else. She would have wanted only one thing at that moment: to be able to squat as she once did on that wall which had encompassed the garden of her youth, to have the power once more to experience that wordless and blind soaring on the cool wave of air. Just that. But this was something she could not do—would never again be able to do.

Such were the thoughts and the inner debate of the prone, unstirring woman on the rock. (And as often when we decide in this way that our eyes have "opened" to something, what it usually means is that we have shut them to a hundred other things.) She felt alarmed and tried to stop her errant mind. No, you shouldn't dwell on it, at any rate not here in the sun! Close your eyes firmly and be carefree, at least try not to think.

This is good. Like this. Screw the eyes down tight, forget that you have them. Forget who or what you are, how much space you occupy, where you came from, or where you are going. Give yourself to the basic and simple things that do not change, or at any rate not so swiftly; to the rock on which you lie, to the sun and the blue sky above the darker sister-blue of the sea. Wipe out every thought and all carping and fault finding, drift away beyond the reach of desire and comparisons. That's good. Good—but it doesn't last long.

From time to time, turning over from one flank to the other like a bed-ridden patient she would open her eyes and experience a quick stab of pain as from a pair of wounds. Her short glance would alight on a young woman, or a girl, sure of herself and without a thought of her body, emerging from the sea with a toss of her wet hair, or else getting ready to jump in. All at once she would think again: "Ah, if these women knew how quickly it all goes and how soon..." And just as abruptly she would break off in the middle of the thought. "What am I whining and crying here for! What do I care about other women, about the whole world for that matter!" But her mind would be off on the same old merry-go-round, the thoughts would chase back and forth and whirl so sharply that each conclusion would be the opposite of every other. And why shouldn't I care? This thing that's happening to me happens to every woman on earth. Surely not one of them remains young and beautiful—they all go through it! Once more, there would be a subtle shift in the logic. Yes of course it happens, how wouldn't it? It happens. But maybe not to everyone, and not in this way? Not like this! And then she would realize with a kind of bitter and surprising clarity that such aging was typical of people who were ashamed of growing old, that a body living only for itself and because of itself was unfortunate, that the full extent of its misfortune became apparent to it only with the onset of old age.

She tried to push these thoughts away, but couldn't dispel the insane one that stood out and apart: Not like this! She felt it as a steady weight on her chest, a hard, dark bell-clapper swinging to and fro with a sound like a never-ending moan, since all the attics of her mind only swelled its echo. Not like this! She beat her forehead on the soft padding of the towel, beneath which there was the eternal stone.

Not like this! Merciful God, not like this!

With a shock, she caught herself whimpering inwardly. Her failure to smother, or at least muffle, the "miserable helpless devil" in her made her frantic. Lately, she had fallen into the habit of picking some meaningless words and repeating it over and over until it became a gloomy refrain, a wail that sent her whole body quaking and which only she could hear. She hated this whimper of hers, yet caught herself at it every other moment. She trembled at the thought that one day it might grow audible, pass her lips, and that one of the people around her might hear it.

The quiver made her flesh creep. Her body grew colder and icier, despite the warm rock under her and the August sun above her. The chill started in her toes, real and excruciating, then climbed and spread, numbing her innermost tissue, and joined finally with similar icy waves that had started out of her elbows and the nape of her neck. Soon she was a piece of ice, her skin encased in gooseflesh. With a last effort she asked herself: Where could all this blood have drained to? The only thing still alive in her was her mind, and this mind informed her that she was lying somewhere among people, like a strange oasis of darkness and frost in the white heat of rocky ground and seething air. The thought made her want to run, to hide herself from the world and this daily exposure. But it was too late for retreat; it would only fan the shame and the horror. The last way out was to vanish. To vanish unnoticed, completely, for ever, in this ice age of the earth, together with all the earth's oceans and continents.

But this powerful and bitter urge to vanish would set off, in the very center of her body, there in the vault of the parting ribs, an infinitely tiny spark that would presently quicken into a flame, minute in compass but terrible in its intensity, which would spread gradually and push out the cold as it grew into a fire. At last, the frost inside her would be transformed into a blaze. Through the mist and the heat waves she would ask herself: "Where does all this blood come from? Where is it gushing out of, and why is it so hot? I'm going to burn up!"

Yes, this too was a way to limbo. There was nothing left but to vanish—yes, to burn up, to scorch this body that had let her down so abjectly, twisted her whole life into the very opposite of what it had always been, of the only thing it was capable of being. To consume oneself utterly, to the last particle beyond recall, in the all-powerful, clean, honorable, irrevocable fire! To burn oneself without a trace, to annihilate oneself in the general conflagration of worlds, like a blaze within a blaze! But still, she remained conscious and did not vanish.

She lifted her head languidly, opened her eyes. Everything was still there. Everything was the same. With difficulty she summoned her strength for a few crabbed movements in this reality which neither cold nor fire could deaden and destroy. She unscrewed the jar of cream and mechanically anointed that body which had died twice in the same moment, once from ice, the second time from fire, but which was still alive and moving and demanding something. The act of motion calmed her, her gaze came to terms with the familiar landscape and with the bathers scattered over it, with the world that existed unchanged outside her thoughts and independent of the changes in herself. In this world there was room, there had to be room somewhere, somehow, for everyone. For everyone.

In the wake of the insane fire and dreadful cold she now felt the living warmth of her blood and its measured beat in the veins of her neck, like the pulse of a clock that ticked the time for living people and slowly bore her to the regions where there was no suffering.

This brought on the soft lassitude of sleep. Will I really doze off? she asked herself with the fainter part of her consciousness. Right here, in full view of everybody? Will I? But her questions grew fainter. In the last instance what did "here" mean? Who was "everybody"? None of it really existed; all was spirited away by the gentle and yet overwhelming power of sleep, before which the color of

267

the sky and the sea and the light tang of the brine-dusted rock faded away in a cosmic mist, in which colors no longer had names, nor scents any meaning. The mist wrapped her from outside and filled the hollows of her body as if she were an unresisting valley, lifting and lowering her at the same time—wafting her somewhere as the ocean of air wafts an immeasurably tiny mote, without a perceptible movement or sound or any sensation familiar to human beings. At the bottom of that mist she discerned a pale blush, the last vestige of a life in which, she vaguely remembered, there had been unfair comparisons, changes, and questions about youth and age, numbers, names, and visible signs of some picayune human existence. There had been, but they were no more. She knew only one thing: That she was falling asleep on the rock. Sleep—on the rock. What did "sleep" mean? What was "rock"? Presently that, too, melted into the ocean of nonbeing. She slept. Eternity.

She didn't wake up from her short nap with a start but glided lightly to the surface. Transformed and invigorated. The scene around her was unchanged. One heard the waves lapping, and the voices of people that meant nothing and could make no difference. There wasn't anything to be afraid of. No confusion, no bad thoughts! All was real, simple, almost gay. The sight before her was attractive; it gave her a strong sense of well-being. Slowly and lightly, she rose with the movement of a deathless goddess loosening the sandal from one of her feet, as she stood, in perfect balance, on the other. The sandals fell away, first one then the other, weightlessly, making no sound.

She stepped forward, upright and natural, her breasts lifted high (though neither too much nor too little), tucking her hot hair under the rubber cap and fastening the strap under the right ear. She approached the edge of the sheer cliff and, with head slightly bent forward, her arms raised high, dived off in a perfect arc. The sea was cooler, harder and darker than one would have expected. Still, she was not expecting anything. She hadn't thought about it at all. She sank.

When she came up her face bore the bright mask of liquid shimmer. The two slits on the mask reflected the blue, endless and ever-lasting sky, in whose center the sun was blossoming—a fiery bloom that one could not look at. She swam out, climbed the vertical iron ladder, reaching up for the higher rungs with strength and ease, while at each step of the climb there waxed in her a sense of calm satisfaction which had no need either to hide or show itself, which did not think of a goal, and knew no end. Mounting the rock she had abandoned a short while ago, she glanced in absent wonder at the pair of carelessly dropped sandals and then lowered herself (smoothly, like a sea creature) on her knees on the big orange beach towel, almost as if she had come across it unexpectedly. She buried her face in the moist softness of her crooked elbow. Her whole body, together with all it had ever been, or desired, or thought and felt, poured itself into this small nook and found there a moment's peace and sanctuary. Somewhere deep in her entrails she could feel a nameless bliss germinating and sprouting, then growing and branching through her entire trunk, spreading at the same time like a palm leaf, its points fine and keen and reaching all the way to the eyes, pressing and teasing the closed lids from inside like a welling of healthy tears. Perhaps everything was all right after all.

She felt as if she were completely enveloped in a bright, feathery, and yet impenetrable sheath, without a name, unknown to herself. Her wet flanks rose and fell to the rhythm of her still agitated breath, gleaming on the rise, darkening as they fell; gleaming and darkening. She felt herself as light and big and powerful as the world which itself changes and remains always the same, calm and happy in the lap of the benign, momentary respite.

Translated by Joseph Hitrec

The Pasha's Concubine

1

On the very eve of Austrian occupation, Veli-ud-din Pasha, nicknamed Circassian, came to Bosnia for the second time—this time as commander-in-chief of all forces on Bosnian soil. He arrived in Sarajevo early in January, without a harem and with little baggage—a fact that immediately attracted notice. In the bazaar they called him a tramp, a rag picker and beggar. "The stuff he brought with him wouldn't have filled a sack," said the men in the bazaar, "but when he leaves Bosnia, watch out for the load of trunks." But in truth, Veli Pasha's household was disorderly rather than poor. The housekeeping was done by an ailing woman, a Jewess from Bessarabia. She was thin, and bowed before her time; something dusky and melancholy in her eyes was the only trace of her former beauty. The servants were a mixed lot drawn from all parts of the world, good for nothing, thieving, and lazy. The Pasha's residence was on Alaibeg's property at the top of the steep Logavina Street.

Veli Pasha himself had changed greatly in these last eight years. He drank more, except that now he did it even more furtively and in private. He was moodier and more short-tempered than ever before. Although still agile, he had grown heavier; and the hair on his temples had become streaked with gray. His left cheek bore some kind of a red blemish, the size of a child's palm, that imperceptibly but steadily grew larger and thicker, eating more and more into the soft underpart of his eyelid. He often suffered from a pustulant rash in his mouth, and from chest pains. But there was almost no change to be seen in his Circassian profile, on which his forehead, his nose, and his heavy mustache sloped down in one line, tilted as it were at the powerfully carved chin. The eyes, too, were unchanged—dark and symmetrically cut, with a calm and earnest look, the kind one sees in clever children and in truly bold and noble men.

He came from a well-known military family and was an only son. His father had left him a considerable estate. Brave, generous, and handsome, he had advanced very rapidly. However, he had spent the last few years in obscure garrisons along the Russian frontier, returning to Istanbul from time to time to sell his legacy, piece by piece.

Ten years ago, he had been transferred to Bosnia, as a colonel at Bijeljina. But since Hafiz Pasha, the commander-in-chief at the time, had been a good friend of his and also a distant relative, he spent more of his time at Sarajevo than at Bijeljina. He was popular with all the officers and foreign consuls, and well known for his horses and picnics in the hills above the city. Nevertheless, even though his good command of Russian enabled him to learn Bosnian quite well, so that he had no trou-

ble communicating with the local people, they took a
dislike to him right from the start, for he could be
haughty, brusque, and forbidding. And since those early
days the leading Turks of Sarajevo remembered him
with anything but pleasure.

In the Provincial Council, where the foremost no-
blemen of the land bickered interminably with the dawdling civilian governor and with venal high army officers, he often cut short their speeches and threw them
into confusion with his curt, practical, army-style questions. And so it came about that he began to feel an increasing contempt for them on account of their foolish
jingoism, narrow-mindedness, and idle chatter, while
they in turn began to hate him and speak ill of him. Stories were told that he had plundered all the towns in the
Caucasus, that he was in debt and a friend of the Russians, that he indulged in drinking orgies with the English vice consul, and swilled wine and ate pork. And he,
in his turn, gave them more and more cause for hatred
and calumny. Showing no interest for anything in the
world except his soldiers and his horses, he was unscru-
pulous and merciless and, when his army needed something, had no qualms taking it from the Turks and
Christians alike. He fined the Sarajevo Jews at every opportunity; but when his soldiers helped themselves to
the hay in the Sarajevo meadow that belonged to an important bey, there was hue and cry among the members
of the Council. In vain did the governor, a relative of
his, implore and admonish him to keep in mind the
touchiness of the beys. Summoned to the Council to
explain the incident of the hay, he gave a short speech

the likes of which had not been heard before. To the accusations that he was a drunkard and a bully who took what belonged to other people, he answered calmly and with a sneer:

"I like to drink, but no one has ever seen me drunk. I don't look for squabbles, but, by Allah, I know how to fight. I have no money or credit, not a puppy or kitten to my name. I fear Allah and serve the Sultan—now what do you propose to do about it?"

Here he turned to the dignitaries and, with the practiced sangfroid of an old cavalry officer made an unexpectedly obscene gesture.

Soon after this he was recalled to Istanbul and reassigned to the Russian frontier.

And now, even though he had come back as commander-in-chief of the entire Bosnian army, he no longer showed his old interest in military affairs, or his former obduracy in his clashes with the civilian governor and the beys. At Travnik, he maintained several detachments of cavalry and two battalions of Albanian foot soldiers. These units were the only ones he was concerned with, the only ones he personally visited and inspected. He utterly neglected the Anatolian troops in Herzegovina, and had not the slightest wish to see the battalion of Turkish regulars at Sarajevo itself. Whenever the commandant of that battalion, a portly major by the name of Uzunić, came to report to him, he would gaze past him with an absent look and invariably leave all his questions unanswered. In this he was so unaffected, adept, and full of dignity that no one knew how to deal with him or dared to break his silence.

Otherwise, among the local people there were only two with whom he occasionally met and talked: Mulaga Merhemić, the oldest of four Merhemić brothers, a reputable merchant and a quiet, upstanding man; and Mullah Suleiman Jakubović, a dervish of the Mevlevi order, a devout monastic but a sincere, outspoken, and cheerful person. Jakubović had a small room at the far end of Čumurija, where that Street meets Tašlihan; the room had a large window which, like a store shutter, was open to the street. Here he sat cross-legged all day long, reading and praying, receiving visitors, giving advice, or else simply gazing into the street, cordially saluting passers-by of all faiths, shouting an occasional polite greeting. And here, too, Veli Pasha often stopped his horse to exchange a few words with this lean dervish who had an unusual way with a sentence and talked freely on almost any subject with a certain wise and jovial pungency.

With the civilian governor, Vizier Mazhar Pasha, he met rarely and talked little, and then in a kind of good-humored and flippant tone that was not entirely free of contempt.

He avoided the meetings of the Council, and on the rare occasions when he was forced to attend he would sit motionless and without a trace of his old intensity, gazing over the heads of the Council members with the same absent and inattentive eyes, forgetting everything and hearing no one, while all the time, with bated breath, he would cock his inner ear to the blight that was burrowing and gnawing dully at his left cheek and spreading to the still-healthy part of his face.

A few weeks after his arrival, Veli Pasha went to Travnik to inspect the garrison. He spent there two days in all. He hardly went anywhere and completed the inspection in no time.

Although February was still in its first week, the air had suddenly grown balmy, bringing with it an unexpected touch of spring. There was a cracking of ice and a roar of new torrents, the house eaves dripped in a day-long whisper; and all night long water gurgled and ran down the streets, which began to show their underlayer of stone. The play of the new sun and rising vapors sparked a bluish, swaying radiance in the air that brightened all things.

In the forenoon of the second day, as he was returning from the drill field, the Pasha and his escort found themselves in the bazaar. They rode cautiously over the thawing ice. It was a market day, and in front of the Garić Bakery their way was blocked by some peasants' horses laden with wood. While the flustered farmers began to hop and skip around the stubborn horses, the Pasha cast a glance into the bakery. Next to the closed brick oven stood the old baker Ali, stoop-shouldered, with rheumy, wizened eyes out of which tears kept oozing on his great white mustache. At the wide-open shopwindow, among the bread loaves and pans of meat and pies, was his daughter Mara. On her knees and propped on the counter with one arm, she had stretched the other for a platter on a shelf underneath. When she heard the shouts the soldiers and the stamping of the peasants' horses, she lifted her head, and the Pasha, seeing her wrapped like this around the counter, fell in love with her round, childish face and her merry eyes.

When he rode that way again in the afternoon, the bakery was deserted, the window half-shuttered, and on the sill was a purring cat with singed white hair.

He gave orders that the girl be found and brought to him. The noncommissioned officers and the town constables ran eagerly to carry them out. He stayed over till noon of the third day, when they reported that the matter could be arranged. The girl had no one except her father. Her mother had been the well-known Jelka, named Hafizadić after the old Mustaybey Hafizadić, who had kept her for several years and then married her off to this Garić, a quiet and simple-minded young man, to whom he had also given money to open the bakery.

The Pasha left some money and entrusted the matter to his old acquaintance Teskeredžić. And toward the end of March, on another market day, they brought the girl to him at Sarajevo.

The Pasha had not been wrong in his judgment. She was the kind of woman he had always sought and particularly esteemed, the only kind that still attracted him. She was not quite sixteen. She had big eyes of a dovelike shade and muted porcelain luster, which moved languidly. Her hair was quite fair, heavy, and thick, such as was seldom seen on women in this region. Both her face and her arms were covered with a fine, light down that was noticeable only in sunlight. What was unusual about her was that even those parts of her skin which were not exposed to the sun and air, were not uniformly white and dun, as is usual with blonde women, but her whole body glowed with a bright, burnished hue that changed only in the shadowy hollows or with a sudden and irregular onrush of blood, when it turned even richer. Her hands were perfectly childlike, short and pink.

The Pasha was buoyed up. In the first few days he was occupied only with her. He also found it pleasant to think that now too, as once before, he could tell by an outstretched hand the kind of woman her owner was, and her true worth. Had he brought her in earlier, it would have been no good; while three to four months later, it seemed to him, the bloom would have been over. This was exactly the right time. She was cut off from her own kin, frightened and isolated, dependent only on him. At times she appeared to him like a young animal which, driven to the edge of a precipice, quivers in her whole body, her pupils contracting. This fanned the passion of his love and, in the contradictory ways of the male heart, evoked in him the impulse to be generous, to make her happy, to protect her.

She lived not far from the Pasha's residence, in a separate cottage which he had rented and furnished. Except for her visits to the Pasha, she went nowhere and received no visitors, save for Hamša the Gypsy, who kept house for her, and Baba Anuša from Bistrik, who was distantly related to her and who lived with her two grandchildren in great poverty. She spent all her days in two poorly lighted rooms, doing those sundry little chores that are so inconspicuous and yet so easily fill a woman's day. At dusk the Pasha's equerry would come for her, and she would wrap and veil herself up to her eyes and then, with a bowed head, accompany him to the Residence.

In the beginning, after they had just brought her from Travnik, she felt utterly lost. Physical pain took complete hold of her; and it was only when this pain, after the first few nights, began to fade that there arose in her mind, like a torment, a vague yet dark and nagging thought of sin and shame. She was afraid of the Pasha, she loathed that Jewess of his, Sarah, and shied away from daylight and from people. She could not sleep, yet even in her dreams felt herself damned.

Nevertheless, she gradually came to terms with Sarah, who was taciturn and good and who did her work and helped in everything with a kind of melancholy friendliness. Getting accustomed to the Pasha and his caresses was harder; even after the initial pain and fear had faded, she accepted those numbly, in childlike bewilderment. But after a while she began to get used to them. She grew especially fond of the smell of his skin. It was seldom that she could look into those unusually steady eyes without a certain timidity, or into that face with its dreadful patch of blight on the left cheek and its dark drooping mustache that was always a little damp and quivered when he spoke like tufted grass in a dark forest pond. But the waftings that his body sent out attracted her more and more, they thrilled and delighted her; and she inhaled them for hours with her eyes closed, her head resting on his chest or in the palm of his hand.

The anguish came back to haunt her only at night when, as it often happened, he sent her to sleep alone. She would then wake up several times with a clear realization—such as can only come in the dark—of what and who she was now, and with a mouth choked with

279

sobs she would press her face between the quilt and the pillows and stammer:

"Turk…!"

In the darkness, the racking thought would assume the shape of eternal punishment and hellish torture, not of earthly shame and ruin as in the daytime. But the next evening she would again face the Pasha with blushing cheeks and a wordless smile that seemed to be made entirely of glistening white teeth and sparkling eyes.

So it went every evening. He would come from an army exercise, or from a ride, flushed and a little sweaty, and she would wait for him with her hands crossed on her breast. He would then undress; Sarah would bring cold water, and a maid would take away his boots. After he had washed and cooled off, he would ask them to open the door and all windows that commanded a view of Sarajevo and the Trebević mountain. He would sit like this in the cool draft until Sarah brought a bottle of *mastika* and a tray of olives and thin strips of bread. Later the equerry Salih would come in with the *narghile* on which the lighted tobacco heap would smolder a dark red, while in its crystal bottle, on the limpid surface of water, there would float two crimson cherries. Then Sarah and the equerry would vanish, and from an adjoining room Mara would return, prepared, and sit on his lap. Between the two of them, this was called "sitting in the box." And next to him, indeed, she was so small, and would snuggle so closely, that all of her could fit comfortably between his crossed legs.

While it was still daylight, she would, sitting thus, rummage through his box of pictures and photographs, in which she found unusual delight and excitement, and which he explained to her only on rare occasions.

Here there were many photographs from the time when as a young officer he had taken part in the various commissions that set the common frontiers with Russia. On all of them she indentified him easily—slimmer, with a smaller mustache and a face not yet disfigured. She admired the Russian officers, splendid men in white blouses and caps, and timidly inquired about them. These questions he answered more willingly, for through them she would touch his weakness for everything that was Russian, a partiality he had acquired during long years of life in the garrisons along the Russian frontier, and in consorting with the Russians, and which all his life he had harbored like a secret foible. Among the pictures were also lithographs of hunting scenes and ships, sent to him by an English friend, whose snapshots, invariably sporting a pipe and a pair of dogs, kept cropping up. There were street scenes, too, and views of Istanbul and Smyrna, and of the gloomy town of Akka with its ruined battlements.

And even when twilight began to deepen, they would be sitting quiet and motionless like that; she inhaling the familiar smell, he feeling the imprint of her small ear, with its invisible ring, on his bare chest. They would hardly stir, and talk little; save for an occasional smile and mock threat on his part when she would start to nibble the hem of his shirt. Over her inclined head he would drink glass after glass of *mastika,* or blow rings of whitish smoke from his *narghile,* in the restless water of which the two crimson cherries kept bobbing. So he drank and smoked and, over her blond nape, watched the slow darkening of the town below and the guttering of cloud after cloud on the mountains.

And when the dark was complete and on the steep roads of Bistrik and Megara clusters of tiny lights flared up, and the stars surfaced in the sky, she would get up, light a candle, and remain waiting by the door. If he said, "Are you sleepy?" she would nod and withdraw into the other room, leaving him by his bottle and candle. But if he said, "Shall we, daughter?" she would go up to him, help him to rise, and they would go together into the room to lie down. Except that this happened less and less often. Usually he sent her in to sleep alone, while he stayed behind to drink, sometimes for many long hours.

Lying in the dark, she would listen to every sound from the glazed verandah and wish that she could be with him, and not have to sleep; at the same time she trembled at the thought that he might enter.

Often she would get up and, shivering all over, peer through the keyhole. (No sooner was she thus a few paces away from him, than he seemed to her strange and forbidding.) She would watch him abandon his *narghile* and put away his amber bead-string, then reach for an oval mirror with an inlaid handle and a frame of gilded bronze, and take a jar of silver nitrate from a box and dress the purple bruise on his face for long minutes, scowling from pain. Before his crossed legs there lay a long, gleaming knife, resting on its back, the sharp side uppermost. And this carefully placed knife, which looked as if it might tip over at any moment, seemed to have the effect of further subduing and mesmerizing his already cramped and infrequent movements. After which he would once more resume his frozen posture, staring into the night and draining his glass at ever shorter intervals.

Seeing him so glum and stiff, with the string of beads, the knife, and the mirror beside him, she felt as though he were performing an inexplicable rite and making an offering to something arcane, horrible, and utterly evil. She would shudder and grit her teeth, yet wouldn't budge from the door until her breasts turned cold and her feet fell asleep. Only then would she slump on the pillows, exhausted, crushed by a feeling that there, behind that door, her soul had also perished.

On waking next morning, her sense of dread would be undiminished. But as the day advanced and the afternoon drew nearer, her curiosity and desire would wax stronger and stronger, until at last, fully dressed and wrapped, and with a kind of aching impatience, she would start waiting for the evening, for the night, for the torment, and for all that had to be. And the dusk would find her "in the box," with a lapful of scattered pictures, timidly asking, "What's on the other side of the sea?" "What kind of people are the Russians?" "How's it that you can take pictures of saints and people?" And everything would be repeated over again.

One other thing troubled her greatly: that she didn't go to church. She dared not and didn't know how to tell him that. But in the veiled and never openly acknowledged give and take that was now developing between them, he remembered it himself and told her, one Friday, that she ought to go. She blushed deeply and only nestled closer to him. And the following Sunday a special attendant of the Pasha's accompanied her to the foot of the church walls, and there waited for her until the Mass was over.

She came back with her head bowed even more abjectly, shaking with muffled sobs. She had often enough, during the day and at night, mused about her life and her shame, but none of it had ever been quite so real and dreadfully clear as during those two brief hours which she had spent in church.

As she had appeared on the church portals, all heads had turned toward her. Old and young women, under red or multicolored kerchiefs, looked her up and down and then resumed praying, their chins on their chests. Hatred and scorn closed in from all sides; so much so that she froze and stopped in the middle of the church. No one wanted to step aside and make room for her. She fell to her knees as in a dream, not daring to lift her eyes either at the altar or at the wall above it on which there was a painting of a haggard and sallow saint—not of Our Lady, as in her church at Dolac. Even the sexton going the rounds with his copper collection bowl gave her a wide berth. And Fra Gregory, during the service itself, gave her a cutting, wrathful, implacable look whenever he turned around. At the end of the sermon, he added several words which she did not understand but felt clearly were meant for her, and which signified the climax of her shame. And so she had knelt in the middle of the church, doubled over, her clenched fists on her pounding heart, burning with a fire that almost scorched her eyes. She could not remember when and how she had managed to walk out, or found the attendant and followed him home.

Afterwards she vainly tried to calm herself, and bathed her face in cold water; her eyes were swollen from crying, the face full of red blotches that would not go away. The Pasha noticed the change right away, but couldn't draw a word out of her; all she did was tremble and press her tightly clamped mouth into the muscle of his arm. In the end he understood what had happened. Early next morning, he sent for Fra Gregory.

Fra Gregory was summoned for midday, but as the times were troubled and full of uncertainty, and he himself was curious and apprehensive, he dropped in at the army riding school at Kršlo much earlier than he was due. Just at that moment the Pasha was standing in the barrack yard and studying the canter of a horse which a syce rode around the ring. He waved his hand, and the syce took the horse away. To the friar's greeting, he answered without any introduction:

"And why don't you let that creature of mine come peacefully into your place of worship and pray to God according to her law?"

Fra Gregory mumbled something about his vocation and about the girl's soul, but Veli Pasha interrupted him sharply:

"What've you got to do with her soul? I don't want to hear about her soul, and I'm not asking about it, but about your church and about last Sunday."

After this Fra Gregory, frail and gaunt, his head barely level with the decorations on the Pasha's chest, mustered his old nimbleness and eloquence in which there was always an equal measure of wheedling and threat, of humility and pugnacity, and which seldom failed to achieve some success. But this time nothing was of any avail.

That morning the Pasha was fresh, alert, and quick with thoughts and words, as he had not been in a long time. He held his whip under his arm, and in the light of the forenoon his big white hands showed brightly against the black uniform. Fra Gregory vainly exerted himself with long Turkish phrases; he could not finish a single one.

"Never mind, no matter—I didn't call you for that. She will come again next Sunday, when it's time to pray, and if you don't make room and receive her like any other female…"

The friar again began to speak about religious rules, and about the folk who kept to their ways.

"Never mind, never mind. I can't wrangle with your folk around the church. You are their headman—it's you I know."

Fra Gregory made pointed allusions to the foreign consuls, to the political situation in the country, but the Pasha broke in decisively:

"Go and tell that to the Vizier!"

And he clapped his hands for the syce to bring his horse out of the stable. Two other young men appeared and got busy around the horse, inspecting the girth once more and holding the reins. First the Pasha mounted his horse, and after him his sergeant-major. The animals started to prance, and Fra Gregory stepped aside. Before riding out of the gate, the Pasha turned over his shoulder once more:

"Let it be as I say, priest, so that you too will be at peace and alive and healthy on Sunday."

He spoke this more softly, though firmly and from a great height, as seagoing men on ships and riders on horses are wont to do.

Fra Gregory, in his tough and indestructible doggedness, wanted still to say something more, but the riders vanished beyond the gate, and he remained thus, with an arrested gesture and unfinished words, beside a couple of soldiers who were wiping their palms on their canvas aprons and looking at him dully.

Yet Mara not only didn't go to church any more, but was incapable of praying even at home. As soon as she would think of God and prayer, the incident in the church would be resurrected in her memory and at once the old cramp would stiffen her jaws and chill her breast, so that she would break off praying and give herself entirely to fear and to her shame. The Pasha at first urged her to go, but later even he forgot about it. For he too, in the last four days, had become more withdrawn and was apt to retire into pensive silences.

In this way the spring months went by.

In the meantime, unknown to her, strange things were happening in the city, and there were changes afoot that would alter the course of her life.

2

Summer arrived, and with it warm showers during the night and clear skies and sunshine in the daytime. The bloom on the hillsides was over, the gardens were blending into the dark greenery. The market stalls blushed with the Konjić cherries, which were big and watery and cracked, as always when the year was rainy. The summer gave every indication of being mild and fruitful.

Yet the bazaar was worried and restive. Business was slow, money scarce and its value unstable; imports were irregular and beset with difficulties. The peasant avoided buying what he needed, and hesitated to accept Turkish paper notes for his produce. Among the Christians there was an ominous silence. Rumors constantly spread that the Austrian army was poised on the river Sava and was only awaiting orders to cross; and while the Austrians were so deployed, four Bosnian battalions had been idling for many months on the outskirts of Istanbul; other Bosnians, prisoners of war and scattered at all points of the compass, were writing home from Russia, Transylvania, and Bessarabia. The bitterness of the populace was turning against the Ottoman authorities— against the Vizier to begin with, and then against his chief army officer. The people gathered in shops and cafés; there was a growing chorus of whispering, the kind that usually precedes action, and which kindles a vague excitement among the masses and kills every desire for work. In the shops, surrounded by worried and attentive listeners, the hodjas read Turkish newspapers, translated and explained the news. In Hadji Ivo Livajić's warehouse, Fra Gregory Martić secretly translated the Budapest newspaper *Pester Lloyd,* while in the commercial center of the city Stevo Petranović, a former teacher at the Serbian school and now in the service of the Italian consul, went from office to office, his pockets bulging with Italian newspapers. Following a few paces behind him went the clerk of the Austrian consulate, Herkalović, a well-dressed and portly man from Lika, telling everyone in the dignified manner of a bureaucrat about his Empire, its might and its order. Storekeepers of all four faiths listened, smoked, shook their heads, but said nothing themselves. Courteous to the point of insincerity, and used to many evils and changes, they heard and noted every word, but when their turn came to express an opinion they steered the conversation to health, which, after all, was the main thing and the greatest boon, and to this year's crops, or else took cover in vague reminiscing about the past. And meanwhile, each thought his own thoughts, thoughts that were nursed in private and remained unvoiced, but which every man lived with, and for which, when necessary, he would fight, spend whatever he possessed, even give his life.

Toward the end of June, rumors of an imminent Austrian occupation came so thick and fast that the jitters, especially of the Turks, could no longer be disguised.

On Friday morning, a deputation of some thirty Turks, representing merchants, agas and artisan guilds, went to see the Vizier to seek assurances about the critical situation and draw his attention to the grave Christian danger from Austria, and to demand the return of Bosnian troops to Bosnia and the recall of Veli Pasha.

Hoping to soothe them with a long speech, the Governor kept them at the Residence an unusually long time. Seeing that the deputation had not returned, the bazaar, distrustful and irritable for many months past, could not contain itself but flared up like one man. There was a sudden banging of store windows and stanchions. From all the lanes and alleys artisans came milling and marching, as if by a previous agreement, toward Sultan's Bridge. The general bitterness and exasperation were at last set in motion, and found expression; everything happened as if by itself; the crowds melted together as if into a ready mold.

At the head of the throng marched Salih Vilajetović, named Hadji Lojo, flanked by his escort of some ten fugitives from Nikšić, homeless desperados. He was bony, haggard, and tall, with legs and arms that seemed much too long for his body; his face was creased with deep, sensual wrinkles and overgrown with a sparse beard, and the gaze of his big blue eyes was disconcertingly rigid. He wore tattered student pants of a dark satin; his chest was bared and hairy, the shirt ripped and stained with mulberry juice. He was muttering some sort of prayer; from time to time he would stop and reel around to face the mob, which would halt also. The men from Nikšić would then fire their rifles into the air, and a thin cloudlet of smoke from their shots would hover, as if unfurled, above the head of their leader, as the myriad tiny bits of paper with which their rifle barrels had been crammed would flutter down on him like snowflakes. Following the silence that followed the volley he would, with arms outspread, intone several words in a deep voice, to which the crowd answered with shouts of acclaim; and then he would continue on his way. He stopped and turned around like this several times.

"We don't want the Istanbulis to fatten their bellies on us!"

"Noooo…!"

"We don't want traitors to sell Bosnia to the infidels!"

"Nooooooo…!"

And this word, which apparently suited the crowd's temper and mood best, caught on with lightning speed and the men kept repeating it furiously, in a quickening rhythm, not even listening to what their leader was saying.

"Noooooo!"

In this fashion they reached the Residence. Here the shooting increased and the whine of sharp bullets could be heard. Most of the shouting was against the two hated pashas.

Hearing the running fire and the noise, the frightened Mazhar Pasha promised the deputation all they had asked if only they would go out and calm the mob. And indeed, when the deputies walked out, the crowd began to subside and go home. But the more restive among them marched around the Residence and gathered in front of the army riding school. There the yelling was confined to protests against Veli Pasha, and the mob called for the disbanding of the Bosnian battalion and demanded that the people be supplied with arms.

In the large balconied haíl that sometimes served for receptions and celebrations, Veli Pasha was sitting with his adjutant, Major Saffet, silently puffing at his *narghile*. When earlier that morning the Governor had asked him to come and attend the deputation, he had declined. Now he sat as if he didn't hear the yelling of the mob. His face was pale, and the lesion on his left cheek had turned purple. To the excited Ismet Pasha Uzunić, commander of the Travnik garrison, who kept asking what was to be done, he replied that everything needful had been taken care of. Ismet offered to go out and pacify the crowd, and wanted to know what to tell them.

"Tell them that I have hauled out my field guns, that my cavalry is ready, and that at the first attempt to enter the barracks I shall order fire."

Whereupon Uzunić did something unexpected. It was an instance of that sudden and unpremeditated bravery that appears in ambitious men when their vanity overcomes both their fear and their common sense. He ordered that the gates be opened and rode out to face the astonished mob. He was in parade uniform, on a white horse, with a drawn sword in his hand; behind him rode two other officers. Taking advantage of the crowd's momentary astonishment, he began to tell them how the Sultan's eye never closed but kept a steady watch on security abroad and on the internal peace of the state, and how they, although acting in the best of faith, would make a terrible mistake if they tried to anticipate the Emperor's thoughts and outbrandish the Emperor's sword. Here, somehow, he managed to

weave in an obscure victory of his in a skirmish on
Black River, and mentioned the ancient glory of the
Sarailis, and requested them to disperse and wait for the
Sultan's call.

Since none of their leaders were present, the crowd
faltered and started to go away. Breathless with excitement, Uzunić came back to the hail where, without having changed their postures, the Pasha and Major Saffet
were smoking. He wanted to boast of his success and
tried several times to recount his speech, but the Pasha
maintained a stony silence and didn't wish to show even
with a glance that he was listening.

A couple of days after this incident—it was a Sunday,
the last day in June—Governor Mazhar Pasha convened
the Council.

Forty-two of the city's leaders took off their sandals
on the steps in front of the Residence, and sat down,
according to their years and rank, in the great hail. No
one spoke, save for an exchange of greetings. At the
head of the hail sat Mazhar Pasha, even sallower than
usual, full of high-sounding, empty words; and indeci-
sive as always. On his right was Kostan Pasha, a tall and
sickly Armenian, his face set, as always, in an expression
of grave and tense attention; on the left was Veli Pasha,
and right next to him sat Brigadier Ismet Pasha Uzunić,
fat, red-faced, looking pleased with himself.

After a lengthy and undistinguished introduction, the
Governor admitted that he had called them in order to
give them "grave and fateful news," namely, that yesterday the Austrian consul had informed him that at a
meeting in Berlin it had been decided that Austria

should occupy Bosnia, "perhaps even Herzegovina," and that Turkey had agreed to it.

In the back rows loud muttering was heard. The Vizier, who never once in his life had spoken a single truth, clear and whole, began, as if alarmed by his own words, to modify and soften them with the statement that this was only a consul's advice and that he had received no information of any kind from Istanbul; rather than make any decisions now, they should discuss possible courses of action in an emergency and meanwhile pacify the common folk.

The muttering grew louder, and out of it rose the voice of Hadji Hafiz Kaukdžić. He had a pink face set in a short, thick, and pitch-black beard, and pudgy white hands like a woman's, and these provided a strange contrast to his booming voice and ever-burning, severe eyes. There hadn't been a vizier in Sarajevo in the last fifteen years with whom he had not clashed and whom he had not accused of slackness; and he never let pass a meeting of the Council without making a speech against the neglect of religious precepts and against dangerous concessions to the Christian populace. In talking to him, everyone chose his words and took care not to provoke and anger him. Many could still remember one such Council meeting some ten odd years ago, in which it was debated whether or no to allow Christians to install bells in their churches and to ring them in towns where there were Turks. One young Osmanli, a scribe of the Governor's, maintained that they could do so without infringing on the laws of the holy Koran. Hadji Hafiz, quoting from a huge book, argued that they couldn't and that no

Muslim should live in a town where "bells were banging." The scribe cited his reasons, the sputtering Hadji
Hafiz his own, meanwhile bristling more and more at
his opponent. At the end of it all, in front of the Governor and the whole assembly, he whacked him with that
book over the head so hard that the frail scribe had to
be splashed with water and doused with sherbet before
he came to himself.

Now, also, Hadji Hafiz spoke at great length about
the jeopardy of Islam, about enemies within the land
and without. Glaring steadily at Veli Pasha and at
Uzunić, he demanded that the "Sultan's generals carry
out those things for which they are appointed, and
which the Faith and the Sultan ask of them," and that
they equip and mobilize the army and organize popular
resistance.

He was abetted in this by the hodjas and poorer members; the wealthier and more distinguished ones sat still,
with an air of inscrutable dignity. The assembly was particularly eager to hear the words of Mustaj Bey Fadilpašić,
a portly and ambitious nobleman who sat at the head of
the hail. Ordinarily, he would go around like a goatskin
full of laughter, always spouting jokes and epigrams, and
shrewdly hiding behind them what he really thought, or
what he didn't know. But now even he sat in worried silence; the fat on him was quiescent, and only the cunning
small eyes on the full pink face never ceased flitting.

After the Governor had spoken briefly, there was an
embarrassed silence, interrupted by Ismet Pasha Uzunić,
whose disjointed sentences didn't make much sense. He
was followed by Kostan Pasha the Armenian who, like

all clever and timid people, seemed to be torn between his timidity and his irrepressible wit and could not come to a realistic conclusion.

There was another pause; one heard only the mumbling of those in the last rows, and the fidgeting and rasping of Hadji Hafiz. At that point the governor himself looked across at Veli Pasha, but the latter was gazing fixedly through the windows, at Bakia, where white summer clouds were peering over the hilltops. Mazhar Pasha cleared his throat.

"Esteemed effendis, let us hear the opinion of the military commander."

At that Veli Pasha turned slowly in his direction and began talking without any preliminaries.

"Honorable Vizier, you will understand that I cannot explain to these people and to this overwrought hodja"—and here he pointed to Hadji Hafiz and waved at the Council, then at once turned back to Mazhar Pasha, not bestowing another glance at Hadji Hafiz during the rest of his short speech—"I cannot, as I say, begin to explain what the army needs, and what the imperial army can and should do. This is neither their business, nor would they understand it…"

This created an uproar, in which Hadji Hafiz was again most vociferous. When the voices quieted down, Veli Pasha finished his speech: In the defense of the country he would undertake only what was ordered by his superiors in Istanbul, and he would put down all meddling by the bazaar in military affairs, and all rebellion, with guns and cavalry. That was all—and nothing could again budge him out of his immobility.

Once more Mazhar Pasha held forth in long, learned sentences of which less than half of the assembly understood every other word; but if his oratory did not salve their souls with its lengthiness and vacuity, at least it wore them out. The Governor wound up the meeting by saying that they should await clear orders from Istanbul, and until such time try and quell the excitement of the people.

Meanwhile, the majority of the assemblymen were more inclined to rebellion than pacification. The insulting words of Veli Pasha had veered the undecided ones, whose number was always great, to Hadji Hafiz and the malcontents. They were now in the majority and were plotting, by signs and whispers, to organize another meeting that same evening. The few beys and wealthier men who were not for drastic measures seemed anxious to get home as quickly as possible, and avoided giving any opinions or promises. As they were leaving, only Salih-aga Šahinagić, a rich and reputable man, known for his sincerity, generosity, and honesty, spoke his thoughts aloud:

"You are a learned man," he said to Hadji Hafiz, "and you know that in all things the leaders have to be ahead of the people, and that without it there's nothing. How could loafers and riff-raff make war on their own? That has never happened, and never can."

Still excited, Hadji Hafiz interrupted him and again said something about the ruin of Islam.

"But I too can see, my dear Hadji Hafiz," Šahinagić went on, "that there's nothing good in the air as long as the imperial army and the beys sit on their haunches

297

while refugees from Nikšić, naked and barefoot, stomp and brawl around Sarajevo, and coopers and gut cleaners take it into their heads to recruit an army. I simply wonder at you and those monastics of yours. Where do you get your confidence? What are you thinking of? May the Allah help us!"

Not deigning to reply to him, and surrounded by a throng of men who shared his views, Hadji Hafiz was concerned only with one thing—to arrange a decisive meeting with Hadji Lojo and Muhammad Effendi Hadžijamaković, which would depose the Vizier and all Turkish authority and put together an insurgent government.

So ended the session of the Council that marked the beginning of rebellion, and decided the fate of the girl from Logavina Street.

Some days previously—when the Turkish merchants had sought an audience with Mazhar Pasha and complained about the grave situation, about the Bosnian army units, and the danger from the Christian riff-raff, or from a certain Christian country—they had, without mentioning names, hinted at two leading culprits, Kostan Pasha, an Armenian and thus a Christian, and Veli Pasha, a despot and drunkard who cared nothing for the security of the land. Even then Mazhar had telegraphed the High Porte, demanding the recall of both. Now, after the last meeting, he telegraphed again insisting that at least Veli Pasha be removed. As it happened, this telegram crossed another one from Istanbul, in which Veli Pasha was recalled and replaced by Hafiz Pasha, who was supposed to arrive any day from Novi

Pazar. Mazhar Pasha breathed a sigh of relief. He perked up even more when he saw that Veli Pasha had taken the news calmly and was all set to depart at once with no intention of interfering in Bosnian affairs. He wouldn't even wait for Hafiz Pasha's arrival; he knew that "desk officer," and "diplomat on a horse" quite well. When told about the squadrons of horse which the new commander-in-chief was bringing with him, he only smiled and told Mazhar Pasha:

"If he brings more than twenty mounted men, I will personally groom all his horses for a whole year. You'll see."

From Friday till Tuesday, Veli Pasha made his preparations for departure. He visited all the consuls, but made a point of spending more time with the English. Among local people, he took leave only from Hadji Mulaga Merhemić and from the Mullah Suleiman Jakubović, in the latter's own cell.

At home everything was being moved and packed, but Mara continued to come every evening as before. The Pasha said nothing, and she dared not inquire. At night she got even less sleep than before, fretting and asking herself what had happened and what was to become of her. She understood nothing of what was going on. During the day she listened fearfully, as to a distant echo, to the clamor of the mob that gathered in the city below, and at night to the shooting and calls of the sentries as they mustered and changed. She realized that Sarah and the inmates were getting ready for a journey. All this merely deepened her dread and bewilderment.

It was only on Monday afternoon that Veli Pasha spoke of his departure for the first time. The house was already completely dismantled and it echoed with a hollow sound. That afternoon, he was sitting as usual on the glazed verandah, in the draft, wearing his lounging clothes, when she came in, as she did every day, shut the door, and sat in his lap. It was only after he had smoked his *narghile* to the end, and after an exchange of small talk (during which her ear was cocked tensely to the clatter of the maids' sandals and the creaking of the baskets that the houseboys were roping in the large room on the ground floor) that he told her he was "going away" tomorrow morning, and then promptly passed over it as though it were something trivial and incidental; he started to tell her how she would be "well off," how the house rent had been paid for a whole year, and how he had arranged for her to get whatever she needed in the Merhemić store, and if there was something they didn't have, Mulaga Merhemić would give her the money to buy it elsewhere.

"And if you would rather go back to your father in Travnik, just tell Merhemić. He will make it his business to send you. But no matter what, you won't be too badly off. Until this blows over—and later we'll see…"

Here he paused, as if at a loss for words. She had hung her head low, but the moment he stopped talking she looked up again for fear he might think that she was crying. And until now he had used the word "daughter" only once in addressing her, at the very beginning (the way he used to say, "Shall we, daughter?"), and had made it sound as though it were a slip of the tongue, for from then on he spoke dryly, matter-of-factly, without changing either his tone of voice or his facial expression. And with all that she neither heard nor understood him; everything that was happening and being said these days she saw and heard as if through a dream; to her, all of it together was one single blow, a blow that took away her breath and sight. Would she still continue to eat and pay for things as if nothing had happened? After all this, was there anything she could still do or say? Here, he was going away, but the shame remained. Taking the horses and servants and the dogs with him, but leaving *her* behind.

Going—leaving behind.

She felt a great emptiness in her breast, something hushed, abruptly stilled, throughout her body. Only two points, in the two temples, beat fast and out of rhythm, misting her vision.

Going—abandoning.

They stood facing each other. He spoke a few words and, holding her left arm, stroked her hair and cheeks briefly, after which he quickly pulled away and clapped his hands. Sarah entered, led her out, and gave her a box with some presents. Resting her hand firmly on Mara's shoulder, Sarah led Mara through the large room downstairs, while Mara, unable to hide her trembling any longer, clutched the box to her body in an unconscious cramp.

One of the houseboys appeared, and they loaded all of her bundled linen on his back. Sarah accompanied her all the way to the courtyard gate, leading her and supporting her, and there kissed her on both cheeks with her thin, cold lips. As in a dream, Mara began to walk down the street, most of which lay in the shade; behind her went Salih, the one who always used to call for her and take her back home, and another young man who, bent low, carried her pillows, a bulging eiderdown, and her house robes. Salih helped her to unlock the door of her cottage and remove the bolt. The porter sat down on the threshold, blew loudly, and untied the carrying rope. The bedding fell open. They put the box next to it on the floor, exchanged glances, greeted her awkwardly, and then vanished.

She looked around the room and, when nothing stirred or made a sound any more, fell first to her knees and then, with all her weight, face down to the floor. The cramp that had tightened her jaws until that moment let up suddenly, followed by a spate of tears that all but choked her. She wanted to cry out, to call a high and sacred name, as she used to when she was a child, but through her lips there came only a howl—drawn out, hoarse, and quaking—and her tears mingled with saliva on her chin. She wanted to catch her breath a little, but the tears welled up again and again, from her very innards and up into her throat, and, choking, she clutched at the bedding with her fingers and upset that box from which baubles scattered in all directions, all the time struggling vainly to utter Our Lady's name.

She remained like this till the following morning. She just managed to drag herself to the window, lean her head against the wall, and close her wakeful eyes. Around her everything lay unpacked and in disorder until Hama the Gypsy arrived at her usual hour.

That same morning Veli Pasha was leaving town. The baggage cart, together with Sarah and the houseboys and maids, had already set out from Bakia at dawn. They were escorted by mounted men. The Pasha meanwhile rode off to the riding school, and there once more inspected his horses and the detachment that was to go with him. As always in the early morning, he was fresh and alert, his eyes sparkled and he talked easily.

The day was well advanced, the people were leaving their houses and the shops were being opened, when the wooden bridge on Čumuria rumbled under the Pasha's horses. There were twelve mounted men all told, and they rode in a long file. At their heads was the Albanian sergeant—major with two buglers; five or six paces behind him came the Pasha, followed immediately by his adjutant, Major Saffet, swarthy and dull-faced; then came three junior officers and, finally, four Albanian horsemen. They were all neatly turned out, fully armed and equipped, with bulging saddlebags and capes folded in tight rolls behind them. Before riding through the narrow Čumuria, the Pasha halted to greet Mullah Sulei-man Jakubović once more.

The day before when he had taken his leave of him, the man had looked pale and oppressed. His usually wrinkled face had been drawn and pinched, and his bright, ever-smiling eyes had had a sad and uncertain look. He was evidently very sick. He hadn't complained about anything, but had spoken about the "transience of things," about death, and the vanity of this world. When the Pasha mentioned his departure, he had become upset.

303

"All of you are quitting! To whom will you leave Sarajevo, and us in the boiling cauldron? Off you go, each on his own, and may Benevolent Allah grant you ever good, but we here can't look forward to anything good any more. We've become heathen, at loggerheads with each other. Now we're waiting to see who'll come from beyond the borders to set us aright and baptize us!"

"But the beys are debating in the Council and Hadji Lojo is collecting an army," Veli Pasha had said with a smile.

"That's just it—the time of the Hadji Lojo has come! In the good old days they went around in chains and pounded stone—they didn't sit in council or recruit armies. But then, I suppose, if one just lived long enough, one might see the end of them too. They'll shout a bit, fire a shot or two, then run home to their wives, who'll lock them up in the storeroom. And should the Austrians remain in Sarajevo even a couple of years, they'll be the first ones to put hats on their heads and scramble for crucifixes and stuff themselves with pork. Ah, my good Veli Pasha, there's hardly a man left here any more, just hungry ragtag and bobtail, and greedy beys. Now each one will have his fling, and as for us, dear friend, what has been— has been."

And lowering his voice as in prayer, he had recited Ibn Abass's prophecy about the terrible "last times when the heart of the true believer shall melt as the salt melts in water, and nothing shall be of any avail."

This morning, too, Mullah Suleiman sat on his narrow window sill, and when he saw the Pasha, he rose to greet him. The Pasha reined in his horse and gave him a military salute; and after he had ridden past and turned the corner, Mullah Suleiman remained standing like that and prayed with open palms, asking Allah to "help and protect this traveler, a true Muslim and man of noble heart."

They rode on through Tašlihan and Predimaret. Most of the shops were still closed, especially those belonging to Christians and Jews. Here and there a Turk was squatting in his shopwindow, but the merchandise had not yet been arrayed on the window shelves, and was inside the shop, so that, if it proved necessary, the place could be shut in a hurry. In Baš Bazaar, there were some bread and sweetmeat vendors and a crowd of loiterers, and they all turned to look at the horsemen who rode slowly and solemnly as in a parade. In the Coopers' Market a few hammers could be heard, and from Green Maidan, where the troops used to assemble daily, came a growing murmur and muffled yelling. It was impossible to make out what they were shouting; one could only hear occasional single voices and the answering roar of acclaim from the mob— a drawn-out chorus that hovered above the town, waxing and waning one after another.

"A-a-a-a-a!"

Riding up through the Kovači, they slowed down and their horses came closer together. Gripping the back of his saddle, the Pasha swiveled around and spoke to Saffet in an undertone:

"The Austrians will pound them into the ground, and I'm only sorry it won't be me who'll do it."

They kept climbing and the city gradually spread itself out beneath them, with its blue smoke above the houses and thin mist above the plum orchards, and

every few moments the air shook with the cheering of
the insurgents.

"A-a-a-a-a..."

They rode out beyond the Višegrad Gate. In a green
sward beside a spring some ten armed Turks were sitting
on the grass. They were insurgent pickets. The sight of
the horsemen threw them into confusion and set them
whispering. A few rose to their feet; the brass-edged
butts of their new Winchester rifles flashed in the sun.
Thus they glared, without saying anything, until the
horsemen rode past.

The city disappeared from view, all sounds faded
away. In the peace of the morning, all that was heard
were the gurgling of springs and the cascade of
Mošćanica Brook in the gullies. The path was straight
and soft, partially vaulted by sagging oaks and trees of
late-ripening pears Acorns, still green, lay on the ground
and burst under the horses' hoofs. They halted by a
spring to water the animals. Way down below they could
see the last tiny Sarajevo café, carved into a steep slope.
On the clearing in front of it were sprawled several men,
beside their cartridge belts, rifles and, presumably,
brandy cups hidden in the grass, for they were obviously
drinking—another good-for-nothing insurgent picket
that had sought haven here, for the insurgent government in the city had prohibited all drinking, vagabond-
age, and loitering. A couple of the men were holding a
red bitch for a shaggy dark-haired dog that was hopping
around her, and were having their coarse soldiers' fun.
Seen from that height, the spectacle had something particularly loathsome and unnatural about it; perhaps be-

cause at that distance one could not hear their voices
and guffaws, and it seemed as if they were going
through their motions in complete silence and dead se-
riousness.

The officers talked quietly among themselves, scoff-
ing at this Bosnian army engaged in mating dogs. The
Pasha was quiet. The morning was well advanced and, as
always, he was beginning to lose his feeling of freshness
and to succumb to his habitual ill-humor. He grew more
and more irritable. As the sun rose higher, it seemed to
him that the gloom and bitterness within him were also
waxing. Words came harder to him, and lifting his lids
needed more effort.

The path rose again and became stonier. The sun began to burn; the path heaved upward more violently.
The horses snorted and sweated. Thrashing their tails,
they picked their foothold gingerly and slipped every
few seconds on the smooth stone, sending up sparks
with their hoofs.

Two of the officers began to curse, mopping their
sweaty faces.

"Fuck their sisters and their Bosnia! What kind of a
country is this! You climb and climb and break your feet
like you were trying to reach the sky, and when you get
to the top, there's nothing! More rocks and mountains!"

"Phew! A foul country!"

And they would fall silent again and ride on, sullen
under the broiling sun.

3

On the same day that Veli Pasha went away, Mara moved to Baba Anuša's house in Bistrik.

Earlier in the morning, when Hama had arrived and found her weeping and disconsolate beside her scattered linen, she had barely managed to raise her up and force her to wash her face and take hold of herself. The good-hearted Gypsy even cried herself, as, at the slightest provocation, do those women who have worn themselves out with hard work and frequent child-bearing. And, through her own tears, she comforted the girl with countless petty and contradictory lies: how the Pasha might come back; how she would go to her father in Travnik; how she would get married and settle down quietly here in Sarajevo; how she was young, pretty, and fresh as a dewdrop; how she still had Baba Anuša, and herself, Hamša.

"A-a-ah, if I were your age I'd do nothing but sing and dance."

In the end she managed to persuade Mara to change and go with her to Baba Anuša's, where, if she felt like it, she might stay for a few days to calm herself and recover a little; while she, Hamša, would look after the cottage.

After midday, she set out with Hamša and her youngest son, who carried her bundle. As they were crossing the Miljacka by the Latin Bridge, they met some armed Turks marching briskly. She bowed her head in fear and her eyes fell on the shallow, pea-colored water and on the small pebbles at its bottom; the sight made her yearn for a whirlpool that would swallow her up without a trace.

They found Baba Anuša in tears, and the house full of women. Under a threadbare quilt whose stuffing was falling apart, lay her grandchild, a girl of about ten. In a corner sat a small grandson, slightly younger, with a big belly, gnawing on a wet cob of cooked corn. Because both her son and daughter-in-law had died last winter, within two months of each other, Baba Anuša had taken the children into her house. She had always been fond of tippling, but since the death of her only son she had become a complete drunkard. Her poverty prevented her from buying as much plum brandy as she needed, so she bought a cheap spirit in the bazaar and melted her own sugar and made a kind of drink that was called *sagrdan*. She ate hardly any food, but walked around the house all day with pouchy eyes, her head tied in a kerchief. She neglected the children, with the result that they spent their days loafing in the streets, coming home only to sleep. This was particularly true of the girl, who had freckled cheeks and a hint of something cunning and brash in her eyes, and was developed beyond her years.

That was how yesterday, already in the early morning, she had gone out to mope around the refuse heaps and steal fruit from other people's gardens. Dressed in a long shirt of coarse calico, she had separated from the other children and sauntered to the top of Bistrik. The streets were deserted and all house gates shut, as people stayed indoors on account of the rebellion. There she met two young men. One was Salčin, from Bistrik, an epileptic and a thug, pock-marked, burly, with a crippled left arm and a forehead that was always bruised. The second was from another district, a slim youngster, well dressed, strapped in a massive cartridge belt, and armed. When he saw the girl, the epileptic called out "Hey little one!"

Standing by a fence, she watched him without batting her eyes, rubbing one foot against the other, and she did not move. He then produced from his sash a big lump of sugar and showed it to her.

"Come here and I'll give it to you."

Glancing from the sugar to his face and back again, she came on slowly, holding four fingers of her left hand flat against her mouth. But as she approached, he backed away up the street. She faltered, with distrust in her eyes and movements. He stopped, too, and stretched his hand out even more.

"Here's the sugar. Here."

Seeing that she did not stir, he took out of his shirt a heavy black key and, with its heavier top part, knocked off a small piece of the sugar. She came up gingerly, like a magpie, and took it. As she bit on it and crunched it, she kept gazing at them. When she was finished, the epileptic held out his hand again.

"Here's some more."

The girl approached, and he backed away, only to halt again and knock off another few morsels and give them to her. So he lured her, as one lures a stubborn ewe with corn. The other young man walked by his side a few paces away, glancing around him every few moments. In this way they finally reached Berkuša, where there were no houses but only a deserted stone quarry, now overgrown with nightshade and thistles.

Salčin climbed a stone mound, from which a part of Sarajevo could be seen. The other young man stood in a ditch below him. The girl alternately looked behind her and then lifted her greedy eyes toward Salčin, who squatted on an overgrown rock and held the sugar in his hand. He broke off one more lump and she came closer to take it, but as it was too far up, the second young man reached for it and gave it to her. And as she stood there with her mouth still full of sugar, he threw himself on her, pulled her down and vanished with her in the undergrowth of the ditch. At first nothing was heard but the scraping of the gravel and the creaking of his bandolier; but very soon the girl began to sob, then scream and call for help. He must have clapped his hand over her mouth, for the screams were muffled and came intermittently.

Salčin meanwhile continued to crouch on his rock. His mouth was agape; the calves of his legs, on which he was squatting with the full weight of his body, twitched and trembled. He remained like this for a long time, staring wide-eyed into the hole under him. All of a sudden his eyes glazed over, he let out a dull, smacking sound, threw out his arms and fell into the ditch beside them. From down below one could hear the noise of his gagging and of his trashing legs. The little girl had fallen completely silent.

When, some time later, the other young man reappeared in the sun, his face was blanched, his knees and elbows coated with brown soil. He put on his cartridge belt and dusted himself off, then went back into the hole and pulled out Salčin, who put an arm around his shoulders to support himself. There was blood on his, nose, his lips were blue and twisted, the hair matted, and on his chest were specks of froth and saliva. He had trouble breathing and his eyes lolled helplessly; he could barely drag one foot behind the other. Thus they vanished among the houses.

The sun rose higher, flooding the quarry and the weed-tufted pits with ever more light. In the hollow of that ditch, the girl lay on trampled grass and torn earth. Her shirt was pulled back over her head, and her child's body, resembling a small object, squashed and lifeless, seemed of a piece with the sharp, near-white rocks basking in the sun. Above it the flies were buzzing. In the sun-drugged silence one could hear how, in the city down below, the mobs were rumbling and threatening and how from time to time hundreds of voices blended into a long, indistinct cheer:

"A-a-a-a!"

That afternoon Baba Anuša, having waited long and vainly with her lunch, sat down to eat with her grandson. The boy sipped the thin broth with a good deal of noise, but refused to eat the barley bread, which was hard and leathery, made of a coarse-sifted flour and full of prickly chaff. To tempt him, the old woman crumbled the bread into the soup and, using a spoon, quashed it into pulp at the bottom of the bowl.

"This is how a Turk sinks in hell, there!"

The little one liked the game; he helped his grandmother and pressed piece after piece to the bottom of the bowl, then fished them out and ate them mashed like that. Occupied thus with the child and the meal, Anuša never even heard the steps on the stairway. The door suddenly flew open and people brought in the little girl.

She had been found unconscious by some Gypsy women from Berkuša who had gone to gather wood, and the district clerk had recognized the child and ordered them to take her home. Now she lay wrapped in wet rags soaked with vinegar, and did not regain consciousness. She was full of blue bruises, mumbled deliriously and from time to time moved her arms, but from the waist down her body was numb and stiff, as if paralyzed.

The women came and went, shed tears of sympathy with Baba Anuša, debated among themselves, but not one of them knew what to do. A few suggested getting some medicine from the Jew at Predimaret, others recommended calling a doctor, while a third group was all for calling a priest, or reporting the matter to the authorities. Outside, in the city, there was open insurrection; the stores were shuttered, the officials had run away, and Lord alone knew where the priest and the doctor were hiding. Everything was cut off, left to its own devices, and everyone felt helpless.

Mara stood by the oven and looked about her in bewilderment and fear. They were all busy with the little girl, and no one seemed even to notice her.

In the end, after a long and futile palaver, the women left. It had grown dark, but no one thought of lighting the candles. The little boy had fallen asleep in his corner, with an uneaten crust of bread in his fingers. Baba Anuša was sitting in the middle of the room and, with practiced movements, preparing her drink, decanting it from one pot into another. The room filled with an acrid and unpleasant smell, as from sour bread. Lying cramped on a narrow, hard sofa in the dark, Mara could make out the quilt that covered the little girl and which was silhouetted against the window as round, still mound. Thus she fell asleep.

She woke up some time at night. The room was bathed in moonlight. The old woman was still sitting in the middle of the room, with a compress on her head, but she was strangely animated, rocking and flailing around her with her arms. She took off her compress every other moment and soaked it in water, while mumbling some disjointed and meaningless words.

"Bless and cross, bless and cross."

She put on and took off compress after compress in this manner, and then all at once she would begin to sway her upper body and sing in a low voice:

"My Jesu-u-us, sweetness mine!"

Tongue-tied and chilled by fear, Mara listened to the whispering and watched the demented movements. She could not understand anything, but felt that something ugly and dreadful was being done here; it was again as if a rite were being offered to something that was evil, something that struck numbness and terror into one. She could not sleep, and dared not reveal her presence. And she made up her mind to flee as soon as dawn came.

Before the women started to gather again, and before Baba Anuša had sobered up, Mara stole away with her bundle and ran down to Bistrik. There were no women in the streets. In front of the huge building of the Austrian consulate there was a row of carriages guarded by armed horsemen. She set off in the opposite direction, staying close to the shuttered stores. As she reached the bottom of Bistrik and was about to pass by the military riding school, she heard a clamor and, from the top of the little knoll on which she happened to be standing, saw a large crowd of people below her. In the center of Atmaidan, the corpse of a Turkish officer lay on its back. His uniform was in tatters, his chest bared; around it was a litter of torn-up papers, a sword sheath, a fez. Cursing and swarming around the corpse like wasps, angry insurgents were kicking its flanks and groin. Mara quickly averted her head and set off in another direction, toward the Latin Bridge. There, still trembling from what she had just seen, she looked once more at the yellowish water with its pebbled bottom and decided at last to do what she had contemplated during the night as she lay on the hard sofa at Baba Anuša's: to go to see Fra Gregory. To do what was hardest and most terrible, and thus forestall every other evil.

In the Latin Quarter everything was quiet. She knocked on the door by the side of the church; but for a long while there was no answer. Eventually, from the adjoining house, an old woman shuffled out, led her into her own courtyard, and from there, by way of two small doors, one through a fence, the other through a wall, they came into the courtyard of the Franciscans.

Here the gravel was white, the hedges trimmed. The old crone led her tip a steep stairway, and they found themselves in the spacious reception hall, draped with curtains of white cloth. Suddenly Mara saw Fra Gregory before her, and she faltered, not letting the bundle out of her hands. He was walking diagonally across the hall with a brisk and firm step, and held an open breviary in his left hand.

He walked to and fro several more times, as if not seeing her; while she remained stock-still, with a single thought in her head: This was it—that most terrible thing! Finally he stopped, closed the breviary with a snap, and turned to her.

This is it, the most terrible thing, she kept thinking as she looked at him and saw, as if through a mist, his clenched knuckles rapping the breviary, his spreading arms and the agitated whipping of his white waist cord and heavy rosary, and his eyes boring into her, brown, cutting, implacable beneath their thick brows.

"Do you know what you are now in the eyes of God and in the eyes of Christian folk? Dung, dung, full of stench and maggots!"

He thundered on, telling her how with her own hand she had reopened all the wounds of Jesus, which had already healed, how she'd made Our Lady weep, spat on the cross and the Holy Host. He glared at her, terrifyingly close. And before those eyes and words she felt as if all of her were shriveling and whittling away, as if there were no ground under her, as if before so much shame her body were disappearing, melting away, existing only in her consciousness, like a dark spot that no amount of effort or pain could wash out.

So she swooned and foundered more and more, as in a miasma, in this thought of damnation and eternal punishment that was the ultimate solution, almost some kind of a respite. And when she thought the end of everything had come, he startled her and rallied her once more with words about the Savior's endless mercy, which was greater than all the sins of mankind, greater than all evil and shame. He spoke about a long penance, about contrition and forgiveness; yet even then his eyes did not become milder, or his words softer. And this penance appeared to her so harsh and inaccessible, and she herself so helpless, that it seemed to her it would be easier to sink utterly in that darkness of damnation and punishment than to think, say, or do anything. But the friar kept darting around her, lashing her with words, and jolting her out of her swoon.

"If you were to bathe the church crucifix with your tears year after year, and live on bread and water, you could not wash away your shame nor make up for the evil you've done."

After which his talk would again take on a vague note of conciliation, which indeed had to come from some quarter, at some time, but which, she felt, was incapable of lifting or comforting her.

She was recalled out of her faint by the rumble and clicking of the clock; a colored Turkish clock, with leaden weights, chimed the hour of noon. Fra Gregory stopped abruptly, knelt down on a *prie-dieu* by the window, crossed himself, and started to pray aloud.

"Hail Mary, full of grace, the Lord is with thee, blessed art thou among women, and blessed is the fruit of thy womb, Jesus..."

When he reached the middle of the prayer, he paused and shouted at her without looking over his shoulder:

"Why aren't you praying? Tell me!"

She obeyed mechanically; took up the prayer and, stammering and swallowing, recited the second half, as was the custom during vespers and vigils.

"Holy Mary—Mother of God—pray for us sinners, now and at the hour of our death."

He joined her once more:

"Receive this servant of our Lord. Let it be as Thou commandest. Ave Maria."

When it was her turn again, she prayed a little more loudly and collectedly. And when in a sharp and clear voice he began the concluding prayer, she felt bold enough to lift her eyes.

Bowed, with a wreath of grizzled hair on his head, his hands clasped around the dark, leather-bound breviary, above the rosary which had pleated itself and become entangled with the white cord of his waist string—he, too, it seemed to her, was doing something mysterious and serving someone, he alone knew whom. This now seemed less unfamiliar and less dreadful, but in its own way just as baffling and upsetting, like those weird night watches of Veli Pasha and Baba Anuša. What was more important—here, too, her soul had been humbled and crushed.

When they had finished praying, he called the housekeeper in a steadier and quieter voice and told her to take the girl to the kitchen. And so she walked out, shivering and stumbling from hunger, from lack of sleep, too much crying, and from utter incomprehension of all that was happening to her.

Fra Gregory also was getting ready to abandon his apartment and seek shelter in some consulate or other. The night before a group of insurgent Turks had looked for him and called his name, but he had hidden himself in the Pamuković house, in the neighborhood. That day also, as soon as the sun went down, he walked over to the Pamukovićes, by way of the garden and through the back fences. There, in conversation with the old Pamuković, he decided finally to move in the next few days over to the French consulate, since the consul, Riveux, a talkative and unusually amiable man and a good Catholic, had offered to give him shelter. The same evening Mara's fate was also decided. She was to come to the house of Pamuković and work there as a maid until the rebellion quieted down and the church could be opened again, so that she might perform her public penance, on a Sunday, during High Mass, in front of the people.

4

The Pamuković houses were not far from the church, in the same Latin Quarter, but close to the edge of it, with the result that they faced in two directions: one toward the Latin Quarter, the other toward Čumuria. There were two of them, whiter and considerably larger than the rest of the homes in the Quarter. The main entrance faced the river Miljacka, and opened into a great courtyard. In the middle of the courtyard grew shrubbery, planted in a rectangle, and within it, at the center, were clusters of small flowers; along the edges of the yard, by the walls, there were evergreens and bushes of a silvery flowering plant called *igda* that gave off a heady and stifling fragrance. Here was the main house of Pamuković, two stories high. Jutting out the entire length of the house, and resting on white pillars, was the large drawing room, its windows painted a pale blue.

Under this main house there was a passage into the second courtyard, which was even bigger, though spread with a coarser gravel, lacking flowers and decorations, where wreaths of onions and drying red peppers hung on the walls. There was the second Pamuković house, smaller and more squat, but just as clean, immaculately whitewashed, with colored windows. At the far end of the yard was a building called the *mutvak,* a simple one-story dwelling containing the kitchen, storerooms, and servants quarters. Behind it, separated by a fence, was a third yard, small, dark, and damp. This was the place for the unloading of hay, wood, fruit, and of everything that the tenants and share-croppers brought in. Stables, too, were there, and vats, barrels, and all kinds of scrap.

All this Mara saw but could hardly register, for her knees were wobbly, her head swam, and her lids drooped from lack of sleep. But one thing she sensed right away: this was a great, splendid, and rich household that could not be compared with anything she had seen thus far; not with the ramshackle house of Alaibegović, nor the half-empty rooms of Veli Pasha, let alone the house of her parents in Dolac or the awful hut of Baba Anuša from which she had fled that morning.

They led her into the kitchen in the last courtyard, where the maids and daughters-in-law were preparing dinner. Here she put her bundle on the floor and stood, like one condemned, by the door jamb. The women studied her with unabashed curiosity. Old Jela was the only one who found a word for her and tried to make her feel less unwanted. When the time came for supper, she sat down with Jela and two other maids at a low, round table. She kept lowering her eyes, misted from shame and lack of sleep, and her hand trembled; and at the same time she was embarrassed before them for not being able to eat, and picked at her plate every now and then, even though she didn't have enough strength either to chew or to swallow. She was relieved when the meal was over and she gathered that she would sleep with Jela in the same room.

She lived through the first few days in a state of wonder and confusion. She helped in the work, both in the kitchen and in the yard, although both Jela and the maids preferred to observe her and question her than to give her work. And she kept pushing and hiding her thick, unruly hair in the kerchief and feeling ashamed of her body. For that reason she liked it best when they gave her a long chore which she could do alone and withdrawn from others; like shelling peas, pleating onion wreaths, or combing wool. Sitting in the corner of a cubicle next to the kitchen, she would then watch the Pamuković house with its lofty drawing room, which was not built of wood and sagging but stately and resting on arches that tapered down to white columns. She tried to imagine how the interior was furnished, what sort of

321

people were they and how they lived. But she rarely saw any of the Pamukovićes; and the less she saw of them and knew them, the better she liked to watch those white columns and windowpanes which were never thrown open and behind which, as it seemed to her, life was better and people were of another kind, the kind that knew no poverty, no misfortune, and no shame.

As time went on, she had the opportunity to see one or the other of the Pamukovićes; but there were many of them, and from those she met she never heard a word or received a smile; they simply walked through the courtyard, or stalked quickly through the drawing room.

That was how she got to know Auntie Andja, sister of the old Pamuković, who had her apartment in the smaller house. She lived there alone, for she had no children, and her husband, Simeon, kept an inn on Kiseljak and only occasionally came to Sarajevo. She was fat and red-faced, with dark pouches under her eyes and incipient wrinkles; she wore shiny loose pantaloons of heavy black satin, which rustled when she walked.

Later she met the two unmarried daughters, and also the daughters-in-law and sons as they chanced to go by. The older daughter was in her late twenties, willowy, rosy-checked like all the Pamukovićes, but past her bloom. The younger was still an adolescent. She still laughed loudly and stammered in her speech; her face was pale, with dark rings under her eyes, and her look restless. Yet she, too, was losing the marks of childhood with each new day and in her gait, visage, and accents, beginning to resemble the other Pamukovićes. The two older daughters-in-law were already like them in every respect. It was strange how they'd taken on all their characteristics: the steady and disdainful gaze, that frosty edge in the voice, the ramrod walk and gestureless speech. Only the third and youngest daughter-in-law was different and a contrast to all the inmates. She was called Nevenka.

One day Mara had a fleeting glimpse of the old woman Pamuković in her drawing room. She was walking slowly, flanked on one side by her younger daughter and on the other by a daughter-in-law; but she was not leaning on them. She was huge, heavy, and could hardly move. Her hair was swaddled in several dark scarves, and her big breasts hung loose in a thin shirt of a silky fabric. The face was laced with red and bluish veins, and bloated with a double row of thick pouches, above which there stared a pair of vacuous, completely round eyes without any lashes.

It was less often that Mara could see the men, who spent their days in the shops, came home late, and went away early. In them, also, as in their womenfolk, one could see that gloomy and ponderous dignity of movement and glance. But Mara believed that those things, like some kind of a shadow, were inseparable from wealth and being a gentleman. And as she combed her wool she continued to muse about their life beyond those windows and columns, full of security, order and dignity, quite different from her own.

Then Jela and the youngest daughter-in-law, Nevenka, took to dropping in and working with her. From their talk and the stories each of them told, the truth about the Pamukovićes begun slowly to dawn on Mara: she learned that they, too were beset with trouble and misfortune, like all the other people she had known till then, like her own mother, Hafizadić, and the old Elias Garić, like Veli Pasha and Baba Anuša—save that they bore it and concealed it in their own fashion. Some of the things the two women told her made her blood run cold, even though frequently the details escaped her, or she happened to listen with half an ear and spent the time thinking about herself. All the same, their long tales and laments made her realize more and more clearly that even behind those big windows and columns life was not good, that this home, too, concealed the same inexpressible thing that was driving her from house to house and tormenting her day and night.

Jela was short but corpulent, with a sallow and puffy face. She was past her fiftieth year, and had never been married. There was some kind of a secret behind this, which, for all her garrulity, she took care to hide. She had served the Pamuković household for thirty-seven years, and now virtually all of it depended on her. Wrapped up to her chin in a great many scarves, in summer and winter alike, she bustled in the kitchen all day long, preparing things and giving orders. At the age of sixteen, she had been seduced by the younger brother of the old Pamuković, an impetuous and beautiful young man who later went abroad and perished somewhere. Since then she had remained in this house, as a maid. Never leaving the kitchen, forever scurrying on the same round of chores, she had withered early and become quite dull. She was in the habit of talking aloud to herself. The Pamukovićes and their household were her whole life and her whole world. She remembered when the old Pamuković had married, when the daughters-in-law had come into the house, when the children and grandchildren were born, when anybody died or was sick. All of them, from the day they were born, had gotten used to her as to an object. She worried about everyone, but nobody worried about her; no one knew whether she ate, slept, or was ill; and if they didn't have to call her, they might have forgotten her name too. In her talks with Nevenka and Mara, she spoke of the Pamukovićes and their lot as of some evil that could not be changed, and which had to be put up with.

Much more alert and eloquent was the daughter-in-law Nevenka. Mara found it hard and unpleasant to look into her fevered black eyes, and talked to her always with a certain sense of unquiet and fear. She was, indeed, not afraid of her, but of the Pamukovićes. And Nevenka, in turn, connived to remain alone with her more and more often, and told her increasingly detailed stories about herself and about the family.

Frail, pallid, brisk in her walk, Nevenka loved to talk, yet always took care to lower her voice when one of the Pamukovićes approached. A poor girl, daughter of a mason, she had come to this house against her will. No one, including herself, knew how it came about that the youngest Pamuković boy saw her in church one Sunday and promptly fell in love with her, or how he managed to overcome his parents' objections and bring her to the house as his bride. She was childless in the first two years, and became pregnant only this past spring; she was now in her sixth month. In that same little room behind the kitchen where Mara combed wool, they had furnished an apartment for Nevenka, in which she now wove cloth for her baby. She was preparing a swaddling outfit, and humming all day long. The song was typical of women at work; neither the tune nor the words had a beginning or an end. When the yarn snapped or the shuttle stuck, the song would cease too; as soon as the shuttle moved again and the loom clattered on, the song was resumed, in faster time. When she got bored with it or her back began to ache, she left off work, sat down next to Mara and, while combing the wool, started to talk: of how she got married, of how she had lived these last two years in the Pamuković household as a barren woman, and so forth. The wool crackled and scraped, the teeth of the carding comb chattered, and Mara, with her chin on her chest, listened as she singled out and dwelt, with a certain bitter satisfaction, on the ugliest and most shocking incidents of her married life. Mara was terrified by what she heard, and even more by the thought of having to hear something more dreadful yet. She would have given anything if the young woman had suddenly burst out laughing and told her, chortling, that none of it was true, but only a horrible tale. And still the daughter-in-law talked and talked, and interrupted herself only from time to time, when she burst into tears. Since her hands were in the wool, she did not wipe her tears but simply averted her head, so that the tears streamed soundlessly to the floor. At those moments the embarrassed Mara bowed her head even lower, while the young woman, having cried herself out, would go on with her story.

The tale Nevenka told was this: After they had seen each other in front of the church two or three times, young Nikola Pamuković had come with his father and old Matan Boštor to ask her hand in marriage. It was the afternoon of Annunciation Day. When the suitors had departed, her mother, who had been ailing for several years, called her to her bedside and embraced her. Although her legs were paralyzed and she lay motionless on her pillow, the mother spoke with her usual calm and an unwavering strength in her voice and eyes.

"Child, I'm not giving you away so that you will have it good and easy, but because it's fated like this, you understand. That house is hard and wicked. You will not starve for bread but for a good word and a kind look. Still, you must go through with it, and a time will come when you'll tuck them all in your waist sash. You won't have it worse than I had it with your father. Be obedient to them and look after your husband, but hold your own. If things ever get bad and you really can't go on any more, you know where our doors are."

Then she kissed her on both cheeks and on the hair, and made a quick sign of the cross over her, as if forestalling danger. And the girl was on her knees by the bed, in her light pantaloons and dark waistcoat—frail, tiny, her head lowered. She did not cry, but she was pale and clenched her teeth with an effort, so that her chin would not tremble.

In the next few days the usual formalities and courtesies were exchanged, all rather hasty and lacking spontaneity, as when a rich house condescends to receive a poor mason's daughter. Four weeks later, she was mar-

ried at an early Mass and taken to the Pamuković house.
She was received by the sisters-in-law with that cool,
wounding civility peculiar to rich people.

After the wedding, she waited the customary seven
days, not saying anything to anyone, and on the afternoon of the eighth went to her mother, all wrapped up
in shawls and bowed down, accompanied by a maid.
Quietly she entered the house and her mother's room,
but the moment the latter put her arms around her, she
slid to her knees in a fit of sobbing that threatened to
suffocate her. An unexpected, harrowing, and, for that
small body, unbelievable howl filled the room. No matter how much the old woman tried to soothe her, she
could not come to herself, but only beat her face on the
floor and drenched the old carpet with her tears and
spittle. When she calmed down a little, she wanted to get
up, but her mother wouldn't let her and pulled her
closer instead; and as the girl vainly tried to wrench herself free, the old woman loosened her dress and began
to examine her. Then she gave a cry and started to curse.

"Oh God, what did that heathen Turk do to the
child! Oooh, that Pamuković beast! The monster!"

She wailed and cried like this over each bruise she
discovered, while the young one shivered under her fingers, tiny and naked like a shorn sheep. They remained
together till sundown, and then the old woman called
the Pamuković maid.

"Go home and tell your mistress and Auntie Andja
that we have no one but this one child, and that I
thought I was marrying her into a Christian house, not
to a brigand. And if their son wants his wife, let him

come for her, so I can ask him where he learned to break a poor mite's bones."

And her large, shiny face blazed in the evening light.

He came the very next day, looking pale, and left looking even paler, leading his wife behind him. And so Nevenka returned and stayed among the Pamukovićes as a "domestic enemy," a secret adversary and a mute victim. In the course of time, that flight of hers was forgotten. She went to visit her mother only on Sundays, and by no means regularly. She began to help in the housework and gradually got to know the Pamukovićes, and their home, and the life in it. This became for her a source of many miseries, which not only gave no sign of diminishing but gave rise to new anguish.

From the day they had brought in her dowry chest— cheap, gaudy, brass-shod, and secured with linchpins— and placed it among their furniture, which was bulky, dark, and without a touch of brightness or color, she had always felt before them, and before every one of their things, a sense of shame that gnawed at her very innards, but this she would never admit or show to any-one. She saw their strength in all they did and said, and saw that everything on them and around them was theirs, grand and fine. Yet she couldn't bring herself to give them credit for anything. All through the day, and even at night, she mentally quarreled, with them and made comparisons; and this need to compare herself with them ate at her, consumed her, and never quite left her. Yet, racking and torturing herself in this way, she slowly got to know the Pamukovićes, and learned many new and terrible things.

She saw that they wronged everyone, gave quarter to
no man, that they liked no one, and were hated by the
whole world, even though the house was frequented by
the town notables and the priests. They fought even
among themselves, though with "silent gunpowder," as
the saying went, and the daughters and the in-laws stole
from each other, dickered, and taunted one another long
after the lights went out at night. She learned that the
old Pamuković sometimes stayed up till dawn over his
ledgers and accounts, arguing with his eldest son, so that
throughout the next day he would be incapable of
touching anything except coffee and tobacco. She saw
that each of them, on reaching a certain age, developed
an open wound on his leg or arm, and secretly bathed
and salved it nights. That was the reason they tried to
marry off their young early. She learned that the old
woman Pamuković had seizures almost every month,
that she locked herself in her room, allowing no one to
come in, and howled and raved and threw herself on the
floor, and afterwards lay in bed five to six days, moaning
like someone mortally ill. She saw a great many hidden
evils, until one night there was revealed to her, in all its
terror and beyond a vestige of doubt, "the thing about
Simeon."

He was Auntie Andja's husband. In her fortieth year,
she had felt a passion for him and had married him; he
was her third husband. Born at Travnik, he was considerably younger than she, of a sallow complexion, a loafer
and blasphemer who drank night and day all over Sarajevo and the outlying suburbs. She loved him as only
women in her years can—morbidly, maternally, uncon-

ditionally. She concealed and glossed over his outbursts, and gave him money for fresh carousals.

One night Simeon came home in such an uproar that it was impossible to hide it. He babbled and kept crashing to the floor like a piece of timber. Sprawled on the ground, he rolled his eyes, his face alternately yellow and ashen, and babbled on even as they tried to hush him and raise him up.

"Oh, oh, pray to God! Make an offering of holy salt! I met a Turk in Ferhadia—squint-eyed, with crinkly hair, in a hansom cab. Black horses and black driver—black, the lot of them. Get into the hansom, Simeon, says he. But I didn't feel like it. Come on, get in, sit down. So I get in. And he breaks into a gallop right away…"

Here Simeon twisted to one side and scraped the floor with his forehead.

"Oh, oh! He rides and rides, till we come to Miljacka. Then up and over the dam and right into the river! I yell and try to stand up, all for nothing. And he gets me across to Čumuria—more dead than alive! Then he disappears, with his cab—into the thin air!"

And again he beat his forehead on the ground and shook in his whole body, while the women sprinkled water and made signs of the cross over him, whispering prayers, coming and going on tiptoes, humming like bees.

"Save us, Virgin!"

"Immaculate Mother!"

And Nevenka, paling and shivering from the cold, from interrupted sleep and fear, watched it all from her window. And in all that horror and disgrace she could

not help noticing the fine pleating on Simeon's pantaloons and the elegant way in which his embroidered
shirt sleeves settled around his bloodless wrists; and
how slender and handsome the sisters-in-law looked in
their thin nightshirts of silken cloth.

Some time after this, the Apparition began to follow
Simeon to the very gate of the courtyard. Jela told her
that she had seen It with her own eyes, that It was really a
Turk, cross-eyed and frizzle-haired, with his fez askew
and his left eye half shut. Nevenka thought about It all
day long; and her sleep became fitful from so much
thinking and fear. She would wake up suddenly during
the night and listen to Andja and the other Pamuković
women struggling over Simeon as over a fallen soul. The
Apparition tugged at his brocade waistcoat to get him out
of the courtyard, calling him back to more revelry, and
the women pulled him back into the yard. Andja was the
boldest. She swung at It with her rosary and its crucifix,
using it like a whip, cursing in a shrill and choked voice.

"Away, infidel scum, leave my man alone! In the
name of Holy Trinity, don't touch this baptized soul!
Back to hell with you, devil!"

Simeon teetered like an upended log of wood between the flailing women and the motionless Turk, who
stood in the shadow by the gate. And Nevenka leaned
out over her window sill and pressed her face to the
wooden bars to better see and hear, although she shuddered from cold and terror and bristled with gooseflesh
every other moment. For long hours afterwards she
would be kept awake by her fear and, even more, by her
gloating and selfish thoughts.

In this intimate contact with the Pamukovićes and
their relations, yet actually quite isolated and left to herself, Nevenka brooded increasingly about everything
about her. Her as yet callow mind took her off along
paths that were too complex for her, and which until
then she had never dreamed existed. Her first and most
persistent thought was: Where did so much evil come
from? Without a spark of goodness, without compassion, devoid of tenderness for anyone or anything that
was not the Pamukovićes'? She waded through this evil
of theirs as through a darkness, and couldn't see the end
of it, nor the sense, nor the reason for it. Pure evil. And
when she was through thinking such thoughts, which
she was adept at starting and expanding but not at disentangling and solving, she would slump helpless and
crushed before the realization that the Pamuković depravity and ugliness would never be denounced and
made public, but that they would remain like this, respectable, powerful, redoubtable, each in his place, till
the end of time.

"No one can ever touch them!"

Look, they sin, poison each other, rot away; they
humiliate and are contemptuous of everyone, and they
hate each other; they are greedy, shameless, and owe
money, yet each one of them holds his head high, steps
boldly, looks around him undaunted, eats well, wears
fine clothes, is not abashed or afraid of anyone, does
what he wants, takes whatever he fancies.

"No one can do a thing to them!"

And when the lot of them, the way they were, at last
found themselves in the other world (her weary imagina-

tion often traveled as far as that), she felt quite certain—
no matter how much they had sinned—that not a single one of them would cast his eyes down before the
radiance of God's face, and that even up there they
would find their way to the top, separate themselves
from others, and carry on as they pleased, obeying their
own laws. Vainly she tried to think of a way in which
she might put them out of countenance and topple
them, justly, as they deserved. And when she tired of
such brooding, when the flagging thought coiled into a
circle and began to eat itself, another, contrary thought
would suddenly appear above it: that, despite all of it,
this state of affairs could not continue, that somewhere
there had to be someone who will unmask them, punish them, annihilate them, and accord justice to her, to
her mother, to Jela, Mara, and all those whom the Pamukovićes scorned, devoured, and trampled. With
these thoughts she racked and mortified herself to the
point of utter exhaustion, and still they kept returning
and jarring her out of sleep and rousing her to new
torments.

She could find peace only in prayer. Here there was
no solution either, but prayer spun a kind of sheath
around her, in which she was, if not safe, at least protected, though the thought of them and their evil would
penetrate even that. It occurred to her sometimes that
they, the Pamukovićes, might be saying the same prayers
and speaking the same words, and she resolved to find
words and prayers that would apply only to herself, and
which they would never be able to find out and speak.
And she would often lull herself to sleep breathing such

prayers in a hot whisper into the edge of the quilt—
prayers made up of new, grave and sweet words.

It was only here that she found what she craved so
very much, a realm in which one truly and honestly
knew who was right and who was wrong, and could tell
the mean and foul from the good and pure—except that
all of it usually melted away somewhere between sleep
and waking. And next day the rankling thoughts would
start again.

But even at that, having discovered "their true face,"
she found it easier to suffer both their contempt and the
hitherto unbearable gap between her own simplicity and
poverty and their lordly ways and haughtiness. The more
she learned and suffered, the more comfort and relief
she found in her musings and prayers—relief that she
never suspected a person could find in himself. Realizing what kind of people they were, she got used to looking at the problem in this way: on one side the Pamukovićes, in their wicked strength and comeliness, and
on the other she herself, with God and God's justice as
allies. And so she toughened inwardly.

Her greatest bane was her husband. Before his spite
and rancor she was still terrified and dumbfounded,
though ready to defend herself. At first he had not
drunk much and had kept early hours, but she knew and
felt that he hated her, secretly, deeply, ever since that
day when, after her initial flight, he had brought her
back from her mother. And when the first year had
gone by and she had not conceived, he began to drink
more often, to return home at dawn, or even the following day.

Once he went to Kiseljak to join Simeon, and came back only after midnight of the third day. Not expecting him any more that night, she had gone to sleep. She was startled awake by a hoarse voice. Jumping up and flinging a wrap over herself, she helped him into a chair. He was muddy, covered with soot, spattered all over with wine and food. She strained hard to pull off his soaking boots, while he, blinking, stared at her with eyes that were not so much drunk as vicious. Suddenly he jerked his leg and drove his booted foot into her chest. She crashed backwards, cushioning her fall with her hand.

"Nikola…"

But he interrupted her hoarsely and wrathfully, drawling the words through a mouthful of spittle.

"You barren bitch!"

"Niko, what are you saying?"

He snarled out an obscenity, involving her mother, but never finished his oath, for she hit him right across the face with the loose boot. With his arm raised to protect himself, astonished more by her unexpected boldness than by the blow itself, he remained stock-still. But then, as if suddenly sobered up, he sprang to his feet and, the way he was, one foot bare, the other shod, started to chase her around the room. Rumpled, bent, his arms outspread, he staggered about as if trying to catch a bird. Since she was quicker than he, she gained the door, rushed across the hall and stopped in the shadow of the stairway. He came after her, muttering unintelligible oaths. She ran down the stairs and into the yard, where the first light of the day was already noticeable, and crouched behind the waterwell. She heard him shuffle and stumble down the steps, his one boot thudding as he went. He stomped around the yard.

"Where are you? Come out, I tell you!"

After discovering her, he started to chase her around the well. She was faster and more nimble, but he went on darting and lunging even though he kept banging himself against the corners of the stone well. At times he would stop and wait in ambush with his arms open. So they faced each other—he on one side, she on the other. In the silence, only their panting could be heard.

"Jump into the well, bitch!"

He kept growling this, but under his breath, almost in a whisper, until suddenly she found her tongue, too, and replied in a changed voices much clearer than his.

"Your old mother Pamuković is a bitch!"

"What!"

After which the furious chase around the well started afresh. But when he lost his balance and stumbled, she took advantage of it and fled to the smaller courtyard, where she hid between the vats and barrels. Barefoot and lightly dressed though she was, she waited till the sun rose and then went back and lay down. Next morning life went on as if nothing had happened. Yet, from that day on whenever he took it into his head to rush her either in drunkenness or for any other reason—and this he often did without any provocation—she would defend herself stoutly, then run away and lock herself in until he had sobered up or calmed down. And their combats were neither seen nor heard by anyone.

It was only in the third year, this past spring, when she had already begun to lose all hope, that Nevenka suddenly conceived. She was overcome more by the joyful unexpectedness of it than by the pregnancy itself. It was as if the three years of secret tears and desperate vows had come back once more, metamorphosed into an excruciating rapture of victory. She said nothing to anyone, but went around the house with bright eyes, doing her work with unaccustomed zeal. The barren woman was jubilant. And the inmates noticed the change, and understood. Her exulting heart sometimes all but choked her, and she had to clamp her mouth with her fingers not to scream from defiance and joy. In the end the long waiting, terror, and reproach, followed by sudden happiness, made the whole thing more of a pain than delight.

One day the old dowager Pamuković called her in and started to tell her, in a roundabout fashion, that it was time for her to begin worrying about swaddling, cradle linen, and little frocks, and to leave off heavy housework. Pale and resolutely calm, Nevenka made as if she didn't understand. The old woman bit her lips. The daughter-in-law exulted. Nevertheless, it was agreed that an apartment would be furnished in the small quarters behind the kitchen, where from now on the young woman would weave until her seventh or eighth month, after which she would only sew. And so here she was now, spending the greater part of her day beside Mara, while in the big house in front they were content not to see her, not to have to avert their eyes before that gravid belly and expectant air of hers.

Evening came on as Nevenka finished telling her story, and it was only then that Mara summoned enough courage to look her in the eyes. In the gathering dusk her sallow face was quite colorless, the lips thin and drawn, while the eyes, darker yet and more glowing, full of hatred, stared absently through the window. Her look, as if piercing through both the Pamuković houses, was lost somewhere in the distance.

Seeing her so rapt and still, her legs oddly spread out with the empty, naked, and sharp-toothed carding comb in her lap, Mara had the impression that Nevenka was plotting something that she, Mara, could not know but which she guessed was to bring vengeance, unquiet, and endless trouble in its wake. She was afraid of all the things she had just learned about the Pamukovićes, and of the young woman herself, even of the child that was yet to be born. Oppressed by her dread and incomprehension, she contracted inwardly, pressed her hands to her chest and hung her head even lower. But Nevenka seemed not to notice her, and went on staring absently through the window, utterly engrossed in her memories, and thoughts of revenge and of the child.

There were other things as well, new and unfamiliar to her, that bewildered Mara. Those visits, above all. Although she lived in a small room in the kitchen building, she nevertheless saw, when her work happened to take her to the front yard, the people who came and went. As soon as the daylight faded, Fra Gregory would arrive; and even though he never spoke a word to her, his presence always disturbed her. Another visitor was old Hadji Ivo Livajić, thin and clean-shaven, his hair trimmed short as though he were a Muslim priest; then the brother of the Pamuković dowager, Matan Boštor, a huge and stout old man, gray as a sheep, with a blotchy face. He once came across her alone in the yard. Stopping, he gave her a long look which she could not understand, but from which she shuddered all night. What did they tell him about her? What did he want? Was he sent to question and punish her with that look of his jaundiced old eyes which, like those of predatory animals, veiled over languidly every other minute and yet saw everything with terrible clarity? And if not that, why did he stare so long and hard? All this was beyond her, something she did not know how to unravel. She knew only her sleeplessness and torment.

One of the visitors of whom she was not afraid was Dr. Ketchet, a Swiss in Turkish service. Small and gray-haired, he would smile already from the courtyard gate and greet her cheerfully. She had not seen such a reassuring smile either among the Christians or the Turks— on no one, in fact, save this foreigner. And she felt that she didn't have to be afraid of him. In recent weeks, however, he came less and less frequently, and disguised in Turkish clothes of all things, which gave him an absurd appearance and a diffident bearing. But she was always pleased to see his face, with its smile and an open, somewhat worried look.

On the whole, however, she feared all these visits, no matter who came, for she was wont to connect them, like all the other things that happened around her, with her own person, or with incidents and changes that might develop and embroil her.

Besides these visitors, she saw another foreign and unusual face. Right behind the stables there was a high fence that separated the Pamuković yard from the garden and house of the family Telalović. In that Telalović dwelling was the English consulate. Through the cracks in the board fence one could see the building and the wooden porch erected on columns overgrown with bougainvillaea. One day Jela and Nevenka showed Mara, through the fence, the English vice consul walking up and down the porch. He was young and sturdy and pink of face. He wore some sort of a long house robe of dark satin with lapels and piping of maroon silk.

The two women told her that this vice consul was crazy, that he often sang and woke up the neighborhood at night, that he collected Gypsies, beggars, and half-wits. All that was deranged, cretinous, maimed, all that crawled naked and barefoot in the alleys, he collected and brought home; there he gave them presents, dressed them, forced his houseboys to bathe them and cut their hair, and played strange games with them. Some of those fools had the temerity to come uninvited, while others wouldn't come near a second time for any money and would run the minute they saw him or his boys. And he often roamed through the most Godforsaken alleys, in high rubber boots and a long leather coat, and invariably led several leashed dogs that were very old and ugly, "as if they'd been bred in hell."

After that Mara used to go alone behind the stables and watch the Englishman through the board fence. She was afraid both of the foreigner and of being found out by one of the Pamukovićes, but still she went, especially in the late evening. The porch was then in a glow of the setting sun. The consul strolled briskly up and down.

Sometimes he would pause and throw his head back, and she would see the sun kindle his purple robe and his eyes flash as if with a kind of madness. But the most outlandish thing was his hair, light brown and luxuriant, streaming over his temples and cut in a straight line at the nape of his neck, as on a schoolboy. Observing how, with his unnaturally tilted head, flooded with sunlight, he gazed toward the west, she imagined that he, also, was performing some kind of a rite whose meaning she could not divine, and which filled her with the familiar dread associated in her mind with everything she had seen at Veli Pasha's, Baba Anuša's, Fra Gregory's, or Nevenka's—and, beyond that, with a peculiar and aching curiosity.

Presently, one after another, the visitors stopped coming. For a while yet she saw Matan Boštor, but then he too dropped out of sight. In the city, the rebellion was in full swing, the bazaar deserted, and all houses shuttered up. Marijan, a syce of the Pamukovićes, who used to go with the horses to Kiseljak every Sunday, went no more. Lolling and smoking around the servants quarters, he talked about the Austrians who had already reached the town of Jajce, with artillery and a great deal of equipment, and about the Turks who were planning to wait for them at Klokoti. They all listened to him attentively and in fear, but to her the whole thing seemed so distant and unreal—those towns as well as those people getting ready to go to war—that she hardly felt any dread. Then she began to be awakened at night by the calls of entries from one shore of the Miljacka to the other, and by the bagpipes and yells of the detachments marching through Čumuria. Occasionally she would sit up with a start and jump out of bed with a scream, so close seemed to be the one who yelled. Once it was a man somewhere outside the front gate, shouting in a thin and terrible voice:

"Ya hayun—ya kayun!"[1]

In the silence that followed both the footfalls and the low murmuring of those who echoed the cry could be heard. Then the quiet was again shattered by the calls of the patrols. Pair after pair of dissimilar voices would chorus one another, as if in some kind of a game.

"Yek dur Allah!"[2]

"Yek dur, yek!"[3] a second one would answer, as if to prove he was awake.

As her heart pounded away, she waited for new voices and tensely stared through the darkness in which Jela's shadow could be made out. Jolted out of her sleep also, Jela was sitting on the edge of her bed, praying with her rosary and trying to calm the girl.

"Cross yourself, child, so that the Lord may humble the Turkish fiends. Then go back to bed and sleep."

But she could find no peace for hours, what with that ceaseless shouting, and it was only toward dawn, when the voices grew less frequent, that she curled up and, overcome by tension and fatigue, drifted off into a profound and sweet sleep.

---

[1] *Thou who art from the beginning:* one of the epithets for Allah, that also serves as a battle cry.
[2] *Allah is one!*
[3] *One and only!*

Once, just before daylight, she dreamed an unusual, dream: that she was playing with a ball in some kind of a strange and spacious meadow. Dark-green grass grew over the meadow and underneath the soil was soft like on a day after a generous rain. The ball was small and blue, quite like the color of the sky, so that up aloft it blended into the light of the sky and disappeared in it. Thus each time she tossed it she felt an anxiety: would she catch it again? This fear sent a tingle through her breasts and brought on an aching and delighted laugh that she was powerless to stop, and which made her quite dizzy. All of her interrupted childhood and stunted youth came now to cavort down the length of the meadow. And as she careened along and lifted up her arms and eyes toward the ball and the sky, she felt as if her innards were straining to take wing and soar aloft somewhere. This made her pant and swell throughout her body, so that it seemed to her she would burst at any moment and float away into the distance. Yet she continued to run, to toss the ball and catch it, laughing and almost blinded by ecstasy; and in the midst of laughter all of her seemed to scatter into the radiance of the huge day.

Next morning, she was still under the spell of the dream. She still felt a little of that pleasurable tingle and lightness in her breasts, and something bright and rest-less behind the eye lids. Indeed, she hardly remembered just what she had dreamt, but only felt a great relief, as if in the darkness that surrounded her a bright window had been sprung open.

That same day, as she sat in her room and combed wool, she heard Jela and Nevenka talking in the kitchen

about Simeon, Auntie Andja's man, and gathered that
because of the uprising he too had fled from Kiseljak
and returned home. In the afternoon, she remained
quite alone. There was no one in the kitchen either.
Since the building was low and the window in the small
room rather tiny, and the courtyard enclosed with a high
wall, the room grew dark early. Outside, it was still daylight; the red glow of sunset fell directly from the sky
and filled the entire yard. At that moment the door
opened slowly and unexpectedly, revealing an oblong of
crimson glow on the yard gravel and, in the door, a red-
haired man with a puffy and flushed face. He hesitated
for a second, then shut the door behind him. In the
careful and soundless way in which he closed it there
was something that froze the blood in Mara's veins. It
was Simeon.

"You're the little one from Travnik, eh?"

His voice was hoarse and deep, he had difficulty
enunciating words, but he made an effort to give his
watery and bloodshot eyes a set look of amiable kindness.

"A little compatriot, eh? Look at her."

Seeing how he was slowly pushing the wool aside
with his foot and trying to come closer, she got up
frightened and backed to the wall. There she stood up to
her knees in wool, her palms pressed desperately into
the wall, the blood drained out of her cheeks, eyes di-
lated. He was still mumbling words that made no particular sense, while awkwardly shoving the wool out of
his way, when the door opened and the crimson light of
the courtyard fell in a shaft across the wool and over the

345

pair of them. Auntie Andja stood in the doorway. With his back turned, Simeon could not see, nor did he hear the door open, and he went on mumbling:

"Little one from Travnik, now don't you be afraid," while trying to edge closer.

Not bothering to shut the door behind her, Andja grabbed him around the waist and pulled him back. After the first shock of surprise, the drunk tried to wrest himself free, while mumbling on. But his wife was stronger and she dragged him away cursing under her breath:

"Come here, you philanderer! You don't need a Turkish concubine!"

Left alone in the semi-dark room, the girl did not move from the spot for some time, then slid down into the wool heap and repeated, inwardly, the word—*concubine*. Only once in her life had she heard that word: When some woman, during a quarrel, had hurled it at her mother across a street. Since they had taken her from Travnik, she too, in her bad moments and during sleepless nights, had been thinking of that word, in which she felt there was something as if blue, giving, and evanescent, but at the same time deadly; she had thought of it, it was true, but had never heard it flung at her by anyone, nor had she dared to pronounce it aloud to herself; it had not been spoken even by Fra Gregory in his worst anger. Now it had been voiced, and she reeled under it as under a final blow.

She was startled by Jela's voice; back in the kitchen, the woman was calling her to come and lend a hand. She rose, shook the wool off her dress; she worked and moved around the kitchen till late in the evening, feeling chilled all over.

That night, sleep would not come. Through her numbness she heard the clatter of some horses, the shouting of patrols, the clamor of the insurgents. Jela, who had no inkling of what had happened that afternoon, got up twice, tried to soothe her and fetch water to wet her temples and chest.

Next morning she could scarcely drag herself into the kitchen. No one noticed that her face was changed and her eyes restless and strange. That same night Simeon tried to hang himself twice. As the day was dawning, Auntie Andja no longer knew how to contain him and called in the young Pamukovices to take turns watching him. The whole house suddenly withdrew into itself and fell silent, more oppressively so than usual. But Nevenka brought the news to the kitchen, and talked quietly to Jela. Mara could not make out what they were saying and only caught a remark of Nevenka's as they were parting.

"Satan put the yoke on him long ago!"

In a lower, but hard and dry voice, Jela added:

"When the Devil puts his rope around a man, it stays on for good."

Hearing this, Mara could not bear to eavesdrop further, but fled to her little room, full of uncarded wool, and banged the door shut after her. The moment she was alone she slumped into a chair, let her arms drop at her sides, and hung her head as if for a blow. She made no sound and shed no tears, but merely froze in the dread that enclosed her like air. After she had rallied a little, she began to pick up the wool with cold fingers and stick it on the comb. Working slowly and vacantly, she felt at times as though she were seeing herself on her knees, with outspread arms and a bowed head, voiceless and without tears. Every now and then she could feel her blood in turn coursing and freezing in the nape of her neck, the muscles twitching on her arms and chest. There was a steady hum in her head; her sight in turn darkened and flashed with painful and unbearable sparks. She was seized by a terror she had never known; as if someone had shut the door behind her and there with her, in the darkness, was the terrible Simeon and her mother Hafizadić. She strove with all her strength to think of something she might clutch at and which would guide her back among those whom the devil had not roped in. She wanted to call someone, but could not remember anything any more; neither Jela's nor Nevenka's name, nor her dream of last night. The only thing that occurred to her was that yesterday, when she was in the stable, she had seen a rope dangling from the rafters. It was the loose end of a halter, thin and sturdy, made greasy and smooth by the drovers' hands. She sprang up and set off toward the stables. She crossed both courtyards without meeting anyone, but before she reached the stable her strength gave out and she stumbled in that narrow, damp and always murky enclosure into which all kitchen slop was emptied, where the cobblestone was usually wet, greenish and mildewed, and where some kind of white and repulsive toadstools grew along the fence. This was the most outlying and hideous nook on the Pamuković property, and here she slumped to her knees and burst into tears once more, without warning, in a copious, heartfelt, childlike fit of crying.

Blurred by the welling and unstoppable tears, the resurrected images passed before her in a streak: her mother Hafizadić, the old Elias Garić, then Veli Pasha, with red epaulettes and a silver-inlaid dagger hilt; then Fra Gregory, quick to work up an anger; then Sarah, Anuša, Jela, and Nevenka... Picture dissolved into picture and faded away, and over them appeared that haggard and austere saint from the altar in the Sarajevo church; but he too melted away in a tear and was replaced by Our Lady from the chapel at Dolac. Holding a fold of her blue gown in each hand, she walked toward Mara, but slowly and with a strange air of gravity. Unable to wait till she came near, Mara fell prostrate on the stone and reached out toward her; resting the weight of her body on one hand, she stretched the other to clutch the hem of the gown and pull it over her head.

"Cover me, Sweet Rose, shelter me! Hide me from all of them, all of them. They've dragged me all over—the Turks and our people, both. They've pulled me apart. I don't know anything. I'm not guilty. Don't let me out of your hands!"

She cried out through her tears, at the top of her voice. And the voice was not the same, but rose up from the base of her throat, clear and firm, as it had never been before.

One of the maids working in the kitchen heard the sobbing and the voice and glanced through the window. She ran out immediately and called Jela. In the yard they were joined by another maid and by Nevenka; together they hurried behind the stable. Finding the girl prone on the ground, they stopped in horror. She was pitching from side to side, her face on the muddy cobblestone, her tiny hand grasping convulsively at something above her, as if trying to pull it over herself. They called her name, but to no avail. On the mud-smeared and utterly distorted face there was not the slightest spark of consciousness or understanding. She did not cease her disjointed wailing and moaning, and showed no restraint or embarrassment. They led the pregnant Nevenka away, to spare her the sight. Jela rushed back to the house for the holy water and the consecrated salt, while the maids, crossing themselves, averted their heads and backed away, dismayed, step by step.

5

From that day on the daughter of the Travnik baker and Veli Pasha's mistress struggled almost continuously with apparitions and hallucinations.

The times were becoming more difficult and turbulent. It was hard to know what to do with this girl whose mind was rapidly disintegrating, and so she remained in the Pamuković house, kept there on sufferance and out of pity. She was quiet, except that she wept a great deal and for no apparent reason. Both Jela and Nevenka cared for her as much as they could, but the girl refused food, didn't want to wash or change, and, like a cut sapling, wilted and withered with terrifying speed, shriveling and disappearing before one's eyes. Her face, whose beauty had once seemed indestructible, grew haggard and coarse, her eyes lost their luster, the mouth grew ugly. Only the hair, thick and fair, kept its old sheen and luxuriance; and rumpled and unkempt though it was, it looked like the adornment of an imperishable beauty. But with time it, too, began to coarsen at the ends, to mat in sweaty knots and lose its color. It seemed incredible that so much beauty could waste away in so short a time.

In a few weeks all that remained of this girl who had combined in herself the charm of a child and the beauty of a woman, was a pathetic, dull-eyed wretch, dressed in rags, after whom urchins would have scampered in the streets had the Pamukovićes only let her out of the house.

And even Jela, who in her time had seen a good deal of evil and had become inured to sickness and slow death, was shaken and baffled in the face of such a disaster. But there was something in this misfortune that perturbed this hardened and prematurely aged homebody even more: the demented wisp of a girl, "wrecked by a Turk," as she put it, was about to give birth to a child. There could be no more doubt about it. Right after that first fit, as she had washed and undressed Mara, Jela had realized that the poor girl was pregnant, and no longer in her early months either. Jela, who had never had a home of her own or known happiness and family, who had experienced man once in her lifetime, and only as a brutish horror, became all concern and excitement at the prospect of children and births. Now all at once she had to do with the moody and embittered Nevenka who was about to start her labor, and with this sick girl who was only a few weeks away from it.

So much evil and suffering, and all of it still breeding and multiplying at every step!

Staggered though she was by it all, Jela did not lose her presence of mind. She looked after Mara, soothed and comforted Nevenka, who was in her last days and apt to be an intolerable burden to herself and others. All this Jela did and bore alone, not saying anything to anyone, knowing from way back that words were useless, that she could expect no help from the others.

Meanwhile, in the Pamuković house the women were whispering and the men were making arrangements. They filled the house with grain, dried meat, and all kinds of provisions. According to the advice conveyed by Fra Gregory, they prepared two large bed sheets in order to hang them out as flags on the two house gates the day the Austrians entered Sarajevo. For, the latter had already marched past Klokoti and it was clear that they would continue unhindered all the way to Sarajevo. And Sarajevo was getting ready to put up resistance.

The city, which for a long time now had resembled a camp and a chaotic anthill, was receiving its first wounded, whose tales injected new excitement into the inhabitants. It was as if everyone were filled with an awareness of the importance and solemn greatness of each day and each hour. Everyone went his way with a dark face, armed and dignified, and each man felt prompted to carry this solemn rigor to the others. The Council forbade the sale of brandy. Constables were arresting young loafers on the streets, marching them off to the arsenal fortress to unload and pack ammunition there, or, when that was done, to loll around there similarly unemployed. Except that each man was eager to do something for the common cause. The mosques were thronged with people, alms were given out generously. No one kept track of lunch or dinner; one ate wherever one happened to be, and somehow there was plenty of everything. Few men slept in their own homes, but, rather, at various picket posts and assembly points; and the one who managed to doze off couldn't even finish his catnap for he would be jolted awake by a rifle-shot or a drum or a cry of *Yek dur Allah!*

Still, little more than a distant echo of all this reached into the servants quarters where Jela was caring for the two pregnant women. Nevenka had grown so heavy and weak that she could hardly move. It looked as if she would never part with the child. The members of the Pamuković family grew noticeably kinder and more solicitous toward her, as if they were only waiting for her delivery in order to announce her complete equality with all the other Pamukovićes. But the daughter-in-law was getting to be increasingly sullen and less accessible; she refused to accept the least favor from them, and their attention. And had she been able to follow the dictates of her own heart, she would have hidden herself, when the time of delivery came, in some remote and forsaken nook of the quarters and there given birth without a sound and without their help, and never even shown her baby to them.

At long last, in the middle of August, Nevenka bore a male child which, though tiny, cried in a strong voice and greedily demanded food.

Two days later, the first guns boomed out above Sarajevo. By noon, the artillery fire came thick and fast. The air shook ominously. Since the Pamuković house towered above the others, its high roof ridge stopped many a stray rifle bullet. Through the steady roar of the field guns one heard clearly from time to time how the lead shot hit the roof boards and how the latter crackled under it. The entire family moved down to the ground floor of the big house, and was ready to descend to the cellars if necessary. The servants were particularly terrified. Only Jela scampered unafraid now and then across the yard between the house and the quarters.

Since the artillery fire had started, Mara had been screaming and sobbing without letup in her room. This frightened and bewildered the Pamuković servants even more. It was only in the afternoon that her wailing ceased. Jela, who throughout that time had not rested for a moment, rushed into the main house and whispered something to the old dowager Pamuković: although barely in her seventh month, the Pasha's concubine had given birth to a child.

As the day drew to an end, the guns fell silent, while small arms fire grew scarcer and more distant. Even before dark, loud music of the Austrian Jaegers could be heard in the city. Both gates of the Pamuković homestead were flung wide open, and the older men went out into the street.

In the quarters, water was being heated, herbs and medicines readied, and Jela shuffled around briskly, preoccupied with tending the baby and its mother, as if inside the house and outside it, and in the whole wide world, there was nothing greater or more important than what she was doing now.

Delivered before its time, Mara's child responded weakly to the cold and light of the world in a feeble voice and with a few puckers and twitches, and promptly expired. Old Marijan rummaging among the wooden cases in the storage bin, chose an empty box on which the stamp of some Austrian nail factory could still be seen, and in that box he and Jela buried the child whose life had lasted a bare half hour. Since the presence of the army made it impossible for them to go to the cemetery that day, Marijan tucked the box under his arm, carried it into the garden, and buried it under the tallest plum tree along the fence.

As soon as she would complete her ministrations to Mara, Jela would immediately go over to Nevenka and continue working by her side with the same zeal and efficiency. The child was healthy and Nevenka was feeling well, but she had no milk to give. Jela fed the child skillfully, as well as she could, but seeing how Nevenka's milk would not come, she took the baby one morning, carried it into the small room where Mara lay in bed and placed it on her swollen breasts, holding it with both hands. The sick girl neither resisted nor touched the child, but with closed eyes and averted face let them do what they wanted with her. In this manner Jela fed Nevenka's child twice a day, until she noticed that Mara had fever.

From that moment, Jela nursed the sick girl for six days and nights. On the evening of the sixth day, Mara breathed her last, without a word or prayer. They buried her next day in the cemetery in Carina.

The funeral was attended by all the servants—three boys and two maids. When the rites were completed, the sickly and embarrassed chaplain wrapped his books in a piece of cloth and went away. The boys put the finishing touches to the grave, while the maids whispered prayers and gazed absently at their clasped hands or at the fresh earth. Marijan erected a makeshift cross and then sat down beside it. A little farther away sat Jela; her eyes were still glued to the mound in front of her, as intensely as if she were looking at something in the distance. She was about to finish her brief prayer for the soul of this girl from Travnik when all of a sudden, from the invisible road that ran behind the cemetery wall, they heard voices, footsteps and a clatter of arms and chains. First the boys, and then the two girls too, broke off their praying and went up to the wall. The boys at once climbed over it, while the girls, after mounting a stone heap overgrown with thick and scorched bramble, watched the scene on the road from inside the wall.

Muhammet Hadžijamaković, the dark and sinewy Kaukdžić, and another pair of reputable townsmen, all fettered to the same chain, were walking past as fast as they could; they were flanked by Austrian soldiers in full equipment, and at the head of the column there rode an officer on a white horse. They were taking them to the place of execution. In a carriage that brought up the rear sat a hodja and some people from the Council.

The boys went forward to the edge of the road to see better; the girls leaned over the wall, holding hands and clinging to each other in fear.

By the grave, which already lay in a summery shade, there remained only Jela and Marijan. Jela had finished her prayer and wanted to get up and call the others, but found it hard to abandon the grave. She thought of Mara and her fate, and of that tiny creature buried without a name and a cross under the plum tree in the Pamuković garden. Absently she went on praying. The words came welling by themselves, and they in turn deepened her melancholy. It had been many years since anyone had seen her shed tears; now she wept and loudly prayed to God to protect and keep safe all women, unhappy companions, and martyrs.

Marijan, who had learned to drink in the company of Simeon on Kiseljak, was quick with tears, and also with words. Seeing Jela cry and whisper, he too began to weep and talk.

"Oh, oh—" he sighed, not quite knowing what he wanted to say. "Oh, we buried a sinner, we buried a poor soul. Each of them took something from her, and now there's no one to feel sorry for her and shed a tear over her. Oh, shame!"

He hung his head and was silent for a while, then suddenly burst out and with a heavy tongue, all twisted with emotion, cried, almost yelled out, as though revealing and admitting something unexpected and dreadful:

"Jela, we buried one of God's angels—an angel!"

Jela came to with a start, interrupted him gruffly and, wiping her wet eyes, called to the girls who were still watching the procession of condemned men marching down the road. In a quieter voice she admonished them

357

not to forget anything by the grave, and to close the gates of the cemetery properly.

On the way back, Jela walked in front of them, with Marijan at her side, and talked with him about house-work and about the need of finding as soon as possible a strong and healthy woman who would be able to suckle Nevenka's son, the youngest Pamuković.

Translated by Joseph Hitrec

Anika's Times

D uring the sixties of the past century a strong desire for knowledge, and the better life that education brings with it, penetrated even the most remote regions of Bosnia. Nothing, not even the mountain Romanija or the river Drina, could prevent this desire from reaching Dobrun and enlightening its parish priest, Father Kosta Porubović. And Father Kosta, a man already advanced in years, casting a glance at his only son, Vujadin, a pale and timid boy, came to the conclusion that at any price his son must get an education. Through some friends, merchants in Sarajevo, he managed to send him all the way to Sremski Karlovci "to catch at least a year or two of theology." He caught just about that much, for toward the end of his second year Father Kosta suddenly died. Vujadin returned home, was married off, and settled into the priesthood in his father's parish. In the first year of marriage his wife gave birth; true enough it was only a girl, but they had many years ahead of them, and it seemed certain that the Porubovićes would sustain the priesthood at Dobrun for many a generation to come.

However, all was not well with Father Vujadin. Nothing specific could be discovered, nor was anyone sure that there was something wrong, but everyone sensed a certain strain between the priest and his parishioners. This strain could be attributed neither to the youth nor to the awkwardness of Father Vujadin, since as time went on the tension grew rather than diminished. Vujadin was of fine stature and handsome, like all the Porubovićes, but lean, pale, and unusually subdued, and, in spite of his youth, there was an aged, gray quality in his voice and eyes.

Around 1875, only a few years before the Austrian occupation of Bosnia, Father Vujadin suffered a great loss: his wife died while giving birth to their second child. From that time onward he grew ever more remote from the world. He sent his little girl to his wife's relatives at Višegrad, and he lived alone in a big house next to the Dobrun church with but a single servant. He performed the rites regularly, attended funerals, officiated at baptisms and weddings, read prayers when requested to do so, but he did not chat or drink with the peasants in the churchyard, or jest with the peasant women, or argue with debtors over their taxes. The townspeople, who were in any case suspicious of a silent, morose man and decidedly favored healthy, talkative priests, simply could not get used to Father Vujadin. They would have forgiven him any other failing more easily. The women, who in these villages determined a man's reputation, good or bad, said of Father Vujadin that there was a thundercloud over his forehead; they disliked going to church, and always brought up that "wild Father Kosta."

"Dull and lost, that's what he is," the peasants complained, forever comparing him to his father, the late

Kosta Porubović, who had been fat, cheerful, but wise and eloquent, on good terms with the peasants and the Turks, with the humble and the strong. Father Kosta's funeral had been a great common sorrow. Older people could even recall Vujadin's grandfather, Jakša, called Djakon, or Deacon. He, too, had been quite a different man: a *hajduk* in his youth and proud of it. When they asked him why he was called Deacon, he would reply cheerfully:

"Ah, my son, when I was only a deacon I joined the *hajduks*, and since every *hajduk* must have a nickname, they started calling me Hajduk Deacon. So that name stuck with me. But later on, as years went by and honors struck me as arrows strike a horse, it was embarrassing to be called a *hajduk*. So '*hajduk*' fell off me like a tail falls off a frog, and I remained simply Deacon."

He was an old man with thick hair and a big beard which grew sideways and did not go gray but remained reddish and unruly until his death. Wild, headstrong, and cunning, he had true friends and fierce enemies among Christians and Turks alike. He enjoyed drinking and had an eye for women until his old age. Even so, he was much liked and respected.

And so it was that, hard as they tried, the peasants could not figure out why Vujadin was the way he was, and not like his father or grandfather. In his lonely life as a widower Father Vujadin was sinking lower and deteriorating further. His beard grew thinner, the hair on his temples white, his cheeks fell in and somehow turned gray so that his large green eyes and ashen brows no longer stood out on his face. Tall, straight, and stiff, he spoke only when absolutely necessary, in a deep voice without color or animation.

As the first priest with even a smattering of education in the more than one hundred years in which his family had served the Dobrun church, Father Vujadin realized full well the extent of his awkward nature and manner. He knew what people were looking for and what sort of priest they wanted, and understood that what they sought was the exact opposite of what he could provide. This knowledge tormented him, but it also stiffened him, and in contact with the parishioners his conduct became all the more rigid. Little by little this rigidity transformed itself into a deep, uncontrollable disgust for these people.

The general weariness of a widower's life, as well as its many renunciations, rapidly widened the rift between Vujadin and his flock. Long before he lost his wife he had suffered because he could not approach them, warm up to them, mix with them. Now this suffering was intensified; he was forced into a position of deliberately concealing many things from them, and in the process grew increasingly distant. Even before, every look and every word had been a torture, a burden, and a painful combat. Now it had become a danger, too, and the fear that he would give himself away made him even more insecure and suspicious.

So his loathing for men grew, settled in him and, like a hidden spleen, poisoned him with a hatred both incomprehensible and unconscious, but real enough nevertheless. This was the secret life of Father Vujadin. He hated himself and his torment. There were days when, downcast and grayish, he would stand by the window, hidden in the shadows for a whole hour, lying in wait simply to get a glimpse of village women passing by on their way to the river to wash their laundry. And when he had spotted them and seen them disappearing behind the willows, he would turn away in disgust and walk back into the stuffy, half-empty room, giving the women most disgraceful names. This irrational hatred would rise up into his throat, he would lose his breath and with it his speech. He spat loudly, unable to find other relief or expression. Then, in the stillness of the stifling summer air, he would regain his senses, and, catching himself in this last violent gesture, would recall his terrible curses and freeze in terror. A shudder would race up his spine and into his skull, and he would be seized by a chilling thought: He was losing his mind.

These fits were tearing his whole being apart, and it had become almost impossible to carry on his own daily life, to say nothing of his duties as a priest. Less than half an hour after this seizure, he was supposed to talk with the peasants; and there he would sit, pale, with a fixed look and a hollow voice, trying to answer their numerous questions, arranging days for baptisms, prayers, and consecrations. And the difference between these two men—the one lying in wait in the shadows of his room, and the other, Father Vujadin, giving advice to the peasants in the churchyard—was such that he was bending under it. The inner pain was producing convulsions; he would bite his mustache and run his fingers through his hair, possessing barely enough self-control to prevent himself from falling on his knees before the peasants and breaking into a scream:

363

"I am losing my mind!"

And while he was talking with the peasants he was constantly reminded that they were comparing him with his late father and all of his relatives. And he began to hate his father and all of his relatives.

Everything that happened to Vujadin only increased his hidden bitterness and hatred. Every day spent in loneliness and every contact with men only strengthened a hatred that was becoming identified with his own body, with all of his movements, desires, and thoughts. The hatred grew larger and overshadowed everything within him, forming the substance of his life, more real than anything else, the only existence in which he moved. Bashful, like many descendants of good, old families, honorable and straight by nature, he concealed his condition as well as he could. Constantly torn between the two realities, he made superhuman efforts not to lose sight of the reality that others see. But the day would come when that inner life would assert itself and Father Vujadin would cross over to the other side, to that strange land to which for years his whole inner life had urged him: into the sphere of open madness, visible and clear to all.

This was indeed what happened in the fifth year of Father Vujadin's life as a widower. Early one morning he went out into the fields and stood around watching the men at work until lunchtime. On his way back, he was surprised to see, in a clearing among the fir trees at the foot of a cliff, a group of strangers. There were five in all: an engineer, two Austrian officers, and two women. A little distance away grooms were watching the horses. A rug was spread out and the strangers were sitting on it, the men bareheaded, with their jackets unbuckled, the women dressed in light frocks that dazzled the eye with their whiteness. Father Vujadin paused a moment, and then quickly climbed a little way up the nearby cliff and leaned against a twisted, half-fallen fir tree. He was perspiring and his heart was beating. Concealed behind the tree, he fixed his eyes on the strangers below him, whom he saw from an odd, slanted perspective. The sight perplexed and excited him, like an image in a dream. And as in a dream, the sight seemed to suggest unlimited possibilities, the more implausible the more likely. The strangers were eating and, in turns, drinking from a glittering metal cup. This, too, excited him. At first he was frightened that they might discover him, fully aware, as he still was, of how embarrassing and ridiculous it would be for the strangers to find a priest stretched along a twisted fir tree gazing so intently at these two women. But little by little the last residue of propriety and embarrassment abandoned him altogether. He did not know how long he had been there absentmindedly stripping the bark off the fir tree with his fingers; it might have been for hours. At last, one of the women, who seemed to be the younger of the two, rose and started up the hill with the two officers. She passed directly underneath him, so that he could see the top of her head. As she climbed, awkwardly using a walking stick for assistance, her hips were swinging, and on her white face, chapped from the wind and riding, red spots were visible, as sometimes appear on the faces of healthy people after food and drink in the fresh air. The other two were stretched out under the fir tree, having covered themselves with the rug on which they had been sitting.

As though the scene had come to an end, the priest suddenly regained his senses, pulled himself together, and started on his way home, carefully avoiding the couple lying under the fir tree, and full of anxiety that he might be noticed by the three strangers still climbing up the hill.

It was well into the afternoon. In answer to the inquiries of his servant, Radivoje, Father Vujadin mumbled something quite incoherent, lacking even the concentration to offer a plausible excuse for his tardy appearance at lunch. Walking through the empty house, he felt an immense heaviness; the earth and the day itself weighed on him like lead, and life seemed to him like embers and hard wood, without sap and without sweetness. His fingers were sticky with resin. He felt a violent thirst. His eyes were tired, his stride heavy. He ate his lunch and then fell into a heavy sleep.

When he awoke, he felt even more inert. He could just barely recall his encounter with the strangers in the woods, as though it were some distant pain. He left the house, and, taking a short cut up the cliff, reached the pine wood. He looked down; there was not a soul left at the clearing in the fir trees. The sun had set. Scattered paper and ripped tinfoil lay in the grass, glimmering in the twilight. In the soft earth he could discern the traces of women's shoes, deep and oblique and, to his eye, incredibly small. He followed the traces that mingled with men's footprints and those of horses' hoofs, at times losing them and then spotting them again. Absorbed and bent over, he walked as though searching for something he had lost. Blood rushed into his head. The approaching darkness further obscured the path and the footprints. He arrived at a crossroads where the trail ended and a road began. Here they must have mounted their horses, thought Vujadin. The scene was deserted. It was already quite dark. In the still bright skies a diagonal wooden post, used as a landmark in the daytime, was outlined. He rushed down the bumpy road, staggering along the fence that followed the road, feeling the burnt edges of the field that crumbled under his feet. The night was clear, but the heat had not relented. Breathing was difficult; the air was stifling, as if there were an iron vault above his head, in the dark. He crossed a trickling stream which, however, offered no coolness or freshness. He found himself suddenly in his own plum orchard, not far from his house, whose contours could be seen in the dark. Stupefied and exhausted, he slipped to the ground. He rested a short while, and then, abruptly, the image of the women he had seen that day was before him again, and with that image a question: Did I really see them, or have I merely imagined it? This question, ordinary and simple at first, slowly began to torment him. Excited, he jumped up. Was it real or wasn't it? Yes, it was; it was. And he was about to slump down into the grass again, but he paused and looked around.

It was dark, the dull and heavy darkness of the village, in which a sound can be heard across great distances, but lonely and awesome like the last spell of the dawn. And again the question rose with a painful throbbing in his temples: Were the women real or had he made them up? He shuddered each I time the question renewed itself.

Terrified, he started back toward the crossroads. He stumbled in the dark and finally reached the wooden post and took hold of it with his hands. He bent down and began feeling, for footprints in the clay, slightly moist at that spot near the swollen brook. He knelt down, running his fingers across the earth once again, trembling with fear, and burning with the desire to find out whether the day's images derived from fancy or reality. He could gather nothing from the touch of his fingers.

"I saw them! I saw them!" he mumbled to himself, as he raced down to the clearing; and there, too, he feverishly ran his fingers along the ground, trying to penetrate the dark with his eyes, hoping to catch sight of the paper wrappings he had seen, or thought he had seen, in the twilight. At last he had to give up the search. He walked slowly to the plum orchard, as though doomed, his confidence in his own senses shattered. He lay face down on the coarse, warm grass for a long time, his arms spread as though crucified, nailed down by the immense weight of his own muscles and bones. The sound of voices startled him, and broke his half-conscious dreams. A fire was burning on the threshing floor of his neighbors, the Tasićes, and peasants were gathered around it. In the glow of the fire, the shapes of men and women could be seen, milling about and again disappearing in the dark. The voices were alternately high and low, but he was too far away to catch the words.

The Tasićes were about to spread the wheat on the floor. During the great heat waves, when the daytime breezes were so slight that they could not scatter the chaff, threshing was often done at night. A breeze invariably blew in from the mountain glades around nine o'clock.

To one side a fire was going. Young girls were holding aloft burning torches to provide light for the workers, long white sleeves hanging down their outstretched arms. They were motionless, except for the movement required, every so often to switch the torch from one hand to another. The peasants were flinging the grain into the air with their shovels, and in the red glow Vujadin could see the grain fly up and fall to the threshing floor, like heavy rain, while the chaff sailed slowly away and, carried by the wind, dispersed and was lost in the dark.

Father Vujadin's excitement, which had been growing in him all day long, was stirred up again and reached a new peak. He trembled and stammered aloud:

"They won't keep quiet, even at night, but wiggle about in the dark, swinging their torches and waving their sleeves and skirts."

A whole series of images came before him: the foreign women whom he had watched when hidden behind the fir tree; the twilight; the tottering search for the footprints that vanished in the dark; and now the hollow night and the fire which illuminated the forms of men shoveling and women gliding along and waving their arms. Thus, his whole secret existence appeared before him, full of that suffering and torment which had turned into hatred. Gone was the last trace of the other existence: Father Vujadin performing services in the church, listening to the peasants, going to town on market days while women and frightened children make way for him and kiss his hand. There was nothing now that could restore this existence and prevent him from giving expression to those desires to which everything had been driving him. Mumbling to himself like a man who was being pursued, he crossed the plum orchard with almost unnatural speed, and, racing through a dark corridor in his house, found himself in a room overlooking the churchyard and the Tasićes threshing floor. Knocking against furniture as if unaware of its presence, Father Vujadin felt his way to the wall where his hunting rifle was hung, loaded at all times. Seizing it instantly, and without even placing it properly against his shoulder, he fired in the direction of the illuminated threshing floor. There was something pleasing in the pull that wrenched his arms as though the rifle were about to leap out of his hands. Even the recoil that struck him violently against the chest was comforting. It was only after he had fired a second barrel that he heard shrieking, followed by long cries. The torches swayed and then fell, the workers fled, leaving only the fire on the threshing floor. Male voices could be heard, but above all the wailing of an old woman tore the darkness:

"Jovan, my son, they are killing us!"

The shots fired at the Tasićes threshing floor that night signaled the decisive breakthrough of Father Vujadin's secret existence. He looked around in the dark, and found a huge knife on a shelf; clutching it firmly he fled into the night.

He waded across the river Rzav, which at that time of the year is quite shallow. Reaching the other side of the river he sat down, breathless and exhausted, in the sand among the young willows. Still mumbling to himself, he cooled his chest and forehead with water, as though he were dressing a wound.

The following day the news spread through the villages that, in his insanity, Father Vujadin had fired several shots at the Tasićes and then fled into the woods on the other side of the Rzav. The story was hard to believe, and no one could either understand it or explain it, especially among the townspeople, who had more respect for Father Vujadin than did the peasants. Although the peasants accept everything much more coolly and simply, they were perplexed by what happened, and even pitied him in their own way. Meeting on their way to the market, peasant women would pause, ask about each other's health, and then mention Father Vujadin, crossing themselves and begging the great and merciful God to protect them and their own.

Višegrad was full of gendarmes at that time, sent to round up the Nevesinje rebels. Before long they were all combing the countryside, tracking down Father Vujadin. Peasants told the gendarmes that they had seen him in a certain forest, in rags, barefoot and hatless, with a knife in his hand, prowling like a beast of prey. But by the time a patrol arrived there was no trace of the priest. He had fled into the mountains, where, frightening off bands of shepherds, he would warm himself by their fire. One such fire, which could be seen from afar, betrayed him. When the gendarmes arrived just before dawn, they found him asleep, the fire having nearly gone out. They were forced to bind him since he resisted capture.

The next day the gendarmes walked Father Vujadin through the town. His hands chained behind his back, he strutted unnaturally fast. His bare head was thrust back so that his long, grayish hair fell down his shoulders. He clenched his lower lip with his teeth and his eyes were half shut. On that face, turned up to the heavens, there was nothing insane, only a deep martyr-like pain. It was only when he lowered his glance that his bloody eyes betrayed a dull look without understanding. Everyone pitied him. The women wept. The authorities were embarrassed.

The gendarmes had been reluctant to bind him, but when he was released from chains he had put up resistance and tried to run. So he was dispatched to Sarajevo in chains. There, in a large hospital on the Kovači, in a half-darkened room, he lived for ten more years, unaware of himself or of this world.

With the unfortunate Father Vujadin the Porubović family came to an end. A stranger came to the Dobrun parish. And when Father Vujadin finally passed away at the Sarajevo hospital he had been long forgotten. Among the peasants he was mentioned only in passing. ("That happened during the summer Father Vujadin went mad....") In the town, on the other hand, Father Vujadin's fate caused more of a stir and occupied men's minds and thoughts for some time to come. For them it represented some hidden curse, an affliction so unexpected and curious that in commiserating with the unfortunate priest they had forebodings about their own fate and the fate of those close to them. Everyone sought a cause and an explanation for this misfortune, hoping in this way to set their minds at rest, to dull a painful memory. But in spite of their efforts, they could not recall anything in Father Vujadin's life that might explain his strange end. Vujadin's fate continued to confront them, stark, simple, and inexplicable; a cheerless child, a lonely youth, an unhappy man.

At last, the memory of Vujadin and his affliction began to fade, even among the townspeople, but it would continue to evoke memories of other disasters and other times long since forgotten. In talking about the Porubović family, for example, they would not confine themselves to Vujadin and his father and grandfather, but would go back to his great-grandfather the famous Dobrun priest Melentije, and, through him, to Anika's times.

Mullah Ibrahim Kuka was the first to mention Anika. He was a man who liked to appear scholarly and mysterious, but was in fact an idle, kindly fellow and an ignoramus who lived on the reputation and income of his grandfather, the renowned *mutavelija* Mullah Mehmed, a wise and learned man who lived be a hundred and one. Among the collection of books and papers left by Mullah Mehmed there were several yellowing volumes in which he had recorded everything that took place in his town as well as world events of which he had any knowledge. Floods, crop failures, wars near and distant were recorded here, as well as eclipses of the sun and the moon, mysterious signs and phenomena in the skies, and everything that in those days excited the *kasaba* and the people in it. Next to a report that in a town in Germany the devil was born (and since he turned out to be only a foot long he was stuffed into a bottle for all to see), there was an item about a Christian general by the name of Bonaparte who had crossed into Misir with the extraordinary idea of waging a war against the Sultan. And a few pages farther on there was a description of how the *rayah* had risen in the province of Belgrade, and how, incited by evil people, they committed rash deeds. Next to this item there was the following entry:

"That same year a young woman, a Christian (God confound all the infidels!), was overtaken by evil, and created such commotion and gained such strength that her evil reputation spread far and wide. Numerous men, both young and old, had gone to her, and many a youth had gone afoul there. And she placed both authority and law under her feet. But someone was found to deal with her, too, and she was crushed according to that which she deserved. And people were again put straight and were mindful of God's commands."

Mullah Ibrahim read this entry to the people gathered in a coffeehouse, and the elder men tried to recall what they had heard, a long time ago, in their childhood, of Anika's times, of Anika's warfare with the Christians and all the secular and spiritual authorities, and especially of her struggle with the Dobrun priest Melentije. Much of this had long ago been forgotten, but when her story was brought back to light it was much discussed, and, indeed, the expression "Anika's times" was later used as a point of reference in conversation.

This is what happened.

I

In the *kasaba,* where men and women resemble one another like sheep, it happens sometimes that chance will
bring a child, as the wind brings seeds, who is depraved
and stands out from the usual order of things, causing
ill-luck and confusion, until it is cut down itself and the
old order re-established.

Anika's father was Marinko Krnojelac, a baker in
Višegrad. As a young man, he was well known for his
almost feminine good looks, but he had aged quickly
and let himself go before his time. One day—he must
have been about forty at the time—he was out in his
plum orchard when he came upon a peasant who, with
his son, as it happened, was stealing plums from Krnojelac's trees. And picking up a wooden stake, Marinko
killed him, right then and there. The child ran away. The
police seized Marinko that same morning. He was sentenced to six years in the Vidin prison, near Sarajevo.
Travelers reported that they had seen him there with
other prisoners hauling limestone to Žuta Tabija, their
chains rattling.

Marinko spent four years in the jail in Vidin. When
he came back to Višegrad he brought with him a new
wife. His first wife, with whom he had had no children,
had died while he was serving his sentence. He took up
his baking again, and lived quietly, as he had done before the disaster.

His second wife, called Andja, was much younger
than he; bent at the waist, she had a tired, still expression in her eyes and something foreign in her bearing.

The townspeople neither liked her nor respected her. It was generally believed that Krnojelac had found her in the prison, and they called her Vidinka after the prison. It was in vain that Marinko tried to prove this story false and to convince them that she was the daughter of a baker for whom he had worked after leaving jail.

This woman was Anika's mother. Marinko had had another child with her, a boy, older than Anika. He was pale, thin, and tall with sweet, smiling eyes, but quite feeble-minded. They called him Lale. He spent his childhood next to his mother, and later worked with his father at the ovens; he never went out with other boys, never drank, smoked, or looked at girls.

No one could quite recall the date of Anika's birth or the manner of her upbringing.

Next to her withdrawn, unsociable mother, she grew up a tall and thin girl with large eyes full of distrust and pride, with a mouth that looked too big for her small face. She grew, but only upward. Her mother tied a scarf around her head in such a way that no hair showed at all, which made the child look even thinner and more peculiar. Stiff and angular, the little girl walked with her head down as though ashamed of her own height, her lips defiant and tight and her eyes lowered. It was not surprising that so little attention was paid to the Krnojelac girl, who was not much to look at, rarely went out, and even then only on brief trips to her father's shop.

A long and damp winter that had begun very early was capped by an unusual Epiphany, without ice or snow. The procession had to wade through mud. The church banners glistened and the people's eyes blinked in the premature, unhealthy sun. The water from which they drew out the cross was green and quivering, as in the springtime.

As the procession entered the church there was another surprise: Krnojelac's daughter. Although still slender, the thin little girl had changed considerably over the winter. Her skin was milk-white, her bearing straight, and she was generally filled out; her eyes had become larger, her mouth smaller. She wore a satin pelisse of unusual cut. Townspeople turned to look at her, wondering who this young girl was and why she had come to church alone. Indeed, it seemed as though she had arrived from another town, from a strange world.

Anika slowly walked through the crowd with a new stride, looking neither around her nor at any of those who were staring at her, but straight at the gate of the churchyard toward which she was heading. At the gate she almost collided with a handsome young man, a certain Mihailo Nikolin, called Stranac—that is, Foreigner. The two were a trifle embarrassed (he more than she) by the manner of their encounter, but they proceeded to cross the doorstep, one next to the other, almost simultaneously.

The Sunday following the Epiphany, Anika and Mihailo met by the same church gate. But this time it was not by chance; Mihailo had waited for her and approached her directly. If the townspeople had been surprised by Anika's sudden transformation, they were equally surprised by Mihailo, who had never gone out with girls, but who now not only waited for Anika but escorted her home as well. The *kasaba* could not stop

talking about Krnojelac's daughter, who had so unexpectedly become a young woman, and had done it so
well that she stood out, in most striking fashion, from all
the other women of the town.

Anika's first appearance among the townspeople
confused her as much as it did them. She began observing everything around her with new eyes. And as though
she had become aware of her body for the first time, she
began caring for her looks and preening herself.

The spring started out slowly and timorously that
year. When the weather was good, Anika went into the
yard, breathing deeply, her eyes blinking. Walking tired
her, but when she went back into the house her room
seemed so cold and dark that, shuddering, she went
right out again. And when the sun set behind the wall of
the yard and the shadows deepened, she raced up the
hill to higher ground to catch the warm sun once again.
On chilly days, when the skies were dark and sleet was
in the air, Anika stayed in her room, lit the stove, and sat
down next to it, staring into the fire. She unbuttoned her
dress and placed her hand a little below the armpit,
where a young girl's breasts begin to separate from the
ribs. The skin is tight there and particularly smooth. She
would press that spot for hours at a time and watch the
fire and the little openings in the stove that are like eyes;
and all the while she was saying something, as if conversing with the objects in the room. But when her
mother called her to do something, and she had to
withdraw her hand, button up, and step out of the
house, she was startled, as though a trance had been
broken. And when she came back and again sat by the

fire, she could not settle down for quite a while; it seemed to her that she would never again be able to find that spot on which she had held her hand; it was as though not long ago something precious had been snatched from her by the wind and carried away.

So Krnojelac's daughter lived immersed in thoughts about herself, taciturn, indifferent to everyone, but growing shapely and more beautiful every day. The girl's time passed swiftly and mysteriously: the summer, the autumn, and again the winter. On Sundays and holidays Anika went to church, accompanied by a pale, fragile girl from her neighborhood. At first Mihailo met her regularly in the churchyard and exchanged a few words with her. But in time, other young men approached her. The following winter the beautiful and tall young woman, who had by now completely outgrown the timid, skinny Krnojelac girl, had become the chief object of men's desire and women's gossip.

That same winter Marinko died. His son, Lale, took over his father's business and continued working. Although young and feeble-minded, he proved himself a good baker and kept his father's customers.

Anja, who had lived like a shadow until that time, grew thinner and even more bent. Her daughter, whom she had never liked and with whom she did not get along, had reached the age when girls become self-centered and withdrawn, without consideration for their parents or their surroundings. With her husband's death, Vidinka's only link to this town had vanished. She ceased talking almost entirely. She did not weep. She observed everything around her with a detached look and passed away that same year, quietly and unobtrusively. Anika was not even given a chance to put away the mourning clothes she had worn for her father.

Their aunt, Plema, moved in with them, so the girl was not alone. Plema was the late Marinko's half-sister, an old, half-blind widow who had had a turbulent and unhappy youth, but a youth now so distant that no one, including herself, could recall just what was involved. So, there was Anika, with her half-witted brother on one side, and her half-blind aunt on the other. The death of her parents had created a vacuum around her. The mourning clothes only served to emphasize her great beauty and curious disposition.

She was a head taller than her brother, and was still growing and developing. Indeed, she was constantly changing. Her look became free, her dark eyes acquired a purple tone, her skin became whiter, her movements slower and more natural. The *kasaba* speculated about Anika's future marriage. So did the young men at church. She watched them all indifferently and listened to them quietly, but said little herself. And when she did speak it was in a subdued, husky voice, almost without opening her full but pale lips. Her frequently monosyllabic statements left not even the slightest echo behind them, but faded away and perished immediately after they had been spoken. It was her appearance rather than her voice or what she had said that left the strongest impression.

And the more curious and mysterious she became, the more the *kasaba* talked about finding a husband for her. Mihailo's name frequently came up.

Mihailo had come to the *kasaba* six years earlier as an apprentice to Master Nikola Subotić, after two years spent tending the Subotich store in Sarajevo. Master Nikola traded in cattle and hides, and since he had a great knack for business, he would have been among the most prosperous of merchants had it not been for two passions that undermined him: loafing and gambling. He could not settle down anywhere. While still young, he was left a widower and never remarried. A man of great courage and uncommon strength and intelligence, he had had a good deal of luck both in business and in gambling. Among his lucky strokes was the decision he had made eight years earlier to hire Mihailo as an apprentice, and later as a partner, with a salary of three *groschen*. While Master Nikola was constantly on the go, risking his luck at cards, which leaves one empty-handed in the end, Mihailo ran his house and kept his store at Višegrad, working steadily and dividing the profits honestly. Such steadfast behavior had finally gained for Mihailo the respect of the *kasaba*. Initially, of course, the townspeople had received him as they did any stranger, with hostility and mistrust. But he had acquired the two things that make it possible to maintain oneself in the *kosaba:* property and position.

He lived in his master's house, which was kept by an old woman who had been Master Nikola's housekeeper since his marriage. Capable and literate and devoted to his work as he was, Mihailo not only assumed a larger part of his master's work, but the responsibility for it as well. His work habits aside, it seemed as if he were doing his best not to distinguish himself in any way from the townspeople. He did everything the other youths did: went out, drank and sang with them. Efforts were made to marry him off, but he refused all offers, either by jesting about it or through silence. Therefore, it had been a great surprise when, two winters earlier, he had started seeing Anika; but it must be said that it was an even greater surprise when, that spring, he suddenly stopped seeing her altogether. The *kasaba* speculated about what had happened between Krnojelac's daughter, who was such a mystery to them, and Mihailo, about whom they also knew very little. And they were left guessing. Not a soul in this stale *kasaba* ever succeeded in finding out what had separated Mihailo and Anika, for none of them could have imagined what was concealed behind the quiet and diligent façade of Master Nikola's partner.

Mihailo's family was from Sandžak, but his grandfather had left Sandžak and moved to Prizren. The family had been gunsmiths for generations. At Prizren, Mihailo's father acquired a substantial fortune following this craft. One of his brothers had been a priest, and since Mihailo was literate and liked books, they wanted him to follow the same line. Besides, after four generations of working as gunsmiths, the family was living in comfortable circumstances and sought a certain refinement befitting its wealth. However, Mihailo's father had died while still a young man, so Mihailo went into the gunsmith trade together with his brother.

They worked and lived together. Mihailo's brother was twenty-three years old, but he neither sought a girl for himself nor would he allow his younger brother to marry before he did. Since Mihailo strongly desired a woman he suffered a great deal, but he was too embarrassed to come into conflict with his brother over such a thing. In a state of constant torment, he stopped one day at Krstinica's roadside inn, called a han in this part of the country. He was on his way back from his small estate at Ljubižda.

It was still hot and there was no one at the han except for Krstinica herself, a buxom redhead of about thirty. While they were talking, she came very close to him. His whole body quivering, Mihailo extended a hand which met with no resistance. At that moment her husband, Krsto, showed up from somewhere. He was a sickly, morose man, completely dominated, as it turned out, by his healthy and alert wife. She whispered to Mihailo that he should come back the following evening. That night he slept little. When he arrived at the han, breathless and agitated, the following evening, he still could not believe that this was possible, that it would really happen. And, indeed, when she greeted him and showed him the way to an isolated room, it seemed to him as though an insufferable burden had been lifted and that God's whole beautiful world had opened before him.

Twice again that month he went to Krstinica secretly at night, and returned unseen into town. He never gave a thought to Krsto, who, it is true, was only a shadow of a man; nor did he pay any attention to what Krstinica said about the future, her terrible fate, about the pity God would take on her, and how He would free her from this burden at some point.

When Mihailo arrived at the han for his fourth visit he did not find Krstinica at her usual place by the fence. After a short wait he heard sounds of a violent quarrel coming from the same isolated room in which he and Krstinica had spent nights together. He stiffened with fear, but somehow made his way to that room, and, opening the door, saw Krsto and Krstinica wrestling with each other. Krsto was holding an ax in his right hand, but his wife had clasped him in such a way that the hand holding the ax was completely rigid and helpless. Panting from their exertions, both were uttering abuses and fragmentary sentences from a quarrel to which this struggle was evidently the climax. Aghast and astonished, Mihailo reached the doorstep just as Krstinica somehow managed to bring her husband to the floor. She fell with him, not releasing even for a split second the hand in which he held the ax. She fell on top of him as the snow plunges or the water breaks, aiming herself at him like a rock hurled from somewhere, and pressing him with her hands, chest, knees, with all her strength and weight. Krsto thrashed his legs frantically in an effort to free himself, and she spread over him even more firmly, so that she was holding him down with her whole body, even with her chin. Unwilling to remove from him even the smallest muscle and thus relieve the pressure, she cast a glance at Mihailo and yelled under her breath, as though to preserve her energy:

"Legs! Hold his legs!"

Had he sat on Krsto's legs? And had he let Krstinica pull the knife attached to his belt? This was the eighth year that Mihailo had asked himself this question, every day and every night, as he ate and as he slept. And more often. And every time, after an emotional turmoil, he would reply to himself that such a thing was beyond belief, because one must not do such a thing, could not do it. And then a darkness would come over him and in the darkness he would tell himself the truth: that he had done it, that he did sit on Krsto's legs, that he had felt her pulling out the knife and heard her stabbing Krsto three, four, five times, at random, as a woman would, between the ribs, in the sides, the hips. Yes, he had done that which was beyond belief, which it was impossible to do. And this horrible and shameful deed stood before him at all times: unchangeable and irremediable.

After Krsto's murder he had dashed outside and had sat down on the trough in front of the han. The bubbling of the fountain in the stillness of the night sounded to him like thunder. He had placed his hands in the cold water.

Still trembling, he had pulled himself together, and suddenly understood what he had seen and heard inside the han. This horrible deed! So this was the true meaning of his month-long passion, of that vast happiness that had swelled inside him and had been spilling over, without a moment's anticipation of evil. And, strangely enough, instead of thinking of the horror and disaster that had taken place before his very eyes and in which he had had a share, his thoughts had reverted to his month-long happiness, wishing to deform it and shame it. For suddenly it had become clear that, from the very beginning, it had all been just as horrible, shameful, and merciless as the final deed itself. There was not a trace left of the thirst for love and happiness which had surged in him for a whole month. He was now involved in a larger event, in which he was an element without meaning and imperceptibly small, and yet the cause and the instrument of the final tragedy. Between Krsto and Krstinica there were big accounts of which he had known nothing, and which they had been disentangling for a long time—and now everything had been abruptly cut off, ended. He felt betrayed, shamed, robbed, permanently crushed, as though he had been caught in a trap, dragged there by a husband and wife, each for different reasons, as part of a deep and ancient hatred which was greater and stronger than all three of them. That was his happiness.

He was startled by the sound of Krstinica's voice; she was calling to him, almost in a whisper, from the half-opened door. He rose and walked over to her. She held on to the door with one hand and held out his knife with the other, saying in a factual, dry tone:

"I've washed it."

Clearly aware of what would follow if he accepted the knife from her hand, he stepped abruptly to one side, and with a powerful blow of his hand struck the woman: she let go of the door and fell back into the room with a dull thump. He left the door of the han half open. Inside a candle was burning quietly, casting a faint light on Krstinica, who was lying unconscious next to Krsto, whose dead body was already covered with a rush mat.

Mihailo quickly reached the road. The fountain was bubbling noisily and the trough spilled over with a splash.

Mihailo reached town before dawn, intending only to change his clothes before giving himself up to the authorities. But when he reached his house, walked through the yard and into his room, looked over the familiar objects in it, and realized that everything was exactly as it had been when he left for the han the night before, a new conviction rapidly took shape: that he should not report himself to the authorities, for in arresting him they would be taking an innocent man. He was guilty, to be sure, and in a most serious sense; but he was not guilty of the crime that would be charged against him. The gendarmes would be incapable of making this distinction, and he would be forced to defend himself from them, to strike and kill once again if necessary. A fever of excitement overtook him, shattering his strength and dimming his eyesight; but his decision not to report himself and to resist arrest was clear and unequivocal. He made up his mind to flee town immediately.

This unhappy young man, whom his father had intended for the priesthood, judged himself and others that morning, and was great in his misfortune and just and infallible in his judgment. But if he was infallible in his judgment of men, he was less so in his judgment of time. Measuring everything by what was going on inside himself, it seemed to Mihailo that time had passed much more slowly than it had in fact.

He was changing his clothes and making hasty preparations for his flight when his servant, Jevra, entered his room to tell him the strange story she had heard in the *kasaba,* which, it turned out, had already opened to business. Apparently that very night a band of robbers had attacked the Krstinica han, killing Krsto and wounding Krstinica. In spite of her condition, Krstinica had been able to describe the attack in some detail, including a reference to the "Greek bandits" who were involved.

It was too late for Mihailo to leave town, unnoticed; he decided to stay at home a little while longer to await confirmation of Jevra's story, which had come to him like a miracle; and if he should see a policeman or any authority at his gate he would flee through the garden toward the willow thickets.

Later in the day he made a cautious trip into town, firmly determined to kill or to be killed if any suspicion were cast on him, or if a policeman should so much as approach him.

With his hands on a knife hidden in his pocket, his teeth clenched, desperately controlling his trembling hands, Mihailo walked through the streets, wondering why the rest of the world did not hear the loud beating of his heart. He listened to everything that was said about the attack on Krstinica's han with seeming calm. He even summoned enough strength to add a few comments of his own. For days he lived without sleep and without food, prolonging his life by the minute.

Eventually it became clear that Krstinica would stick to her story about the unseen robbers and that no one doubted her testimony; she was in mourning for Krsto, but continued to run the han. She brought her widowed sister to the house so as not to be left alone. It was only when the danger had passed that Mihailo felt his strength giving way, and he fell ill.

But he did not disclose anything, not even during the period of his most acute fever. In three weeks he was on his feet gain. He came to accept the fact that Krstinica was not going to tell the true story of Krsto's death. And it was with a peace of mind, surprising even to himself, that he started making preparations for his departure— slow and cautious preparations, so as not to arouse suspicion. His brother was by nature a greedy person, which eased Mihailo's departure. By leaving the shop to his brother, and taking only a small portion of his share in ready money, he was able to obtain his brother's approval to go into the world. Indeed, he had worked everything out so carefully that when his departure from town finally occurred it aroused neither suspicion nor surprise.

But as soon as he had passed the first hill, and was out of sight of his own fields and hayloft at Ljubižda, his courage failed him and he lost his peace of mind once again. He believed that he was cursed and felt like a pursued beast. He traveled on side roads, took short cuts and detours, stopped only at little-known inns, and crossed and recrossed his own path—all to throw his imagined pursuers off his trail. But as the real danger disappeared, another danger began growing in him, and a game of infected fancy and disturbed conscience was taking root. He passed near the town of Nova Varoš, where he had relatives, but he did not stop. It was not until reached Priboj that he went into a han for the first time to buy bread and tobacco.

Moderate by nature and brought up strictly by his father and elder brother, Mihailo had smoked little before; but from that time on he smoked constantly and passionately. He discovered that this permanent little flame before the eyes was a blessing and that the same purple smoke which tickles the eyes and the throat made it possible for a man to shed a tear without weeping, and, in exhaling the smoke, to sigh without sighing. So this flame shone before his eyes or burned between his fingers for many years to come. The smoke, always the same and yet forever varied, helped prevent his thoughts from reverting to what he feared most, and in exceptionally tranquil hours guided him into a state of complete oblivion and forgetfulness; it fed him, like bread, and comforted him, like a friend. At night he would dream about smoking as others dream of encounters with those they love. But when his dreams turned into nightmares and he thought he saw Krsto's body or Krstinica's eyes, he would awaken with a cry, seize tobacco as one would a pistol, or as those who do not sleep alone would seize somebody's hand. And as soon as the flint had ignited in the dark, and the tobacco had caught the sparks, he would relax and with the invisible smoke he would blow away the burden from his agitated mind.

He continued his journey, avoiding Višegrad, which was much too near his home. On the slopes of Mount Romanija at the great Obodjaš han, he met Master Nikola Subotić who frequently traveled on the road between Sarajevo and Višegrad. Subotić employed Mihailo as a herdsman, his first real pause since his wanderings had begun. Unaccustomed to the hard life and rough customs, he had to endure a great deal, but all this vanished before one great and singular blessing: that he was once again hard at work with other young men, in the fields or in market places swarming with people.

He spent two years in Sarajevo and on various side trips for Subotić. And it was at this point that, as we have seen, Subotić singled out Mihailo from the other young men and put him in charge of his interests in Višegrad. At first he found this town forbidding, bounded as it was by two rivers and closed in by the mountains. Its people struck him as a scornful and mistrustful lot. But as time went on he grew accustomed to their ways, until he developed a real fondness for the town and its people, almost as if they were his own. In the process his secret torment seemed to have diminished, and life was easier.

On meeting Krnojelac's daughter, Anika, last year, new prospects suddenly opened up for him, prospects which until then had not existed and for which he had not dared hope. The first time in several years a whole day and a night passed in which he did not feel that black and horrible thought spinning through him, the thought in which Krsto's murder and a desire for his own death had become one and the same obsession. The very idea that something in this world might restore to him the freedom he had enjoyed before that dawn at the han was enough to lift him from the earth.

But when the time came for him to go beyond these hopes and dreams, insurmountable barriers seemed to arise before him, of whose nature only he was aware. Shaken and cut down early in his life, he could not find a way to this girl: he would approach her genuinely and cheerfully, and then, suddenly, he would panic and retreat. The happiness and joy felt with Anika was not enough to free him from the terror of the earlier experience. He yearned for Anika's smiles and hungrily followed all of her movements and expressions, carefully measuring them later in his solitude. He was searching for some resemblance to Krstinića, frightened at the same time that he might find it. This, of course, poisoned all of his pleasures, and even began to alter his appearance; it was the cause of his strange behavior toward the girl herself.

So a whole year passed. There was no true understanding between them, and yet there was no break either. Meanwhile Anika was growing more beautiful and more unusual and was greatly admired. Under such circumstances, the break was inevitable; it came the following spring, on quite an insignificant issue.

One day Aunt Plema called at Mihailo's, and told him that Anika wished to see him. He thought it unsuitable for him to visit a girl's home, but nevertheless he agreed to go.

Krnojelac's house was quite luxuriously furnished; more so, at any rate, than other houses in Višegrad. It was not so much its wealth but something foreign and outstanding in its color, furnishings, and carpeting. In this setting Anika seemed to him even taller and more extraordinary. She explained that she had asked him over to find out what plans he had made for St.

George's feast day. There was a curious lack of proportion between her hollow, deep voice, her grave and
milk-white face, and this trifle about which she was in-
quiring. Mihailo's confusion grew. However, they agreed
to meet and he promised to go to the feast "with God's
help."

"I shall be there too, with God's help and if I'm not
married by then," added Anika.

"I don't see how you could get married within the
next few days."

"There are many things I can do."

"No, I don't think you can. I don't think you can."

"You think not?"

This last phrase, strangely uttered, forced Mihailo to
look her in the eyes.

These eyes, always deep, were now as though illuminated from within, clear and opaque all at once; they
flashed with the color of blood, and the passion of tears,
and their expression became sharp, clear, and hard. Mihailo stared straight into those eyes, dazed by their light,
and full of disbelief, waiting for their color to change or
fade away, like an illusion. But the look grew sharper and
clearer, and the glow more intense. A thought flashed in
Mihailo's mind and instantly took shape, and he wanted
to scream, to yell. Anika's look was familiar to him; he
had seen it some time ago, at the han, and in the dreams
of his long unhappy nights. It seemed to him that he was
gazing at Krstinica's animal-like eyes, full of horrible and
unknown intentions; and he wanted to run away, although one could never run far enough. He thought he
might break the hold of her eyes by an abrupt movement

and a violent scream, as he had so often done when confronted by this image in those sweaty nooks in haylofts and roadside inns. But the spell could not be broken, and as he stood there, swaying back and forth between dreams and reality, Anika's question rang again and again in his ears, with a hundredfold din.

"You think not?"

Anika and Mihailo continued to stare at each other, with the intensity of lovers in their first few days, or as two beasts that collide in the dark of the forest, seeing only each other's eyeballs. But even the longest look of love comes to an end. Tearing his eyes away from hers, Mihailo glanced at Anika's strong and beautiful hands, with their fine skin and rosy nails. Finally realizing the full extent of his horror, he was forced to give up any hope of release from it. And so he began to retreat, like a trapped beast.

With great effort he produced a smile designed to delude his enemy, and managed to control himself sufficiently not to run out of the house and slam the door. Instead, he took his leave and walked out with an easy stride, in spite of his deadly fear. The door closed behind him; somehow he crossed the yard, and walked to the town square, deserted at this time of day. The fountain was bubbling quietly. Mihailo approached the stone trough and, sitting down at one end, placed his hands under the stream of water, regaining his senses and calming down.

He spent the next few days struggling with his thoughts, as though with shadows and apparitions. For one whole year Anika had been the core of all his hopes;

now he was losing these hopes, and he felt as if he were losing life itself.

When Aunt Plema called on him once again to ask him to come to Anika, he replied that he could not do so. The day before the feast of St. George she came to inquire whether he would accompany Anika to the feast. "I cannot," he replied, anticipating some terrible reaction, as one awaits a blow. (Like a man who is seriously ill, he could think only of himself; it did not occur to him to wonder, and he could not have guessed, what was going on in Anika's mind during those days.)

Events developed quickly, with deeper and more serious consequences than anyone could have predicted.

St. George's feast day that year was remembered in town as the day on which Anika "announced herself." By the time of the feast of St. Elias, only two months later, her banner was completely unfurled. Anika opened her home to men. She hired two women, village tramps, whose names were Jelenka and Saveta, as her companions. It was in this manner that the reign of Anika Krnojelac began—a reign of a year and a half in which Anika devoted herself to evil and disaster in much the same way that other people might occupy themselves with children, bread, their homes. She ignited men, set them afire, not only in the *kasaba*, but in the whole district of Višegrad. Many details have been forgotten, and many a misfortune was never revealed, but it was not until Anika's times that the people of Višegrad discovered what powers an evil woman possesses.

Little by little the yard in front of Anika's house came to resemble a camping site. No one could keep track of the many who came at night; young and old, bachelors and married men, neighbors from nearby Dobrun and travelers from distant Foča. And there were others who, bereft of shame or reason, came in full daylight and sat in the yard or, if allowed, in the house, or simply wandered about with their hands in their pockets, glancing from time to time up at Anika's window.

One of the most desperate and ardent of Anika's visitors was certain Tane Kujundžija, a thin man with very wide eyes on a worn, tired face. He would sit on a crate behind the kitchen door, saying nothing, waiting patiently for Anika, looking up only when Jelenka and Saveta entered the kitchen. Going past him as though he did not exist, Jelenka and Saveta received their guests and proceeded with them to their rooms. When they threw him out of the kitchen, he would seat himself somewhere in the yard, bashfully smiling at Jelenka as she chased him out.

"Ah, let me be, *bona*. What am I doing to you?"

He would wait in the yard for hours, with a mournful expression, as though he found it hard to sit there for so long. Occasionally he would rise and leave without a word, only to come again the next day. At home he was scolded by his wife, Kosara, a robust woman of peasant stock with eyebrows that ran together.

"Have you been sitting in the bitches' yard again, you ugly duckling? You should have stayed there!"

"Eh, I should have stayed there," he repeated sadly, and his thoughts went back to the yard he had just left.

This indifference drove Kosara insane and she started a dreadful row, but Tane only waved his hand, as though awakened from a dream.

Some of Anika's company were quite mad, like Nazif, a big and retarded youth from the house of a bey. He was a quiet fool, deaf and dumb. He would pass under Anika's window and call to her in his unintelligible language at least twice a day. He offered her a handful of sugar, and she jested with him about it.

"That isn't enough, Nazif, not enough," Anika called from above, smiling. Somehow or other the idiot understood what she had said, ran home, stole some money from his brothers, bought two half-pecks of sugar and returned to the window. Grinning with happiness, he offered her his fortune in sugar. Anika roared with laughter and indicated to him, through signs, that he had still not brought enough, and he left mumbling sadly.

From that day on he came every morning, carrying a basket filled with sugar, as well as additional amounts under his wide sash and in his pockets. Anika soon grew bored with the joke. The madman's persistence angered her, and she sent Saveta and Jelenka to chase him away. He defended himself and then left muttering incoherently, only to appear bright early the following day with even more sugar. They chased him away again. All day long he carried the sugar around the town, twittering and murmuring. Children followed him, teased him, and stole the sugar from the basket which he clutched so passionately.

There were, of course, men who, lacking the courage to come in the daytime, waited for night to make their regular appearance, although many of them had no prospects of even entering Anika's house. They would simply sit there, on the trough by the fountain, waiting and smoking all night long. A man could arrive at night unseen by anyone; and he could leave in the same way. On the following morning a small heap of wood shavings and cigarette butts would appear where he had been sitting. He must have been an unhappy young man, God only knew which one; Anika certainly did not know him, and he knew her only by sight. For they were not all there just to see Anika. Some came simply because they were drawn to evil things, others because they had been from birth lost and tormented. Everything that was questionable, and contrary to God's will, assembled around that house and in that yard. The circle of men around Anika's house was rapidly expanding, and in time embraced not only the weak and the wicked, but the healthy and the wise too.

In the end, there were but few young men in the *kasaba* who had not been to Anika or who had not tried to approach her. First, they went to her stealthily, at night, obliquely and individually. They talked of her as of something shameful and horrible, but at the same time distant and almost beyond belief. But the more they talked and gossiped about her, the more comprehensible her evil seemed. At first they pointed a stern finger at those who went there, but in the end it was those who did not go to Anika's who attracted scorn. Since only a small group of men managed to reach Anika at first try, and the rest had to content themselves with Jelenka and Saveta, envy, male pride, and vanity began taking their toll. Those who had been rejected came again, hoping to make up for the double humiliation of having gone and been rejected all in one night; and those who had been received once could no longer stop themselves, but as if under a spell went back again and again.

The women of Višegrad were unanimously and savagely against the disgrace of the house in the Mejdan and fought Anika defiantly, ruthlessly, as women will, without much reflection. But their struggle was not always easy or safe, and it was in such a struggle that the Ristićes household was ruined.

The old Ristićka, a rich widow with the ability and resolution of a man, had successfully married off all her daughters as well as her only son, a small fellow with rosy cheeks and a quiet disposition, a clever merchant who always sought the company of older men, made money, and looked after his family. The wife his mother had found him was a beautiful, quiet girl from a rich family in Foča. They had two children.

The trouble began at a funeral repast the previous winter, when the women were complaining about Anika and their men. Old Ristićka, having emptied a glass for the soul of the deceased, remarked loudly and defiantly:

"By God, I say, don't let them go. I have a son, too, a good man. But so long as I'm alive he'll never cross that bitch's doorstep."

The very next day these words were reported to Anika, as was everything said about her, and a day later Ristićka received a message:

"Within the next month your son, the good man, will come to me with all of his Saturday earnings in his hands; and you will then discover who Anika is."

A certain restlessness and concern crept into the Ristić house, but this did not stop the old woman. She went on upbraiding Anika, who was, at this very time, at the height of her powers. On the following Saturday the young Ristić, drunk and half carried by his companions, called on Anika with his Saturday earnings, deep in the pockets of his trousers. He lay in front of Anika's door, thrashing his feet, scattering money around, frantically calling out to Anika and his mother at the same time. Jelenka and Saveta hovered over him and invited the curious to come in and take a look. At dawn Anika ordered Saveta to arrange for two young Turks to escort him home.

When the old Ristićka had realized that her son was late for supper, she had made the rounds of the town. Finally understanding that he had, indeed, gone to Anika's, the old woman went home, collapsed in the middle of the parlor, foaming at the mouth, and never again regained consciousness. Her daughter-in-law, a slender, pale girl, with dark hair and large eyes, walked into the main room and, kneeling down before the sanctuary lamp, swiftly crossed herself several times and began cursing Anika:

"I pray to God, woman, to see you mad, driven about in chains; I hope to God to see you become leprous, your whole body covered with sores; tired of yourself; desiring death, but death not wanting you! Amen, oh, great and only God! Amen. Amen."

Then and only then she broke into tears, which surged forth with such power that she was blinded, lost her balance, and crumpled, falling to the floor with all her weight. Groping with her arms, she knocked down the sanctuary lamp and the light went out. Later in the night she arose and slowly began putting the room in order. She washed the floor, wiped the oil that had spilled on the rug, prepared another lamp and lit it, crossed herself three times in front of it, and bowed without a word. She looked at the child who was sleeping in the crib. Then she went over to the sanctuary lamp, sat down under it, and, with her hands neatly folded in her lap, waited for her man.

Everything is known in the *kasaba*, even things one says to oneself; there is no secret of either the soul or the body. The news of the young woman's curse reached Anika the following day. In the afternoon, Anika's servant, a one-eyed Gypsy, called on the daughter-in-law and handed her a kerchief full of silver and copper coins. As soon as the Gypsy woman had handed over the kerchief, she retreated into a far corner of the yard where, full of foreboding, she repeated a message her mistress had given her. Even to a Gypsy this was a terrifying task.

"Anika sends you this. 'Let Ristićka count the coins in the company of her son and daughter-in-law; his earnings are all there, not a penny is missing. She returned to you your man, and she is returning his money as well. She took out only enough to pay for what she had given him. The curse means nothing to her.'"

Next to the women of the town, who all hated her with equal venom, Anika's greatest foe was Master Petar

Filipovac. His son Andrija was among those who called most frequently at Anika's house. The eldest son in the family, an awkward and pale youth, always sleepy and seemingly lost, he showed, however, great energy and persistence in his passion for Anika. He stopped coming home altogether because his father tried to kill him one night, and would surely have done so had not his mother hidden him and saved him. Now he slept in the hayloft, and his mother stealthily sent him food. And all the while she prayed to God and wept, but in secret, for Master Petar had threatened to throw her out of the house too after thirty years of married life, if she uttered but one sigh or shed one tear for the renegade.

The people who truly hated and condemned Anika congregated in the shop of Master Petar Filipovac. They might take a smoke or exchange a few words about something else, but they would invariably return to their major concern: the girl from the Mejdan. In this connection they recalled the story of Tijana, often told them by their elders.

Some seventy years earlier there was a shepherd's daughter, by the name of Tijana, who was well known for her beauty. Casting aside every scruple, she had played havoc with the *kasaba*. Such was the race and the fight to get her that during a great church fair all the *čaršija* shops had remained closed, which had happened before only in time of plague or flood. The Sarajevo silversmiths and the Skoplje merchants came with copper dishes, and left with her both their goods and their earnings, departing as naked as rifles. Nothing could be done to destroy her. But one day she vanished as abruptly as she had appeared. One of Tijana's first admirers was a certain Kosta, called the Greek, a rich young man with neither mother nor father. He wanted to marry her, they said, but Tijana would not hear of it; instead she gathered around her more ruffians than ever, Turks and men of every faith. The Greek withdrew and disappeared from the *kasaba*. It was later learned that he had gone to the Banja Monastery, had become a monk and was pining away. And they forgot all about him. But exactly a year later, when Tijana was in full swing and both God and men had had enough of her, that same Kosta suddenly turned up again. His face was overgrown with hair, and he had lost weight and was dressed in a costume half-monk and half-peasant. He had neither the sack nor the stick of a monk; instead, there were two little pistols tucked in his belt. He barged straight into Tijana's house, burst open the door of her room, and fired several shots at her. But she was only slightly injured, and fled into the street. Running up the Mejdan, she lost her slippers, ducats fell from her neck and pins from her hair. She ran toward a woodland below the old town. Reaching a ditch, she dropped into it, utterly exhausted. The monk overtook her and killed her.

There she lay, all day, her hair spread about her, still holding onto a whip, her mouth wide open; and it almost seemed as if she were watching over the shepherds some distance away. A great black wound could be seen in her blue silk garment. At twilight two Gypsies were sent from town to bury her where she had been killed. The slayer himself disappeared into the forest. No one looked for him. But three days later he was found, his throat slashed, on the mound over Tijana's grave.

While men sat in their shops recounting the past and women were weeping in their homes over current domestic tragedies, the game of feminine evil that Anika was playing went on. It was at this time that Anika began her fight with Melentije, the Dobrun priest, over his son, Jakša, called the Deacon.

II

Anika's reputation had spread far and wide. But it had never occurred to Jakša Porubović, the son of the Dobrun parish priest, to visit her. He preferred rakiya to women, and better than rakiya he liked his freedom and the right to loaf.

Jakša was twenty years old, the tallest and the strongest youth in the *kadiluks* of Dobrun and Višegrad. He had even gone to Čajniče to wrestle with a certain Nedjo, called Kurjaković, and had pinned him down.

Fair and red-haired, with green, bold eyes, Jakša was the very opposite of his father, who was a tall, thin man with an ashen face and a black wrinkle between his brows; he had been gray-haired since his youth. The priest was one of those people who was as much a burden to himself as he was to others, who seem to carry inside themselves from birth to death a heavy thought. His son, Jakša, on the other hand, took after his maternal grandfather, a certain Milisav, from Trnavci, a rich man, jovial and kindly.

The priest dearly loved his only son and was greatly upset by his wild and restless behavior. Jakša had been a deacon for one year now, and his father had pressed him to get married so that he could enter the priesthood. But Jakša did not care too much for the ministry, and he would not hear of marriage. The priest's wife, a good, dark, worn old woman, thrifty to the point of stinginess, now defended the son and then again supported the father. And she wept for both of them.

That winter Jakša had decidedly calmed down a little. He was at home more often, and even allowed his parents to talk about his future marriage, although he himself never said a word. They were expecting a visit from the Bishop of Sarajevo in the spring, sometime after St. George's feast day, and it was the priest's hope that by that time his son would be married and that he could be ordained by the Bishop himself. Toward the end of the winter, Jakša came to Višegrad on business.

He arrived during the big fish runs at the end of February, when thousands of fish come down the Rzav in three great swarms, each one separated by a few days. One such run occurs early in the morning, usually just before dawn, and lasts until noon, drawing everyone down to the river, nets in hand. The children waded in the shallow waters, catching fish in pots or in their bare hands.

These three days have become an early springtime holiday; the homes all smell of oil, and so much fish is consumed that people become tired of it and its price drops precipitously. The last catch, in fact, is usually bought in bulk by neighboring peasants, who take it to their villages, where the fish are stretched out and dried.

Riding along the Dobrun road that morning, Jakša saw the Rzav before him with fishermen and children scattered along it like ants. The sun shone brilliantly, the earth smoked, the fish glittered.

Jakša quickly finished the work that had brought him to Višegrad and was planning to return to Dobrun before dark. But some friends asked him to stop by at a coffeehouse where several merchants' sons were snacking on fish and drinking a mild rakiya. They were jesting with Gazija, one of Višegrad's best fishermen and, like all fishermen, a drunkard. Gazija stood in the middle of the café, holding a soaking net from which a heavy lead weight was hanging; the water dripped onto the floor next to his bare feet. He had sold all of his catch. Wet up to his waist, he was shivering slightly and emptying one glass of rakiya after another. They asked him how the catch had been this year, and how much he had caught and sold, but, like most real hunters, he superstitiously evaded questions of this sort.

"I hear you've made a pretty penny and are preparing to buy a gift for Anika," one of the young men taunted him.

"I, a gift for Anika? My turn will never come—because of you gentlemen!" he protested, rolling a cigarette, and transferring his weight from one foot to another.

The truth is that he was one of many who tried in vain to reach Anika, and they teased him so that they themselves could start talking about her.

Gazija paid for his drinks and left the coffeehouse, still shivering with cold, and muttering:

"That's for you, gentlemen. Such goods are not for me. I live on water."

And they went on talking about Anika.

Jakša saw her that same night. He did not go back to Dobrun again. He spent whole nights with Anika, and it seemed that she received only him. The *kasaba* talked of nothing but the priest's son. Women turned their heads away from him, and men spent their time giving him counsel, gossiping about him, and envying him.

In vain the priest sent messages to his son, threatened and implored. Seeing that he was getting nowhere, he decided to go to Višegrad personally. That did not help either. Then he turned to the *kajmakam*, the Mayor of Višegrad. His name was Alibey.

The son of the rich and respected Jevad Pasha Plevlyak, Alibey could easily have resided at a more distinguished place, or occupied a higher position, but from his mother, who was descended from the renowned Mehmed Pasha Sokolović, who built the Višegrad bridge, he had inherited a great and noble indifference to all things, especially to profiteering and speculating. Twenty-five years ago, when the *kasaba* was enjoying a sudden boom and a brief period of well-being and plenty, Alibey was appointed police commissioner of the *kasaba* at the age of twenty-one. In those days a great deal of trade passed across the Višegrad bridge, and the town was full of goods, money, and travelers; therefore a large police force was needed, in the command of a strong and incorruptible person such as Alibey.

In time trade turned the other way, deserting the Višegrad road, and foreigners were not seen there often. The police force was reduced and many left; Alibey was the only member of the force who did not abandon

Višegrad; he stayed on and became the mayor, or *ka-jmakam*. With his father he went to war twice, to Vlaška and to Serbia, but on both occasions he came back to his position in Višegrad.

He had two homes, the most beautiful in town. Both were on the bank of the Drina, and between them there stood a large garden. The *kajmakam* had been married several times, but all of his wives were dead. He was known for his weakness for women. With the years he drank increasingly, but always with moderation and taste. Despite his age and the irregular life he had led, he still had a slender figure. The sharp and restless features of his youth had, by this time, mellowed into a calm, smiling expression. Between his gray mustache and his big beard, youthfully reddish lips were clearly delineated. He spoke without gestures, but with warmth in his voice and frankness in his eyes. He had a passion for hot springs, and whenever he heard report of a new one, he would go to look it over, no matter how far away it might be. He would frequently have a fountain or a spa constructed there at his own expense.

In the *kasaba*, which had dwindled both in population and in commerce, the *kajmakam's* duties had for a long time been few. With the distinction of a man of noble birth, he was slowly growing old and was living for his own pleasure and for the pleasure of others. He visited his estate at Plevlje, or went calling on his friends, the begs of Rujani and Glasinac.

The *kajmakam* had always felt uneasy about the Do-brun priest, who was as straight and stiff as a plank. When the priest called on the *kajmakam*, Alibey received him coldly, but listened to his complaints about Anika, and promised to investigate the matter. He had also heard about the daughter of the late Krnojelac, and had already received many complaints about her. He promised the priest that Jakša would be sent to Dobrun and the woman brought under control.

Overcome with shame, the priest spent two days at Višegrad, staying at the home of a friend, a frightened, half-blind priest, named Josa. But when he saw that his son was not going to return with him and that the *kajmakam* was not going to help him, he mounted his gentle black horse, and, with a soul full of bitterness, returned to Dobrun.

As soon as the priest had left, the *kajmakam* called in the chief of the Višegrad police, a certain Hedo Salko, and ordered him to call on this Christian woman, to threaten her with prison if she did not control herself, and to send Jakša back to Dobrun forthwith.

Hedo carried out the order. He mounted his horse as on an important and solemn occasion, rode up the Mejdan, and strutted back and forth in front of Anika's yard, yelling sharply to Jelenka, who was busy in the garden. The disorder around their house would not be tolerated any longer, he said, and furthermore, if that miserable son of the Dobrun priest did not go home immediately, he, Hedo Salko, would have a word or two to say to him. Jelenka ran to the house and reported it all to Anika, who instantly appeared at the door, but Hedo, anticipating this, had already trotted off on his high horse.

As lethargic as a court of law and as punctual as its worldly justice, Hedo had for thirty years carried out his duty in this manner. His face was entirely unique, full of deep and unusual wrinkles which had developed in unexpected directions, covering his forehead and nose and chin, swallowing up his thin mustache, and descending like streams of water down his scorched neck. From this labyrinth of lines protruded two round eyes without lashes, giving him the expression of an old horse. Thirty years as a policeman in the *kasaba* had shaped him in this way.

The *kajmakam* was a man who disliked unpleasant things, even in the neighboring *kadiluk,* the man to whom Hedo never dared report a single problem that had not already been satisfactorily resolved. Policemen came and went and were either too easily bribed or too scrupulously zealous. So during the past twenty-five years everything had landed on poor Hedo's head, from crop damage, drunkenness, and the neighbors' rows to the most horrible murders and the biggest robberies. He had distinguished himself as a young policeman, and so became the chief. But soon thereafter he realized that riots, murders, and misfortunes occur as some natural and inevitable evil, and that his, Hedo's, hands and eyes were too weak to cope with them all, and resolve them, punish offenders according to merit. Instead of gradually acquiring a sense of authority and power in his position, he had acquired a superstitious awe of crime, and indeed almost respect for a person who had thought up and then carried out an evil deed. He automatically appeared at every place prescribed by his duty, not to clash with the violator, but to chase him out of his district and into someone else's. In constant touch with human evil and human suffering, he had gained over the years a most peculiar experience, to which he unconsciously adjusted all his actions. On the basis of this experience he had arrived at two seemingly opposed truths, but both equally valid. First, that evil, misfortune, and unrest are constant and eternal and that nothing concerning them can be changed. Second, that every single problem will somehow be resolved and settled, for nothing in this world is lasting or eternal: the neighbors will make peace, the murderer will either surrender himself or else flee into another district where there are other policemen, with their chiefs; stolen objects will be recovered sooner or later, for people are not only thieves but also blabbermouths and informers; drunkards will sober up and therefore one should not tangle with them while they are drunk and know not what they do.

These two maxims guided Hedo in all of his official business. But when a woman was involved in some dispute or crime, this passivity of his turned into complete numbness. In these moments he resembled a man on whose neck a wasp has descended; he stiffens and lets it walk up and down, while he himself does what is most wise: waits for it to fly away by itself. As soon as Hedo Salko came across a woman in the course of an investigation, he would go no further, unless absolutely necessary. Of course this was not done deliberately. Experience had taught him this lesson and instinct had led him to it: to get involved in a dispute in which women are mixed up meant putting one's finger between a door and the door frame.

When Jakša arrived that evening, Anika would not allow him into her room, in spite of all his entreaties and

411

arguments. She had simply decided not to receive him, and did not wish even to discuss it. To all of his ardent words, she replied scornfully:

"Why don't you go back to Dobrun? Your father wants you."

And Jakša answered:

"I have no father. You know that."

"What do I know?" she inquired softly.

"You know well what I have said to you every night and I know all that you have said to me."

He recalled the caresses and confused words; the dawn approaching and her palms covering his eyes.

It was ridiculous and sad to see that huge man re-counting like a woman the details of the past nights But it was obvious that the words had intoxicated him as love itself had, and that he did not know what he was doing or saying. Anika listened to him patiently, without a word, without compassion, but also without derision. He knew he had to leave, but wanted to know when he might see her again. She replied, smiling:

"Well, perhaps at the Dobrun fair, on the day of Our Lady."

From then on Jakša stayed at Zarije's inn. His pride would not allow him to loiter in front of Anika's door. He treated people to drinks and drank himself, sitting motionless, his fists on the table, his handsome head tilted back resting against the wall, his face turned upward to the grimy ceiling as though reading something on it. No one dared mention Anika to him, although they all knew why he had taken to drinking.

Thus he sat for hours, looking at the ceiling, and recalling not so much her words as her silences. He was full of that silence of hers and felt it in his intestines. Even without closing his eyes he saw her sitting on the low *minderluk*, a white scarf firmly tied around her head covering not only her hair but her forehead down to her eyes. Her hands are in her lap; she firmly presses one palm against the other, as though telling a fortune. Her face is large and white, her cheekbones prominent, her eyes, which have become deep in color, are surrounded by a smile which illuminates them. Her silence shortens his breath and clouds his sight. If he could once more sit next to her, he would take that head in both his hands, twist it violently, bend it down to the bed, to the floor, to the grass. But then he recalled her cold scorn, which had made him suffer so much, not because he could not destroy it, but because there was no use destroying it. And he was startled, as if he had hit a wall; his large fists on the table trembled.

While Jakša was thus drinking at Zarije's inn, there were new disorders around Anika's house, of which Hedo Salko pretended he knew nothing. Since she did not wish to receive guests, drunken men rushed at her gate while others, hoping thereby to win her fancy, ejected the drunken men from her door.

Knowing Hedo's weaknesses, the *kajmakam* finally decided that he would have to go to Anika's house himself to see what was causing the trouble. One afternoon he paid her a visit, accompanied by a gendarme who soon returned alone. The *kajmakam* stayed until nightfall. And the next day he came again.

And it could not be otherwise. The *kajmakam*, who had seen many women in his lifetime and had not been without a wide choice, felt that here he had found something extraordinary—a woman of such movements and such looks as had not been seen since the *kasaba* had first entrenched itself in Višegrad, or, indeed, since men and women have known each other and borne children together. This body was not born or nurtured in connection with anything surrounding it; it simply happened.

The *kajmakam* paused in wonderment before so much beauty, as if he had come upon something familiar and long lost—the rich whiteness of her skin, which so completely covered her veins, and from which the deep red of her lips was separated only by a sharp, abrupt line; that same rich whiteness which turned so gradually into a hardly perceptible pink around her nails and under her ears. This whole, large, harmonious body, solemn in its tranquility, slow in its movement, seemingly preoccupied only with itself, feeling no desire or need to resemble others—it was like a rich self-sufficient empire, with nothing to conceal and no need to display its wealth, living in silence and despising others for their need to talk and explain themselves.

The *kajmakam* took all this in with the eyes of a man of mature years who believes that he knows the full value of life and at the same time recognizes that this life is slipping away from him. What woman would have dared put off this man, this Turk, if not Anika herself? But Anika chose not to do so.

The following day, after the *kajmakam's* second visit, Anika asked to see Tane the silversmith, who was still in her yard after these many months.

"Can you write?"

"Yes, I can," replied Tane, and to demonstrate it he spread out the fingers of his right hand, his eyes moist with pleasure.

Tane brought from the shop his ink, pen, and paper. Now he sat on the *minderluk,* Anika next to him.

"Can you write down everything you are told?"

"Well, yes, I think so."

The fury that lives in every idle woman dictated to Anika, and she, through Tane, to the pen. Tane began to write, his whole body leaning to one side, slowly stringing one letter next to the other, and his wrinkled cheek constantly being thrust out, lifting up and down as he followed the movements of the pen with his tongue. Anika dictated:

"You are the priest of Dobrun and I the whore of Višegrad. Our parishes are divided, and it would be better for you to leave alone that which does not belong to you."

Tane, who was already hesitant about putting down certain words, stopped writing altogether at this point, and gave Anika a ridiculously worried look, as though he wanted to be told that it was all a joke and that she was not seriously thinking about sending this letter to the priest of Dobrun. Without looking at him, however, Anika caught him up sharply:

"Write!"

And he went on writing with the same ridiculously worried look on his face.

"Before I was even born, you were jumping the fence at Nedeljkovica's, while her husband, Nedeljko, thinking it was a badger in the cornfield, almost killed you. And today your priestly robes are still being mended in the homes of friendly widows. And I, for my part, have never inquired after your health, or asked about your doings. And yet you felt called upon to send to me the *kajmakam* and his police. It would have been better for you to have touched a snake under a rock. Well, priest, I want you to know that the *kajmakam* has come to me twice since then, and that I have ungirdled his sword as though he were a child, and, old as he is, he held a basin and a towel for me; perhaps you would like to know these things. And since you are worried about your handsome son, there he is at Zarije's inn; shaven like a bridegroom, it is true, and dead drunk, but that doesn't matter; take him home by all means; he will sober up, his beard will grow, and, as far as I am concerned, he can even become a bishop."

She paused. Tane recovered his breath. He could just barely manage to follow her, although he had left out many letters and whole syllables too.

Anika's letter to the Dobrun priest was known in the *kasaba* the very next day. But after the *kajmakam's* first visit, the town could no longer be surprised. It was even said that upon learning the latest news, the Dobrun priest delivered vespers wearing his robes inside out, the candles burning upside down.

It was believed in the *kasaba* that no human act could alter this situation; they must await God's hand. Even

416

so, Anika managed to turn the *kasaba* upside down once more.

On the day of Our Lady, a great fair was held at the Dobrun church, to which peasants come in large numbers, even from the most remote villages.

Anika, too, had decided to go to the fair; she left for Dobrun at noon of the day before, riding with Jelenka on quiet well-fed horses, a servant following behind them. They rode through the side alleys, but even so the news that Anika was on her way spread quickly through the *kasaba*. Men moved about and twisted their necks to catch a glimpse of her as she set off on the steep road below Stražište. Apprentices and novices ingeniously conceived of jobs to do in the attic, climbed up and looked through the attic window to see Anika disappear behind the hill.

Following Anika on a lame horse, which, in his hurry, he had hired from a Gypsy, was Tane the silversmith. Paler than usual, with a long face, he followed Anika, riding right through the heart of the *čaršija* without shame or embarrassment. He paid no heed to the laughter and mockery which greeted him; perhaps he did not even hear their cries. But after he had disappeared behind the hill an uncomfortable silence came over the town. The men had withdrawn into their shops and were trying to busy themselves with whatever was at hand. And many of those who only a few minutes earlier had laughed at Tane were now devising some pretext by which they might unnoticed follow Anika. Some decided to go to the villages to buy hides, others to Dobrun on urgent business, and still others set off for the market at Priboj. And when night fell, young men stole away, taking short cuts in the same direction in which the older men had already gone. Many of them were still boys and had no hope for themselves, but it pleased them to lose a night because of her and to tumble among the crags along the Rzav.

Tane caught up with Anika and her escort at Čelik's bridge. Jelenka scolded him, but Tane only grinned and gazed at Anika as though expecting her to say something.

"What have I done to hurt you?" asked Tane.

Jelenka was furious. She halted her horse.

"This is what you have done to me. You are sitting on top of my head. We've had enough of you at Više-grad. Why do you have to follow us? Go home and rock the cradle for your wife!"

While arguing, they were both watching Anika, but she was riding ahead, not looking back or indicating in any way that she was listening to them. Jelenka angrily spurred her horse, and caught up with Anika. And Tane, with his head lowered and his reins limp, rode in step with them.

So they rode for about a hundred paces, until Anika stopped her horse and turned abruptly. Tane found himself face to face with her, their horses bracing one another. Her face was glowing from the heat, framed with a thin white kerchief whose ends fell over her shoulders. She was smiling gently, childlike. Tane felt the skin on his face tighten. His teeth and his pale gums appeared, his sad gray eyes became moist.

"Tane, I bought some lemons at Medjuselac's, but forgot them by the door. Go back to Višegrad, I beg of

you, and get them for me. You will catch up with us before we get to Dobrun."

Grinning with happiness, Tane barely understood
what she had asked him to do.

"Lemons ... at Medjuselac's ... I am going, I am
gone!" He turned round instantly and sadly rode toward
Višegrad, vainly spurring the gypsy nag, who was impervious to blows. Once or twice he turned back to see
Anika's long white scarf as she and Jelenka disappeared
toward Dobrun.

As soon as Tane had left, Jelenka burst into laughter,
she was so amused by Anika's cunning. But Anika only
rode on, smiling, not saying anything. The servant had
gone ahead of them and was waiting in the shade.

The next day the Dobrun fair opened and soon
was in full swing. It was said that Anika had arrived,
but no one had seen her during the morning service or
around the church in the afternoon. In the boisterous
and excited crowd Tane the silversmith could be seen,
roaming about, looking sadly right and left. Drunken
peasants pushed him and stepped on his toes, but
he continued walking all morning, carrying the bagful
of lemons which he had bought yesterday, out of his
own pocket, when he realized that Anika had not forgotten anything at the store. Toward nightfall, Anika
appeared with Jelenka. They walked to the middle of
the churchyard, entered a large tent set on an elevated
platform, and seated themselves. As soon as he had
heard of Anika's arrival, the priest, beside himself with
anger, announced that he would approach her personally, and order her to leave. But the church elders

stopped him and said that they themselves would speak to her.

A huge crowd of men, however, had already gathered around Anika. When the elders appeared, they were greeted first with laughter, and then with abuse. Anika acted as though she neither saw nor heard this tumult. The church emissaries tried to get to her so that they might throw her out by force, but a wall of drunken young peasants instantly formed between them and the two women. The elders were squeezed back against the fence in front of the priest's house, and just barely escaped through the door.

It was almost dark when the elders and the priest himself came down the stairs. But the mob was so large that the door was blocked, and they could not make their way out of the house.

When matters are most confusing, people least know what they want. They rushed from Anika's tent to the door of the parish house and back again. In truth, the actual rushing was confined to several drunken young men, while the rest of the mob only swayed with them. The men from Lijesko, who find a cause for a scuffle at every church feast, threatened and shouted more than anybody. Happy this year to have found so noble a target for their fury, they shouted with double strength:

"No, we won't let you!"

"No, we won't."

The Limić brothers, the best known among the Liještani, loosened their belts, gnashed their teeth, brandished their knives, and needlessly assured one another:

"Brother, I am with you...."

Night had fallen completely. A little earlier Jakša had
arrived from Višegrad; he had struggled with himself all
day, and when he could stand it no longer, he started for
Dobrun. Everyone gathered around the illuminated
tents or around the fires burning on the plain. Those
who were very drunk disappeared into the fields, vomited, groaned, and talked to themselves along the fences
in the dark. By the door of the parish house, there was a
constant din, of which nothing could be understood.
The priest stood there, black and pale in the light of a
torch that someone held behind him in the corridor. He
rose to speak, tried to advance, but was held back by the
church elders, and the noise was such that he could not
hear himself. There was no trace of fear or confusion on
his face, but only wrath and wonderment. For a long
time he tried to speak and to approach the drunkards.
Attempting to stand on his toes and to break free of the
crowd, the priest suddenly stopped in his tracks, his
glance falling on the middle tent, the most brilliantly lit
of them all. In the red glow he saw Anika's upright and
proud figure, with Jelenka on one side and Jakša, who
had just entered, on the other, bent toward Anika with
his arms outstretched, with a gesture full of tenderness
and devotion, a gesture both shameful and inexplicable
in the eyes of his father.

The priest pushed aside the people standing near
him, and rushed up the half-dark stairs into his room.
His wife, who was trembling on the porch and striking
her forehead, weeping with hopeless shame and twofold
sorrow, rushed up behind the priest, followed by several
of her women friends. Some relatives and the elders

joined them in the room, while others tried to stop the mob from breaking into the house and up the stairs. In the dark room they found the priest removing a long rifle from its place on the wall. They caught up with him by a window from which, in the middle of the swaying mob, Anika's fiery tent could be seen. Jakša was there, still bent, and Anika sat in the middle like a finished portrait. The elders clasped the priest around the waist, and his wife reached for the rifle, but he held onto it with great determination. As they wrestled with him they tried to calm him down:

"Father, Father! We plead with you!"

With horror in her voice his wife whimpered hoarsely and quietly.

"I implore you, for our sake, for God's sake!"

Finally they managed to drag him back into the dark room, from where the yard outside could not be seen. At last he let go of the rifle which he had held in his raised arm. His wife fainted. While the women busied themselves with her, the men took the priest into another room on the other side of the house.

Outside the din had subsided and the mob was dispersing. Drunkards quickly forgot the priest, and, finding a new cause for an outburst, were fighting among themselves or with their relatives. The relatives, for their part, were loading the drunkards on horses like goods, or leading them away between them down the road. Only a few remained in front of the tent, blinking and staring at Anika, sweat reflected on their foreheads.

Anika, too, was getting ready to go. She refused Jakša's offer to escort them to Višegrad. In his confusion and helplessness he was bitterly and repeatedly asking her:

"And the *kajmakam* comes to you all the time?"

Anika listened and replied absent-mindedly, as if she were thinking of something else:

"Every evening, Jakša. How come you haven't seen him? Or perhaps the *kajmakam* stays out of your way?"

Jakša winced at this insult. She continued softly, in a quiet voice:

"Or perhaps you stay out of his way?"

As though not thinking about what she was saying, she added:

"He will come to me tomorrow, too, right after supper."

By that time hardly anyone was left in the church-yard: innkeepers and candy and food vendors were putting their goods and utensils into the cases on which they had been displayed. The fires were going out, sprinkled with water or simply abandoned. In the dark the sighs and moans of drunks were still heard. And now even those sounds were receding. Only a few of them lay in a nearby ditch as though struck down in battle.

In the priest's house lights flickered in the windows as torches and candles were moved from one room to another; women were whispering to each other, serving coffee and rakiya to the men. The priest had regained control over himself and was talking with the men, but the talk was constrained, as though it were after a funeral. Finally, the remaining visitors rose and took leave of the priest, who was doing his best to appear self-possessed and calm. Two women stayed with his wife for the night.

After they had gone, the priest remained in his room for a while, and then, getting up, walked across the house to the window facing the churchyard and the Tasić home. Hearing his footsteps the women were full of foreboding. But not a sound was heard from him any more. They assumed that he had decided to take a nap in the large room, which was cooler and better ventilated than his own.

The priest locked the door, lit a candle, and seated himself before it. The candlelight illuminated his chest, his beard, his wide gray face, with eyes like dark holes. Outside, the dogs barked. The churchyard was in darkness; on the other side of the brook, by the Tasić house, a few torches were still burning. With his hands in his lap the priest sat as though watching over a dead body.

His rage had subsided, his thoughts had been put in order, but the pain had grown. He could not bear the present state of things, so he sought support in past memories, in the time *before this*. He had been a priest at Dobrun for almost thirty years. Living in the church and with the people, he had seen and could still remember a great deal of evil, but he could not have anticipated this—that he would live to witness, in his own blood and on his own threshold, this depravity, coming invisibly and unexpectedly, tearing into parents' hearts, spitting in their faces, a malignancy that can in no way be prevented or driven away, neither through outright struggle nor through death itself.

Suddenly a new and painful feeling of boundless pity broke through the complete vacuum that was forming within him. He felt pity for man's brood, for the air they breathe, for the bread they must eat. His pity went to that big crazy child Jakša—for the humiliation and the disgrace into which he had fallen. Sitting on a trunk, cowering like an orphan, with his face in the palms of his hands, he started to cry for the first time in his life, loudly and without restraint. Powerless and disarmed before so much evil, shame, and injustice, he was choking through his clenched teeth, trying in vain to overcome and stop his tears. It seemed that those tears had brought everything to life and shaken everything inside of him. In convulsions, his head dropped to his knees. But suddenly he grew greatly disturbed and rose unexpectedly; and with all his mind and all his soul he cursed the harlot, this horrible creature without shame or reason.

III

Anika returned to Višegrad that night, in the moonlight. Jakša followed immediately after her. The next evening, while the *kajmakam* was visiting Anika, someone took a shot at him from behind a fence overgrown with ivy. Alibey's right arm was slightly wounded; the same evening Jakša vanished from the *kasaba*.

Anika sent her Gypsy to Alibey's home to inquire how he was faring, but the servants chased the gypsy away with sticks. Anika did not worry about it too much. She knew that the *kajmakam* would come to her as soon as he had recovered, and sooner if she asked him. Her visit to Dobrun had convinced her that she could do anything she pleased. The *kasaba* was equally convinced.

It was September. Jakša had fled to the forest above Banpolje, and every night his fires could be seen from the town. He would not return to Dobrun and he could not return to Višegrad. Hedo Salko was sent out to capture him, but got nowhere. Soon they stopped pursuing him altogether; and Jakša's fires continued to burn above Banpolje, half an hour's distance from the town. Everyone in Višegrad knew they were Jakša's fires, and Anika herself sometimes came out into the yard to watch the first flames, which always appeared at about the same time as the first stars, growing bigger and redder, conquering the darkness of the hills and the heavens above.

While Jakša was hiding in the woods, the Dobrun priest lay in bed at home, pale and still, like a dead man. His weeping wife sat next to him day and night. She begged him to say something, anything, to give out orders, but he went on biting his lips, drowning in his white beard and mustache, his look faded, rigid, and lost.

The *kajmakam* spent the evenings in his garden on the Drina, drinking with friends. He would order his police to go out and seize Jakša, only to forget the whole matter the next moment. His wound healed quickly. From Sarajevo came two guests, two well-fed Turks.

During the day the three of them sat gambling in the *kajmakam's* garden by the river. They ordered soldiers to set yellow pumpkins afloat on the river, which they used as targets for shooting contests. As soon as it grew dark, gypsy musicians began to play. The guests had brought with them firecrackers, purchased in Austria, which were fired at night. These new and unheard-of games excited the whole town. Children would not go to sleep, but waited until the firecrackers had been set off from the garden. The townspeople watched with misgiving and wonderment as the red and green sparks scattered under the summer sky, broke and fell to the ground like a brilliant rainfall, leaving the land in a darkness more dense than before. And all the while Jakša's fire burned in the mountains.

Anika did nothing. She no longer received anyone. Toward the evening she locked the garden gate and ordered Jelenka to sing for her. Jelenka had a sharp, high-pitched voice that carried through the whole *kasaba* from hill to hill. Anika sat next to her and listened expressionless and without a word. It was said that although she had humiliated the priest on his own threshold and subordinated the whole town to her will, Anika was still neither calm nor pleased. The only word they had of her came from a drunken Turk who was camping in front of her house and would not leave, and whose words were repeated in the *kasaba* with awe and fear.

This Turk was a rich and wild fellow from Rudo. When sober he might be found at the han and around town; but soon as he got drunk—and that was not seldom—he went up to the Mejdan, straight to Anika's gate. From day to day he grew increasingly mean and surly. He assaulted Jelenka and Saveta and the men who came and waited as he did. He yelled underneath Anika's window, threatened, and thrust his knife into the gate. One evening he again brandished his knife in the yard, shouting at the top of his voice that he would kill someone that evening. Anika herself appeared, dressed lightly in white stockings and without slippers, and approached the Turk.

"What is it? Why are you screaming? What do you want?" she asked in her low husky voice. Her face was still, except for her arched brows. "Whom will you kill? Go ahead, kill! You think anyone is afraid of your knife, you peasant fool! Go ahead, kill!"

The Turk's eyes were stock-still; he was chewing and swallowing so that his long reddish mustache and his sharp, unshaven Adam's apple were quivering. He forgot that he had a knife in his hand, that he had ever said anything, and stood there as though waiting for her to kill him. Anika pushed him out of the yard and slammed the gate behind him.

It was said that on her way back through the house— as she was passing Jelenka, Tane, and a young man— and still cursing the drunken Turk, she had muttered loudly to herself:

"Whoever would kill me would do me a great favor."

In this scene of evil and confusion there were two griefs of which no one in the *kasaba* knew anything. Two men were tormented, suffering each by himself and in his own way, secretly and in silence: a torment shared with everyone, but which to them had a special depth and meaning. One was Lale, Anika's brother, and the other Mihailo.

Lale had left home when Anika's behavior first became notorious. Nor was he seen any longer in the *čaršija*.
He lived and slept in his bakery shop. When someone
accidentally mentioned his sister, his bright boyish face
would cloud over and his eyes would fix themselves rig-
idly on one object. But almost instantly, he would shake
his fair head, covered with flour, and his usual feeble-
minded smile would return to his face. Humming quietly
to himself, he went on punching quickly and automatically the monotonous patterns on the bread loaves, as his
father had taught him to do in his childhood.

That was Lale, Anika's brother. What was on his
mind, or how much this feeble-minded youth suffered
in that half-dark' room behind the big stove, no one
knew.

Mihailo lived in Master Nikola's house, which was a
little way off the *čaršija*, not far from the Krnojelac bakery. Since Anika had taken to this way of life, Mihailo
had gone on trips as often as he could, but while in
town he could not help overhearing the talk about
Anika, and he knew everything that had happened.

Master Petar Filipovac, who had chased his own son
away from home, and who was no longer on speaking
terms with either his wife or his daughters, was exceptionally fond of Mihailo. They frequently got together
early in the morning, in the shade of Master Petar's
shop. Most of the *čaršija* shops were still closed. It was
peaceful. Gloomy and bloated, Master Petar spoke in his
hoarse voice:

"See, you are a young man, but I tell you that the say-
ings of old people still hold true: In every woman there

is a devil that must be killed, either by hard work or through childbearing. A woman who escapes both should be done away with."

And as though they had never discussed it, Master Petar's voice would rise, and he would address Mihailo with one and the same complaint.

"Mihailo, brother, a thing such as this has never happened in our town."

Mihailo would remind him of Tijana, or Saveta, who had been known for evil long before Anika, but Master Petar would interrupt him:

"By comparison to this one, Tijana was a saint. If Saveta were the only problem, the town would sleep peacefully. There has always been some Gypsy or slut, and her place known: with soldiers in the ditches. No one looked at them or paid any attention to them. But this! Don't you see what's going on? She has shamed the church, won over the authorities, and will finish us all off. And no one can do anything with her."

"No one?"

"No one, by God. In our *kasaba* she is today both the pasha and the bishop. We should all roast in hell because not one of us has the courage to kill her. Those who sit in an ambush along the road have done less evil than she has."

Once more Master Petar enumerated her evils and wicked deeds, referring briefly to his own son's misfortune, at which point he would only wave his hand and silently swallow his bitterness. Mihailo tried to comfort him:

"A day will come when there will be an end to her too."

"No, there is no end to such a woman. She will carry on for as long as she likes. You don't know us, or this *kasaba*. We can resist every evil, but not *this*. She is riding us and no one can shake her off."

With this phrase Master Petar ended all of these talks to which Mihailo listened thoughtfully.

If this embittered old man had known the anguish these talks caused Mihailo he would doubtless have sought another companion, or would have mulled over his misfortune alone.

Mihailo sometimes wondered where he found the strength to move among these people, to work and to talk with them, without losing his control. Watching Anika all this time, his short-lived and quickly betrayed hope of redemption turned once more against him. Disgusted with himself, he wondered how he could have believed, even for a moment, that what had happened at the han could ever be erased and forgotten.

Years ago, in Sarajevo, he had seen a Serb stab a Moslem in the street. The stricken man never looked back to see the murderer whom others were chasing, but started slowly and solemnly for the first open door. He walked as though counting his steps, without looking at anyone; he was pressing his wound with both his hands, clearly feeling that he would live only as long as the knife remained in the wound.

Mihailo saw Krsto's murder as his own death, inevitable and imminent, and understood that it had not been redeemed even with eight years of suffering. He, Mihailo, had been mortally wounded that night. These eight years have been like the few steps the Moslem took to the first door, his eyes downcast, both hands on his wound.

Mihailo took pity on himself.

"The time has come to release the knife from the wound. It is no use deluding oneself."

He could no longer recall when it was that he first lost his ability to distinguish between Anika and Krstinica in his mind, the two women had for a long time been one and the same person. Indeed, any woman he desired or possessed became one woman: tall, buxom Krstinica, with her reddish hair, powerful arms, and blazing eyes.

On a hill above him, within calling distance, lived a woman who, more than any other, reminded him of Krstinica; and, like Krstinica, she had raised his hopes and then, after a brief and torturous game, had revealed herself for what she was, confirming all his forebodings.

Brought up by a wise and honest father, sensitive by nature and yet hard inside, Mihailo was capable of great suffering; yet he knew how to conceal these feelings. But his torment had now grown to such proportions that concealment had become almost impossible. Shame hovered in sight like an apparition, more painful and more horrible than death itself. And the torment penetrated even the most trifling details of everyday life.

With childlike persistence, he returned to certain details again and again. For instance, he was convinced that he would have felt better had he taken the knife from Krstinica's hands when she had offered it to him. But having left the knife at the han, it was as if it were pawned to her, forming a link between him and the horror from which he had fled that night. And whenever he heard the word "knife" mentioned, accidentally and in no relation to him, he would think to himself:

"She still has my knife."

This incomprehensible game of conscience slowly conquered Mihailo's whole existence.

In his frequent settling of accounts with himself, there was one horror he did not think possible: dreaming the same dream repeatedly, always in the full awareness of what had happened in the previous one. He no longer remembered his first dream of this nature, but sensed that each repetition added something to reality, some detail, some trifle to an increasingly sharp image. The image slowly condensed, separated itself from his dream world, approached reality, and infiltrated it imperceptibly.

This was his dream: the morning is bright. He feels its freshness and coolness on his face, in his mouth, on his whole body. He walks upright and solemn under the impact of a certain decision which is so immense that he cannot grasp it, but only feels its great weight. It seems that the alleys and squares are emptying before him; only the weight of his decision is pushing him ahead. Thus he passes by Krnojelac's bakery, from which Lale's cheerful singing can be heard. He climbs up the Mejdan. Anika's yard is full of bright, fresh flowers. The door of the house is open, inviting one to enter.

What desperate effort Mihailo made, both in reality and in the dream, not to cross this door, not to pass that threshold. For years he had made work for himself and traveled, even when he did not have to, simply to stay away from this yard. He had been successful in this for a long time, but now he felt that he was no longer in control. He would forget business arrangements, arrive late for appointments. Realizing that he was becoming absent-minded and negligent, he was frightened, as though he had discovered that he had a disease.

There was perhaps another possibility: to leave everything before a disaster occurred, to flee into the world, a man without honor, a criminal. If his problem had been real, his enemies visible, he would have done so. But as things stood, where would he flee? The object of his fear would await him on every road, in every town.

He even considered sending a letter to Anika, threatening her, begging her to go away, for her own sake, for the *kasaba*'s sake, for his sake. But he instantly understood the futility of such a communication.

He frequently thought of Lale. He had always been attached to this handsome, simple-minded youth. Between him and Anika's brother there had always been a certain attraction, a mixture of affection, distrust, and brusqueness. After his talks with Master Petar he frequently thought of Lale. It seemed to him that, as Anika's brother, Lale saw it all and felt it all, and that perhaps he should be the one to disarm and defeat her. Passing by the bakery early one morning, Mihailo called on him. He found Lale singing loudly and punching the full, white loaves with a big, black knife. They chatted, as much as one could chat with Lale. Mihailo would bring Anika into the conversation, but he got nowhere. Lale continued smiling like a happy idiot, talking about the flour, the water, and the bread.

Thus Mihailo lost all hope of involving Anika's brother in his torment. Everyone was slipping away, leaving him with Anika. Everything was driving him forward and only occasionally could he step back to measure the distance he had traveled along the road down which he was sliding imperceptibly.

It was a beautiful Višegrad autumn. Mihailo sensed that he would soon be on his way; this, too, had come imperceptibly. He woke up one morning full of thoughts of departure.

While washing his face a little later at the fountain in the yard, he suddenly uttered the word "farewell" into a handful of cold, cheerful water, and immediately spilled the water, and his thought went with it.

Mihailo was taking leave of everything around him. One day he went up to Anika's Gypsy, whom he saw often in the *čaršija*, and said to her in a natural tone of voice:

"Ask Anika whether I may come to see her tomorrow morning; I can only come when no one else is there. I have something to tell her."

The Gypsy vanished. Mihailo shuddered a little and looked around as if seeking help or advice. But for the rest of the day he was composed. He worked carefully on his accounts and cleaned up around the house. Just before sunset, he started toward Stražište, the hill on which he had so many times welcomed the evening with his friends.

He climbed slowly, and sat down in the clearing above the Turkish cemetery, laid on the ground next to him a flask of rakiya and some food. He slowly struck a piece of steel against the flint and delicately held the burning cigarette between the fingers of his left hand. He could not take his eyes from the smoke which rose in front of him, blocking his view, whirling around and disappearing slowly into the still air. There was still a faint gleam of sunlight among the fir trees. Below him the smoke lifted slowly from among the black and the red roofs of the white Višegrad houses. One flooded arm of the river Rzav reflected the skies and the willows along its bank.

Mihailo also saw many things that were not visible from this spot: the shop doors, the house gates with the large polished stones outside on which the children played, the men, their glances and their greetings.

He drank a cup of rakiya, but forgot about the food. The smoke was turning purple, and rings hovered in the air a long time and slowly grew thinner. In the twilight all things seem to retain their shape longer. And Mihailo inhaled the smoke a and the air, the Višegrad air, looked at the houses, the sharp peaks of the mountains and the glades, to all of which he had been linked for many years now. As he was thinking, the peaks disappeared and were enveloped in the dark blue glow which precedes the night.

It was now six years since he had come to live among these hills and with these people. Here he had once again found his place among men. Here he had extended his roots, here his life resumed. How he hated to change his shape and break his rhythm once again.

He took a few puffs on a cigarette, and the smoke hovered over the town, where fires were being started in the homes. He continued to draw on his cigarette, and in his chest he felt a humming caused by the rakiya. At the horizon, near where the sun had set, the clouds were a burning red, illuminating a glade on the top of Janjats mountain, a glade that Mihailo had never seen before. At that point, as though at a given signal, he arose and descended into town with the dark.

He went straight home. He pressed on the yard gate and felt its wooden padlock—that same worn gate that he had been pressing for years and whose peculiarities and faults he knew so well. The door to the house was half open and a fire was burning inside. Crossing the yard, he suddenly started, as though he had tripped over something. Standing by the barn was Anika's one-eyed Gypsy. Embarrassed by his own bewilderment, he went over to see what she wanted. She spoke first, almost in a whisper:

"Anika wants you to come to her house tomorrow morning, as early as you can." Then she walked off, softly, almost in audibly.

That night he put all his papers in order for his partner, Master Nikola. It was dawn by the time he had completed his preparations. Mihailo had not slept, overcome by a quiet ecstasy which had shortened the night and eradicated every reality.

Surrounded by steep tall mountains the sun arrives late in Višegrad. But long before the sunrise the *kasaba* is reached by an indirect light, which seems to fall from the very center of the skies. It was in this quiet light that Mihailo crossed the yard, threw a bag over his shoulder, as he often did when going on a journey, and set out for the Mejdan.

The streets were deserted and looked wider and brighter. He passed Lale's bakery, but heard no singing from it, which was unusual at this time of day. In fact, the bakery was closed; it looked lonely and dark, like an old tomb. But everything else in town seemed to be in its place.

The trail up the Mejdan was deserted. The skies looked like a burning field from which the sun would soon rise. Under the eaves the doves were cooing. The doors of many houses were open and black, as if the inhabitants wanted the darkness to leave by the door.

Anika's gate, too, was wide open. High up in the steep garden above the house Jelenka was hidden in the greenery, picking string beans and singing like a cricket.

As soon as Mihailo entered the house, his eyes fell on the fireplace. Among the ashes was lying a black baker's knife, bloodstained up to the handle. It was the same knife he bad so often seen in Lale's hands while talking to him at the bakery.

Astonished, confused, as if it were one strange dream within another, Mihailo walked slowly to the door of Anika's room, opened it without hesitation, and stood there. It was a small, neat room, covered with rugs. Two cushions from the *minderluk* were out of place. Anika's body lay on the floor. She was dressed; her vest and shirt were pierced between the breasts, and she looked as though she had died quietly, without the tortures of death. She looked even bigger than usual, stretched out on the floor, her back on the mattress and her head on the pillows against the wall.

There was a flower in her hair. No blood was to be seen anywhere.

Cold with fear, Mihailo raised his hand to cross himself, but paused and with the same raised hand shut the door to Anika's room. As he was leaving, he looked once again at the bloodstained knife in the ashes, which lay there in the stillness as things do that have been dead for centuries. He turned around and, with a deep shudder, picked up the knife, wiped it off first in the ashes and then against the wooden frame of the hearth, and tucked it under his belt, next to the big knife he himself had taken with him that morning.

Outside, the sun was rising and Jelenka was singing high up in the garden. The fountain was bubbling loudly. The crazy Nazif had already seated himself for the day on a low bench beneath the window, arranging heaps of sugar around him, mumbling cheerfully. He did not even look up at Mihailo as he passed him, walking fast toward the brook over which the shadows of the morning still hovered.

Anika's death changed Višegrad, as it had to. The speed with which everything was restored to the old rhythm was indeed almost hard to believe. No one was curious to know where the woman had come from, why she had lived, and what she had wanted. She was harmful and dangerous, and now she was dead, buried, and forgotten. The *kasaba,* which had been momentarily deranged, could again sleep peacefully, walk freely, and breathe regularly. If a similar blight should occur—and it will at some point—the *kasaba* will again resist it, succumb to it, struggle against it, break it, bury it, and forget it.

439

Hedo Salko conducted an inquiry into the murder. Jelenka, Saveta, and the gypsy were questioned and beaten, needlessly of course, since they were all telling the truth anyway.

As it turned out, Anika had wanted to be left alone that morning. She had given the house a thorough cleaning, and had barred everyone from it; she sent both the gypsy and Saveta to Vučine to call on a certain woman (a trip of several hours) and ordered Jelenka up into the garden to pick string beans, telling her not to return until she was called.

The Gypsy revealed that on the same evening that she had delivered Anika's invitation to Mihailo, she had called on Lale and given him the same message:

"Anika wants you to come for sure, tomorrow morning, as early as you can."

Lale had given her no reply.

Why had Anika asked her brother, whom she had not seen in such a long time, to visit her on the very morning for which she had asked Mihailo? Was this an accident, or had she been preparing a trap and a surprise? And which one of the two killed Anika? The Gypsy could explain nothing, and neither could Jelenka or Saveta, for Anika talked rarely to them, and certainly never revealed her plans.

Jelenka could only report that from the hill she had kept a close eye on those who came and went, and that she had seen Lale enter first and that sometime later she saw him run out of the house. This did not surprise her, for she knew that Lale was a little mad. But then Mihailo entered; he stayed inside even more briefly and left the

440

house with a firm stride. Although she was very curious to find out what had brought Lale, with whom Anika was feuding, and what business she could have had with Mihailo, of whom she had seen nothing of late, Jelenka did not have the courage to leave the garden until she was called. But she ran down when she heard the wailing of an old woman who had come across Anika's body accidentally while offering cloth for sale from house to house.

Peasants said they had seen Lale above Dobrun, on the road to Užice, while it was generally known that Mihailo had left in the opposite direction, along the Sarajevo road. The knife with which Anika had been killed was never found.

Everything was unclear, confused, and seemingly beyond explanation. Hedo Salko welcomed the confusion, because it meant that he could bring to an end an inquiry that could reveal nothing, corroborate nothing, and that, if the truth be known, no one was in need of, and no one had asked for.

The *kajmakam* spent two or three weeks at Plevlje with his relatives, and later returned to Višegrad and went on living as he had always done, for his own pleasure and for the pleasure of others. It is true that, sitting in his garden, smoking his *narghile* and gazing down at the fast river Drina, he sometimes thought of the Christian woman from the Mejdan. "Miraculous! That nothing should be left of so much beauty!" This was, at any rate, the theme of his meditation. But he did not believe that there was anyone in the *kasaba* with whom it would be worth discussing these things.

And the rest of the town was rapidly recovering and taking on its customary appearance. The women were more cheerful, the men more tranquil.

Master Petar Filipovac's son made peace with his father. He held his head lower, suddenly grew heavier, sprouted a thin, long mustache, bent his legs at the knees, and so tottered around the town. After Christmas they will marry him off.

Master Petar was the only one among the men of the *kasaba* who sat ill-tempered and grim in his shop, just as before. He felt deep sorrow for Mihailo, an odd young man who must have kept hidden some great torment. And when the *charshiya* men said how lucky it was that the *kasaba* was rid of Anika, he only waved his hand:

"That one will poison us even in her death, and it will last for a hundred years. Mark my word, her poison will be in us for a hundred years."

But he was the only one who spoke in this manner. Even at the home of the Dobrun priest things took a turn for the better. After Anika's death, Jakša had started to cross into Serbia, but on his way he learned that his father was on his deathbed. Suddenly he changed his mind. Arriving a Dobrun at night, he went straight into his father's room, kissed his hand, and was given forgiveness and the blessing. His father sent him immediately to Trnavci, where he was to wait until the storm had blown over. Shortly afterward the priest was well enough to ride into Višegrad. There he found out that the *kajmakam* had no intention of persecuting Jakša. Hedo, for his part, pretended he did not know who had taken a shot at the *kajmakam*. Everything was forgotten as if by secret agreement, and everything was settling itself as though by a miracle.

Jakša was married the following summer, and his father lived to see him ordained and installed as his successor in the Dobrun parish.

Lale's bakery and Krnojelac's house have been taken over by the municipality and are rented out. Other people live and work there now. Few even remember the children of Andja Vidinka. And Mihailo, too, is being forgotten. Only his former master and partner, Nikola Subotić, thinks of him. Having lost Mihailo, he found it necessary to settle permanently in Višegrad, for there was no one to replace him in his shop. He travels less and gambles less. It seems that illness was gnawing at him anyway. Now he chats with Master Petar Filipovac, who comes often to see him in the early evening, after the heat has subsided. In a large handsome yard, they spread out a rush mat along the boxwood plants above the fountain. Drinking rakiya, they often talk of Mihailo.

"The man fell as though into muddy waters," says Master Nikola in his deep, hoarse voice, "and if he were my own son it seems to me, I could not feel more sorrow."

And he blesses a hundred times the salt and the bread which he and Mihailo had eaten together. An immovable spark glitters in a corner of his eye, a tear that has never rolled down, but has sparkled every time the talk moves on to Mihailo, as though it were always the same tear.

Translated by Drenka Willen

A Family Portrait

fter 1919 reception rooms in the houses of wealthy Belgrade merchants' homes began to change and, with more or less success and consistency, were transformed into salons following the urban taste of the time. Not only was the cheap, excess, furniture removed, but so were *Pirot* kilims and enlarged, colored oleographs of patriotic paintings. This was all used in other rooms, or even thrown into a closet or the servants' quarters amongst old and unnecessary things.

In May 1944, after the second heavy American air bombardment, by a strange coincidence I spent the night in a partly destroyed house which belonged to such a merchants' family. It happened that I slept in the cramped maid's room, on the hard bed where many Slovenian girls and *Totice* had slept, serving in this wealthy house over the last twenty or so years.

Agitated, worried, and sleepless, yet unable to read, by the light of an improvised lamp I first looked over the meager furniture and then the cluster of small and large objects discarded by this household over time that lay in one corner, coated by old dust and a new layer of plaster from the shock of that morning's explosion.

Here was a whole small world of voiceless yet eloquent odds and ends which time and people deemed unfashionable and useless: broken toys, fans with snapped ribs, chipped phonograph records, expired calendars, cracked shells with a color picture of Dubrovnik or Opatija on their mother of pearl inner surface, advertisements for Viennese firms and French spas and sanatoria, printed invitations for long past performances, and "Dance Cards" from old balls. The biggest of these objects, and the one which most attracted my attention, was a large family portrait in a heavy, gilt frame.

It was a photograph of a married couple, from somewhere in the nineties of the last century, enlarged as much as possible and retouched to the point of absurdity. The photograph was even tinted. The particular expert who had even signed it had also taken care to give the face, eyes, and clothing of the married couple colors which do not much resemble those we see in life, but roughly correspond to the idea of the color a wealthy man's face, eyes, and clothing ought to be according to convention. But he had applied this special coloring care and skill to the garnet brooch and gold chain of the lady and to the medals—of St. Sava and the Red Cross—hanging on the husband's chest.

My eyes kept returning to that portrait. When at last I fell asleep, I had some vague dreams about it. And when the first light of day woke me, I spent a long time watching the reflection of the bright Belgrade dawn and the first morning hours on the portrait. I had the opportunity to look at it thoroughly and, it seems to me, I "read" it well. And thus today it is not difficult to present to you the personalities from that large "picture," since in itself, a picture—regardless of what our artists might say—conveys a lot through its style, craftsmanship and taste, but the faces shown on it, for one who knew them alive or knows how to revive them, are even more eloquent in their speech or in their silence.

That portrait shows the owner—Nikola K. Dimitrijević, nicknamed and once generally known in the marketplace by the name "Kapa," and his wife Natalija, Madame Nata, neé Kamenković, as they were in life, she in her forty-first and he in his fiftieth year.

Brought back to life and out of their frame, they would look roughly like this.

The wife. Let us begin with the wife, since it is with her anyway that everything from wedding to grave began and ended in this house. She is a woman with dark oily skin, short, with two double chins, and sharp whiskers, with abundant and numerous layers of fat in unusual amounts and unexpected places. The dress is made of "crème"-colored silk, according to the latest style of the time, with a low waist, narrow, cut low around the neck, very unsuitable for her short, stocky figure. Black eyes of a cold brilliance, and somewhat yellowish whites. A small bent nose catches the eye; it is lost in the fat face, still oily under layers of powder, just as her thin lips are pale under the thick rouge, lips which do not show teeth either when she speaks or when she smiles. (A long time ago someone said that "for the Kamenkovićes a smile is as good as a gold coin, and they do not waste gold coins, rather they keep them for themselves.") Because of the great obesity of that whole body, the feet and hands are tiny and seem weak, but looks are deceptive. There is nothing in her or about her that is not powerful and tough. Barely suppressed energy causes the whole woman to shake and dance as on a wire; it seems that one can hear raw power within her throbbing like a mighty unseen and well-oiled engine. She has something offended, angry, in her voice, expression and whole demeanor. She does not shrink from anything, and no one surprises her, she never restrains herself, saying whatever she thinks, the moment she thinks it, sparing no one and considering nothing. For what she thinks is for her the truth, what she says is the law, and what she does is just.

The skill to be selfish, hard, unpleasant and unkind, and to have continuously only one's own interest in sight, that first and most immediate interest which concerns us most directly, that skill, developed through generations of provincial traders, was realized in Madame Nata to perfection, to the point of absurdity. For in order to have all that she has, and in her circle to be able to do all she can, it is not remotely necessary to be so arrogant, aggressive, harsh and malicious. Long since deceased forebears, some of them under constant threat and therefore merciless and relentless toward everyone, and others always cautious and angry, speak through her in a ghostly tongue and guide her incomprehensible acts invisibly. All the characteristics which she displays, have been developed gradually in many long-since deceased Kamenkovićes and passed on to their descendants, as they struggled in the marketplace with competitors, un-trustworthy villagers, corrupt authorities, customers and swindlers of all kinds, and she brought them into the world, together with the estate she inherited, mastered and developed them into maniacal forms. These charac-teristics—a dark and fateful inheritance—completely redundant and senseless in her circumstances and her time, make of her wealthy life a wasteland, grief and hate—and of herself a monstrous creation, evil and wicked toward everyone.

Madame Nata was born like this and this is how she lived, not like a separate and independent person, but rather as a sample of the Kamenković clan. Only in the state administration and church records was she regis-tered as Dimitrijević, but that was a pure formality, an empty convention, but she knew, as did the whole world since she repeated it tirelessly and demonstrated it in everything, that she was and remained, and in others' eyes existed only—as the seed of Kamenković. As such she married a rather short but handsome, no longer all that young, merchant in the haberdashery business, Ni-kola Dimitrijević Kapa.

It was a marriage without reproach according to all the norms of the *čaršija*. He—a man without shortcom-ings, a trader at the difficult beginning of his career, who needed only good and solid support to break into the ranks of the most prominent people in the haberdashery trade. She—a girl from a rich and influential home, who needed a man of another class and a name in order to bear children and expand the posterity of the Kamenk-ovićes, albeit from the maternal line. The Kamenkovićes accomplished everything that they could by themselves so that the effort as well as the fruit of the effort remained in the family, but for this task they had to seek, with great regret, a stranger and introduce "foreign blood" among them. But for this reason the marriageable girls from the Kamenković house labored instinctively so that the indispensable stranger, their husbands, started to resemble the Kamenkovićes as soon as and as much as possible, he adopted their views and habits, their way of life and doing business, down to their slightest movements and expressions. Their husband must think and speak like the Kamenkovićes, or else think nothing and keep quiet for life.

This Kamenković girl, the black-haired, plumpish, and always frowning Nata, completed perfectly the task of transforming one living man into the moveable property of the Kamenkovićes, in the established, traditional style of the family which all the Kamenković girls since the inception of the dynasty until today could envy.

As soon as they returned from their wedding the bride showed her true face and in a lawyerly fashion used the first opportunity to assume the principle position right away and seize all roles in the home and marriage.

The affectionate and considerate man suggested to his new wife that they should do something small for his uncle and aunt, who had both provided for his training and helped him so much while he grew and learned, and now were very happy with this marriage and loved her already like a real daughter. The woman jumped up and refused rudely. The mere realization that other people, in addition to this indispensable male and husband, could also get involved in their world, made the Kamenković girl inside her bristle, and the bride, taciturn until then, spoke out unexpectedly, animatedly, harshly and bluntly, in a voice (and maybe words, too) of some distant great-grandmother Kamenković:

"You can't be serious! What's wrong with you? Do you know who we are?"

(Master Nikola's uncle, a good-natured fellow just like him, did not take the bride's attitude to heart, but his wife, who was insulted as never before, could not forget or forgive Madame Nata for her behavior toward her poor relatives and had no desire, to cross the threshold of their home, even for their *Slava*.)

And as on that first day, with that trivial family matter, so it was until the end of time, with all affairs and with the most important questions, and in response to everything that Master Nikola could say, advise or suggest, there was always one and the same gruff and scornful answer—"You can't be serious! What's wrong with you?"—always the same ill-will and inflexibility.

At first he tried to contradict her in his gentle, soft Valjevo manner and haberdashery merchant's way, to explain and persuade, but he quickly saw that it was a futile and hopeless effort. He saw that not only did his thoughts and suggestions not matter, but that he himself meant nothing, that in reality he had not married one girl, but all of the Kamenkovićes, living and dead, that they had overwhelmed and enslaved him and that from this point forward he must live *for* them, live *their life*, he was condemned until death to be only and simply a

451

Kamenković son-in-law. And what could he do against this tempest of a wife who was not able to think or feel anything that was outside her family circle, who had no regard for anybody and was not afraid of anything? What could he do? Nothing, evidently!

She had a physical aversion to anything that was not Kamenković blood, even towards her husband, and towards him personally she would control that aversion only to the extent that he was a son-in-law and husband. Nor did she know how to bow her head in church, and when she laid her offering on the church plate, she placed her coin in an empty place, separate from all the other money, and the expression on her face would say:

"This is for you, God, from the Kamenkovićes. But, be careful, don't mix that money up with who knows whose small change."

She commanded and policed as naturally as she breathed and walked, and as long as she lived she could not and did not know how to do otherwise.

She bore two daughters in the first four years of marriage. That was all, they had no more children. And those two little girls, with their characteristics of the Kamenković race, resembled their mother from birth, and with every day and month came to resemble her more. They did not look like their mother the way children look like their parents, no, this was a completely organic, mechanical resemblance, the way small fish resemble big ones and differ from them only in dimensions. This was a small biological miracle that was discussed not only among the neighbors but in the wider circle of the Dimitrijevićes' acquaintances. The owner of the next-door shop, a scoundrel and old bachelor, would say to his friends, whenever the conversation turned to this:

"Why are you surprised? You know well that in that house in everything, especially in that, only the women's side has its say."

Master Nikola himself just watched how the new versions of the Kamenkovićes developed in his house; he observed the blind and unhindered progress of that natural process, and at times it looked terrible to him and filled him with superstitious horror, and at other times it seemed grotesque and incited violent and painful laughter in him, which nauseated him, but which he did not dare let out, since there was no means or prospect of him being able to explain it to the other members of the household.

The girls grew up together like twins, and next to the mother like copies next to a prototype. They were both short and dark, even at thirteen and fifteen each of them already had pillows of fat hiding muscles of quick and sharp reflexes, with a tightened mouth and a little line of fuzz in place of her mother's whiskers, an angry and offended expression on her face, and a commanding scornful tone in her voice.

When the older daughter, who was named Poleksija like her grandmother Kamenković, was nineteen years old, Madame Nata found her a husband, a prominent contractor who had become wealthy quickly and unusually by rapidly building and then cleverly reselling a houses in the center of Belgrade. But it was not fated for Madame Nata to see her grandchild, nor to give away her second daughter in marriage. In her forty-second year, when she seemed both to herself and to others to be at her strongest and healthiest, she became rapidly ill from a very serious sickness. It began with a minor incident and was barely noticeable, but developed quickly and dreadfully.

One day, Madame Nata had an argument with a certain coachman. (As the years went on, she had become tighter with money, sharper with her tongue and more inconsiderate to others.) The coachman had wheeled over on his carriage a few wardrobes that Madame Nata had inherited from an old aunt. She demanded that the things must be brought into the house in a roundabout way, through a side yard so that it would not dirty her main entrance, and the coachman kept insisting that this was not part of the agreement and expected that he and his helper be paid extra for this unforeseen effort. This prompted the mistress of the house to call the coachman a *hajduk* and a robber, to which he answered, sizing her up from head to toe, and asking with a deliberately insulting, calm arrogance:

"Has anyone, Ma'am, ever given you a good thrashing?"

And when the lady, with a vehement shriek which rang through the hallway, rejected this unthinkable and fearful thought, the coachman added, even more calmly and more insultingly:

"Aha, you see, that's unfortunate. That's exactly what you need!"

"My, my!" shrieked Madame Nata still for a while after this quarrel keeping both of her hands somewhere under her navel, because from this coachman's question she suddenly felt a strong pain near her stomach, something like a sharp stab, from the mere thought that it could occur to anyone, that one of the Kamenkovićes could be beaten, and that there was a man living who dared say it aloud.

The incident with the coachman was somehow resolved and quickly forgotten, as were many of Madame Nata's other outbursts and conflicts but from then on, that pain in the stomach area stayed with her, occurring more often, day and night, and for no special reason. The family physician recommended a clinical examination, but Madame Nata sharply refused. Her husband encouraged her more and more to seek treatment, but she responded to him in her constant and perpetually the same tone:

"You must be joking! What's wrong with you? Shall I fill the purses of those charlatans and pickpockets who call themselves doctors?"

But when it became obvious that Madame Nata was wasting away steadily and ever more rapidly, when the pains became unbearable and her skin assumed a particular grayish-green color, Madame Nata nonetheless went to the clinic. There, after the initial consultation, the doctors concluded that Madame Nata was suffering from cancer and that an operation was imperative, if not already too late. Initially she refused, as she always refused everything in life, but then, under the pressure of the pains, she nevertheless conceded. When they operated on her, it really was too late. ("Cut her open, took a look and immediately sewed her back up," reported Master Nikola's aunt vengefully, whom Madame Nata refused to acknowledge as an equal member of the family.) She lived all of three weeks after the operation in pain that even strong doses of morphine could not relieve.

Thus Madame Nata died in her forty-third year of life, and unexpectedly simply and quickly disappeared from the home in which she had seemed, always and to everyone, eternal and all-powerful. And after her death, she was surprisingly rarely mentioned, as though everyone was trying to forget her. Yet, Madame Nata was mentioned longest by Master Nikola's incurably offended aunt. Even six months after Madame Nata's death, when Master Nikola's uncle returned from the cemetery where Madame Nata's memorial service was held, she welcomed her good-natured husband with the words:

"So even Kamenkovićes die, do they! I've been thinking about it all morning, and what I'm about to say isn't nice, but God did well, for otherwise in a hundred years' time they would have multiplied to such an extent that they would rule half the world."

The husband. Nikola Dimitrijević came to Belgrade when he was nine. The villagers of his region never wanted to send their children away from home, but there were always exceptions. The little boy's parents both fell ill and died the same winter; his relatives turned out to be bad and quarrelsome people, but his father's younger brother lived in Belgrade and he took the child there with him, looked after him until he finished primary school, and then sent him to learn a trade at a well-known haberdashery shop on Knez Mihailova Street.

That uncle of Nikola's, Sava, was an exception in the village and in the family. As a child he demonstrated an unusual desire for books and learning. They let him spend a year at the Valjevo Gymnasium, since he had threatened to run away from home, and at school he showed such diligence and such a memory that the professors, who saw in him a child prodigy, never let him leave the school. They speculated what would become of him. A scientist, a great mathematician, or a philologist? Maybe a politician? All this was possible since Sava studied all subjects with the same interest and received equally excellent grades. Always smiling, modest, and hesitant, the boy was without specific resolve or clear goal. And the more he developed and advanced, the more that indifference grew—towards everything both at school and in life, a strange inability to show anywhere or in anything either an active desire or youthful passion. Thus he finished six grades, as many as there were at the Valjevo Gymnasium, and his professors made sure that he did not stop halfway and they enabled him to transfer to Belgrade and finish school. The quiet and jovial boy graduated from school with excellent marks. But then, when financial support at the university had been secured for him and when all he needed to do was choose his subject, to the general surprise of those who knew him and had helped him through school he refused categorically to continue his studies and took the position of an archive official in the Ministry of Agriculture. Simply, he himself put an end to his further development, education and advancement in society. And in a year or two the "exceptionally talented young man" was lost in the gray mass of the Belgrade minor bureaucracy. Some incomprehensible shyness hindered the whole life of this young man who had been withdrawn since childhood. Just as others pushed forward and propelled themselves to higher posts ardently, with all of their resources and by all possible means, he pulled back and fled just as ardently and persistently from everything, in the hope that nobody would notice him, that he would not stand out in any way, that he would live unmentioned and unknown. And he succeeded in this too. An excellent student and the pride of the Valjevo Gymnasium, Sava Dimitrijević remained a clerk in the archives, and all his "gifts" and wide-ranging knowledge were buried in polite, smiling silence.

Being more diligent and talented than the others, he advanced rather quickly and ultimately became the head of the archive. He married a Novi Sad girl who had been sent to relatives in Serbia; she was not a beauty but educated and well read, a girl of lively speech, who spoke in a cultivated language, choosing her words with care, but also in a somewhat mannered way and with a kind of guileless affectation. After their first child, who died soon after birth, they remained childless.

Nikola spent two beautiful years of his boyhood in the home of this married couple, and after that experienced the somewhat more difficult life of the apprentice. But the young man was diligent and obedient; resembling Uncle Sava in many ways, both physically and morally—he endured and mastered everything. Thus passed the difficult years of his apprenticeship, thus passed the still more difficult years as an assistant, and finally came the time when Nikola opened his own shop and married into the rich and, in the merchant world, prominent, Kamenković family.

This was the turning point of Nikola Kapa's life, insofar as what came after his marriage to the Kamenković daughter could be called life. As we have seen, his wife devoured him; she did not swallow him up as the females of certain insects swallow their mates, she depleted him from the inside, emptied him out and left only a thin façade, and what remained of the man named Nikola Dimitrijević Kapa, lived, that is he continued to trade and cautiously but steadily to expand and build up his shop, established his household and acquired prestige and prominence in the Belgrade *čaršija*. And he did all this not as an independent, separate individual, but as the husband of Madame Nata Kamenković and the father of her children. That was the only way he existed in the eyes of his wife and the entire world, even his relatives. That was the one and only way that he could exist. There was no room in his life for anything else, from the smallest living creature to the dead.

Early on, he would sometimes go secretly to Uncle Sava's. (They had been living for a long time now in their own little house in Senjak, which they had bought with his savings and her handsome inheritance from Novi Sad. The neighborhood was undeveloped, but Sava planted a beautiful, spacious garden where he kept bees. It was that year, after twenty-five years of service, that he put in for retirement. Always withdrawn, they now lived an even more withdrawn life, growing old, comfortably, quietly, side by side.) Already on one of his first visits, Sava's wife had asked, looking straight at him with her nearsighted, kind eyes and stressing every word, as if she was on stage:

"Are you, at least, happy?"

"Of course I am, Aunt."

"You're not, Nikola, and you can't be. I see that, and so I must say it. But what can be done? This is your burden, you can't throw it off, and you must carry it as decently as you can. You're right."

Hearing this, Uncle Sava only blinked in embarrassment.

Madame Nata soon found out about these visits, and Nikola had to give them up as well, "for the sake of domestic peace"; he visited his uncle only twice a year, on his *Slava* and for Christmas.

This is how he became entirely and completely enslaved.

Skinny, quiet, gaunt and stiff, pale and prematurely gray, with eyes that appeared bigger and darker because of his pallor, polite, proper and kind to all, he was always dressed formally and as though for a funeral: in a black suit, a starched shirt with a high collar and dark tie, and black dress shoes. This is how you could have seen him either in the shop or on the street, where he doffed his black, always new-looking hat deeply, in response to every greeting.

This is how he lived, that is, this is how he moved about for over twenty years, changing nothing in his in life and practically not himself changing at all. Then, after twenty-four years of marriage, Madame Nata died unexpectedly.

When such people whose very existence means pressure on all those around them, disappear suddenly and unexpectedly, a bizarre silence and a major disturbance in the balance manifests itself for all those for whom that pressure was an integral part of their life. Suddenly, Master Nikola found himself at an unimagined and dangerous crossroads: should he continue on the same path of his current existence and follow his wife, or should he stay and, if possible, continue his life interrupted with marriage, in other words live his own life for himself. The emptiness into which his wife had disappeared dragged him towards it like a deep whirlpool, but the shred of character that nonetheless remained somewhere in him, kept him alive. For a time, it was unclear in which direction he would go. He lost even more weight, became still quieter and thinner, like a lost man, but then he nevertheless prevailed.

A year after his wife's death, when he had married off the other daughter to a young, able man of his profession, and he was alone, Master Nikola started to stand on his own feet again and recover. But that was neither quick nor easy.

A man who is unexpectedly and prematurely released from long imprisonment initially always undergoes a crisis, more or less severe. Such a man, prior to returning to his previous unfettered stride and movement, goes through a long period of readjustment. During this period, three phases may be roughly established. Phase one: wherever he goes and however he moves, the man seems to hear behind him the steps of the guard following him, and he would need only to turn around to see him. Phase two: walking freely along the streets, the man feels as though something is missing; he no longer hears footsteps and no longer feels that as soon as he turns around he will see the previously constant shadow of all his movements and outings—the armed guard at his heels. This bothers him, unnerves and frightens him in its own way. And finally, phase three: the man stops hearing steps behind him and no longer feels as though he is being followed, but this does not bother him because he no longer even thinks about the guard or the time of his imprisonment. This means that he has not only survived the incarceration but also got over it and managed to recover from it. It is only then that the former prisoner can say he is once again a free man who moves about freely. (Perhaps all of these phases are not exactly like this or this clearly delineated or separated in each individual, but undoubtedly everyone has at least a bit of each.)

It was similar for Nikola Kapa. But in the end he recovered completely.

"Have you seen how lively Kapa has become?"

"Indeed, he really is lively."

"What do you mean, 'lively'? The man has been resurrected!"

This is what was said throughout the *čaršija* and amongst his acquaintances. But Nikola did not wonder what was being said or how people interpreted things. He simply lived.

Gone was that sense of a vague, oppressive burden which he had borne from the beginning of his marriage, like a heavy, hidden torment. He did not ask himself where it had gone, rather how it could have existed. And then, he did not ask himself anything, he forgot that it had existed. He felt only that a great mortal weight had fallen away from him, that dark, bare mountains had parted and the world was open before him. And that was enough for him. He sought nothing from that world. He lived a small, modest life. The house, in which for a quarter century no one had dared open a window, put a log on the fire or move a chair without Nata's permission, was now free, spacious, and cheerful. Not only did the servants breathe a sigh of relief and calm down, but so did the furniture and walls of the house.

Master Nikola got up early, because he wanted to. He sat on the terrace under the arbor. On the wall there was a long row of pots full of flowers. A small, white, loveable dog placed at his feet. These were things that had been unthinkable, since Nata was a resolute opponent of flowers, claiming that they cost money, required work and dirtied the house yet did not serve any purpose, while she loathed dogs, as she did cats and all other animals, not tolerating them even in the house next door. It was here every morning that he was brought first a glass of water and a cube of sugar; here he ate breakfast, breathed freely and watched everything peacefully and joyfully.

He went off to the shop, but increasingly as a visitor, since he was ceding the business little by little to his younger son-in-law. He rarely visited his daughters. The older one already had two children, a boy and a girl. Master Nikola watched them growing, dark, stocky, vociferous, and aggressive, still undiluted Kamenković blood. He tried once or twice to caress them, but the children resisted or turned their heads away indifferently, especially the little girl. She had only just begun to walk, but she already waved her hand in a commanding fashion as though she was about to speak and say something sharp and unpleasant beginning with the words—"You must be joking...!" "Nata! Naataa!" thought Master Nikola to himself, but without fear or agitation. Let them grow and multiply, none of that had any longer power over him or could change or ruin anything in the life that had opened up before him. Others will fight and struggle with that; he was saved and—living.

He went most often out to Senjak to his uncle. The small house, which had once been alone, was now surrounded by small villas, but Sava's garden which he had nurtured for twenty-five years already, was now a dense orchard through which no noise from the street nor neighbor's gaze could penetrate. Sava had long ago passed his seventieth year, but was a healthy and vigorous old man, as often happens with people who were quiet and reserved in their youth. His aunt had also passed her sixtieth year, but was agile and eloquent, liked books and spoke a refined and sophisticated language as before. She had filled out and become prettier with age, as often happens to women who were not pretty when they were young. Both were completely gray.

Here, in the dense, well-tended garden, not far from the beehives, which had become a veritable apiary, uncle and nephew sat, half in the sun and half in the shade, chatting about everyday things. The aunt brought out a snack for them which they ate slowly and with relish.

Sava cut small slices of bread with a pocket knife, in the manner of villagers in the Valjevo region. His wife scolded him, but with a smile and no hope that she would wean him from the habit. (Reproaches between such old and harmonious spouses are harmless, without edge, they do not clash, rather they glide easily like those white pebbles which a river has smoothed and polished to perfection over the years, so that they bind the couple together rather than separating them.)

Bees hummed around them, a fresh, mixed fragrance rose from the grass. Nikola Kapa felt alive and that he was free and joyful.

Master Nikola died joyfully in the fourth year of his life and freedom as a widower. He died from a heart attack, feeling no pain or illness, he slipped away in a moment, as he sat on the terrace of his house. In the glass of water beside him, a cube of sugar dropped into it was dissolving and sending upward tiny, fine bubbles, like sparks.

Translated by Daniel J. Gerstle

The Snake

O n the white road that cut through the Glasinac
Plain as far as the eye could see, an elegant yellow phaeton was moving slowly, drawn by two
rather small but lively blacks in a spanking new harness.
Seated in the coach were two young girls wearing identical gray mantles of light silk and wide-brimmed straw
hats on which the veils had been raised and drawn back.
In front, with a pipe between his teeth, sat the driver, a
native of Kranj. His red beard and whiskers and bushy
eyebrows were coated with dust of a flourlike whiteness.

The girls, Agatha and Amelia, were daughters of
General Radaković, traveling from Sarajevo to Višegrad.
A month ago they had both arrived in Sarajevo, where
their father had been on duty since spring.

Their father, a gray-haired but slim and red-cheeked
man, belonged to the Viennese family of Radaković that,
for more than one and a half centuries, had supplied the
Austrian Empire with high-ranking officers. Originally
from the province of Lika, they had long since become
Germanized and had, in the fifth or sixth generation,
come to regard themselves as genuine Viennese. With a
certain archness, they claimed that they were descended

from some Bosnian princes, and in their family coat of arms, which each of them wore engraved on a massive ring, were supposed to be heraldic indications that bore out their claim. Beside his Croatian surname, it was possible that this legend too had contributed to the general's appointment that spring to the post of division commander in occupied Bosnia, with headquarters at Sarajevo.

Now that the mild September weather had set in, the general had begun an inspection tour of his garrisons on the eastern border. Višegrad was to be the base from which this tour would be conducted. He planned to remain there two or three weeks. The Višegrad commanding officer was an old acquaintance from Vienna, a veteran bachelor and an amiable rake who had long given up the hope of advancing his career and was now assigned only to easier duties in outlying garrisons where he might gratify his passion for gardening and organizing mess rooms and officers' quarters—the one passion left to him from so many foolish and expensive ones, which had earned him a bad name among his superiors while at the same time making him popular with fellow officers, with women, and with moneylenders. It had been his suggestion that the general bring his family, and he took it upon himself to arrange their quarters ("the best available, considering the place and circumstances"), and to furnish house help, organize the hunts, and plan suitable diversions for the ladies.

So the general had set out with his wife, two daughters, and his son, a cadet at the military academy and now on furlough.

They had left Sarajevo early the day before. The general, his portly wife, and cadet son were riding in the heavy black landau which the Sarajevo firm of Saračević rented only to leading notables and for grand occasions. The daughters, both grown up, had connived to travel separately in the general's coach, which was light and gaily painted. They were thrilled at the prospect of spending two whole days together and of being able, while passing through wild, unknown country, to talk undisturbed and to their heart's content; they were unusually fond of each other, even though the only thing they had in common was their beauty.

Agatha, the older sister, was of a quiet and sober nature, even-tempered and dependable, always occupied with some business of the family or home. Her Viennese friends jokingly called her Caritas, for she had, while still a young girl of sixteen, founded her own society for helping the poor. She was one of those girls for whom personal happiness was not the first and last thing in life, and who in seeking happiness would find it in the service of others.

Barely a year younger but just as lovely, Amelia was somewhat frailer and paler. She had been nicknamed Ophelia. She was very musical and fond of books and entertainment. Ever since her "coming out," she had suffered (there is no other word for it) from a complicated and hopeless love for a childhood friend, a cool and self-contained young man who would have driven into a convent even a hardier type than Ophelia. Amelia did not enter a convent, since those things were not done any more—the year was 1885—but she continued to suffer because of the young man, or, more accurately, because of her love for him, as from a secret and lingering disease. Hidden wounds take longer to heal, and the one person in whom she could safely confide was this sister of hers. Agatha responded with patience and genuine sympathy, and was ever ready to understand, soothe, and offer comfort.

The girls had been inseparable since childhood. When their father was stationed in small garrisons in Hungary and Galicia, they had gone to the same boarding school near Vienna. Later, he had served five years at Prague and Vienna, and they had spent their first adult years in those two cities.

Now this remarkable and breathtaking ride over the wild Romanija Mountain and along the endless Glasinac Plain gave the younger sister a rare opportunity to confide in the elder. After a lengthy and particularly agonizing whispered confession, she broke down and started to cry. In the middle of that sun-baked plain, sketchily edged by blue mountains in the distance, her anguish sounded even more distressing and hopeless than usual.

The older sister gestured at the hulking back of the driver, reminding her that one should not give way to emotion in front of servants and that there would be time enough to cry later, then drew her gently to herself in order to calm her. After a quiet cry on her sister's shoulder, the blond girl lifted up her head. Her face seemed transfigured in the September sun. They exchanged smiles that were almost identical in the beauty of their teeth and lips and shiny eyes, but one seemed to say, "Isn't it better and easier now?" and the other, "Yes, it is, my dear, but it hurts all the same and always will."

Now, as their carriage continued on its course, they were enchanted with the air and the wide expanse of the changing landscape. The landau carrying the rest of the family had fallen behind by almost an hour's ride.

It was getting toward noon. The road dipped imperceptibly. Here the plateau appeared to sag a little and for the first time they felt the mugginess of the day, which seemed more like midsummer than early autumn. On both sides could be seen scattered cattle sheds built of dry gray logs. The lonely and empty structures gave an impression of utter neglect. There wasn't a human being or dwelling anywhere in sight, not a tree or cultivated field or cattle, or a single bird in the torpid air. From this shallow lowland the road began to ascend again in a wide curve. The horses slowed down and their breathing grew more labored. And when at last they had pulled the carriage to the highest point of the rise, the plain reappeared once more, though no longer as smooth and uniform as before. Now it was tilting slightly and was fringed on both sides by small mounds and dimpled ridges covered with low undergrowth in the hollows.

On a little flat to the right side of the road they saw a small knot of people. Two of them were peasant women, bending over something on the ground. Both sisters saw them at the same moment. As they drew nearer they realized that the women were busy with a small prone child. Next to them stood a small boy. The women and the boy turned to stare up at the girls as if they were apparitions.

It was obvious right away that the small girl who lay on the grass beside a fire was feverish and very sick. The sisters knew only how to say "Good day" in Bosnian and beyond that they were unable to make themselves understood. They called the driver. He was reluctant to leave the coach, but after securing the team he went up the rise and began to act as interpreter.

The child had been bitten by a snake while rounding up her sheep in the bushes. (Both sisters froze in momentary confusion and fear as if they themselves had stepped on a snake.) This information was conveyed by the weeping younger woman, the child's mother, who gasped between words as though she were laboring uphill with a heavy burden. The older woman was a charm healer from a nearby village. She squatted beside the little girl, whispering.

The charm healer was known as Smilja the Serbian. A ruddy, powerfully built woman with big dark eyes, she was the healer and fortune teller for that entire region. The sudden appearance of the two foreign ladies did not disconcert her in the least. She went about her ministrations with perfect composure, yet also with a total concentration that brought to her features the calm and compassionate expression seen on the faces of good doctors. Her patient would undoubtedly have found her presence reassuring, were it not for the fact that more than three hours had elapsed since the accident and the child had already passed into that typical state of utter apathy common to snake-bite victims—eyes shut, lips tightly compressed, face of an earthen color, breath short, skin cold and clammy. The sorceress had observed all this at the start, and was concentrating all the more zealously on the tiny, all but invisible wound on the girl's swollen leg. Calm and unruffled, she was gazing at the wound as if it were some secret text. From time to time she would trace, with the long thumbnail of her right hand, a wavy line around the wound resembling a spiral thunderbolt that was supposed to represent the broken black stripe on a snake's back. In a low but steady voice, she recited some verses in which it was possible occasionally to make out the rhymes, but the rest of which was lost in a prayerful whisper. Then, lifting her head and rocking over the wound, she recited in an undertone:

> *Early on Sunday Lena made her way*
> *to the meadow for a sheaf of hay.*
> *In the hay a yellow snake*
> *bit Lena and made her cry,*
> *Her mother tried to soothe her:*
> *"Little Lena, fear no harm,*
> *your mother will find a charm:*
> *Milk from the wild doe yonder*
> *and apple milk to seal the wonder."*

This was followed by a rhythmical chanting of jumbled and meaningless gutturals, punctuated by a solemn blowing of her breath first directly into the wound, then into the distance, and finally in all four directions of the compass. When it was finished, the sorceress calmly rose to her feet, as though all were now in the best possible order, and began to untie the knotted end of a short towel and take out some dried snake herbs that were to be wetted with saliva and then applied to the wound.

The older sister watched the stern, matter-of-fact woman with disapproval. She felt that one ought to protest against such superstition, make a determined stand against this witchery and offer instead some sensible treatment and genuine medication. But she remained standing as if chained to the spot, as if on climbing down from the coach she had immediately stepped into a tepid and sticky quicksand in which one moved only with the utmost effort and where every thought foundered and vanished the moment it was born. She had to brace herself and summon all her strength to move closer to the scene.

. The child lay on her left flank now. Her long white shirt was thrown up over her knees, her left leg thrust out sideways and already noticeably swollen. The bite could not be seen, though it must have been somewhere just above the ankle, for that was where the blue-green circle was, fiery around the edges. The child was moaning softly and every once in a while her whole body shook as in a hiccup.

After moving closer, the older sister gazed long and fixedly at the inflamed leg. Her fine dark eyebrows had come together, which gave her face an altogether new and unnatural expression. Disturbed by it, the younger sister joined her and asked in a hushed voice:

"How does one treat a snake bite?"

Still staring at the sick child, Agatha seemed not to hear the question.

She had seen illness and poverty in the slums of Vienna, on her periodic rounds in the company of other members of her organization. But this—this was something new and quite horrid. There, one had always known what was lacking and also the possibilities of help, at least as far as practicable. There it had been a problem of saving children from bad parents, alcoholics, or from an illness that was easily diagnosed and prescribed for, in which only the money for the pharmacy was lacking, or of patients who needed a better diet or a change of air. But what was one to do here? This plight seemed to be beyond anyone's grasp and intervention. Scowling as before, Agatha asked question after question, which the driver translated haltingly.

What had they done about it so far? It turned out they had squeezed all the blood they could from the wound and tied a tourniquet above the knee and then sent a boy, the little girl's older brother, to the village for brandy. Wiping her tears and sweat, the child's mother motioned vaguely at a point in the distance where the village was supposed to be. Now they were waiting. There was nothing else they could do.

"Do you have any rum or brandy?" Agatha asked the driver.

"No, miss. I don't drink or carry the stuff when I'm on the job."

Agatha would best like to have sent both of them packing, the spellbinder with her unctuous face and the driver who seemed as if he were secretly gloating over the fact that there was nothing anyone could do, and to roll up her sleeves and do something useful. But she stood there helplessly, fretting at herself and at everyone around her.

"One can't let a human being die like this," she said under her breath, not knowing herself whom the rebuke was meant for. She went down on her knees, poured some cologne water on her handkerchief and gently began to mop the child's forehead and face. The girl only moaned louder.

"Alcohol, of course! Only alcohol can save her," she said under her breath, as though it had only just occurred to her. Then she turned to the driver. "Please turn the carriage around at once and go back as fast as you can to meet father and mother. Ask them for the cognac flask and come back quickly. Quickly, do you hear?"

But speed was not congenial to this driver from Kranj, who was wont to regard the young mistress's activities among these Bosnian peasant women as something exaggerated, slightly unreal, and altogether senseless, much like those drunken cutups of gentlemen officers when they urged him to drive faster at some ungodly hour over rough and tricky roads. But he turned the coach around and started back. To Agatha it seemed that he was crawling.

Throughout this time Amelia had stood to one side and, with a sense of uselessness, watched her "big" sister. Now that they were alone they could look around and take stock of the situation. In the oppressive heat of midday the little peasant group appeared wretched and pathetically lost on the scorched plain. The women stood there as if made of stone. The child's mother kept glancing westward, toward the village where the life-saving brandy was supposed to come from, but the glance was tormented and empty of hope, as if the village were half a world away. The spell-woman quietly waited for her work to take effect. The little boy stared on dully, while the stricken girl lay in her dirty, grass-stained shirt, her swollen leg stuck out stiffly.

"Will she die?" asked the younger sister in a voice full of fear.

"Not if we can give her enough alcohol in time," the other replied in the tone of an expert.

The silence was complete—broken only by the child's muffled, continuing moans. The sun beat down mercilessly. The vast gray plain seemed to have swallowed the coachman. Time stood still, hot and immovable, like the misery and suffering that surrounded them.

"My God, Agatha, what kind of a life is this! What kind of a country, what kind of people!" whispered the younger sister, trying to still her own deep unease.

Agatha's eyes were on the horizon, on which the carriage was supposed to appear momentarily. Steadily, mechanically, the child's mother was drying her invisible, inexhaustible tears.

Suddenly the child gagged and doubled convulsively, then vomited without lifting her head off the ground. The mother leaned down and propped up her head, while Agatha wiped the child's mouth with her lace handkerchief. The spasm racked the tiny body a few more times, after which she grew still and deathly pale. Her breath sounded shorter. Agatha pulled up the shirt and saw that the belly was also beginning to swell. There came off her a rank and sickening smell of excrement, as the food had poured out of her from all sides.

Agatha rose and asked by sign language if they had any water. On the grass lay an earthern jug, and from this they drained the last few drops, indicating that there was no more to be had for miles around. When she asked for a small spoon to pry open the child's tightly clamped teeth, it took quite some gesturing for them to understand each other; and again the answer was in the negative.

"Nothing—not a blessed thing," Agatha said as she wiped her fingers on the handkerchief her sister had handed her. In the face of so much helplessness her goodwill began to fail her too.

She folded her hands and with a mounting sense of impotence looked querulously at the sorceress who crouched on the dry and parched ground, unshakably calm and confident in her nostrums and magic which, judging from the looks of her, were already at work and were bound to help, if God willed it. Agatha began to relent toward her and was in half a mind to ask her to get on with her spells and charms, seeing how there was nothing else to be done, anything but slouch there so impassively while the venom raced through the child's body and spread havoc with every passing minute.

The younger sister was apt to imitate the older unconsciously. Now they both stood with folded hands and waited, like the two peasant women, for the help that was supposed to come. Now they, too, were beginning to feel a little as if they had always stood forlorn like this, helpless and superfluous under the vast sky on this interminable plain of stunted pastures that was empty of any vestige of human habitation or activity save the dingy, ramshackle cow sheds which looked for all the world like a discarded stage setting. They felt as if they were poor and squalid themselves, embroiled for untold ages in some drama of primitive shepherd life, with a leaden weight on their heads, on their eyes and all their limbs, rooted in a cosmic seizure in which only the hidden evil in the child's body continued to live, pulsate and ravage unimpeded.

In silence the mother wiped her tears and sweat and then, between expelled breaths, began to emit short laments of which the sisters understood not a single word and yet perceived the full meaning.

"Oh, poor unhappy me! Hoo-ooh, everything comes down on my head. Hoo-ooh, what a cursed wretch I am!"

And again she would lift her head and scan the horizon for the boy who some three hours ago had gone for the brandy and was dawdling as if he were fetching Death itself.

Finally, the bright-yellow coach reappeared on the highway. Agatha nervously waved her handkerchief at the driver, urging him to hurry, but the man was a congenital laggard whom nothing could change. He brought along a flat crystal flask with a silver cap that served also as a peg.

They barely managed to loosen the child's cramped mouth. Into it Agatha poured the cognac slowly and carefully, afraid lest the girl bring it up again. As soon as the child would start to choke, she at once withdrew the flask and waited. In this way the flask was gradually emptied of cognac. Some ten minutes later big drops of sweat broke out on the child's forehead, her eyes cleared and her cheeks came out in a flush.

Through the driver Agatha explained to the women that the child should be kept awake at all costs, that they were to massage her forehead and chest and raise up her arms periodically to encourage breathing and stimulate the heart. They nodded and promised to do it, but in their awe forgot either to thank her or bid her good-bye. The little group remained unchanged, save for the two extraordinary foreigners in their bright city finery.

The girls quickly took their seats in the carriage, which promptly started down the road of the plateau. Some distance behind them the dusty and lumbering landau had just come into view.

The terrain grew more and more uneven. The plain heaved and sloped downward at the same time. The swelter grew more intense. Thin spurs of red earth began to border the road on both sides and low, scraggly undergrowth became prevalent: dwarf juniper, hellebore, briar, hawthorn, and nameless tiny thornbush close to the ground itself. The landscape rapidly lost that grandeur and melancholy beauty usually found in a plain that meets and joins the sky in a soft unbroken line; it began to look somber and frayed, poor somehow and lacking proportion. The horses trotted faster. The driver spurred them on, anxious to outdistance the landau to spare their honors the dust he was raising. With a forward tilt, the light carriage fled along the dust-filled ruts making hardly a sound.

The sisters gazed ahead in oppressive silence, lost in the languor of the landscape and of the stuffy afternoon. How different, how crisp and invigorating had been that morning on the same Glasinac Plain when they had chattered about this and that and Amelia had eased her heartache with a good little cry!

Her eyes riveted on the driver's shoulder buttons, Agatha continued to scowl just as she had done over the sick child a while ago. Now the expression gave a new cast to her features, both aloof and alarming. It cowed Amelia, who, glancing mutely and anxiously at her sister, longed to be able to say something, anything, that would break the heavy encompassing silence, yet dared not for fear of making her wise big sister sadder yet. Shyly she put a hand on Agatha's. As if she had been waiting for the gesture, Agatha bent her dark head to her sister's shoulder and closed her eyes. Observing her from the side, Amelia saw the quivering lips and the long dense eyelashes straining to hold back tears. Touched to the quick, she gave her an awkward hug and said:

"No, don't cry. There's nothing to cry for. Please don't. A fine big sister you are, carrying on like this."

In an unconscious echo of her older sister's gesture earlier that morning, she drew her attention to the driver and wordlessly implored her to control herself. Agatha quickly checked herself and dabbed her eyes, but just then her tears came welling with an unstoppable force and she again dropped her head on her sister's shoulder and said in a smothered, trembling voice:

"Oh, I told you in Vienna what kind of a country we were going to. Now you've seen what it's like. Not a wretched thing under the heavens—I kept telling you about the poverty and wilderness—the ugly, indescribable squalor. I did tell you, didn't I? It's awful, absolutely awful!"

"Darling, calm yourself, please." Flustered, the younger sister tried to comfort her. "Don't be a child. Remember how Count Prokesch used to say you exaggerated everything—and that Turkish proverb he used to quote to you: He who weeps for the whole world won't have any eyes left. He knew what he was saying, he'd lived long enough in the East. The world's full of misery and backwaters like these, and there's nothing you or I can do about it."

"Ah, nothing, really nothing. But one should at least make an effort. Somebody ought to try—at least a little—because like this it's impossible, impossible for them and for us to live. It's too horrible for words."

"But that's neither your fault nor mine," said the younger sister with an edge of exasperation in her voice, herself close to tears.

"No, of course not," answered the older sister dully. But she immediately corrected herself. "Really, I don't know any more. Not our fault, that's very easy to say. In the end it turns out it's nobody's fault, but look how the people live and what they do. You saw it with your own eyes. Somebody must be to blame or else how could this horror exist? Such horror!"

With a tenderness at once childlike and grave, the young one put a hand first over her sister's mouth, then over her eyes, as if to snuff out the tears. In doing that she herself dissolved in tears, brought on by a vague

sense of shame, anger, and grief over her sister's outburst, impelled by the instinctive egotism of young,
beautiful, and spoiled women who understand and endure tears only in relation to their own pain. Her feelings presently coalesced in one urgent wish: That this
weeping of her sister's cease and that all talk of misery
and bad luck be silenced forthwith. In a chiding and irritable tone she whispered through her own tears, even
while pressing her sister's head to hers:

"Don't cry, Agatha. Calm yourself, I beg of you. The
driver is listening. Really, I don't understand you. Bosnia
isn't worth crying about. Please don't! I can't bear to see
you crying. I can't."

Huddled like this and mingling their tears the sisters
crossed the Glasinac Plain, oblivious of the driver and
of the whole world. The plateau soon came to an end
and was replaced by steep mountain country. The road
began to drop noticeably and the vegetation on both
sides thickened. The brakes made a harsh scraping noise
against the coach wheels.

Translated by Joseph Hitrec

The Tanners

Almost lost within the spacious and lively *čaršija*, there exists a short, narrow street which does not have its own name rather it is referred to as the branch of the Master Craftsmen's Guild. Here are only master tanners and craftsmen specializing in soft footwear, the latter being smaller and newer. (Fifteen shops in all.) They sit cross-legged with bowed heads, styling and cutting leather, making buttons and attaching them, assembling equestrian equipment, and there are also those that simply cobble shoes and their shops resemble more an ordinary large box that is merely attached to a proper workshop. Nonetheless, all of them—including their little passageway—are, all in all, part of the *čaršija*, living its life and breathing its soul.

The shops' eaves are low and the street is narrow, making it look more like a covered space into which sunshine and noise from the *čaršija* penetrate with difficulty and only occasionally. There is both a lot of humidity in this street, and some damp and somber silence in which the monotonous beating of the craftsman's hammer is totally incorporated. Only occasionally and exceptionally does a loud shout break through from a passerby or someone who, like the clients, sits along the shop window to casually discuss their purchase and haggle over prices with patience and dignity.

A peasant from Sarajevo Polje kept turning in his hands a lovely and decorated leather bag and quietly inquired as to its price. Sixteen *groschen*, responded the craftsman. The peasant was silent for a while, as though unable to gather his wits from astonishment; remaining silent intentionally for a long time after in order to show how aghast he was by such a high price, then even more quietly than before, as though recovering from a blow, says:

"Sixteen, you say?"

"Exactly!" responds the craftsman, but in fact, he did not actually utter the word, rather he expressed this with a decisive movement of his chin.

The peasant turned and looked over the leather bag from all angles, inside and out whispering something, while the craftsman continued his work with a scornful absent look on his face. The peasant's whispers slowly transformed themselves into words and then very quiet speech. He said that, in passing, he had seen this same leather bag for thirteen *groschen* at another craftsman's shop. Without stopping his work, the craftsman coldbloodedly responded that he was mistaken not to have purchased it on the spot.

"Thirteen, by God Almighty," swore the peasant, "the same as this one!"

"Thirteen, possibly, but the same as this one—no way."

There was once again silence which was only reinforced and stifled by the clatter of many hammers striking in unison. Its loud waves floated in the air and crashed into one another or collided with the resonance which rebounded from across the street. In the end, all these noises mixed and cancelled one another out creating the loud characteristic rhythm of a working day above the humid and dark street which the sun's light never illuminates to the end.

The peasant sat there for some time more, arduously and hopelessly thinking of a way to engage this craftsman in bargaining, until he ultimately found the strength to tear himself away from the shop window and move on.

There is not much news nor are there many changes in this street. Commotions are a rarity. Perhaps that very day the Sarajevo Police lieutenant would pass, followed by a constable, tapping their swords on the cobblestones, returning greetings to the left then to the right and calling some craftsmen by name. If they stopped at any of the shops, the owners would politely make room for them to sit and immediately order coffee but if they were to pass without stopping, they would all happily see their backs, since these men do not like to lose work time; and contact with state authorities and its representatives is avoided as much as possible.

The most change and unrest brought into that world, from time to time, is Stanka; a slender, strong young woman—cut thin at the waist—with the innocent and sweet face of a blond beauty. She is the servant of a wealthy man in Varoš. When she is going to the marketplace or returning from it with a full string bag, she often passes through this little street. She is always accompanied by an older woman or a young boy, no matter how small he may be.

Two neighbors, tanners, were sitting each in their own shop, separated only by a wooden fence made of spruce planks which had been separated by time. When the young lady approached, as if summoned, they both raised their heads a bit and drifted with their regard from the ankle upwards, along the silhouette of her *dimije*, her waist, up to her bright face and lowered eyes. These were immeasurably fast and short moments.

The young woman had already passed, and the two tanner neighbors sat numb, their hands motionless on their work, looking off into the direction in which she had disappeared. They did not see each other, but they heard one another.

"Oh, beautiful creature! Mercy, people, God's beauty!"

"Shame she's of that religion!"

"But, when I see her looking like that, I forget who is of which religion."

"You're right. Who can even think about her religion?"

All of this is said with a hollow voice, more or less each man for himself and more guessing the words as opposed to actually hearing them individually.

The young woman moved on; the wave of excitement that followed her began to subside. The young tanner called out:

"What's that you said?"

The man on the other side waved his hand.

"Oh nothing, neighbor."

Silence and the banging of tools.

There are also those that are younger and less re-strained and less cautious—Huso the cobbler, for ex-ample. When the young woman passes by, and as though hovering disappears around the corner, he throws down his hammer, lowers his feet from the win-dow sill and briskly puts on his slippers as though he was going to go follow her. But alas—it is understood—he does not go, for the road in pursuit of beauty, which irreversibly passes us by does not exist. He does not go, instead he remains pensive for a few moments, then throws off his slippers, lifts his feet on to the shop win-dow and folds them under himself, and returns to his work—but now with his hammer he mercilessly pounds the outstretched leather in from if him, filling the tan-ner's alley with an echo.

This Huso's hot-tempered start in pursuit of fleeting beauty, the sudden deflation and the return to daily chores and set old habits are parts of a long-time estab-lished scene which repeats itself from time to time, al-ways similar but never the same. This brings some life and joy into the low and dark store-workshops. Every-one laughs, more or less loudly and openly. Even the old reputed craftsmen snicker, but behind their mustaches. They would never do or dare what this cobbler does, although it is not nice to laugh, each one of them—in himself—is happy that there is someone who dares and does.

Besides the buyers and passers-by, regular guests of this street include both beggars and the *čaršija*'s fools, toward whom everyone here behaves in a restrained manner with a sort of compassion and superstitious attention. Sometimes one of those disturbed people would pass by singing or rudely shouting, but the craftsmen continue their work, patiently and quietly waiting for that misfortune and misery of insanity to either finish singing its song or fall silent, or together with its song quiet down and disappear around a corner.

But when a blind or crippled and deformed person in rags whom destiny has rejected from the orders of healthy and capable people, stops at a shop window, the craftsman immediately takes from the wooden box without a lid a small copper coin and carefully places it in the extended hand whispering something inaudible without raising his glance. In addition to his small coin offering he adds his composed and solemn gestures along with a prayer-like whisper as his contribution to the protection from all evils which can at any moment fall on any living man.

So in work and dealings, in conversation, sometimes in laughter, and in the changing faces known and new, comes lunch time when the craftsmen, again calmly and patiently, eat what has been brought to them in a copper-covered plate by someone from home. That way the afternoon passes by even more quickly, and the traffic dies out and work dwindles. Almost unexpectedly, shadows chill and dull the daylight, indicating here that dusk is drawing near. The craftsmen then abandon their work aprons, dress and put their shoes on and withdraw to the back of the workshop to count their money and place it in a special leather bag. The apprentice collects the tools, and the leather scraps, loose threads and cords are crammed into a corner. Metallic articles retain for some time more their borrowed shine.

Then begins, as though according to an ancient ritual, the serious and sacred moment of the closing of the shop. The assistant or apprentice lifts and lowers the wings of the double-door and pulls the door latch through over them, but the last part of this important operation is performed by the master craftsman himself, who personally puts the big lock on the end of the latch, locks it and returns the key to his belt; he does this conscientiously and calmly, as though casting a spell, moving his palms over the lock and the planks upon which it hangs; in the somber fading light, his faces takes on a calm expression like that of a man who considers that he has passed a good day today and done all that was in due order and worthwhile, and here even as he does so, deflecting all thoughts of robbery or fire or some other mishap and trouble, that the night is always capable of bringing about, and without words, he entrusts the *čaršija* in which all of his goods and estate are located to the protection of good forces.

The sky is still light over the tanners' alleyway when the craftsmen disperse to their homes, which are, generally, scattered about the hillsides around the city, at Vratnik, over Kovači or over somewhere near the top of Bistrik. With a large bag on their right shoulder, carrying what they have acquired during the day for their homes or their children, they slowly walk up the steep road; and the more they climb, the more they enter into parts of the city which are still illuminated.

When those who are a bit elderly tire, they sit down next to a fountain on a square and white stone, as if it were a regular and ready rest-stop. They roll and light tobacco, and following the tobacco smoke with their glance, they look at the spread-out city in the valley below and the last rays of sunlight that are setting, somewhere behind Hum. Then they go in their thoughts again over the dealings of the day. One recounts his daily receipts or adds up the outstanding loans, another unravels some unpleasant encounter or thinks about tomorrow's worries; and yet another, throwing a glance in the direction of the fire blazing around the setting sun, will once again see the young beauty that passed through the tanners' street this morning. He watches her, taller and more beautiful than ever, as she walks across the entire horizon like an apparition, and also sees the folds of her *dimije* made out of the evening glow and fine clouds fluttering and intertwining above the blazing crater into which the sun sinks, where they too are consumed one by one as if by the flames of the burning stake.

Translated by Savka Gajić

The Game

It was warm and light outside. Like a motionless stage set, the sea, adorned by a row of pale green tamarisks, engulfed the entire view. On the open veranda of the large restaurant stood a long row of small tables covered in crisp white tablecloths. Lazar sat at one of these tables, alone. There were two young people at the table across from him. The man was facing him, and the woman, who was closer, had her back to him. The man was blond, with long hair; he had a broad, well-groomed face and was carefully dressed. She wore a light, loose-fitting dress with red stripes. The woman blocked Lazar's view of the man, he saw him only from time to time, and then only partially, when he moved to the left or to the right. But Lazar saw her well, even if only from the back. She had thick, healthy hair, a full but still slender neck, and a straight spine. This was youth.

When he lowered his eyes, down the wooden back of the chair, he caught sight of her two feet, bare, in flat loafers, on the parquet floor. Fine ankles, not too weak, not too strong. Her skin was youthful and dark in the muted shadow of her wide skirt and the chair. Everything was usual and ordinary, only the lively movement of those feet held his attention. The woman kept taking her shoes off and putting them on again. One moment she would remove one foot from its loafer, next the other, then both at once, only to hide them happily, a few moment later, in their soft red shoes.

The woman's entire body was practically motionless. She did not move her head or her shoulders, nor did she gesture with her hands as she spoke. And it appeared that she was not even speaking, or that she spoke very little and very quietly. But the young woman's feet, not too big and not too small, somehow estranged and isolated in their refuge, did not rest for a moment, nor did they allow her shoes to rest.

That pair of bare feet and pair of red loafers moved like four figures in a puppet theater where some unseen puppeteer, skilled and daring, moved the figures with invisible strings according to some unknown script, to the rhythm of some inaudible music, in the spirit of a fantastic theatrical production. The parquet floor, and the four legs of the chair draped over on three sides with the wide silk skirt, formed the stage on which those four puppets performed their hidden play, visible only from Lazar's seat.

From where he sat, it looked as though the woman was not at all interested in the conversation, or in love, or in walking; the main and only important thing for her was *the game*.

It appeared that all of the life of the woman's entire motionless body was in her legs, or, to be exact, in her feet. They would enter, for a moment, into their shoes, only to exit right away, one after the other, or both at once. And with them the woman performed a strange pantomime, whose meaning Lazar tried in vain to decode or guess. Her two bare feet would circle around, each one separately, as if sketching, and then immediately erasing, incomprehensible and strange symbols. Then they would come together and embrace, press together and caress one another in their tender, innocent game. But this did not last long either, because they would suddenly begin rubbing, knocking each other and colliding in mischievous and angry ways, like two badly brought up children. Once again they would separate, and the beautifully formed, hollowed out soles of her feet, fresh and unworn because they did not carry a heavy weight and because they had not for a long time, would start their game again. They bent at every joint. They stared at one another, grinned and frowned, glared and scowled in angry grimaces. With this sudden change, her feet would lose their beauty and freshness, and suddenly appear old and wretched, wrinkled, even a little unclean, with something animal, monkey-like about them. Immediately afterwards, those feet would change even more, and in their endless movements traversed the entire span of natural development, from the lowest species to man. They were fins, then the undeveloped limbs of some extinct species of reptile, then clumsy paws, then back to the feet of the boldly upright biped. And all of this without any transition, without order, swift, abridged, disjointed.

And then everything would stop. The young woman's feet now rested peacefully one next to the other, her soles straightened out and became motionless, powerful and smooth, as if sculpted.

Then those human feet, becoming again what they really were, began to go through new changes and metamorphoses. Pressing the floor firmly with their toes, they suddenly became short and shapeless, filled with blood—that lowest, supporting, enslaved part of the body which bears one's entire weight, which is condemned to carry this weight until the end of time, and which never leaves the ground except to jump, and then just for a blink of an eye only to fall back down more heavily and painfully. But the game did not end there. In the subsequent chain of transfigurations, they easily and briskly separated themselves from the earth that otherwise enslaved them; they became thin, changed color, grew pale, and fluttered for a while, like wings, which, as long as they live do not know contact with the ground. Then they became animated, pliable, as expressive as hands, now healing and generously good, now lustfully soft and sinlessly clean. And it could somehow be concluded (he did not known how or according to what) that from them emanated that vague, odorless, fresh scent which only a woman's body can sometimes have for the man who desires her.

But this, like everything else, would last only for a short while, like the inevitable passage from one game in exchange for another. A new restlessness would soon possess those feet. And, bare as they were, they would begin to sweep the parquet floor and with that acquire a sort of sober, careful, domestic expression. And promptly the woman would nervously search for her shoes, find them, try to put the left one on the right foot and vice versa. Then she would abandon her attempt, raise just one with her big toe and balance it for some time. But then the other foot would capriciously disturb the balance, toss the slipper far up and then blindly and excitedly search and draw it towards her.

The performance continued like this and it was impossible to predict how long it would last, where it would go, what would become of those two small feet and what they would turn into during this game which they played only with themselves and only for themselves, on their sheltered and covered stage with Lazar as the only, coincidental and unsuspected spectator.

And throughout this whole time, the young woman's entire body was and remained motionless. Hers was the straight and still posture of a girl with a good and strict upbringing. Not a single muscle moved on her, not a single strand of her thick hair, not a single flounce of her light silk skirt. And their conversation was quiet and discreet; not a single word they uttered could reach even Lazar, who sat closest to them. Nothing. Only the feet under the chair played their strange and incomprehensible game of pretend.

Lazar ate slowly and carelessly. And as he ate he did not stop watching—unobserved—the foot game which nobody apart from him could notice, and guessing from it what this young woman's face looked like and what was the nature of the conversation between her and her friend at the table. (Whenever he would raise his eyes and manage to look at his face for a minute, it was calm, happy, drawn into a satisfied smile!). Did the game of those feet follow the meaning of her words? Or did they answer to his? Or perhaps it was neither, but the expression of her unspoken thoughts and hidden feelings? Something that she herself did not suspect and did not know? Or, finally, were those feet performing only for their own sake and for themselves, independently of everything that the two of them said, wanted, and thought?

He did not find an answer. At one moment he looked away from the performance under the chair and glanced at the clock—he flinched. He saw that he would be late for the boat if he did not leave right away. He quickly finished his lunch, and not waiting for the end of the performance, which probably never had an end, got up and set off for the shore. As he walked past the young couple, he did not turn around or glance to see what the woman with the restless feet looked like. He would never see her again, either from the front or from the back.

But he never forgot the performance.

Translated by Natalia Ermolaev

An Ivory Woman

My friend told me this story:

I bought it from a Chinese man who was cheekily obsequious and who crowed like a bird. I remember clearly, it was getting dark. I had just calculated that this day marked exactly seven months of my living in that stifling city, alone and dissatisfied, and I was rushing home to get off the street as soon as possible, where, in the autumn fog, I was constantly plagued by the same thought—that all these people would one day be skeletons. And the countless crowds of them, surging and murmuring slowed me down.

That's how I felt every evening, as frustrated as young people who go home too early. But this evening promised to be more cheerful, as though I were less lonely. In my right pocket I was carrying a woman made of ivory.

By the time I arrived home, the fire had gone out; the room smelled of coal. I rang for the servants and called them, but to no avail. It was one of those evenings, when everything is a problem and nothing is in its place. The oranges were without juice. The girl had forgotten to pour the water. Then I remembered the woman in my pocket. I pulled her out and placed her on the table beneath the lamp. The shadows arranged themselves nicely. Her shoulders and cheekbones glittered. She looked as if she were smiling. She had been carved skillfully, like all those gods, dragons and monkeys that the Chinese sell. The gloom and my bad mood seemed to lift.

Reading in bed, I would occasionally glance at her, studying her, a small, bright, graceful thing, in the circle of light beneath the lamp. I read for a long time, until the book became heavy and the lines broke up and merged. I thought that I heard the book fall and it occurred to me that I should turn off the light, but I was too tired and it all seemed impossible and too far away. In any case, that's when something happened that demanded my full attention.

Out of the grey light, the small woman made of ivory was growing and coming closer to me, ever larger and closer, until finally she sat down on the bed beside me, laughing and without greeting me, as if she had been there all along, had only stepped out for a moment, and had now come back.

I wasn't even as surprised as I should have been. I just sat up a bit against the pillows. Then the woman, still smiling, spoke.

"I just knew it had to be like this. It was all meant to be. Where would you be without me?"

I started to get confused.

"My God," she said, "how long we've been apart, and never a word, while my heart was full; yet all through that long wait I always believed and I knew we would meet, and that you were made for me, and I for you."

"But…"

"Don't, don't say anything; you were hard-hearted. How could you hesitate for so long?"

"But…"

"But it's all right now. From now on all we have we share; our lives, our work, our death; from now till eternity!"

"But!"

But the woman was becoming increasingly fervent.

"Yes, from now we will live, create, suffer together …"

In my consternation and distress, which was beginning to turn into despair, I almost shouted what was least on my mind.

"But, you're made of a bone!"

"Wha-a-t am I?!"

And the woman bristled and tensed, as though heading for a furious scene and a scandal.

"What am I ma-d-e of?!"

"Of ivory…I mean, from…"

She screamed as though wounded. I propped myself even higher, so that I was half sitting. After that first scream she was now only whimpering.

"Oh, oh, how the world has corrupted you, how numb you've become! Oh, you cannot understand love and goodness, you cannot make anyone happy."

I nodded in agreement, hoping that the uninvited temptress would leave me alone, but she wasn't even looking at me, instead she continued excitedly.

"Don't you see? That's exactly why I can't leave you; I must sacrifice myself and remain beside you, because you are so bad, you are ill, but I will take care of you as a mother does, a sister, eternally..."

At that point I realized there was no hope, no escape. And, I was overcome with a horror I had known only in rare, terrible dreams. For I knew how powerless we were in the face of human stupidity and selfishness when they took on a touching and lofty form. But still, I collected myself and resolved to use all my strength to get rid of her. Yet, she was speaking so quickly and hysterically that I could not understand anything she was saying any more; only, whenever I heard "eternity" or "remain eternally," a deep abyss would open before me and each time I would be paralyzed with terror, and fall silent again. I even thought of driving her out, but my arms and legs were paralyzed. I was barely able to find words.

I spoke like a man fighting to survive. I explained, incoherently, that she was made of bone, a mere doll, that I had bought her with my hard-earned cash, and here she was persecuting me, I mocked her for being ridiculous, wanton, Chinese. Finally I was yelling at the top of my lungs.

"So, you burst into my house from god knows where and unload your feelings! You choose me for your good deeds! Me to share your stupid eternity and me to help finish the work I'm barely able to complete myself?! Get out of here this minute! Out!"

I don't remember everything I said to her in my fear and with the ultimate intention of insulting her so much that she would leave. But she just stood there shaking her head in pity, without moving an inch.

I tried crawling from my bed, but suddenly I noticed the woman beside me start to expand. I cowered closer and closer and closer to the wall, and when she pushed against me, I began to pull away. But the woman was expanding ever more, until she lost all shape, and filled the room like ashy, lukewarm smoke.

I ran through the house, but her smoke quickly filled both the house and all the streets, and when, consumed with fear and panting from running, I pressed against an old wall at the edge of the city, I noticed how with appalling speed, like a sea or lava, the smoke was barreling towards me. Suffocated and helpless, I lifted my head towards the sky, but the sky too was covered. Above me, as around me, was nothing but thick clouds of heavy, stifling smoke. Eternity.

Seeing that I could neither fight nor run, I howled as loudly as I could with every last bit of desperate strength. And then, as if by a miracle, the fog around me began to lift and dissipate, and through the thin smoke I thought spotted a small circle of greenish light. Then I awoke.

I rubbed my eyes, still plagued with uncertainty. My heart was pounding in my throat. The air seemed heavy and stuffy. I was soaked with sweat. I sat up. Under the lamp, which I had forgotten to turn off, stood the small woman made of ivory. The shadows lay nicely on her and the lit up surfaces were smiling.

My whole body shuddered and my hands were still trembling, as I picked her up. I opened the window. It seemed I would not be able to shake off the nightmare until I heard her shatter into pieces on the granite cobblestones below.

It was a late city night, without stars or clouds, made up of a damp darkness and silence which was frightening. I drew my arm back and threw the woman with all my might onto the street, and waited, trying to hear her fall and break. I waited, but I could only hear the hollow beating of my heart, together with my short, but frequent and steady breathing, but I did not hear the ivory woman crash onto the stone, or break. I felt goose pimples all over again. I waited, but the woman never hit the ground. The hair on my head turned as cold as ice and ached. I looked at the peaceful lamp, then at the dark street. Where did she go? Were ghosts playing an invisible game with me? I thought that for just a moment, because immediately afterwards my clear old consciousness returned: there are no such things as ghosts, and everything that happens to us is just one single, all-embracing reality. Completely numb, I closed the window, sat down by the lamp and bowed my head at the thought that I was certain to meet her again somewhere.

Believe me, I still tremble from the devil's work that night.

Translated by Biljana Obradović and John Gery

Jelena, the Woman Who is Not

From the Outset

In the still, silent air of a summer day there came from somewhere an unexpected and invisible movement, like a single, solitary wave. And my half-open window knocked several times against the wall. Bang-bang-bang! Without raising my eyes from my work, I just smiled like a man who knows everything around him well and lives calmly in a contentment that is beyond surprises. Without a word or a sound, with just a movement of my head I made a sign that the joke had succeeded, that she could come in, that I was awaiting her joyfully. That is how she always comes, with a charming joke, with music or a scent. (The music of a single, chance sound that seems unusual and significant, the scent of a landscape or a north wind hinting at the first snow.) Sometimes I hear an indistinct conversation, as though she were asking someone at the street door the way to my apartment. Sometimes I see only her shadow, slender, inaudible, passing my window, but again I do not turn my head or raise my eyes, so certain am I that it is she and that she is about to come in. But I revel in that fraction of a second in a way I cannot describe or express.

Afterwards, of course, she never does come in or appear before my eyes which have never seen her. But by now I have grown used to not expecting her and sinking entirely into the bliss of that endless moment of her coming into being. And I have recovered from the fact that she will not appear, that she does not exist, as one recovers from an illness one suffers from only once in one's life.

As I observe and recall over the days and years her appearances in the most varied forms, always strange and unexpected, I have succeeded in finding a certain pattern in them, a kind of order. Above all, the illusion is associated with the sun and its progress. (I call it an illusion for the sake of you to whom I am telling this, for me it would be both ridiculous and insulting to call my greatest reality by that name, which in fact means nothing.) Yes, she appears almost exclusively between the end of April and the beginning of November. During the winter she very rarely comes, and if she does it is in connection with the sun and light. And then, as the sun grows in strength, so do her appearances become more frequent and more vivid. In May they are rare and irregular. In July and August almost daily. But in October, when the afternoon sun is thin and when one drinks it in endlessly and tirelessly, as though one were drinking thirst itself, she hardly moves from my side as I sit on the terrace, under a web of sun and the shadows of leaves. I feel her presence in the room in the barely audible rustling of the pages of my book or the barely noticeable creaking of the parquet. But mostly she stands, unseen and unheard, somewhere behind my shadow. And I live for hours in the awareness of her presence, which is far more than anything I can be granted by my eyes and ears and all my feeble senses.

But when the sun's path begins to shorten and the leaves are becoming sparse, and the lightning streak of a squirrel whose coat is already changing darts up the shiny smooth bark of a tree, the illusion begins to fade and disappear. The minute sounds I have become accustomed to hearing behind me in my room become increasingly rare, the jokes known only to carefree youth and the eternal world of dreams cease altogether. The invisible woman begins to weave herself into my shadow. She vanishes and expires like ghosts and phantoms, without a sign or farewell. She never existed. Now she is not.

Based on my long experience, I know that she sleeps in my shadow as on a miraculous couch from which she arises and greets me at random, unexpected moments, according to a logic it is hard to make out. Capricious and unpredictable, as one might expect of a creature that is both a woman and an apparition. And exactly as it would be with a woman of flesh and blood, from time to time she brings into my life suspicion, anxiety and melancholy, with no explanation or respite.

So it was last autumn. The end of October came. I believe it was the last day of the month. For the second day running, there was a strong wind. It did not abate even at night, like an executioner who has to settle accounts with flowers, leaves and branches. Torrential rain came with it as its assistant. A dark red glow in the western sky did not foretell anything good, hanging cold

and still like a witness to ensure that this bloody business of destruction, dispersal and washing away was carried out exactly. I went down from the mountain where
I had been staying to the sodden Alpine hamlet to re-
serve a seat on the next day's train and sort out everything I needed for the journey. On my way back to the
house, I was passed by huge blue buses full of people.
The tourists were abandoning the mountains in frenzied
flight. The healthy color they had acquired from the
height and the sun covered their faces like a mask
through which their anxious eyes peered and under
which one could make out a frightened pallor.

When I entered the lobby of my apartment, it was already swathed in half-darkness with which a single window, still red from the evening sky, was struggling helplessly. My luggage was there, ready for the journey.
Among the suitcases, with her head on the largest of
them, her face turned to the floor, lay Jelena. In the half-
dark, I could not make out details, but there was no
doubt that her whole posture suggested a woman felled
to the ground by great sorrow and overwhelming tears,
sobbing over the things prepared for the journey.

I shuddered and at the same moment reached instinctively for the light switch by the door. A white light
blazed, instantly extinguishing the red window, and
flooding the hall and everything in it. On the floor there
were two small suitcases and one large one with my
mountain cape of dark green cloth lying on top of them.
It must have slipped from the coat rack and fallen onto
the suitcases below it. I felt the chill that had gripped my
body begin to recede. I entered the room, turned on all

508

the lights, and began to sort out the last few things. Forcing myself to move calmly, I went back to the hall as though looking for something. At the threshold, I shuddered again. But everything was where it should have been, under the white light, the suitcases and the cape lying on them. It was all natural, intelligible and easily explained.

I ate a meager supper and slept uneasily, and first thing in the morning I was sitting alone in the train taking me down to the foothills and then to the town.

December came, those grey days before the end of the year when single people decline invitations to evening parties and sink ever more deeply into their intolerable solitude, as into cold water or a sinister forest, hoping that, if they surrender completely to it, they will pass through it as quickly as possible, escape and emerge into a joyful clearing.

One night I was sitting alone in my room, working. The large room, with its many windows, was inadequately heated and, as the night wore on, the room became increasingly cold. In order to warm up, I moved a small table to the end of the room, where there was a miserly stove. From there I happened to catch sight of the recess where my suitcases were stored. A small table lamp cast a little circle of light which only partially lit the recess with the cases. Interrupting my work from time to time, I glanced absent-mindedly at the top suitcase, which was in the light, with its metal trim and brightly colored hotel stickers, and, like bruises on a body, the traces of porters' impatience and days and nights spent in baggage vans. Suddenly I thought I saw a blond woman's hair on the nickel clasp. I jumped. Firmly woven into the lock was just one hair, blond, and hard as a piece of broken wire. I did not dare approach and touch it because at that moment I was gripped by the same dread that I had experienced two months earlier in the lobby of my Alpine apartment.

So, after all, someone must have been lying on those suitcases, her hair loose and her face in her hands! I hovered round that discovery for a few moments, and then, as though following an order, I moved the table back to its old place, together with the lamp and my papers. The recess was left in half-darkness behind me. I had withdrawn instinctively from that painful game which I had not sought and which I did not control.

I felt still colder. I forced myself not to think about my recent discovery. But even when I succeeded, I was obliged to realize that I was incapable of thinking about anything else. I have never liked excessive sentiment or those unclear, dubious states of mind in which our imagination so easily takes us off along its misguided and barren paths. That is why this whole business angered and tormented me. In order to get my own back, I wanted to punish her with contempt, ignore her and no longer vouch for her. But in fact this meant that I had to keep thinking about my contempt, and continue to torment myself. Nothing helped. All that was left was my bed, which, like a tomb, covered every torment with oblivion, healing it, although increasingly imperfectly. Ah, if only *to lie down* were the same as *to fall asleep,* life would not be what it is: death without peace or certainty. Far away and more inaccessible than the greatest treasure and boldest world record, sleep lay somewhere in the distance, an ocean of sleep, while I was dying for one single drop of it. To fall asleep, to sleep a dreamless sleep, the sleep of the dead, in which there was no suitcase, nor weeping, nor a woman's hair, nor women, whether real or ghostly!

The darkness and my vain effort to fall asleep wore me out and unsettled my consciousness to such an extent that I began to lose a sense of the dimensions of my body. My own palm, on which my left cheek was resting, appeared to me like a scorching desert without end, without a blade of grass or water. In my exhausted consciousness, I felt as though I had been lying like this from time immemorial and that the thought of a woman's blond hair was only one of the countless dreams I dreamed, as I lay awake. That idea gave me the strength to pull myself together and turn on the light.

How small and confused the world of tangible things is compared to the scorching, limitless expanses of insomnia! How blurred and ugly is everything that the open eyes can see! The whirlwind abruptly revealed by the painful earthly light began to spin increasingly slowly. Finally, everything came to rest, each in its rightful place: the door, the large mirror, the divan, the desk, the telephone.

I got up. With the uncertain step of a child who knows the names of the objects around it, but not all their characteristics, I set off through that reality of a lower order. At the back of the room I turned on another light, on the wall. In the recess lay the luggage, motionless and illuminated. My eye fell on the two

511

nickel clasps of the largest suitcase, slipping from one to the other. No trace of a woman's hair. I turned on the desk light as well and sat down on the chair where I had been sitting before I went to bed and caught sight of the strand of fluttering hair. From that perspective the reflection of a bent, fine line of light could be made out on the left-hand clasp, resembling a strand of blond hair. And that was all.

I switched off all the lights one after the other again and approached my bed, which under the glow of the small lamp on the bedside table looked like a war zone or the tragic aftermath of a great geological upheaval. I straightened the pillows and smoothed out the sheet, the arena of nocturnal battles, turned off the last light and lay down. It must have been at such a moment that the idea of resurrection from the dead first occurred to a person. I felt shattered and small, the pitiful remnant of the man who had entered this room about ten o'clock the previous evening and sat down to work, cheated and humiliated, twice over: once by an apparition and then by reality. What still remained of me, after all of this, was able to lie still, like the empty shell of an eaten shellfish, left untouched. And I fell asleep quickly and soundly, but it was not the kind of sleep I had so craved before I got up. It was the unconsciousness of an unnecessary, rejected body.

All the trials, all the expiation and all the torments of life can be measured by the strength and duration of the insomnia that accompanies them. Because daytime is not their true territory. Daytime is simply blank paper on which everything is noted and written down, while the bill is paid at night, on the wide, dark, scalding fields of insomnia. That is where everything is resolved and erased, finally and irrevocably. Any pain that has been overcome disappears like an underground stream, or burns up without trace or memory.

The winter wore on. The strange, painful business with the weeping form on the luggage and the strand of hair in the nickel clasp was happily forgotten. The vision rarely appeared.

One bright morning, I was standing in front of the mirror combing my hair. Just then I thought I caught sight through my fingers and the locks of my hair, as through a lattice, of Jelena passing through the room behind me. She slipped like an indistinct shadow the whole length of the mirror. And before I was able to get a good look at her, she disappeared in the polished edges of the glass where the gold and dark blue reflections of the winter morning were caught.

One day I took a walk out of town. I stopped on the river bank and walked across the stony bed right down to the water, which was flowing rapidly, a murky green. Winter water, barren, with no fish, no insects, no twigs or leaves, with no half-nibbled fruit dropped by children somewhere as they bathed, water sharp and merciless as a weapon. Leafless bushes and frozen willow. On the opposite bank, inaccessible and rocky, scattered pine trees. The winter afternoon, always shorter and colder than one imagines it is going to be, suddenly became cold and grey. A wind began to blow up from far off, harbinger of dusk. I clearly saw the pines on the opposite bank bending under it, one after the other. The wind

513

which was drawing closer to me lifted a fine shadow, like dust, from the pines, the rocks and the water, carrying it onwards, like an increasingly dense and dark wave, ever more rapidly. Finally, the shadow was blown right up to me, where it condensed and straightened into a figure. If I had shifted my glance barely perceptibly to the left, I am convinced that I would have caught sight of Jelena's hand and the end of her grey sleeve. But I would never do that. I stood with lowered eyes, without stirring, completely preoccupied with her unexpected presence.

That is how she appeared to me last winter. That is how she appeared a moment ago, at the window, with a spring breeze. In what form shall I meet her again? Where will I be led by the illusion of her, dearer than anything and more dangerous than any real-life danger? When the time comes, will she be placed in the same grave as me? At this moment I think that then, when I and my shadow become forever one, she will fly out of it, like a butterfly from a chrysalis, and take off through the world to visit the windows of the living. That is what I think now.

Traveling

Someone started talking about traveling. Then the topic was taken up by the whole group. Everyone joined in, sometimes two people at once. The good wine, which they were drinking in moderate sips, enlivened the conversation.

"I love traveling," a young man said all at once, un-expectedly and softly, but with a smile containing sub-dued excitement and the thrill of departure.

This youthful smile stirred me and prompted me to relate something of my travels as well, but to myself. It was an unspoken monolog, which flowed soundlessly beneath their loud exchange, like an underground stream.

But who does not like traveling? Talk to women and young men and you will see. Look into the hearts of older, serene folk, who do not speak of their desires, and you will find the same passion, faded, with no hope of being realized, but alive and enduring. Perhaps one can say that everyone likes traveling, or at least thinking about it, as his other, more beautiful life. But when I say that I like traveling, I have a real and particular reason for it. It is on journeys that I am most often aware of Jelena, who appears so seldom. That is why I like travel-ing alone and why I travel often. As soon as summer begins to ripen, a kind of vigor, which may come from within me or from the worlds around me, raises me up-wards as moisture raises seedlings towards the light, and I travel: I drive, I sail, I fly. In other words, I am happy because I could not say where I am.

It is at such happy moments that Jelena may appear. How, when and in what shape or disguise, I could not say because I can never foresee it nor am I able to ex-plain it to myself afterwards.

It happens that I meet her just as I set out, as though she had been waiting for me. As soon as I have settled into the compartment, in a seat by the window (pale green upholstery, with white lace on the headrest), the train starts moving, taking a few moments to emerge from the scattered, mournful suburbs. When expanses of gardens and fields begin to flow and stream past the large compartment window and when the mass of fences, trees and telegraph lines twist and whirl as they come to life, I turn my eyes away from the seat opposite, which is unoccupied as though waiting for someone. I keep gazing into the distance and I know that all these landscapes and objects transformed by speed into a fluid, swirling mass are condensing into the form of my lady companion. I gaze into the distance, at the dark outline of an oak wood at the edge of the horizon or at a farm etched half on the earth and half in the sky. At the same time I know that the being whose mere presence brings me immeasurable joy, which grows in incalculable proportion every minute, is already here, opposite me, becoming steadily more real. Is it not, then, the same thing to be looking at a distant point on the horizon or at the face of a woman coming into being before me? For the joy of her increasingly felt presence, because she exists just as she is and as it has been granted me to see her and have her beside me—this joy is so great and it grows so terribly quickly that it floods and erases our features, the landscapes and the distances around us, it spills over the sharp line of the horizon, falling like rain beyond the world. And the great miracle of this joy lies in the fact that any moment I can stop this tide of happiness, return it and limit it to our two bodies and to the narrow space of the compartment in which we are traveling. But just a few seconds later, the flood of happiness begins again and the two of us merge into it, together with the compartment and the whole wide world.

So I am borne on this cosmic swing, in breathtaking sweeps, from one perfect bliss to another, from Jelena's and my presence to our disappearance along with everything around us into the joy of general existence. And there is no stopping, even for a moment, at any point on this endless arc, because we are always either sweeping upwards or descending.

Yes, Jelena is here now, in the corner of my eye, on the edge of the wide horizon, which dissolves, shifts and tumbles in rapids and waterfalls—motionless and silent, but already alive and real. The wide, serene and free gaze of her eyes as they come into being has not yet sharpened and focused into a specific look. That is how young women observe the world with their pure, calm eyes, from bodies that have the freshness of mountain air and the sap of bluebells. Those eyes, which move slowly and change their expression imperceptibly, as the sky changes color, resemble part of a globe, which, softly illuminated from within, suggests unknown but imagined parts of continents and oceans. The gaze of those eyes never rested on me alone and, as they looked at me, I was able to delight inexplicably in all they saw, because those eyes laid out before them the unknown regions of innocent worlds, in which what they could see of me was absorbed. They moved and shone with the indifferent precision of celestial changes and at the same time they confused my senses and lured them along unsuspected paths and into enchanting delusions.

It has only happened rarely in my life, contemplating the greatest, most exceptional sights which earth and sky together spread before us, that I have experienced the same dancing and shifting of my enhanced senses and their infinite increase, to the point of the simultaneous awareness of phenomena which, outside those festive moments, we come upon and feel separately, each for itself. (Such moments have no name and leave behind them only a pale trace, in the memories of our everyday existence.)

So it was once, standing at a height of 3,400 meters and looking at glaciers and the apparently motionless brilliant sunlight on them, that I suddenly *heard*, rising from them, an infinitely delicate sound, a music, which the ear can barely make out and cannot retain. And, on another occasion, I stood on a sunless autumn day, under a grey sky, lost on a steppe that stretched from my feet to the indistinct horizon of the sky's vault. And as I listened to the soft, sharp sounds and whines made by the grass bent by the wind in thin grey waves, I suddenly *saw* on the crests of those endless waves a sheen which the eye, accustomed to the phenomena and sights it had seen up to then, could barely notice and grasp, but which seemed not to have come from the sun.

On such journeys with Jelena this, otherwise rare, merging of the senses was continual and entirely possible, it happened with the ease of a dream and the speed of a thought. And that is how it was this time as well.

When, on a bend in the track, the sun shifted and appeared on Jelena's side, she closed her eyes for an instant. Then I saw her strange, heavy eyelids, covering living worlds, shining with their own flame, which made her eyelashes, unable to contain all that radiance, glow with soft reflections of dark, molten gold, a miraculous iridescence.

While her eyes were closed, I observed her forehead, cheeks and neck. An indistinct halo, an intense but barely perceptible glow, hovered round them like a summer haze around ripe fruit, its edges fading in the moving, fluid landscape evoked, broken up and dispersed in the eyes of the traveler by the speed of the train.

So we sat silent for a long time, covering the miles, she in the nature of her being and origin, and I in the indescribable rapture of her presence, which grew, overflowed and swept away anything that could have been thought or said.

There was only one moment when I could not resist my desire. I forgot myself and interrupted the silence for a second, just long enough to tell her in half a word that I was immeasurably happier than all people on earth who share their days and nights, their bread and board with ghosts, and not as I do—with a real woman of perfect form and appearance.

That was all it took to make the woman who for me personified the vigor and beauty of the world vanish like an apparition.

Opposite me the empty seat swayed to the rhythm of the express train, like a branch from which a bird had just flown. In vain did the train window catch and cut through ever changing landscapes in a constantly new exchange of light and clouds. It all came and went in

519

formless, fluid shapes. And I traveled like the anxious loner I have in fact always been without Jelena's presence.

But it can also happen that Jelena appears in other circumstances and in a different way, but always on a journey, always strangely and unexpectedly.

Sometimes, on the way back from a foreign city, there is an hour to spare between two trains, or between a train and a plane, or a boat and a train. Those hours always have a special color and a special place in our life.

A sunny afternoon after rain. My things are in the left-luggage, the train ticket for my onward journey this evening is in my pocket. All my past life is behind me and all my future lies ahead. An empty space, of complete freedom, opens up. Here, life is good. Nothing is as it was, nor as it will be, but as it might have been and as, by some miracle, it really is. My whole life has suddenly become firm, clear, anonymous, perceptible only through what is of intrinsic worth. Everything has a special meaning and value, what one thinks and what one sees, smells or tastes. Under such circumstances, trifles and chance encounters often have the appearance of important things and great adventures.

I walked briskly and breathlessly from street to street, I looked at store-windows, monuments and buildings, as though I would be able to carry it all away in my memory. I went into stores and bought trifles, gifts to take to my friends back home. I was excited, as though I were snatching something from life or stealing from death. I was taking gifts to others, but I was walking along, filled with joy, as though it were they all around me who were presenting me with precious things, together with their glances and smiles, which are worth a thousand times more than those things. I passed through the familiar city as though through someone else's luxurious orchard. I looked around, did some shopping, excused myself, said "thank you." While before me was constantly the scheduled hour and minute of my departure.

I went into a large, well-stocked stationery store full of people coming and going continuously through the two large doors. It was the time of year when the days begin to grow noticeably shorter. It was still quite light outside, when all at once the store lights flashed on, flooding the whole space with a milky brilliance, in which all objects came to life—the colorful merchandise on the counters and shelves and the faces of the customers and assistants. At that moment I caught sight of Jelena. She was walking towards the cash desk in order to pay. One of the assistants left her place and followed Jelena, not taking her eyes from her. The woman at the cash desk accepted the note absent-mindedly, but when she was about to give back the change and looked up at Jelena's face, she suddenly stood up to hand her the money. Jelena went towards the exit, but the young assistant followed her all the way to the door, with the obvious intention of opening it. But she was beaten to it by an older employee, who happened to be just there. Looking directly at Jelena, he opened the door wide and said loudly and happily:

"It's all right, I'll shut it!"

The woman at the cash desk was still standing, watching Jelena go.

521

I was totally entranced, watching each person change, as if under a magic spell, as soon as they looked directly at Jelena's face. It was only when the door had closed behind her that it occurred to me that I should hurry to catch up with her. Unfortunately, I still had to pay. I quickly shook out my money in front of the woman at the cash desk, who glanced coldly at me, like a number in a whole series of numbers. Jostling people and stumbling, I ran outside. I looked to the left and then to the right. People were milling along the broad sidewalks in both directions; in the street, cars were crawling along in an unbroken procession. It was the ambiguous, transitional hour between day and night. Everything was illuminated, and yet unclear and indecipherable. It seemed to me that a procession of people with masked faces was passing by. Where had Jelena vanished? Which way had she gone? How could I find her? I did the worst and the least sensible thing. I set off to the left, pushing my way roughly through the crowd, and staring every woman in the face. Then I went back to the store and set off to the right. When I had lost all hope, I returned to my starting-point. I stood there for some time, like a man who has lost forever what he most cared about. Everything was hazy and vague, only one thing was clear: no one could be reconciled to such a loss.

I went on wandering for a long time through that lively, bustling part of the city, hauling my little packages and looking around, bewildered. Now and then I thought I saw Jelena disappearing round a corner. I ran to the place and found an unknown woman. I stopped, embarrassed. But a little later it would again seem to me that I could just make out Jelena's form in the crowd on the opposite side of the street. I ran through the traffic, against regulations, but in vain. Everything deluded me. I was steadily losing confidence in my eyesight and the speed of my step.

Disconsolate and weary, I reached the station just before the departure of the train. I collected my things and found a place in an eerily illuminated compartment. I put the shopping into my suitcase. I felt as though I had split in two and that I could see myself sitting still for a long time, with my case on my knee, endlessly wondering whether that really could have been Jelena. Then I pressed down the two locks on the suitcase, firmly and irritably, and as they snapped shut, they spoke out in a metallic voice, one saying "yes!" and the other "no!".

We were traveling through damp darkness and a desolate, unlit region. Jelena would not appear again. Darkness, damp, This was not her element. Ahead of me was a night without sleep, and an immeasurable, savage, deadly desert. It seemed to me that no living creature could survive it or make out its end. But I had to live and wait. To live with hope, waiting. Or even without hope.

To This Day

I noticed some time ago that Jelena was appearing increasingly seldom and increasingly indistinctly, but it took me a long time to admit this to myself. In order not to do so, I contented myself with very little, ever less, hoping always for something more.

So I lived for one whole summer from one incomprehensible, fleeting encounter. As I drove at dusk along a freshly leafy street, one of the loveliest streets in Belgrade, I caught sight of Jelena's indistinct form, dressed in white. She had her back to me. One could just make out that she was in one of those unusual positions that a person does not stay in long. Her pose and behavior suggested to me that she was calling something to someone or greeting someone in the distance. But I did not hear her voice even then, as I did not ever before or since. Whatever it was, she looked magnificent, stretched in space, her body responding to a need unknown to me and wholly focused on the ardent effort to give to someone who was leaving and whom I, watching her, could not see, something more of herself, to hold onto something of that person, no matter how little, whatever the night and distance allowed.

I saw all that in an instant, as one sees at dusk through the shadow of leafy trees, from a car racing down a wide, empty street. It did not occur to me to brake or stop. On the contrary, I snatched, as I passed, the whole of that twilit moment: the leafy crown of a large tree, the sidewalk, the dimmed façade of a white building, and against all that the stretching, warm, summer figure of a woman giving herself unconsciously and unstintingly to something in the distance and darkness—and I sped away with it, my foot pressing on the accelerator, like a robber.

For months afterwards, I carried that image of her within me. It was all always there: the heady May dusk, which lasts a long time and in which everything is full of life, the town in leaf, and the girl in white, her arms extended, bending towards her unseen collocutor—an apparition, but also a real woman, with warm blood, a lovely name and habits that fitted in with mine. It was all there, in front of me, it could all be eaten and drunk, like fruit and wine. But at the same time, there were also my hunger and my thirst, vast to the point of madness, without even the slightest hope that anything would ever be able to satisfy or quench them.

So I traveled through the world, the happiest man with the most beautiful woman, who could only be seen in the twilight of a long day in my solitary summer, filled with denial.

It was only in the fall that it became apparent that my illusions were of shallow root and short duration. And not only in the fall. Jelena disappeared from all my seasons.

Not even traveling seemed to help any more. Whatever it is I would like to flee comes with me, arriving before me at my destination, and waiting for me at the station, leading me to my hotel and accompanying me into town. And what I would like, with a secret, unacknowledged, hope—no longer appears even in my sleep. Jelena is not. Traveling has lost its pleasure and meaning.

My last encounter with her (strange and unforgettable) was, it is true, on a journey.

I was visiting several Mediterranean towns, making short trips on a simple steamer. It was so beautiful that I could not help thinking that I was bidding farewell to all that is called beauty and richness in this world. That thought accompanied me constantly, like muted music under all the sounds of life around me, like an invisible but ever present shadow in the full brightness of a sunny noon. Farewell, light!

In Istanbul I was supposed to meet up with a compatriot. We had arranged to meet in the large fur shop belonging to an Armenian friend of his. When I got there, my compatriot had not yet arrived. The owner of the shop, a sallow-faced man, marked by disease, but tough and a consummate salesman, was busy. I was invited to sit down and wait. So I had the opportunity to observe him from close to as he showed furs to a stout Greek woman, an eastern beauty, who was accompanied by her small and much older husband. A grey, inaudible and almost invisible young man brought out piles of expensive skins, which gave off the icy breath of the dark store-room. The shopkeeper took each fur, one by one, shaking them and opening them out before our eyes, then throwing them skillfully to the ground and spreading them right in front of the tall, large Greek woman's feet, where she stood in the pose of a wild animal tamer. As he did so he pronounced in a steely voice the name of the animal in Turkish, Greek and French, curt and business-like. "mink," "sapphire mink," "mahogany mink, "Indian lamb," "astrakhan," "panther," "ermine," "sable." And to each of these names he added one single word: "fine!," "elegant," "fashionable," "rare!". Piece after piece fell onto the pile; his hard, convincing words fell along with each fur, increasing in volume and significance, as he spoke them in pious rapture, as though he were saying: "Heavenly sun!" "Almighty God!" "Immaculate Virgin!" (In a dark corner of the shop a small icon of the Virgin could indeed be made out!) Sure of himself, his goods and his profit estimates, the shop-keeper caught my gaze as well, but I could not take my eyes off those animal skins.

One after another the unusual furs were spread before me, and with them the forests, farms, steppes and un-known regions where they came from. The world was opening up. My amazement was great and bore me far away. A kind of anticipation was steadily growing in me. At a certain moment—I did not even hear the name of the fur the shopkeeper pronounced—I saw opening up in front of me a pristine, brightly-lit landscape and in it, large and elongated, Jelena's walking form. She was not naked but dressed, as in a trembling net, only in the land-scape through which she was moving: waves, the spar-kling light of sun and water, young leaves. At that instant I saw her, as never before, full-size, in all her glory.

I do not know how long I looked at her, lost and de-lirious. When I came to, the shopkeeper was still listing: "otter," "seal," "Canadian marten," and covering over my landscape and Jelena with more and more new furs.

Since that day she did not appear again, ever.

The time has perhaps forever passed when I used to see her in the light of day, simply, with the eyes with which I looked at all the other phenomena of the visible world. That vision was always brief (a star shooting across a summer sky!), but now it does not last even that long, and it would be better if it did not occur at all.

At the worst moments of the night—and night has always been a bad time in my life—I do occasionally feel something like a hint of her presence.

The four sides of the world disappear, leaving only one, and that has no name. No one knows or wonders any longer what is *below* and what *above,* what is *behind* and what is *in front.* I am alive, but in a world of disturbed relationships and dimensions, without measure or vision. And Jelena is present, but only in that I know she is somewhere reaching out her hand to give me something. And I desperately want to raise my right hand to receive the tiny, invisible object she is offering me. So we stay for a long time in that painful position of one movement begun and one not yet started, and we do not know where we are or what we are doing, who we are or what we are really called. What is vivid and clear in my consciousness is our desire, which we share. That desire tells me that we exist, it is all that connects us and all that we know of one another.

One cannot endure in that position for long; it leads in two directions: either to complete unconsciousness or to waking. This time I wake. I wake into the world of my present life, that is to say: into a world without Jelena. I live with people, I move around among objects, but nothing can any longer summon her.

It was always like this between us: when she is not here, it is as though she will never, ever appear again; but when she is here, then she is present as though it were the most natural thing in the world, and as though she will remain here forever, and nothing will ever change. But now it seems to me that this was a deception, the self-deception of a deceived man. In fact, she does not even know that I exist, and I know only her.

That is how it is, and so—if I admit the truth—that is how it always was. One could say that I always lived on the memory of an illusion and now I am living on the recollection of that memory.

And yet—this must also be admitted—I keep thinking that she could appear once more, and that she should appear. And I always feel closest to that possibility in the warm atmosphere created by a crowd of people in motion.

The lobby of a large hotel in R. A dance from five to eight. I watched dozens, hundreds of beautiful women who were not Jelena pass me—as though someone were slowly and ceaselessly shuffling playing cards. Each of those faces appeared for a moment to be hers, but then it became, hopelessly and irrevocably, someone else's. And I watched each of these women for a moment as though she was her, but then at once she was submerged and borne away with the wave of bodies, as though dead, more than dead, because she was not Jelena, nor could she ever have been.

I found myself increasingly frequently seeking out and visiting places where excited crowds of people gather, on holidays, at festivals, at sporting events. I would spend hours there, troubled by misgivings, observing the endless ocean of human faces with greater attention than the spectacle for which they had all assembled. My excitement was particularly great as I arrived and left. It did once happen that I actually caught sight of her, as I was swept along by a mass of people slowly leaving a stadium—if that could be called seeing, and if the whole thing was not simply a pointless, painful game without end.

First, hesitantly to start with and then confidently, I glimpsed her head. I saw the expression on her face, a mysterious smile. She evidently had something to tell me, but she could not come near me because of the crowd of people surrounding and separating us. I made a great effort to push my way through them. I was getting steadily nearer Jelena. Her expression was increasingly eloquent. I was already imagining finding myself beside her and her telling me finally all that I was waiting for and that she ought to have told me long ago. With re-doubled efforts I was coming closer. At last, at last we were almost side by side. I wanted to question her, I was expecting her to say something to me but the animated clamor made it impossible to make anything out. Like a swaying swing, the mass of people pushed us now to-gether, now apart. At the moment when we were closest, I bent down and turned my head, and she told me something with a movement of her lips. It was a lively, fervent whisper. Judging by that and her expression, it seemed to me that what she wanted to convey to me was really beautiful and important, from time to time I could catch an individual word (not the sound, but its sense!), but the meaning of the whole—I could not un-derstand. I strained feverishly to grasp it and I was quite close to her, it seemed to me, but at that moment her whisper dropped and broke up like a thin trickle of wa-ter over a rock, inaudible and meaningless.

In the meantime, the agitated crowd had separated us again. I endeavored not to lose sight of Jelena's face; I could still make it out; it kept sinking and then reappear-ing in the quivering sea of human faces. She kept on trying to convey to me through her eyes what she had not managed to say, but in vain. All my efforts to resist the weight of the crowd only bore me further away from her face, which was already vanishing among the thousands of others.

Despondently, I let the endless procession of human waves carry me wherever it wanted. It was all just like a dream.

And I must say this, as well.

There was another time after that... I do not know myself whether I should say anything about it, whether it is at all possible to put it into words! Yes, there was a time when I expected a letter from her. That seems incredible and utterly senseless. And it is. And yet, that is how it was. Like a dream.

Of all the countless ways in which she appeared, deceived my senses, confused my thoughts and—vanished, this was the only one that was still missing. But it could not be omitted, and, indeed, it was not. When did that illusion come to me and how did it take hold? I could not say. When I first asked myself that question, I realized only that I had been waiting for her letter for a long time and that was all I was waiting for, at every moment of the day or night, awake or asleep. But at the same time, at each of those moments, I *knew* that it would not come, that it could not.

Who has not had the experience and has it still, on returning home and stepping into the half-dark hallway of his apartment building, of casting an uneasy glance towards the little table on which the postman leaves the mail? For many of us have thought many times about an

unknown or forgotten friend far away and about his unexpected letter with kind, warm messages, which would
have been able to bring more meaning and brightness
into our life. That is one of those vague human wish-
hopes that accompany many of us for years, that never
come true, but they make life more bearable. But in this
case, I imagined this as a real letter from a specific person, with specific contents.

The thought of Jelena's letter came to me periodically,
at irregular intervals and with varying intensity. Sometimes it would disappear for several months, or at least
lie low, like an illness one is unaware of and does not
suspect. But then there would be whole weeks when it
did not leave me day or night. Especially during the
summer. (For summer is the season when a person is
most vulnerable to the arbitrary play of nerves, and
when a mistaken idea most easily settles in us, and becomes fixed to a particular object with extraordinary te-
nacity.) And more than one of my summers was clouded
by my anticipation of Jelena's letter! Whether in the
mountains or at the sea.

A letter! When I hear that word in passing or when I
read it somewhere, I can think only of her and of her
letter. And that letter which does not come ruins all
those I do receive, which real people actually write to
me, undermining their meaning in advance and depriv-
ing them of all value.

I came back one evening from the mountains, tired,
but calm and cheerful. As I passed through the lobby, I
heard someone say my name. I ran to the desk clerk and
asked excitedly for the letter. "No," said the man, "no,

there's been a mistake, there is no letter for you." And he gave me a strange look.

I was dropping with fatigue, but I could not sleep. I did not believe there was a mistake. There must have been a letter, and it could only have been from her. But when I did finally close my eyes and fall asleep, I did not sleep soundly and I did not dream as other people do. I struggled with her letter. I heard the paper rustle, I felt it under my fingers. I strained my eyes and seemed to see individual shapes of letters, but I could not understand a single word. Then I wondered whether she could possibly use our human writing at all. I opened my eyes, wide-awake again, and in the darkness I saw streaks of light penetrating through the parted ribs of the window blinds. And it looked like a letter, with thick, even lines. A letter, but illegible.

I woke like that more than once in the middle of the night, a bitter taste in my mouth, disquiet in the pit of my stomach, furious with myself, with that damned woman whose letter I was waiting for in vain, and with the whole world. I walked over to the window, like a man looking for light and air, and I struck the window sill violently with my hand, incensed and determined to clear away once and for all that web of delusions, in which my own thoughts were entangling me.

"No, she will never contact me," I now told myself. "Why, she does not even have a hand, does not know what pen and paper are, nor human thought, nor human speech; she does not have the slightest inkling that I exist—not I nor my world of expectation. She herself does not exist. I have lost myself looking for her." That is what

533

I said, but at the same time I could see that this had not clarified or established anything. All I felt was pain the palm of my hand. And for the hundredth time my thoughts wheeled round, rushing off in the opposite direction.

"Won't she ever write? Doesn't she exist? But then what woke me, got me up and brought me to this window? And, after all, how do we know what exists and what does not? All right, she won't write, nor could she. Ever. But what if a letter came, tomorrow, with messages...?"

And the circle began again, turning without ceasing, without mercy, without a way out or solution.

What I was unable to solve in my sleep, I often tried to read awake by day. Out walking, or even in the middle of a conversation with people. A piece of white paper would suddenly appear in front of me, covered with black words, And I would be reading Jelena's letter, which I had never received. As I read, the conversation of the people around me disturbed me, like an indistinct noise in the distance, but I read persistently on.

Each time, Jelena had something joyful to tell me in her letter. She would suggest that we meet somewhere, or invite me to spend a day or two in the small place on the coast, where she was staying for the summer vacation. The connections were good, both by train and boat. For example, you can take the boat from ...

Here my reading was interrupted. Someone next to me had spoken a word in a raised tone. I gave a start. The question was directed to me. It required a reply. The letter vanished. My answer was confused.

This happened many times. And my reading was always interrupted just when it came to some specific information, the name of the place or the date. And I would continue the conversation with the people around me, thinking the whole time of the vanished letter, but trying not to be impolite and too absentminded a companion.

But then a time came when I would gladly have forgotten all of that. My torment over Jelena's letter stopped all of a sudden, miraculously. It was lost somewhere in the realms of dreams and oblivion, where it belonged. I would then live for months calmly and cheerfully, working purposefully and energetically. But then again, one evening, who knows how or why, that same thought would come to me again.

That day too will come. The unseen postman will pronounce my name from the stairway, which will seem a revelation even to me at that moment, as if up to then I had not known either who I was or what I was called. After all, a letter! It will have the festive and bright certainty of a holiday. Precise news of Jelena's arrival, or a specific invitation to come to such and such a place, at such and such a time. (In fact, that would amount to her presence!) And I shall respond easily and naturally, as though that moment had not been preceded by years of doubt, illusion and expectation. My joy will be perfect and complete. That moment of complete certainty, with no real foundation, will suddenly raise me up. And the whirlwind around Jelena will begin again. Fleeting dreams of joy again alternating with prolonged, real torments. Thoughts of her absence or her presence overtaking one another, crowding each other out, and bearing me along like waves.

535

Now it is spring. Spring, again! Ahead of me are a hundred and eighty sunny days. I feel as though my hands were filled with marvelous gold pieces, each one like the sun. All paths are open. Breathing is easy.

As I stood there, undecided with happiness, I sensed that Jelena had suddenly come into being behind me. I did not dare turn round. She stayed there for a moment or two without moving (my breathing stopped at the same time), but then she placed her hand on my shoulder. I could not say how or why I felt this. It was more the idea of a woman's hand. It rested on my shoulder like a shadow, but a shadow that has its own immeasurably small, but still real weight, and as much softness and firmness. And I stood enraptured and solemnly stiff.

I do not know when that hand flew away from me, like the shadow of a butterfly, because when I was able again to grasp and know anything, it was no longer there.

But, it is spring. Spring, again. I am enriched, I am calm, and I can wait. Yes, there was nothing, and there is nothing, nothing clear or definite, but nothing is lost or irretrievably and completely excluded. I know that in the world there are many half-open windows, with the spring breeze knocking on them, many reflections of the sun on metal and on water, empty seats in train compartments, bustling processions and brightly-lit faces glimpsed in passing. I sense that there are also thousands of other unknown possibilities and opportunities. I know that she can appear everywhere and always. Jelena, the woman who is not. Just let me never stop expecting her!

Translated by Celia Hawkesworth

Glossary

aga	Originally an officer, later a gentleman and landowner.
bey	High ranking official, a title of respect.
čaršija	Business district or downtown.
dimije	Wide trousers worn by Muslim women in Bosnia.
effendi	Used as an equivalent for "sir" or "master."
groschen	Austrian small coins.
hadji	Person who made a pilgrimage to Mecca.
hajduk	Anti-Turkish highwayman, outlaw.
hodja	Muslim man of religion, teacher.
kadi	Muslim judge.
kajmakam	High administrative official, vizier's deputy.
kasaba	Provincial town in Ottoman Bosnia.
minderluk	Type of sofa.
mufti	Highest religious official in the province.
mullah	Ottoman scholar.
munderiz	Instructor in an Islamic high school.
narghile	Oriental pipe with a long hose.
opanci	Type of peasants' shoes.

Glossary

Porte	Title of the central office of the Ottoman government.
selam	Muslim greeting.
slava	Serbian family patron saint's day.
tekke	Buildings housing a Muslim religious order.
Totica	Hungarian name for a Slovak woman.
vizier	Governor of an Ottoman province.
zurna	Type of woodwind instrument.

A Key to the Pronunciation of Proper Names

With few exceptions, the original spelling of proper names has been retained throughout this volume. The following key will help the reader in pronouncing them:

c = ts as in ca**ts**
č = as in **ch**ange
ć = is a softer ch as in Italian **ci**ao
š = is sh as in **sh**ine
ž = is s as in plea**s**ure
j = y as in bo**y**
dj = j as in **j**ar but softer
dž = zh as in bu**dg**e but harder
lj = li as in stal**li**on
a = a as in f**a**ther
i = ee as in f**ee**t
e = e as in n**e**t
u = oo as in s**oo**n
o = o as in m**o**re

Original titles and
permissions

Ljubav u kasabi (Love in the *kasaba*)
Nemirna godina (An Uneasy Year);
Ćorkan i Švabica (Ćorkan and the German Tightrope Walker)
Bajron u Sintri (Byron in Sintra)
Zlostavljanje (Maltreatment)
Geometar i Julka (The Surveyor and Julka)
Olujaci
Žed (Thirst)
Čudo u Olovu (Miracle at Olovo)
Za logorovanja (In the Camp)
Robinja (The Slave Girl)
Zuja
Ljubavi (Loves)
Žena na kamenu (Woman on the Rock)
Mara milosnica (The Pasha's Concubine)
Anikina vremena (Anika's Times)
Porodična slika (A Family Portrait)
Zmija (The Snake)
Sarači (The Tanners)
Igra (The Game)
Žena od slonovače (An Ivory Woman)
Jelena, žena koje nema (Jelena, the Woman Who is Not)